ISBN:978-1-7395722-0-4
ISBN: 978-1-7395722-1-1
ISBN:978-1-7395722-2-8

Because of you…

For Mum, your support never faltered.
My husband Paul & daughter Maddie, forever my inspiration.
Dr James Cole
thank you for giving me that chance.
My writing career began because of you and for that I'm profoundly grateful.
Dr Brad Gyori
Thank you for letting me tease you endlessly and always seeing the strength in my written word.
For all the victims of Jack, the Ripper may you rest in peace.

To Find a Penny

Lillian Maddison

ISBN:978-1-7395722-0-4
ISBN: 978-1-7395722-1-1
ISBN:978-1-7395722-2-8

Chapter One

December 1888.

He could see her just up ahead, illuminated under the low flicker of the gas lamp. She staggered drunkenly over the cobbled pathway, supported by a nearby wall as she tried to steady herself against its surface. The effects of his wicked concoction had finally taken hold, and he watched in amusement as the girl swayed unsteadily on her feet.

He kept within the shadows, hugging the darkness to him like a cold sibling. She'd fascinated him at the public house, and he'd watched her from a corner. Her skin glowed, her blonde hair shone, and she looked so… alive.

The clatter of horse's hooves and the rattle of wagon wheels could be heard further up the street. A hansom cab pulled over as the driver caught sight of the girl, now slumped on her knees against the wall.

The man's gut twisted in knots as the horse-drawn carriage and its driver rumbled down the street. He took a step back, willing himself to look away, he needed to move on, find another, but his gaze was captivated. She was perfect for the dark rite. He could feel it in his bones, and the sweet chill he so loved ran through him. A seething anger surged through his veins as the moment he had longed for was slipping away from him. He needed just a few more moments and she would be completely at his mercy, a faithful sacrifice to the vile ritual that he so eagerly sought to fulfil. Fury boiled inside him, threatening to spill over like an unstoppable flood of rage.

“You all right Miss?” The driver tied off the reins and jumped down to the cobbles. “Miss?” He walked over to where the girl was slouched and bent down to look her in the face. “Good lord, you ain’t even awake.”

The cabbie glanced around to see if there might be someone around that could help him. “Well, c’mon lassie, not safe for you to spend the night here. Good job I’m going for some grub, you can stay in the cab whilst I eat.”

She groaned as he lifted her onto unsteady feet, and then carried the girl to the cab.

A burning rage bubbled in his chest as he watched the cabbie drive away. He wanted to scream, to let out all of his bottled up energy until it shattered the windows around him. His chance had been stolen and no other opportunity could compare; she was the perfect catch that he'd sought for so long. The man quickly disappeared into nothingness, vanishing like salt into boiling water.

****

Martha’s carriage boots were rubbing her feet and she was cold and hungry. She’d left her daughter, Polly, with a friend earlier so that she could come out and tout some business. Money had been extremely hard to come by since she had left the brothel, but she needed to move on. Her friend had given her some advice. She needed to find a regular stream of clients to bring in cash for food and shelter.

The breeze blew around the corner where she stood on the cobbled street and lifted a tiny, fragile wisp of hair that had come loose from her braid. The gas lamps let out a watery light that wasn't enough to illuminate the whole street, but it was enough for her to see that there was no one approaching. The buildings around her seemed to huddle together for warmth like old men in coats with their hands in their pockets. Martha was so cold, she pulled her shawl tighter around herself. It wouldn't be long before she gave up this foolish notion of waiting for punters and went home, where she could curl up in bed with her daughter. They liked to watch the rain splash against the window or listen as the wind howled outside as they told stories to each other.

A couple walked by on the other side of the street glancing across at her and giving disapproving glances. Martha attempted to pretend she didn't notice the looks of distaste they gave her, but the stares sent daggers through her heart. Despite her best efforts to maintain a brave face, she couldn't help but feel their disdain and it seemed to seep into her pores as easily as water. The gent gave her another furtive look and then cast his eyes to the cobbles. Ha – another punter trying to hide his private rendezvous.' Hypocrisy at its absolute best. Martha shook her head and turned away.

A man coming in the other direction towards the couple raised his hat to the woman and then stood back to let them pass. He watched as they walked to the end of the street and turned the corner, then crossed the road to where Martha stood.

“Looking for some company duckie?” Martha grinned at the man and ran her fingers across her bosom drawing his eye towards her cleavage.

He didn’t meet her gaze, just dug both hands into his pockets presumably for his money. “How much?”

Martha wasn’t bothered that he didn’t attempt any pleasantries with her, she was used to the punters just wanting to get down to business.

The seduction technique was falling short so, “Tuppence lovie, but a sovereign will ‘ave me on me knees too.” She grinned at him again and licked her teeth.

“Where to? Don't want to be overlooked.” He pulled his hands from his pockets and opened them, revealing two shiny pennies cupped between his palms. His brow was furrowed as he nervously shifted his weight from one foot to the other.

“Up to you, duckie, I’m not bothered where we do business.” Martha pushed her hip out. He looks older, maybe forty. She raised an eyebrow in thought and tipped her head to one side.

“Over there,” He pointed to an adjacent alleyway. “Nice an’ dark down the end, no one can see us.” He didn’t wait for Martha to agree, just crossed the street, and disappeared into the gloom.

Martha followed. She repositioned her bosoms making her cleavage more pronounced as she crossed the cobbles. The passageway gave little away, the dark stretched out around her, and she hesitated momentarily giving her eyes time to adjust, not being able to see where he’d gone.

The sound of a glass bottle being kicked on the ground gave Martha an idea of how much further she needed to go.

"Hello duckie, you still 'ere?" She walked slowly, checking every footstep so as not to stumble. "Duckie?"

Silence.

"Duckie, you takin' the piss out of Martha now."

Nothing.

"You're running out of time, Duckie. Hiding ain't free, ya know?" Her words turned icy as they clung to the air like a cloud of frost. "Don't waste my time, I've plenty more customers."

She stopped walking and listened, hoping to hear him. Something brushed against her foot. She jumped and instinctively kicked out and looked towards the ground. Whatever it was squealed in pain and scuttled back into the inky darkness. Martha shivered.

"This ain't funny duckie."

Seconds seemed like minutes.

"C'mon duckie, you're getting me gander up now, I'm wasting time down here with you when I could be earning some coin servicing another punter."

More seconds ticked by.

Then, "I'm down here… just walk towards my voice."

She let out a relieved breath. "I'm on my way Duckie, hope I'm not disappointed." Martha continued walking.

"Oh, you won't be…"

After another few feet, a hand stretched out of the shadows and grabbed her arm. Martha screamed.

"Christ, duckie I nearly peed me britches." She walked in the direction the hand was pulling her and was pushed up against a wall.

Duckie stepped up close to her and kissed her roughly on her mouth, she felt the prickle of his facial hair against her face and his tongue met hers.

She pushed him to arm's length. "Your tuppence don't cover that." She bent and raised her skirts enough so he could see her undergarments. "Give me your hand duckie, I'll shows yah what yah coin gets yah."

He extended his palm towards her. Martha didn't see the blade slide free from its hiding place.

The sharp edge cut across her throat severing her vocal cords. Her eyes baulked and she bought her hand up to the gash, trying hopelessly to stem the bleeding. Her legs buckled beneath her, she slid down the wall and then felt him cut away some clothing.

"Now the ritual can begin." He growled.

Moments later she was still. Martha's blue eyes stared lifelessly into the darkness.

Chapter Two

Three months earlier.

The black door of the townhouse opened. A grey cloud of tobacco smoke drifted out and dissolved into the smog of the city. The crumpled and bloody mess of Captain Oliver Smythe rolled onto the top marble step, assisted by the carriage boot of Ruby Myers. Her red Medusa curls fell from the updo around her face, and her high cheekbones were flushed with anger and disgust. Blue eyes, framed with thick dark lashes, sparkled with hatred. Ruby's petite nose with the nostrils flared and her lips narrowed in a clenched line, hindered her from radiating her usual beauty. She stood at five foot four inches in her stocking feet and with a petite feminine frame Ruby could easily be considered as the weaker sex.

"That's the last time you come to this establishment and get handy with one of the girls."

She spoke with a strong cockney accent.

Another kick. Smythe rolled down the next step. Ruby wasn't done. It wasn't the first time he'd visited and left after giving one of the girls a bad beating, not to mention, expecting more from the service than the girl had previously agreed. She grabbed a handful of his oiled barnet. The devil's strength surged through her veins. She pulled his whiskey-filled carcass by his hair and hauled him down the last two.

Smythe yelped in pain. Ruby didn't let up, he had to learn that all the girls at this establishment were to be respected. She had him on the cobbles. A hard punch to his face followed.

He raised his hands as he tried to deflect another punch.

She dug her fingernails into his cheek and pulled them down. Another yelp. "Not nice is it when a woman fights back." She sneered. "They might not be able to stand up to you, but I certainly can."

She looked around and saw a pile of cold horse dung nearby.

"This'll teach yah, maybe you'll remember when a lady says no to something, then it's no."

"No, no pl-"

"Too late for that, get on yah hands an' knees." She demanded.

She watched him roll and push up into a crawl.

"Miss Myers, I implore you."

Ruby pulled her hairpin from the last of the updo of her hair. She pulled his head back and pointed it at his left eye. "Move."

His bladder evacuated the last of the house whiskey and he whimpered.

"Shut up old man, shit is as shit does."

The captain crawled his way over to the horse dung. He looked up at her, his right eye swollen from the earlier punch. He was on his knees now and hands clasped in front of him.

"Miss Myers, I beseech you. It's the whiskey, it makes a bad man of me. It won't happen again."

“You’re right it won’t. I repeat, no punter comes into my house and beats the girls to a pulp, then expects them to give in to extra vile tastes against their wishes, do I make myself clear?” Ruby waited for the words to hit home, lifted her skirt, put her carriage boot to his chest and shoved.

His face was now inches from the horse manure, “do it again and I won’t stop at this point, your face will be in it, understand?”

“I hear you loud and clear, Miss.”

Ruby didn’t look back as she made her way back to the townhouse, walked up the steps and closed the door behind her.

****

Martha lay motionless on the bed, her body a mosaic of purple, yellow and different shades of red. Swollen eyelids were barely visible between strands of matted hair. Ruby sighed as she wrung out the cloth—the water in the bowl turning pink—and brought it to Martha’s lip. She dabbed gently until the blood stopped seeping from the gash. Martha winced at the touch.

“I’m sorry… he won’t be back.” Ruby said with conviction, her eyes hardening with determination.

“Miss Ruby, it’s not your fault.” Martha peered up at Ruby with her one good eye, trying to offer reassurance.

“You’ll need bed rest for a while, I’ll see to it that the linen is changed, and I’ll have a bath sent up here so you can bathe.” Ruby pushed Martha’s blood-soaked blonde hair off her face and began wiping some of the gore off her throat and chest.

"Miss, it's the punters, sometimes you get a bad un." The girl tried to smile but the swelling made it look like a grimace.

"Not in this house Martha, it's a strict rule the punters have to abide by." She dropped the rag into the bowl and stood. "I have you girls here because I can help to keep you all safe. Not like before, Martha when you and Polly were treated like prey on the streets, lucky to come home every evening and not found dead in the gutter." She walked towards the door. "Punters respect my girls or don't come in."

"Miss, I'm thankful for what you've done to keep me and my little girl safe."

"I know. I'll get Rose to bring up some of her chicken broth and some hot milk, it'll help you to mend. The Doctor will be sent for shortly."

"Miss, I can't afford no Doctor."

"Let me worry about that, you need a doctor to see you. Get some rest, the food will be sent up once the Doctor has been." She paused with her hand on the doorknob.

"Thank you, Miss." Martha lay back against the pillows.

"Oh, and Martha…"

"Yes Miss"

"Next time a punter wants to be wet nursed, just say yes, it does tend to stop a tantrum." Ruby grinned and winked at the girl.

Martha chuckled, wincing in pain as she did so, "I 'fink you could be right, Miss."

Ruby closed the door quietly behind her and headed for the kitchen, which was warm and cosy. The smell of chicken broth and soot comforted Ruby as she put the bowl and bloody cloth in the sink.

"How is she?" asked Arthur over the newspaper.

He sat in a chair near the fireplace and folded the paper into his lap. His well-groomed, lightly oiled dark hair was parted to the left, with the sides swept back. His dark eyes narrowed, and his square jaw clenched as he watched his Ruby.

Ruby frowned but anger burned again in her eyes. Arthur rose from the chair and pulled her into a hug. His six-foot broad frame and muscular arms made Ruby feel safe and protected. Arthur Morris was a good-looking and well-respected gangster, and he loved Ruby deeply.

"Come on, my girl, tell me how bad she is." He pulled back and looked Ruby directly in the eyes. "How bad?"

"He gave her a leathering; she'll be bed-bound for a good few weeks, plus he forced some acts on her that weren't agreed beforehand, vile man. I need to send out for the Doctor, where's Rose?" Ruby asked.

"Already sent her. She took Polly with her too; I think she's trying to shield the child from this as best she can." Arthur ushered Ruby to his vacant chair. "Sit, I'll get you some tea."

"How long has she been gone?" Ruby took the cup and saucer and sipped the hot liquid. It helped a bit.

“I’d say twenty minutes or so, shouldn’t be long now.” Arthur pulled his pocket watch from his waistcoat and snapped open the cover. Eight fifteen. “I must say Rubes if it wasn’t for the fact that you gave him what he deserved, Smythe would’ve had a visit from me and the lads and been given a very hard lesson regarding his behaviour here tonight.” The muscle in Arthur’s jaw tensed and his brown eyes hardened.

They were interrupted as the door to the kitchen opened and Rose came into the room followed by Polly and the Doctor.

“Good evening, Doctor, thank you for coming.” Arthur stepped forward and extended his hand.

The doctor returned a weak handshake, “Where’s the patient? Let’s not waste time with pleasantries.” His eyes spoke of his distaste for the establishment. “Madam, shall we?” He looked directly at Ruby.

Her nostrils flared and her mouth contorted into a hard line at his ignorance. She stood and handed the empty cup and saucer back to Arthur. “Certainly, follow me please.”

The Doctor examined Martha and found her to have, three broken ribs, severe bruising to the torso and face, a chipped tooth, a badly blackened eye, a suspected cheek fracture, and a split lip.

“Quite the job this time Madam Ruby. Don’t you think?” The doctor's hands trembled slightly as he gathered his stethoscope, thermometer, and other instruments into his bag. He snapped the latch shut with a little too much force, then straightened up and adjusted his wire-rimmed glasses. His eyebrows were pressed together in an arrogant frown as he said, “Well, is this sort of beating acceptable? I think not.”

Ruby indicated to the door, “Shall we discuss this outside Doctor?”

He didn’t need to be told twice and swept from the room. Ruby raised her eyebrows at Martha and followed.

“Madam Ruby, when will this stop? This is the third girl in as many months, I-”

Ruby cut him off, “Thank you Doctor,” she glared at him before she led him down the stairs and out of the front door. She stopped on the first step.

A neighbouring couple had appeared on the street and began walking in their direction. Excellent timing. The Doctor stiffened.

Ruby lowered her voice just enough so only the Doctor could hear her. “Firstly, it’s Miss Ruby, there aint no M’dam in this gaff.” Her cockney accent began to emerge.

She stepped closer.

The doctor here was someone with specific desires that only some of the women willingly engaged in. He often walked into the scarlet hallway, a frequent visitor to this brothel, and he knew his way around like he had memorized it.

"Were you and your brother well looked after the other evening, in the private rooms, at the back of the building where every need or desire is fulfilled to your utmost satisfaction? I'd like to think you were as you are both such valued customers here."

The arrogance dribbled out of his mouth and down his chin.

Ruby leaned in towards the doctor, her eyebrows drawn together in a frown and eyes narrowed. "Doctor, I need to make myself perfectly clear. The care you provide to these women here is essential. But I must ask that any opinions, no matter how strong they are, are kept to yourself and also stay within these walls. If it got back to me that you were talking about us outside of this house, it could be detrimental to all of us. This is a very conservative neighbourhood, and if malicious gossip spread it would become too much of a burden to bear, not only for you but especially for your lovely wife." Ruby raised her voice, "Do I make myself understood?"

The couple passing by looked up at them as they heard her. The Doctor glanced at them and then looked pleadingly back at Ruby.

"I take it that the next visit will be more tolerable for you, I do so hate unpleasant atmospheres, don't you Doctor?" She gave the man a tight smile.

The Doctor gave a weak nod, adjusted his scarf, cleared his throat, and began to make his way down the steps.

"Thank you for coming Doctor, give my regards to your good lady." She said to his back.

She nodded at the pair further down the road, who continuously stole glances in her direction. "Rather chilly this evening don't you think?" The couple looked uncomfortable but smiled and nodded in agreement then continued on their way. Ruby went inside and shut the door.

Ruby went to bed that night feeling drained, but sleep was little solace. Meandering through her dreams, the black serpent crawled from its hiding place. It always knew her vulnerabilities, fears, and her secrets. It descended, as always, upon the young girl cowering beneath the covers, wrapping its body around her, and trapping her limbs in place. Despite her desperate pleas and struggles, it held her fast as she fought against it. The more she struggled the more powerful it became, as if trying to make her give up her deepest darkest insecurities by forcing the air from her lungs.

Ruby's eyes flew open, and she felt her nightdress clinging to her skin. Her heart pounded in terror until she found her bearings and realized it was a nightmare. Arthur lay deep in slumber next to her. His rhythmic breathing like a nocturnal metronome. Her heart rate slowed as she moved her body up against his. Instinctively, although asleep, his arm came across her and calmed her, lulling her back into a much more peaceful rest.

****

Ruby woke up early the next morning with the events of Smyth's antics being at the forefront of her mind. She ate a small breakfast and after checking on Martha she left the townhouse. Outside the horse dung still lay in the road. Ruby raised an eyebrow. Was she too hard on him? Did her temper get the better of her again? She adjusted her gloves and began walking down the street. The morning air was crisp and cool. The sun shone low in the sky and filtered through the branches of the trees in a yellow-gold hue. The oranges and yellows were muted with browns, signalling that autumn would be here soon. A brisk breeze rattled leaves along the path, dislodging them from their high perches to tumble across cobbled streets. A luscious fragrance of newly baked loaves and pumpkin seeds teased her senses and her mouth watered. She passed a cart selling seasonal vegetables, the stall holder tipped his hat as she passed.

"Good morning, Miss Myers." His smile revealed blackened teeth.

"Good morning, George." Ruby nodded but kept her pace.

Getting out of the house helped Ruby clear her mind. Other shop owners were beginning to open for their day of trading. She passed another stall selling pastries and she made a mental note to get one on her way home, the idea like a hug from a mother nurturing a new-born. She could hear a newspaper seller shouting the news headlines.

"Whitechapel murder, the victim named."

A well-dressed man approached and held out his hand, “Copy sir? Thank you kindly.” He said as he took the money, and the gent took one of the papers off his stand.

Ruby stopped and scanned the heading.

Agatha Pullman named as victim.

The colour drained from her face and her mouth dried up.

“You alright miss?” The seller looked concerned. “Miss?”

Ruby didn’t move, just stared at the name that jumped out from the front page of the Daily Tribune.

Ruby met Agatha when Ruby used to run illegal bare-knuckle fights. At first, they didn’t get along. Ruby was suspicious of her and didn’t understand why a woman like Agatha wanted to frequent the fights. The girl had a strong, flirtatious personality and a loudmouth. She was able to twist the punters around her little finger. Unbeknownst to the spectators, Agatha would circle the men and wait to get the attention of one man. As the audience watched the two blokes in the ring beat the living daylights out of each other, she’d move in.

With Agatha’s white, blonde hair contrasting with her bright green eyes that sparkled with life and a delicately boned, heart shape face with cupid bow lips she could mesmerize any man.

Ruby watched the woman circling the men like a predator stalking its prey and she knew that Agatha was up to something. She’d finished taking the bets off the late arrivals and decided to step back into a secluded corner to watch Agatha.

Ruby glanced away as the crowd began cheering. One of the fighters had dropped to the ground. The other fighter saw his chance and laid one last punch. He wouldn't be getting up.

Ruby looked back in Agatha's direction and saw her lead the man away. His smirk told her it was his lucky night.

"Jim, take the payments for me." Ruby untied the cords around her waist and handed the betting bag over to a man lent against a wall not too far from her.

"No problem." He said, as he took it from her, and she headed in the direction of Agatha.

Fortunately, the street was quiet as Ruby made her way away from the melee hidden deep in an alleyway. Ruby could just see the pair walking up the street in front of her. Agatha leaned close to his ear at times. What was she saying to him?

Suddenly the man's legs buckled, and he fell onto the cobbles. Ruby stopped, ducked into a shop doorway to figure out her next move. There was no way that that woman would be getting her hands on any of the men's money without an invitation from her first, after all it was her idea of the boxing matches.

Agatha turned the man over and patted him down. She took his change from his trouser pocket and then emptied his inside pockets of any items he was carrying. She pushed everything under her bosoms, readjusted her top and walked away, leaving him flat out on the ground. Ruby bolted from the doorway in an attempt to follow, but Agatha moved quickly and managed to slip away down an alley. When Ruby got there, she'd vanished.

At the next bare-knuckle fight, a week later Ruby had decided to confront Agatha. The fight was being held in an old flour mill, a change of location to stay out of the earshot of the local peelers. The two men were into the third round when Ruby noticed Agatha making her way around the crowd.

Agatha used her usual tactics to gain a man's full attention, let him drink from a hip flask that she carried and after thirty minutes or so began to lead him outside.

Ruby was ready and followed closely behind.

Within a few yards, the man became unsteady on his legs, several more and his legs buckled, and he sank to the cobbles. Agatha wasted no time, squatted next to the chap, and began patting him down. As soon as he'd collapsed Ruby was able to catch up.

"Hey, girl, what'd ya doin'?" Ruby quickened her pace to cover the ground between her and the woman.

Agatha glanced around and for a second froze until she could see her pursuer.

"Nuffin,' I found him like it and was tryin' to 'elp him." Her eyes followed Ruby's approach.

"Don't think so, saw you touting the crowd back there." Ruby tipped her head back in the direction of the fight and then put her hands on her hips. "Your nothin' but a bug hunter." She spat.

The girl slowly rose to her feet, her legs shaking. She nervously peeked behind Ruby to check that no one was in earshot before continuing their conversation.

“A girl needs to eat, don’t she?” She folded her arms and scowled at Ruby. “Anyhows, what’s it t’ you?”

“I run the fights and you’re nicking from my punters,” Ruby answered. “What’d you think you had dibs too?” She glanced down at the man still out cold on the ground. “Slip ‘im somethin’?”

The girl shifted nervously on her feet, her arms crossed over her chest in an effort to maintain a barrier between herself and the others. She spoke slowly, her eyes darting around as if searching for help or an escape route. “What if I did, doin’ him no harm—just messin’ with his things a bit and maybe give 'im a headache in the mornin'. That's all." Agatha smiled smugly, a hint of pride skittering across her features.

“You used Chloral, or knockout drops into that hip flask, no wonder he’s out cold.” She shook her head and dropped her hands to her sides. “If you wanta tout my crowd then you need to cut me in.” Ruby pursed her lips together and pushed out her chin.

“Don’t ‘fink so girly, I don’t share nuffin’ I’ve worked for.” Agatha pointed her right index finger to her temple. “Must fink I’m barmy.” Her eyes shone with defiance.

Ruby shook her head and grinned. She looked the girl straight at her. As she stepped forward, she slipped a small blade from her sleeve, grabbed Agatha's throat with her free hand and shoved her backwards against some nearby railings. The weapon came up under the girl's chin. Her eyes were cold as she looked straight at Agatha's which bulged with fear.

"Yah don't mess with me girly, understand?" The point of the blade pressed on the girl's vocal cords. Ruby tipped her head to one side as she spoke, but her eyes continued to look straight into Agatha's. "Now treacle, do I have yah attention?"

She nodded and tried to swallow, but the blade made that impossible.

"So, you will cut me in thirty per cent, not 'appy then you go elsewhere. Try to stitch me I'll know, dob me into the ole bill, I'll find ya." Ruby didn't drop her grip.

Agatha gave a short nod of agreement.

"Good." Ruby let her go, sliding the blade back up her sleeve.

"Who are you?" Agatha's voice was unusually quiet. "I like to know who I'm doin' business wiv."

"Ruby, Ruby Myers." She watched Agatha's face pale and her jaw dropped to her ripe pippins at the mention of her name.

The girl said nothing, just nodded again. Ruby turned and walked back to the fight.

The arrangement worked well, and Agatha paid up without so much as a quibble. One evening in late summer changed everything between the two women.

Ruby wiped the sweat from her forehead with a grimy cloth and grabbed another bucket of mop water. The only sound in the building was the dull echo of her shoes slapping against the concrete floor, until a door creaked open from the side entrance. A man stepped out from his hiding place, shards of broken glass glinting in his hand and pointed directly at Ruby's face. He took one step forward and for a moment she froze in terror.

"Don't move or I cut yah tongue out."

Ruby could smell his sour breath but didn't recognise the voice.

"Lost yah bet tonight?" Ruby croaked.

He reached out and grabbed her by her throat, his movement swift and sudden.

She could feel his powerful hands squeezing harder and tighter with each passing second. Her throat felt like a vice, the air being forced from her lungs as she tried to gasp for breath. Ruby's mind raced wildly in search of an escape as she desperately clawed at his grip, only for him to increase the pressure even further.

The sensation of helplessness swept over her like a tidal wave, engulfing her in its depths until Ruby felt completely consumed. She was no longer the one in control, instead she was paralyzed by fear, unable to make any decisions or even move as the unfamiliar emotion eclipsed every thought.

"If I goes home without money, my wife will kick me out." His voice was gruff but softened as he spoke of his lady. "Got kids to feed yah see Missy."

Ruby's instinct was telling her this wasn't a violent man; it was desperation.

“How much?” Her voice was a whisper.

“Enough.”

She gasped from the pressure on her throat, and she clawed at his forearm.

“I… can’t…. bre-.” Ruby spluttered. “Ple-” She tapped his arm, but his grip didn’t let up. Ruby desperately gasped for air as her vision blurred and her head filled with a fog of dizziness. Terror gripped her like a vice, squeezing the breath from her lungs. Her heart felt like it was about to burst through her chest while she dug her nails deep into his skin, leaving bloody tracks in her wake tearing away at flesh, as she tried to cry out in fury. She gritted her teeth, determined not to let him win, but the fear had already consumed her whole being. Despite the pain, he stood there still as a rock. With every ounce of strength left in her body, she summoned all her energy to reach up and claw at his eyes.

Then his grip dropped away. Ruby sunk to her knees and gasped pulling in an urgent breath. Her vision cleared and she looked behind her.

He lay on the cold ground, his body convulsing as a fountain of blood burst from an open wound just below his left ear. His eyes bulged, rolling back into his head until they were lifeless and vacant. With one last gasp he reached out to clutch the puncture in his neck, his hand barely holding back the tide of deep red liquid that spilled across his chest. He gargled something incomprehensible through clenched teeth then fell still, leaving death to take its merciless course.

Agatha stood behind him holding a shard of broken glass, blood dripped from the first two inches of its point. The girl dropped it and helped Ruby to her feet.

"Thanks." Ruby stood on shaky legs.

"What was Ernie Stopple doin her Miss Ruby?" Agatha wiped her forearm across her forehead. "Don't want the likes of 'im 'ere." She kicked at his foot. "He's a wrong'un, Miss."

Ruby seethed and her eyes burned with fury when the girl said, "Didn't invite him." She raised her leg and delivered two sharp kicks to the man before demanding, "How'd you know him?"

Agatha moved back a step and avoided eye contact, rubbing her arm nervously. She sighed heavily and mumbled, "Long story. Feel better?"

Ruby wondered if Agatha was trying to soothe herself. She nodded before saying, "I'm listening."

"When I was turning tricks, he was one of my regular punters, nasty bastard, liked to hit." Agatha shivered and gave Ruby a weak smile. "Glad he's done." The girl smirked and she turned away.

"We need to get 'im moved so the ole bill don't find him." Ruby bent down grabbing hold of his ankles. "Agatha, we're too darn pretty for 'angin' so grab the other end will yah."

Agatha did as she was asked and the two women moved him over into a corner and covered the body with empty flour sacks, then dragged over some of the full ones and positioned them so he couldn't be seen.

“Should be ok ‘ere for a bit, I’ll get my Arfur to get rid of ‘im.” Ruby pushed loose hair off her face as she spoke, “he was heavier than I imagined.”

The two women did their best to brush off the flour dust on their clothes.

“I owe you, Agatha.” Ruby put out her hand, “Friends?”

The girl grinned back at her, “Friends.” She said as they shook hands.

In Ruby's reverie, the sky had turned grey like a bruise, as if it too mourned the loss of her friend. The street was busier now, retailers shouting and selling their wares over the cobbles. Several people purchased newspapers as she stood there.

"You alright Miss?"

Ruby’s attention snapped back to the newspaper seller.

“Uh, yes I’ll take a copy.” She reached into her money pouch and handed him a coin. “Keep the change.”

“Much obliged Miss.” He tipped his cap and handed her the newspaper.

She took it and continued on.

Ruby was glad to find the haberdashery quiet that morning. The loss of her friend had shaken her. She was the first true companion she’d had since growing up in the workhouse and it was a shock to think that she’d never see her again.

The polite conversation with Mrs Miller, the proprietor, was the last thing she needed. Mrs Miller had a bright smile, but it was quickly replaced by a mischievous twinkle in her eye when engaging in conversation. She had an uncanny knack for stretching the truth and to an outsider, it could appear that Mrs Miller was just a harmless old woman who liked to chat. But they'd quickly learn that every one of her conversations spiralled into rambling accounts of local gossip until what should have been a two-minute visit dragged on for hours.

However, Ruby liked her and was always satisfied with her purchases. The quality of her dress material and linens were the best in the city, so every time she visited the shop Ruby allowed extra time.

The bell above the door tingled Ruby's arrival and Mrs Miller appeared from behind a curtain at the rear of the shop. Although the store was on the small side every available space was filled with shelves of different coloured materials and silks, stark white linens, and balls of knitting yarn. Ruby knew that Mrs Miller prided herself on her dressmaking skills and hidden behind the drape was where she hand-stitched the dresses that clothed a lot of the people of the city.

"Ah, good morning, Miss Ruby, a pleasure as always." The woman stood at the back of a long glass cabinet that served as her counter. Inside were silk handkerchiefs and a selection of embroidery threads and needles, crochet tools and thimbles. "How are you? And what can I do for you this fine day?" She smiled warmly as she looked, with pale blue eyes, over her small round spectacles that were perched on the end of her petite nose. For her advanced years, her skin showed little sign of ageing and she had a delicate flush on her cheeks. With her delicate facial bone structure and oval-shaped face, she was still a pretty-looking woman. She wore a frilled, high-collared, long-sleeved blouse with ruched cuffs and a dark blue ankle-length tweed skirt. Her grey hair was pinned in a tidy bun on the top of her head. Mrs Miller always looked immaculate.

"Good morning, Mrs Miller." Ruby avoided the first question. "I'm in need of some bed linens please."

"Certainly." The woman came around the front of the cabinet and extended her arm in an invitation to follow her. "May I show you the linens that have just arrived, they're from France?" Mrs Miller walked over to the left-hand side of the shop where some bolts of material were on display. "I'm incredibly pleased with this new collection, Miss Ruby. The fabric is beautiful, and the thread count provides a luxurious feel to the touch." She pulled out some stark white cloth for Ruby to touch. "Please, be my guest and feel the quality of the material."

Ruby removed a glove and ran her fingers across the material. "It is as you say, Mrs Miller, quite lovely. I'm needing two sets please, when could you have it ready for me?" She replaced her glove and walked over to the display cabinet where the handkerchiefs were. "Please can I have a look at the handkerchiefs also? Can they be monogrammed too?"

Mrs Miller lifted the glass of the cabinet and took out the foulards. "For two people, my, my I must say this has been an exceedingly popular line of late, several customers have asked for them. Only yesterday Mrs Gibson who runs the hardware shop just down the street ordered one, a gift for her husband apparently." Mrs Miller placed the material on the countertop, "Do you know the Gibson's at all?"

Ruby noticed the familiar twinkle appear in her eye and knew all too well where this conversation was headed. "Not personally, no. So can they be monogrammed?" She asked, in an attempt to deflect her from gossiping.

"Of course, I just need the initials you'd require. May I ask if it's for a man or a woman?" She slid a piece of paper and pencil across the glass for Ruby to write on.

"Both, actually." Ruby didn't say anything further but took up the pencil and began writing.

The bell above the door sounded out a delicate tingle and Ruby heard someone enter behind her.

"Good morning, Mrs Byford how are you on this fine day?" Mrs Miller said brightly.

Ruby’s stomach tightened at the sound of the name. Could this day get any worse? She could feel the eyes of Mrs Byford burning into her back as she continued to look through the silk squares on the countertop.

“Good morning, Mrs Miller, you can see me now, one has a church meeting to attend.”

“Be right with you, Mrs Byford. Would you like to sit down whilst you wait?” Mrs Miller gestured to a solitary chair positioned at the front of the shop just under the window display.

“I think not Mrs Miller, there is no need to stand on parade with the likes of her.” She tipped her head in Ruby’s direction. “Surely the upstanding people of this community deem priority instead of you bowing down to a strumpet that wears tasteless attire such as the red dress she is standing up in.” The woman stood stock still with her chin in the air.

Mrs Miller’s mouth hung open, “Uh… Mrs Byford…I re-.”

Ruby turned as she answered cutting her off.

“I’m assumin’ that you’re addressin’ me, Madam?” Ruby glared at her, but the woman looked straight in the direction of the shop owner.

Mrs. Byford's arched eyebrows shot up. "My, we are quick today, aren't we?" she said icily. Her pinched face twitched with irritation as she turned and regarded Ruby through narrowed eyes, her long nose pointing down at her like a dagger. Byford’s face looked like she'd just stepped in something nasty as the woman spoke to Ruby with enough bite to show how much she disliked her.

"My dresses are all stitched by this lady, thank you for inquirin.' Can I ask where yours are sewn?" Ruby narrowed her eyes at the woman and then looked her up and down.

Mildred Octavia Byford was always in black mourning her husband's death. She wore an outdated dress and shawl, a comically large hat with a feather and faux grapes attached, and elbow-length gloves. Her most prominent feature was her large, pointed nose. In one hand she carried a tiny velvet pouch, and in the other an ornately detailed ebony cane.

Ruby had trouble keeping a serious expression on her face as she observed the scene. She commented, "This has so lightened my mood after I read about the death of my friend in the news today, please do tell, Mrs Byford who made such a fine outfit?" Ruby shot Mrs Miller a quick look and noticed the woman's attempt to stifle a smile at her sardonic comment.

"The woman's a genius and clearly you can't afford her." Byford's witch-like features screwed up in distaste as she spoke to Ruby. Byford then looked straight at the shop owner, before commenting, "That monstrosity is surely not one of yours Mrs Miller?" Her face looked like a shrew chewing a worm.

Mrs Miller's expression flattened as Mrs Byford sneered. "Really, I'm surprised. Not one of your best then," she said curtly, her lips curling in satisfaction. She gestured towards the newspaper lying on the table in front of them, where 'Martha' was featured on the front page. Her face twisted into a mask of revulsion and condemnation. "Another fallen woman who can no longer spread disease is off the streets," she spat with contempt. “and one more of your acquaintances, Miss Myers, who has been dragged down by her own immorality.” She shook her head slowly, pleased with her own cruel words before looking back to the two women with haughty eyes. Mrs Byford had an air of smugness about her as her gaze shifted between them both.

Mildred's lips curled into a sneer as she attempted to start another argument with Ruby. It was apparent that the townhouse had been having trouble lately, and Ruby sensed Mrs Byford had something to do with it. The woman was known for gossiping about other people's business yet kept her own life tightly under wraps.

Mrs Byford's cheeks hollowed out and her mouth puckered into a sharp circle. She resembled someone who had just eaten a sour fruit. “Do you have some sort of grudge against me?” asked Ruby slyly.

Mrs Byford’s face grew red, and her voice was cold and sharp, “I beg your pardon Miss Myers, or should I address you as Madam.” One of the fake grapes trembled further to the edge of the brim and the feather quivered as if it were a quill taking notes.

"I'm sure I don't know what it is you're implying Mrs Byford."

Mrs Miller tried to interject but Byford cut her off.

"Shall I enlighten you, Madam?" Byford propped her cane against the glass cabinet and then, stood poker straight with her gloved hands clasped in front of her. "I'm quite sure that what I have to say to you is on the lips of many of the people living around here, I just have the courage to speak up." The feather quivered at her indignation.

"Of course, please do." Ruby's eyes glistened with contempt.

Mrs Miller cleared her throat as a way to distract the two women, but it went unheard.

"It is well known about the premises that you own and the debauchery that occurs within its walls." She screwed up her mouth again, "the townsfolk wish that you would pack up this place of depravity," she ranted, "including the fallen women that you house there, and get out of town." Her eyes were cold and hard as Mildred pinned Ruby with them.

Ruby felt a chill as soon as Byford began to speak. Her words were cold and cutting, but there was an unmistakable glee in her tone. Ruby had been here before, and the familiarity of the woman's dislike always made her stomach clench with anger. Mildred was a formidable woman, her voice loud and uncompromising. She had no qualms with expressing her opinion, no matter how polarizing or unpopular it might be.

"Do they now, and whom may I ask has said this? I would be pleased to have a discussion with them at my earliest convenience." Ruby challenged.

Byford's eyes widened as Ruby spoke and her mouth hung open. A moment passed before Byford regained her composure.

"Um… Well… I-I'm sure I cannot say, it would be breaking a confidence." The woman grabbed her cane and leaned on it.

Ruby could sense the discomfort radiating from Mrs Byford, and she allowed herself a moment of triumph. Ruby kept her face impassive, but it wasn't enough - it was time to take drastic measures. She had to made sure that Smythe knew he'd overstepped the boundaries and now it was Mrs Byford's turn to understand who she was messing with. "Well, that is unusual for you Mrs Byford, keeping confidence I mean." Ruby clenched her jaw and her nostrils flared as she tried to remain calm.

Byford didn't let up.

"It is quite one thing to have a place of entertainment, but utterly unacceptable that you have a place such as this, it is ungodly, disrespectful to the district and it is also not a townhouse, it's a, a…" The woman stammered; the feather continued taking notes.

"A brothel?" Ruby finished for her.

The woman's eyes blinked quickly, and another grape hung with the other.

"Quite." Mrs Byford managed to say.

"Ladies, please if we could possibly…" Mrs Miller had walked around the front of the counter.

Ruby looked at the proprietor. "It's fine Mrs Miller." Ruby gave the owner a small nod and turned back to the shrew in front of her.

"Do you really want to get into this debate with me today, Mrs Byford?"

Mrs Byford pulled her shoulders back and lifted her chin as she spoke. "Madam, it needs to be said that this place of ill repute should be removed."

Ruby shook her head with a half grimace on her face and then stepped up to the woman and inclined her head, so her mouth was level with her ear. "Didn't Mr Byford leave you for Scarlet, a very popular addition to my bordello? Wasn't this because she could fulfil his peculiar desires?" Ruby whispered.

The woman's body went rigid. Then the boldness evaporated, as her shoulders sagged.

"Nothing to say?" Ruby hadn't moved from the woman's ear.

"Your establishment is ungodly, Miss Myers, and brings the district into disrepute." Byford weakly retorted.

Ruby shook her head. "Be careful Mrs Byford, there's a lot about your late husband I know, he certainly wasn't the Right Honourable that's for sure." She waited for the words to sink in.

The comment slapped the woman straight in the face and what was left of her bravado dribbled out of her mouth and crawled across the floor towards the shop door.

Ruby squared her shoulders and stood tall, gazing down the length of her nose at the woman before her. She let a sly smile curl on her lips as she willed the woman to understand that she wasn't to be trifled with. “Didn’t he have an embarrassing scar and mole on his person?”

Ruby fought back a smirk as she handed Mrs Miller her money and noticed that Mrs Byford was still standing like a statue, gaping in disbelief at their exchange. With a triumphant grin on her face, she exited the shop and stepped out into the sunny day outside without a second glance back.

Chapter Three

As Elsie stepped off the stage, her boots clicked against the polished wood floor. She glanced around at the now-empty theatre - red velvet curtains hung from sconce walls, vermilion carpets muffled each step of the audience's feet. Gas lamps cast a warm glow over everything, illuminating the tiniest details: the patina of the worn leather chairs, used by the higher paying customers, tucked in an alcove and the slight sheen to the polished wood seats. A cloud of Elsie's perfume lingered in the air, so heavy that it seemed like it could be scooped up with a spoon. Jack the bartender wiped down the bar with a rag, his movements slow and methodical as he checked stock.

"I'll be off home now Jack, love. I'm plain worn out." She wrapped her fox fur stole around her shoulders and then began to pull on her elbow-length gloves. Her pink taffeta dress kissed her feet as she walked, and the monarch train dragged unceremoniously behind her across the floor. She reached behind her, found the loop of fabric, and hooked it over her wrist which lifted it away from her feet.

"I won't be far behind you Els, tough crowd tonight." Jack continued wiping the bar down with a dirty rag.

"You ain't wrong, had to fight one of the punters off me earlier, bloody near tore my dress clean off 'we did." Elsie tutted. "Feel sorry for their poor wives, 'avin them turn up 'ome drunk as lords." She readjusted the stole. "Right, I'm off, see ya on the morrow."

"See ya, Miss Elsie."

The letter had been strange, and she half-expected to find someone waiting for her backstage. There was no one, however, only an unnerving silence. Elsie cautiously pushed open the heavy stage doors, her breath quickening. As she stepped outside, a cold wind blew through the alleyway and swirled around her body like a phantom. On the opposite side of the doorway, a man was slouched against the wall, holding a bottle of beer in his hands. His head lulled on his chest and his legs were straight out in front of him. The bottle was tucked under his left arm and his right lay palm up on the ground beside him. He's no use to man or beast.

A kernel of excitement popped in her stomach, the anticipation making her feel giddy. Her heart raced as she thought of Ruby, her lover, and the night they would spend together. As she walked through the dark streets, the cobbled stones clicked beneath her boots, and streetlights cast a warm glow on everything around her. She smiled to herself, imagining the way Ruby's eyes lit up when she saw her. They had been together for a year now, yet every meeting still felt like the first time. With each step she took towards home, the world seemed to crackle with possibility before finally exploding into blissful abandon.

The lightest breeze ran its fingers over the city, sending both sweet and bitter smells into the air. A few small snowflakes were falling from the sky, joining those that had fallen early in the evening to dapple Elsie's stole with white flecks. Her steps crunched on the stone as she hurried down the street, lit by a large gas lamp glowing like an orange lantern. She pulled her fox fur wrap tight around her neck against the chill of the autumn night and listened for another sound in the city. All was quiet: dogs did not bark at her approach, houses did not creak on their roofs against this late-night visitor, and no drunkard stumbled out from his saloon for a piss. There was nothing but silence except for the old church clock chiming out the hour. Eleven times it tolled, echoing off buildings in different volumes, marking time louder than any cacophonous work song.

Elsie paused at the corner of the road and looked up and down in the hope of seeing Ruby or a Hansom cab approach. Where was Ruby? She always made her feel safe. Elsie shivered. She had to get home, so she turned to her right and continued on her way. Maybe she'll be further up the road. A cat bolted from an alley and disappeared in a passageway opposite. The sound of glass shattering on concrete rang out and then the clatter of metal as the moggy darted into the dark. Elsie put her hand to her chest and pulled in a breath. Fingers of unease ran from the nape of her neck down her spine and the hairs on her arms raised. Home seemed so far away.

She came to the mouth of an alleyway and briefly paused. The darkness reached out and tried to pull her in. Elsie knew she had to pass it to get home. She picked up her step. The inkiness called to her and the opening of the passage to her right yawned. She trembled. Her heartbeat was shallow and fast. All she could hear was her carriage boots as they tapped out the rhythm of her steps. Her dress caught under the heel of her boot, and she stopped to release it. Then she heard the footsteps behind her. She didn't look back, just continued her pace. Nearly past. Relief held her hand as she reached the other side of the entrance. She felt brave enough to turn around to see who was behind her. She strained her eyes but couldn't see anyone in the dark. Where had they gone?

Elsie felt a cold hand clamp over her mouth, muffling her screams. A cloying arm snaked around her chest and dragged her backwards into the darkness of the alley. Her breath came in shallow gasps as panic rose within her, sending adrenaline coursing through her veins. She clawed wildly at the fingers that constricted her, desperately trying to pry the trap from her face, but to no avail. The force of the unknown assailant was too strong and inexorable.

She bucked and kicked in the hope her attacker would let her go. The hand still covered her mouth and nose so she bit down hoping it would free her airways. Her assailant screamed out in pain but didn't let go. She couldn't breathe. They moved deeper into the alley and turned left around a bend. Her lungs burned from her exertion and lack of air.

They kept moving deeper into the gloom. The fingers released her nose. She pulled in a desperate breath. Her brain fired up with the intake of air. She had to fight back.

Elsie thrust her elbow backward, feeling the satisfying thud of contact with her assailant's ribs. Her attacker howled in response and without warning, teeth latched onto her ear like a vice. Elsie's vision blurred as a searing pain shot through her skull, immobilizing her for a heart-stopping moment before she snapped back to reality.

"Stop fighting me!" A gruff voice said.

She felt a hot breath on the side of her neck as her aggressor spoke. She didn't listen. She tried to turn to face him, but his grip was too strong. Where the hell was Ruby? Elsie attempted to scream but her jaw was locked by the grip of the hand. She uttered only a squeak.

"I said stop fighting me!" He growled.

Elsie whimpered and a tear ran down her face. Suddenly the hand moved from her mouth and her surroundings spun. The attacker grabbed her hair, and she felt her face hit hard concrete. She lifted her hand to protect herself. The second hard smack didn't reverberate like the first, but she felt disorientated and stunned. A pain shot through her mouth, and she tasted the copper taste of blood. Instinct made her tongue investigate where she bled from. It found a long split inside her lower lip. The impact had made her bite down and her two front teeth had also loosened from the gum. He was banging her head against a wall.

"Please don't." Was all she was able to say before her face was rammed into the bricks again.

Her eyebrow split with the next blow and blood began to run into her left eye and down her face.

"Struggle again and I'll cut ya." He said almost playfully.

"I've no money." Elsie's mind felt like treacle. Should she reason with him?

"Not ya money I want."

Elsie felt something cold and sharp come up under her chin and she went still.

"Turn around," he ordered, "scream and you're dead." He stepped back.

She kept her hands by her side and slowly turned, frightened of who might be behind her. The blood that ran into her eye dripped off her chin and onto her chest.

The alleyway was too dark to see clearly, and her head still swam.

Her eyes bulged as his hand came up to her throat. A knee pushed her thighs apart.

"Spread ya feet." He commanded.

Repulsive thoughts flooded Elsie's mind. "Please… not that I-" She pleaded. She felt her stomach heave.

"Don't flatter yourself."

She closed her eyes and hoped that it was all a bad dream. The cold steel of the blade pressed against her gullet. She swallowed. The knife stayed firmly against her skin.

"Bet ya thinking why you, ain't ya?" He asked.

Elsie screwed up her face in an attempt not to cry and gave a short nod of the head. She didn't open her eyes.

The attacker lifted the blade. Elsie didn't see it fall.

Chapter Four

The pale light leaking through the curtains woke Ruby with a fresh wave of dread. She had gone out the previous night to meet Elsie, but when she arrived late, Elsie's predilection for punctuality meant she'd already taken off. As Ruby slowly made her way over to Elsie's apartment, fear and guilt weighed down her chest like heavy stones. Yet upon arriving, she found that Elsie had still not returned home. Half of her wanted to stay and wait for her, while an equally powerful urge pulled at her to go back home, in hope that Elsie would be there. When she reached the kitchen table and set down her key cold reality told her differently. Ruby stared at the glowing embers of the dying fire late into the night, trying to figure out why Elsie hadn't sent a message or come by the townhouse.

"Not a nice front page today, Miss Ruby." Polly picked up a slice of bread and butter and took a bite, her eyes dancing with barely suppressed excitement. "Nuva two bodies, one girl named they don't yet know who the 'ova one is." She ran her finger across her throat as she spoke. "Rose, yah seen this?" She shovelled the rest of the bread into her mouth, pointed at the newspaper Ruby had in front of her, then reached over the table for the teapot.

"Polly, what've I told yah about manners." Rose chastised. "Sit down at the table properly when you eat, I'm so sorry Miss Ruby." She pulled out a chair tucked under the table and pointed for Polly to sit down.

"Sorry Miss Ruby, Rose." Polly slid into the chair eagerly, her curious eyes on Ruby, who still hadn't looked up from the paper. The headlines seared into her brain like a branding iron:

Two New Bodies, One Victim Named!

Ruby fought back tears as she looked up from the paper. "The paper says the victim was Amy Glover, I hope this ain't the Amy I know." She looked from Rose to Polly and then back to Rose in desperation.

"Miss Ruby you've gone as white as a sheet."

Rose came around the table and placed an arm around Ruby's shaking shoulders. "Do you think it's possible that it could be 'er?" Rose asked as she pulled out the chair next to Ruby, sat down and reached out for Ruby's trembling hand.

"Rose, I really hope it's not, she was a good girl, Amy." Ruby let go of Rose's hand, put her elbows on the table and rested her chin on her fists. "Polly, can you go and find Arfur for me, there's a girl."

She bought her eyes back down to the paper.

"I'm off for 'im now Miss Ruby." Polly stood, pushed the chair under the table and made for the door at the back of the kitchen. "Be back in a trice."

Rose stood and began clearing the table. "Martha is doin' well, the bruises are startin' to fade some." She loaded the crockery into the sink as she changed the subject. "Might 'en you go up a see 'er today, Miss Ruby?" She threw a quick glance at Ruby as she washed the dishes.

"Umm…" Ruby's mind was buzzing with so many questions, and she couldn't think straight. The news of two girls being murdered had sent shock waves through her already fragile psyche. She wondered if one of the victims was her friend, and if not, who was the second girl? Was it someone else that she had been close to? Her thoughts spiralled out of control, and she felt like she was drowning in a sea of emotions. Fear, anger, and sadness mixed together in her mind as everything became a blur. She needed answers, but the more she tried to find them, the more confused she became.

"Martha, maybe a visit." Repeated Rose.

The mention of the girl's name snapped Ruby out of her thoughts. "What's that about Martha?" She pushed up from the table and brushed breadcrumbs from the tablecloth into her hand, walked to the back door, opened it, and threw the crumbs outside. The cold early morning draft rushed in, and she shivered. "Is Martha mending ok, Rose?" Ruby pulled her hair up and knotted it into a bun securing it with a hair clip.

"Would you nip up and see her? She's getting better, bruising is fading." Rose repeated.

"Yes of course, can you let me know when Arthur arrives?" Ruby put out an appreciative hand and rested it on Rose's left shoulder. "Thank you, Rose."

Rose smiled and nodded at her and continued with the dishes.

Half an hour later a rather cold Polly and Arthur arrived at the townhouse. After a quick visit to Martha, Ruby went and sat in her parlour. She always read her mail at her mahogany bureaux, a gift from Elsie, which she loved and fell even deeper in love with Elsie because of it. Ornate carvings adorned the edges and down the sides, with two cupids engrained on the top above the writing desk. Ruby kept her parlour clean and warm. Her tastes were modest, and she had very few ornaments or possessions around the room. A grandmother clock ticked soothingly in the corner and a round table stood under a bay window, covered with a thick velvet cloth. On top of it was a brass oil lamp with an ornate glass shade, with etchings of leaves and twines that adorned its surface. Two brown leather wing-back armchairs were positioned by the fire, the only furniture of any great value, and stood on top of a beige rag rug. Above the fireplace, one single photo sat on the mantlepiece, darkened, and charred around the edges, placed in an overly large frame. A couple looked out happy and smiling, with three small children standing in front of them. Ruby's late parents and her two dead siblings. The photo was the only possession Ruby was able to save from the fire.

She'd just finished reading the mail when Arthur came in.

"Good to see my girl, Polly told me what'd happened, are you sure you know her?" He stood behind her, stroked both of her arms and then kissed her on the top of her head.

Ruby stood, turned around and encircled his waist with her arms and rested her head against his chest. “I think so, there must be a way we can find out who the two girls are, do you know of someone?” She lifted her head and met Arthur’s gaze.

“There’s a copper at H division that I know.” He went and sat in a chair opposite Ruby’s. “I can have a word in his ear, see if he can shed some light.” He crossed his legs and looked into the fireplace. His arms rested in his lap, he lifted a hand and absentmindedly smoothed his moustache with his thumb and index finger. “He’s usually pretty knowledgeable about the goings on at the pig pen.” His brown eyes watched as the flames danced in the hearth. He dropped his hand and smoothed the fabric of his trousers and looked back at Ruby.

Ruby nervously sat in her chair, the feeling of dread growing inside her. She felt restless, so she slowly stood up and walked to the window, before turning back to face Arty. "I can't shake this feeling that it really is true," she said, her voice quavering. "But I don't want to believe it is Amy."

There was a light knock on the parlour door, followed by Rose. “Excuse me, Miss Ruby, there’s a visitor for you,” Rose pointed over her shoulder with her thumb, “an Inspector Abberline from Scotland Yard.” She frowned and stuck out her bottom lip. “He hasn’t said what ‘e wants, just asked for ya.”

Ruby looked over at Arthur and raised her eyebrows in question.

“Not the contact I know,” he said as he shrugged his shoulders.

“Ok Rose, show him in and any chance of a pot of tea?” Ruby asked then sat back down in her chair.

A smartly but modestly dressed man entered the room. “Good morning to you, both, Inspector Abberline, Scotland Yard.” He said after giving them both a warm smile.

Ruby only nodded and didn’t speak to her visitor, she just sat down in her chair. Arthur took his place with his back against the fireplace and pulled a pipe from his waistcoat and put it in his mouth but didn’t light it.

The room was silent, as though the air had been sucked out with all the oxygen. No one moved and no one breathed, leaving an eerie feeling of anticipation that hung heavy in the air.

“So, Inspector Abberline, what can we do for you today?” Said Arthur. He’d taken the pipe out of his mouth and held it in his hand behind his back.

“I gave your maid my calling card, it has all my details for future reference.” Abberline said as he looked over at Rose. Abberline stood of average height and was of medium build, with greying hair combed back over his head. His beard and moustache were well groomed, and he wore a tweed suit with polished black lace-up shoes. He had a kind face with soft grey eyes, a pale blue handkerchief in his breast pocket, and a sprig of lavender in the buttonhole.

“She’s not a maid, Inspector Abberline, she’s, my housekeeper.” Said Ruby curtly.

“My apologies Miss Myers, your housekeeper.” Corrected Abberline.

Rose pushed her chest out proudly and handed her the small card she was holding bearing Abberline's details. Ruby didn't look at it and passed it to Arthur.

Abberline smiled warmly again at Ruby. "Miss Ruby Myers, I apologise, I assume I've inconvenienced you with my visit?"

"You've assumed correctly, I've business matters to attend to in town shortly, will you be long?" She glanced across at Arthur.

To Arthur's surprise, Abberline approached him and extended his hand to him to shake his, "Arthur Miller, I assume?"

"You assume correctly, I must be honest, I'm a little surprised by the handshake, Inspector." Arthur queried as he shook his hand, then offered him the seat opposite Ruby.

"Thank you. Well, I do like to shake the hand of any new acquaintance, I feel it breaks the ice somewhat, don't you agree?" He dug into his jacket pocket and pulled out a small black notebook and a small pencil with a badly chewed end.

Arthur didn't reply.

"Do you mind if I take some notes, my memory doesn't serve me so well these days?" He glanced at Arthur then at Ruby and produced a small pair of spectacles and propped them on the end of his nose.

"Just so long as I know why you're here, Inspector." Said Ruby.

They were interrupted by Rose who came in and placed a tray with a teapot, cups, saucers, and a jug of milk on the table behind Ruby's chair. "Your tea." She said then scuttled out of the room.

"Thank you, Rose," Ruby said but she hadn't taken her eyes off Abberline. "And?" She asked.

Abberline cleared his throat. "Miss Myers, do you happen to know an Elsie Lancaster?"

Ruby felt a sudden rush of warmth course through her at the mention of Elsie's name. Her cheeks tinged pink, and a flutter of excitement settled in her stomach as memories of their last night together filled her mind. She clenched her fists tightly, hiding the undeniable blush that crept up her neck. Even if anyone else suspected her secret affair with Elsie, only Arthur knew for sure.

Abberline noticed.

"What if I do?" She had no intentions of giving anything away to a copper.

"I'm afraid I need you to be more specific than that Miss Myers." His pencil was poised above the notebook, and he looked at her over the glasses. "What's your relationship with her?"

Ruby's expression was cold and impassive. "Yes, I know Elsie Lancaster, Inspector. Why'd ya ask?" She looked at Arthur who was pulling in a lungful of tobacco smoke. He raised his eyebrows.

"Just answer the question for me please, your relationship with Miss Lancaster?"

Ruby's mouth went dry, and she tried to swallow. "She's a friend, well we're more like sisters actually." She glanced again at Arthur, and he winked at her.

Abberline didn't notice.

"Does she work at the local theatre and sings on the stage there?" Again, he looked at her over his glasses.

"Yes, some of the time." A hard knot formed in the pit of Ruby's stomach.

"And the address of her lodgings?"

"Carter Street, number 56 I think."

"Can you name the theatre for me, please Miss Myers?

"It's the Dragoon Theatre – for goodness's sake Inspector." Ruby's throat tightened.

Arthur cleared his throat and was about to speak but Abberline spoke first.

"Miss Myers, I went into the theatre this morning and spoke to a," Abberline glanced down at his notebook and flicked through some of the pages, "ah yes, to a Jack Hardman and he told me that you were the person I needed to see. I sorry to tell you that Elsie Lancaster was found brutally dead last night."

Ruby's face drained of colour, her mouth tightening as she tried to keep herself composed, a chill ran down her spine; the words seemed to hang in the air like icicles, yet she still couldn't find it within herself to respond.

"Inspector, are you completely certain that it's Elsie?" Arthur stepped forward and took Ruby's hand. It felt cold to the touch.

“Yes, we are sure, Mr Hardman confirmed her identity at the mortuary just before I came here.” He looked at Arthur and raised his eyebrows.

Arthur was still standing next to Ruby and holding her hand. She still hadn’t spoken.

“Inspector, is Elsie at the mortuary on King’s Street?” Arthur asked. “Has anyone actually claimed the body?”

“No one would, her parents are both dead and she had no brothers or sisters.” Ruby managed to say. “I need to go there Arfur, I need to see her right now. Please can you take me?” Ruby tried to stand, but her legs wouldn’t support her.

Ruby felt Arthur put his free hand under her elbow to help her to her feet.

Abberline cleared his throat. “Um, Miss Myers, Mr. Morris, yes she is at King’s Street, but I don’t advise you go to see her in the mortuary, it isn’t pleasant and certainly not a place for a lady to visit.” He looked at Arthur.

Arthur noticed a look of genuine concern. “Ruby, love, did you hear the Inspector?”

She nodded.

“Inspector, with all due respect, if Miss Myers wants to see Elsie, then I see no reason why this cannot be arranged. Is there a place where the body can be moved into another room that is more, er… suitable?” Arthur hadn’t let go of Ruby.

“Don’t say the body, Arthur, Elsie is a person.” Ruby looked up at him, her blue eyes full of tears. “Do you think it could be her Arty?” She said in a quiet voice. A tear ran down her cheek.

"I hope it's not Ruby, love," He glanced across at Abberline, "
but you had it confirmed, didn't you?" Arthur asked.

Abberline nodded, "I'm so sorry to say it has been confirmed."

"I want to go and see her and I am." Ruby slipped her hand from Arthur's and turned to the Inspector.

"Why do I feel like you're keeping something from me, Inspector?" She asked, her voice trembling with fear and anger, "tell me why it's so important that I don't go to the mortuary. What is it you don't want me to see?"

Abberline didn't answer and looked at Arthur for reassurance. Arthur nodded.

"Well, Inspector?" Ruby had run out of patience.

"Miss Myers, I'm afraid it doesn't make for pretty viewing, and I would rather spare you the anguish of seeing such things." Abberline removed his glasses and put them back into his jacket pocket.

"Just give me the truth Inspector… all of it."

"Just tell her Inspector," Arthur said.

Abberline took a deep breath before he spoke "Miss Myers, I'm sorry to have to tell you this, but Elsie was badly disfigured by her killer, so a viewing won't be advisable, also it was concluded by the Doctor after the post-mortem that Elsie Lancaster was with child."

Ruby clasped her hand over her mouth, her stomach rolled like bilge water at the bottom of a boat.

Arthur turned to Abberline and threw him a questionable look. “Inspector, I think you should tell me the further details and I will relay them to Ruby at a later date.” He put his pipe back between his teeth and then crossed to the fireplace.

“Mr Morris, there is little else I can share with you.” Abberline looked apologetic as he stood up and pushed the notebook and pencil back into his jacket pocket. “There is very little to go on at this present time.”

Arthur pulled hard on his pipe, before answering.

“Inspector Abberline,” he said as smoke billowed from his mouth and nose. “Surely there must be more answers than this. Granted it’s not even been twenty-four hours, but have any clues been found or could Jack give you some idea of whom she may have left the theatre with last night?” Arthur drew his eyebrows together in a frown.

Abberline fixed his gaze on Mr Morris, unwavering and serious. His hands were clenched tightly in his lap as he leaned forward. “I can’t tell you any more about the case, Mr Morris. After I leave here, I must go to the Mortuary to discuss the results of the post-mortem with Dr Sequira. I wanted to come here myself because Mr Hardman said that you were Miss Lancaster’s closest friend and perhaps you could’ve provided me with some information on those close to her that I could speak with. However, it appears that is not the case. Rest assured that we will do everything to catch the perpetrator of this terrible crime."

"Inspector, I need time to process what you've just told me, it was a complete shock, Rose will show you out." Ruby didn't meet Abberline's eyes as she spoke.

If Abberline was surprised by the sudden dismissal, he didn't show it.

"Of course, you have my card, if you think of anything that may help, please do get in touch." He walked towards the door. "Oh, and may I say that it was a pleasure meeting you Mr Morris, Miss Myers, even under such horrible circumstances."

Neither replied.

"Good day to you both." He smiled warmly at them, went out into the hallway where Rose was waiting with his coat and hat, and closed the door quietly behind him.

The two didn't speak for several moments, each trying to digest what they'd just been told. It was Ruby that spoke first.

"It's my fault this has happened Arty, I was running late meeting her last night." She looked over at Arthur who had now sat down in the chair opposite. "I was dealing with that nasty punter Smythe, if it hadn't been for him, I'd have been there to meet her for our usual night together." She looked across to the fireplace.

The flames danced and licked at the log that had been placed there.

"Rubes, this wasn't your fault. I'll have a word with my associates at Scotland Yard and Whitechapel H Division and see if I can find out more details. I'll find out if Abberline was playing his cards close to his chest by keeping information from us." He raised his pipe to his mouth again and attempted to take a long draw, but it had burnt out.

"I need to see her Arty, can that be arranged too?" She watched him as he tapped the ashes out of his pipe into a nearby glass ashtray.

"Um." Arthur said absentmindedly. He glanced across at Ruby.

"Arrange for me to see her, is that possible?" Ruby's face looked at him full of expectation.

"I'm sorry darling, I was thinking about contacts, of course, leave it with me, I will do my best." He stood and put his hand out and cupped her chin. "It'll be a cold day in hell when I don't do everything I can to help my girl." He smiled at her and bent to place a light kiss on her mouth.

Chapter Five

Abberline pushed open the door to the mortuary. He pulled out a handkerchief from his top pocket and placed it over his nose and mouth. The smells always turned his stomach.

Four gurneys which all hosted a deceased were lined up against the left wall. Stained sack cloths covered the identity of each one beneath it.

Dr Sequeira was with a female who was laid out on the slab in front of him in the centre of the room. An array of medical instruments was on a trolley on his right, most covered with gore from the dead woman.

On the back wall, behind Sequeira, a sink with one tap was mounted. Water dripped from it intermittently marking the passing seconds as if it were a metronome keeping time for the dead.

The sun shone its autumnal rays through the window on the right-hand side of the room and cast shadowy fingers across the dead woman and onto the trolley of instruments.

"Still find the smells distasteful ole boy?" Sequeira looked up from the woman and threw Abberline an amused look.

Abberline moved the handkerchief just enough so he could be heard. "Aubrey, you know I'll never get accustomed no matter how many times I need to visit this infernal place. Present company and all that." A warm look of greeting could be seen over the hanky at Abberline's mouth.

The doctor chuckled, removed his arm from the woman's chest cavity, wiped his hands on a rag pushed into the belt of his bloodied apron and reached for a hip flask laying on the instrument trolley.

Abberline fought the urge to gag as he noticed some blackened human tissue sliver down its side onto the floor. The doctor didn't notice.

"Nothing like the evacuations of the dead to have you saying goodbye to your breakfast, eh Fred?" Sequeira put his free hand on his hip as he took a deep swill from the flask in the other. "Good to see you, my friend, even if it always seems to be like this."

Abberline nodded and swallowed hard before speaking. "Is this the woman from last night?" He didn't move any closer, doing his best to keep a respectful distance from the naked form on the slab. She may be dead, but she was still a lady when alive.

"What this old girl?" The doctor waved his hand holding the hip flask over the woman and took another swig from it before screwing the cap back on. "No, not this one, she was found dead in her bed," he said as he swallowed the liquid, "She's over there." He lifted his chin in the direction of the four gurneys, "Second one along I think." Sequeira continued to look down into the woman's open cavity, then glanced up again at Abberline. "Have a look if you want, won't be a jiffy." He reached underneath the bottom of the trolley and pulled out some crumpled sackcloth. "Fred?"

Abberline was standing stock still, his pallor spoke volumes. “Would rather not, thanks Doc, I’ll let you have the pleasure.” He dabbed at his mouth with his handkerchief. “Good lord, it’s warm in here this morning.” The Inspector held his breath as he wiped his brow and the back of his neck where perspiration had formed.

Sequeira moved in between the second and the third gurney, lifted the covering of the second and peered underneath.

“Yes, this is her.”

Abberline walked to where she lay and stood at the feet of the deceased.

“Leave the cover in place, there’s a good man,” Abberline said. “No need for me to see anything else.”

“No problem,” Sequeira smirked at his friend’s ongoing discomfort.

Abberline ignored it as he asked, “what else can you tell me since we spoke first thing?”

“Several things actually.”

“Such as?”

“Well, you remember I said that this girl was with child?”

Abberline nodded and raised his eyebrows.

“I hadn’t had time to properly examine the girl.” Sequeira scratched his temple before continuing, “I won’t beat about the bush here ole boy, but it’s not something I’ve come across before. I assumed that this woman had been pregnant as I’d found some foetal matter in the lower part of her vagina. It wasn’t until further inspection that I realised that this couldn’t have been her child.”

Abberline felt the heat rise in his cheeks as his friend talked about the nether regions of the woman. He tried to maintain his composure, but he couldn't keep the look of embarrassment off his face. "Oh, really? And why do you think that?" He asked, hoping to divert the conversation away from uncomfortable territory.

"Well, it's because this woman was born without ovaries." The doctor gave Abberline a moment to digest what he'd just been told before continuing.

Abberline cleared his throat, "So Aubrey, you're telling me that this poor woman was in fact sterile?" His jaw hung slack behind the hanky he still held to his face.

"Of that, I am ole boy." He walked back to the centre slab, picked up a notebook and pencil that was on the instrument trolley and scribbled something down.

"That's as maybe Aubrey, but what about the foetal matter in her lower… um… parts?" Abberline, stumbled over the words, then asked, "how in God's name has that ended up in…" Realisation dropped like a stone into Abberline's mind. "Good Heavens the person who killed her must have put it there. Am I right in my assumptions Doc?" Abberline looked around for a place to sit down but couldn't see anywhere.

“Certainly, seems that way, Fred.” Sequeira had finished scribbling and now patted himself down looking for his hip flask. “Where on earth… ah, there it is.” He noticed it on the slab next to the other dead woman and picked it up and began unscrewing the cap. “I can’t say for sure, but I’d say that the woman that it originally came out of,” he pointed over to gurney number two, “was in the early stages of pregnancy, maybe six to eight weeks,” He took a swig before continuing, “Fred,” he said mid-swallow, “I also found this, it was caught up in her hair.” Aubrey had crossed to the trolley that had all the surgical instruments on. “This, a coin.” He handed it to Abberline. “Quite odd really, ole boy, thought it was a stone or maybe a hair ornament until I managed to untangle it.” He stood with his arms folded waiting for Abberline’s answer.

“What on earth -” The Inspector turned the object over in his fingers, then held it up in the light. “Nothing out of the ordinary minted 1855, but other than that a normal currency.” He slipped the coin into his pocket. “Aubrey?” Abberline’s pallor stopped the Doctor in his tracks.

“I think you could do with some air ole boy.” Sequeira raised his hand towards the doors, “Let’s go outside, shall we Fred, we can talk out there.”

Abberline didn’t need to be asked twice and wasted no time in taking up Sequeira on his offer.

Although the late morning air was still crisp Abberline had to draw in a deep lungful in the hope of settling his stomach. The trees were dropping their leaves and the ground was covered in a carpet of yellows and browns and burnt oranges. He kicked absentmindedly at the foliage, his mind whirred with the information he'd just been made privy to.

"Fred, sorry ole chap, I sometimes forget that not everyone has the stomach for what I do." Aubrey smiled at him and gave his left shoulder a friendly squeeze.

"It's of no matter Aubrey, these things need to be done, even though it's not my favourite part of the job." He felt the coin in his pocket, "And this," he said taking it out and pushing it through his fingers, "has some bearing in the case, I can feel it." He looked at Sequeira and pursed his lips together whilst nodding slowly. "By George, I'll get to the bottom of this, hopefully, sooner rather than later." Abberline's jaw clenched.

"I have complete faith in you, Fred, nothing gets past you. If I find anything further that might be of interest, I'll get word to you. Now if you'll excuse me, I'm needed back in there." He pointed his thumb over his shoulder. "She's not going anywhere, but I've got your colleague on my back wanting some answers." Aubrey turned and walked towards the building.

"Is it Inspector Royal you're talking about Aubrey?" Abberline pushed his hands into his coat pockets.

"The very same, see you, Fred." Aubrey didn't look back as he walked into the building.

Fred lingered outside the mortuary, his thoughts consumed by the women who had been brutally slain. Three deaths in only a few days—he was no closer to understanding the culprit's identity or intent. What bearing did the coin have in the case? More to the point who would be depraved enough to put foetal matter upon the woman's person. Was this the work of a maniac, revelling in their suffering? Or was it an act of revenge against these innocent victims? Why would Royal be pushing for answers so quickly when the information could be discussed over a pint later? So many questions lingered in his mind as he idly turned the coin over in his hand. Abberline was determined to stop this evil before it struck again, but he didn't know if he could do it soon enough.

Chapter Six

Ruby wasn't kept waiting long when she arrived at Whitechapel's local police station. The note asking for the meeting arrived the previous night, just before dinner. A tall, wiry copper delivered it. He'd flushed when he handed it to Ruby, it wasn't until later that she'd realised he was a regular punter for one of the girls.

The room had gone very quiet upon her arrival, and it didn't take a genius to work out that most of the constables were or had been regulars who frequented her establishment at some point. Hypocrites.

Nevertheless, she waited patiently until a skinny, blond-haired copper with bad skin came to show her into Abberline's office.

The Inspector stood and gave her a warm smile, which she didn't return when she entered the room.

The office wasn't very big and cluttered with piles of paper and files stacked on the floor and on the shelves on the wall. A desk had been squeezed into the middle of the room and a chair sat behind it, two other faded green, button-back chairs were placed in front of it. The backs of which faced the fire in the hearth about a stride away. The mantle that was above it had a solitary clock upon it. Beyond the desk, on the other side of the room and no more than two strides from it were a large, lead, lattice paned window. The autumnal morning sun shone through doing little to warm and illuminate the room with its watery light. Even so, the room felt stuffy and oppressive.

"Miss Myers, so good of you to come, please take a seat. Inspector Royal should be with us shortly. Can I offer you some tea, perhaps?" He nodded to the skinny copper still standing in the doorway. "Fetch some tea will you Constable Doyle."

"Not for me thank you." Ruby answered.

Abberline ignored her and nodded again to the Constable, who closed the door quietly behind him.

Abberline turned his attention back to Ruby.

"How are you Miss Myers after the dreadful events of the past few nights?" He searched her face for any expression.

"Is that what you've called me here for Inspector?" Ruby said in a tight voice, her face expressionless. "I've not come all this way-"

Abberline cut her off with the raise of his hand. He stood up and came around to the front of the desk and perched himself on its edge, near to the chair she was sitting in.

"Please, Miss Myers, that is not the reason, I was just merely enquiring as to your wellbeing, is that such a bad thing?" He noticed a flush appear on her cheeks.

Ruby cleared her throat, "Inspector, my well-being is none of your concern, now if you'd get down to the reason as to why I'm here, then I can be on my way." She screwed her lips together and frowned at the man in front of her. How dare he.

Abberline nodded an apology, "Of course, I shouldn't have pried. I was hoping that Inspector Royal would've been here by now, he was told the time of our meeting." He pulled out his pocket watch and checked the time against the clock on the mantel. "M-uh, well I'll begin, and he can always be filled in on the details upon his arrival." He snapped the cover shut and pushed his watch back into his waistcoat pocket, then returned to his seat behind the desk. He placed his forearms on top lacing his fingers together. "Now Miss Myers, where do I start?" He pursed his lips together in thought. "Ah, yes. As you are aware there have been some nasty murders of late. I know one of which was your close friend Elsie-"

Ruby caught him off guard when she interrupted him. "Three of which are my friends." She fixed him with her blue eyes.

It took Abberline a few seconds to collect his thoughts. "Thank you for the information, Miss Myers, I wasn't aware the others were friends of yours too, past acquaintances may I ask?"

"They were but not all had worked for me, one was a friend from a while back." Ruby answered.

Abberline nodded, "I see. I will make sure that this is included in the notes of the investigation." He plucked up a pencil and scratched something on some paper beside him on the desk. "As I was saying, as we are all aware some horrible things have been occurring recently around the district. I must be entirely honest and admit that at Scotland Yard we are at our wit's end trying to get to the bottom of these killings." Abberline shifted in his seat.

They were interrupted by a knock at the door.

"Come."

The door opened and Doyle stood in the doorway. "Inspector Royal for you Sir." He stood back and let the visitor pass him.

"Thank you, Doyle, see about that tea would you." Abberline smiled at his colleague "Royal, so glad to see you." He walked around the desk, took hold of the man's hand, and gave it a shake. "Have you met Miss Myers?" He asked extending his arm in Ruby's direction.

"Can't say I've met her, but I certainly know of her." Royal didn't look in Ruby's direction.

The man was of average height, with a very prominent bulbous nose. He was dressed in a white overshirt worn underneath a grey waistcoat, trousers, and a long matching jacket. The buttons on the waistcoat were strained over his substantial midriff. His double chin sat on the shirt collar and a small black tie around his throat. Red thread veins covered both cheeks. Dark pig-like shaped eyes stared back at her overshadowed by bushy, grey, unruly eyebrows. The thick whiskers that ran down both sides of his face from his large, floppy, ear lobes to his chin were sprinkled with white hair and his grey thatch was heavily oiled. Royal's podgy fingers held his bowler hat which he tossed onto the desk in front of him as he sat down. Not a pleasant-looking man.

Abberline was taken aback by the remark. He knew his colleague could be brash, but he was never usually rude.

Ruby's shoulders stiffened. Marvellous, another arrogant pig to deal with.

Royal walked around the desk and sat down in Abberline's chair, by which, Ruby had no choice but to see exactly the type of person she was dealing with.

Abberline paused for a moment before taking a seat in the chair next to Ruby's. The cushions were worn and the fabric slightly torn, but he made himself comfortable.

Royal raised his eyebrows then shifted in Abberline's chair, grunting in the process and began to absentmindedly fiddle with his left whisker.

"Good, well I've come up with an idea as to how we could possibly find the person or persons that are causing all this terror on our local streets." Abberline paused and looked from Ruby to Royal and back again before continuing. "Now I know that this is probably a tall order, but I was wondering Miss Myers if perhaps you and your beau would be willing to join together with the constabulary to try to bring this horrible situation to a close?" He smiled warmly at Ruby.

Ruby's expression didn't change.

Royal had a deep frown on his face.

"You want me and my Arthur to collaborate with you and…" She let the words drift off. She glanced at Royal then turned her eyes back to Abberline. "I'm not sure that I heard you correctly Inspector, you want to forge a temporary alliance?"

“That is exactly what I’m proposing Miss Myers, yes. I know that you have the means and the methods with the help of your many associates, to find out more on the streets of Whitechapel than could be possible by the police here. I’m under no illusions that your acquaintances are not keen on helping the law with any such investigations, and the locals would rather taunt us than help us. But the networks that the constabulary are normally investigating have the capacity to uncover far more information in an expedited fashion, particularly when you or Mr Morris request it.”

Abberline started filling teacups from a tray the constable had just bought in, as he continued talking. “So, what do you make of this, Miss Myers?” He kept his eyes downcast.

“I should like to see what Mr Morris has to say before I give an answer.” She accepted the cup and saucer that Abberline offered her, albeit hesitantly.

“Don't you want my opinion on this too, Fred?” Royal scooped some sugar into his tea.

"Absolutely! Of course, I'd love your thoughts on it, Bernard." He picked up his cup and saucer and then sat back in his chair. "We usually tend to agree anyway, don't we?" Abberline crossed his legs.

"I'm afraid I don't Fred, what in the blazes do you think it'll achieve? Not for one moment do I think it's at all possible to work at any point with a group of organised criminals. Good grief man, they might take our money without us realizing it, lure us on pointless errands, and even give the criminal we're after information to help them avoid capture. Not to mention the possibility of them sneaking into our beds in the night and killing us." His hand trembled as he spooned more sugar. "Absolutely outrageous. I've always respected you Fred and the way you do your job, but on this, I'm afraid I have to disagree, plain and simple."

Ruby put her cup and saucer back on the tea tray, the tea untouched. The look on Royal's face told her everything she needed to know. He was a copper through and through and hated the world she was involved in, and he made his hatred as plain as the nose on his face.

But there was something more to it than just disdain. He was scared. That much was clear when she saw the way his eyes shifted around the room, searching for an escape. He was a policeman, but he feared her, and this was a new experience for him.

Ruby felt a surge of energy course through her veins. The familiar sense of power was different this time – it was more intense, more alive. She watched as Royal's gaze darted around the room, trying to find an excuse to escape back into the safety of his world. But he couldn't escape without showing weakness and submission in front of Abberline. She saw his hesitation, and she could feel her own strength and control growing.

"Well, my intentions are that it'll help to quickly catch this madman and send him to the gallows." Abberline drank from his teacup, "Obviously it's an unusual arrange-"

"Poppycock man." Royal interrupted, "Surely you don't think for one second that the likes of her," he stabbed a pointed finger at Ruby, "would be even prepared to, to hel-"

"That is quite enough Inspector, I will not sit here and be insulted by you!" Interrupted Ruby as she narrowed her eyes in Royal's direction. "Believe it or not my contacts are trusted and loyal to me, which is something that you're clearly unaccustomed to within the ranks of this place." She hoped her stare portrayed the dislike that she felt about this man.

Royal shot out of his seat, his face crimson, the teacup upending in the saucer, hot liquid splashed across the desk. "How dare you insinuate anything of the kind, I'm more than aware of the businesses that you run Miss Myers and, to be honest, I won't be at all sad when they've sent you to prison or even to the gallows." A vein pulsated in his neck.

Abberline leant forward and placed his empty cup and saucer on the tray. "Now Bernard, let's not be too hasty with our own opinions. As I said it would be helpful if Miss Myers could agree to work alongside us, throwing insults at one another isn't going to do either of us any good." He pulled his handkerchief from one of his pockets and began to mop up the spilt tea.

Ruby fixed Inspector Abberline with a gaze of steel. “It's not my call to make, but if we join forces then I need you both to be crystal clear: the task at hand is all that matters. Nothing else.” She spoke the words like daggers, her voice as cold as ice, leaving no room for misunderstanding. She glared across at Royal, “And Inspector Royal, I’ll tell you now that there is no way I’ll allow you to insult or demoralise me or any of my associates with your crass remarks. You are expecting respect from me and the others that I know, but respect is earned.” Ruby’s eyes were like hot coals as she made her point. “Now Inspectors is there anything else?” Ruby stood up.

Abberline shifted uncomfortably in his chair. Royal’s jaw hung slackly, his face still crimson.

“If I need to speak with you further Miss Myers, would you permit me to visit you at your lodgings?” Asked Abberline. “I do hope that this proposal can be agreeable to yourself and your associates, I’ve no doubt that we both wish to bring these crimes to a close.” Abberline rose and directed Ruby to the door. “Thank you for your time this morning.” He gave her another kind smile as he opened the door for her.

Ruby nodded and then turned again to Royal. “I’d say it was a pleasure meeting you Inspector, but I’d be lying.” She didn’t wait for a rcsponsc as shc nodded once more at Abberline and left the room. Ruby waited until she heard the office door close behind her then let out an animalistic growl. Arrogant bloody pig.

As she stalked out of the station, she could hear Royal's raised voice complaining to Abberline. Outside she thumped down the steps and noticed Arthur leaning against a nearby wrought iron fence reading a newspaper. Anger radiated out of her as she fought back tears.

"Arty, I'm so glad to see you here, how was your meeting?" She said, trying to calm down.

Arthur folded the paper, "Went as expected. You ok Rubes? What's happened? Why are you so angry?" He saw the tightness in her expression.

"I've just had the misfortune to meet an Inspector Royal, is the name familiar to you?" She moved nearer to the railings to let a woman through pushing a pram, the baby inside gurgled happily as they passed.

"I know of him, yes, his reputation precedes him. Not a pleasant bloke by all accounts." He put his hand on Ruby's elbow and began leading her away from the station. "Let's talk as we walk my girl; the walls've ears with this place."

"He did nothing to make me believe otherwise, Abberline actually told him to stop, which surprised me for a copper." Spittle formed in the corners of Ruby's mouth as she still tried to keep her temper, "thing is Arty, I know him from somewhere, his face is really familiar."

"So, what did Abberline say?" He prodded.

Ruby was pulled out of her thoughts by Arthur's question "Umm, something about a temporary alliance between us and the coppers. I guess it would help to solve these murders as we can get information quicker than them." She glanced up at Arthur. "Could that really work? I mean do we really have to go that far? I can't think of anything more repulsive, especially working alongside that Royal bloke." Her face twisted in disgust at the thought.

Arthur stopped in his tracks, pondering the decision before them. "I don't know if we can trust Abberline, Ruby. What if this is a way for Royal to access information about our other activities?"

Ruby looked at him frantically, searching for the answer in his face. "I'm not sure what to do, Arthur. We need to talk it through with the lads first."

"I agree," he said finally.

Ruby hesitated as she looked at Arthur, feeling both concern and fear of what may lay ahead. They had come to a crossroad, one which they knew they must tread together. She slowly looped her arm through his, and with trepidation in every step, they started on their way towards the group of lads who would surely have many questions.

Chapter Seven

In the bar she'd been buxom and brash with the locals, flirting with one then another her dark hair in a messy bun perched on the top of her head was quivering with her every movement. She moved between the drinkers easily and he could tell she had a confidence that many of the others he'd chosen before didn't possess. A plain girl, with hazel eyes and a rounded profile, her cheeks rosy from the warmth of the tavern.

She had a friendliness about her that was portrayed in her face and the girl smiled as she brushed past an old boy as she collected glasses and tankards to take back to the bar.

"You all right Alice? Looking rather ravishing tonight I must say." Said the old man as he watched her behind as she moved between the chairs.

She threw him an exasperated half smile over her shoulder then turned to collect two more glasses from an adjoining group. The old man sat at a table with four other men all of whom were pretty well-oiled. "I wouldn't mind a piece of that for the night, mate." He leant over to the chap seated next to him as he spoke.

"A night, Jimmy, you wouldn't last five minutes." A companion said laughing hard.

The other two men joined in and started teasing him too.

"Well, one can hope." Jimmy took another swig from his pint before laughing along with the camaraderie. "Yeah, yeah, I know, but there's life in the old todger yet, especially with a backside like 'ers on display." Jimmy gave a wink and then stood up and made his way to the bar.

The spectator sat and watched, sipping whiskey from the glass in front of him. Jimmy was an idiot.

He rested his hand on the silver top of his cane warming it in his palm. The clenched fist was a distinctive design from his late mother. How useful it had been of late.

A man began thumping the keys on a piano in the corner of the room and a drunken version of *Roll out the Barrel* began to permeate the chatter from the crowd. The old boy crossed from the bar, a new pint in his hand and sat on the chair next to the musician, patting out a rhythm on the top of his leg.

"If I 'ad me spoons George I woulda joined yah," Jimmy shouted so he could be heard through the din.

The spectator continued to watch Alice as she did the rounds collecting glasses and dodging the frequent wandering hands. The watcher's fist clenched, turning his knuckles white, as the owners of the hands just laughed. Nobody can touch this girl, except him.

She made her way over to where he was sitting and swiped an empty glass on the opposite side of the table. Alice lifted her eyes and looked straight into his. He smiled at her, and she dropped her chin coyly and returned the gesture.

“Good evening squire, can I get you anova drink?” She moved around to his side of the table close enough so he could see the curve of her hips under her skirt and her narrow nipped-in waist.

“Good evening, Alice, would you be a dear.” He placed the glass in her outstretched hand. He saw the look of a surprise because he’d used her name. “It shouldn’t be a shock that I know your name, my angel, it’s been used by the rest of the men in here all evening.”

“It’s nice of you to notice, Whiskey, was it?” She smiled at him again as she turned away and walked back towards the bar.

He nodded at her and sat back in his chair. The perfect sacrifice.

“What time do you finish her tonight, my dear?” He asked as she returned with his drink.

“Why you ask Squire? She said with a hint of curiosity in her voice.

He smirked and raised an eyebrow. “Now that would be lovely.” He said as his eyes traced down her jawline to her neck then onto her cleavage. “Very nice indeed. I’ve lodgings just up the street. We could have some gin to warm us, there’s a bottle with your name on it.” He tipped his head to the side, “That’s if you’d like to?”

Her eyes widened with anticipation as he uttered the word “Gin,” but her manners betrayed only a hint of optimism. "Sounds awfully tempting, however I will only step out with a proper gentleman," she said in a coy manner.

He stepped forward, cane propped against the table and long blade concealed up his sleeve pressing against his skin like an invitation. His confident smile gave way to sheer excitement as he assured her that he was indeed a real gentleman. A sense of thrill flooded through him along with the tingle that he so loved. Yes, this one would be special, incredibly special indeed.

Chapter Eight

Abberline had barely finished his breakfast when a Constable knocked at the front door. His wife Emma answered and showed the lad into the parlour where the Inspector sat eating.

"Fredrick, dear, Constable Dibbens is here, says it's urgent." She turned to Dibbens, "could I offer you some tea Constable? It is rather a cold morning." She smiled and her green eyes lit up with friendly warmth. Her hair still hung in two plaits, but she had dressed in a long brown tweed skirt and white blouse and had an apron tied around her waist as she clucked around the parlour.

Before Dibbens could answer Abberline interrupted him. "Dibbens isn't staying long enough my dear, we'll be on our way in a few moments." The Inspector rose from the table brushing crumbs from his clothing onto the plate in front of him. "Just let me get my coat Dibbens and I'll be along, you can wait outside." Abberline pushed his chair under the table and reached for his coat that was hanging on the back of the parlour door.

"Very good Sir, Madam." Dibbens gave a small nod to Mrs Abberline and left the room to do as instructed.

"Fred, it mithers me so when you have to leave in such a hurry, can it not wait for a few more moments? It does your digestion no good if you rush around after your meal." Emma stood by the table and reached for the teapot. "You should really think about slowing down some." She said as she poured tea into a nearby teacup.

“Now, now dear, police work never stops and you know as well as I do that time waits for no man, especially when it comes to crime.” He kissed his wife on the forehead and stepped back smiling at her. “You’re even more beautiful when you’re fretting.” Abberline winked at her.

“Fredrick Abberline, you have a silver tongue and no mistake.” Emma flushed with pleasure at her husband’s compliment. “Well don’t be too late home this evening, I’m cooking a suet pudding and as there’s been a glut of apples from Mrs Shaw’s orchard, I think I’ll make an apple pie for afters, how does that sound?” She began clearing the table.

“Sounds delightful dear.” He said buttoning up his coat, “now I must be off.” He kissed her once more on the cheek and went outside to meet the Dibbens.

“Right Dibbens, what’s the urgency?” Abberline closed the door behind him and stepped onto the street. He’d made it abundantly clear at the station that police business was never to be discussed around his beloved Emma. She can be spared of all the ugliness that he dealt with every day.

“Inspector, Sir, there’s been another one.” Dibbens stepped aside to allow a nun to pass by. She nodded her gratitude. Abberline tipped his hat.

“Oh, dear god, not another?” The Inspector straightened his hat as he continued walking. “I cannot believe the amount of evil that continues on whilst the rest of us innocent people are tucked up in our beds, Constable.” Abberline shivered, but not from the cold.

“I know what you mean, Sir, and this one is far worse than the others.”

“How in god’s name can one murder be worse than another Dibbens?” Abberline stepped off the pavement to cross the street, being narrowly missed by a Hansom cab in the process.

The driver threw him an angry stare, but Abberline ignored it.

“I’m sorry Sir, I jus-”

Abberline cut him off, “No Dibbens, it’s me that should apologise, I’m a little rattled this morning. These murders are increasingly frequent, that’s four in as many days, and I can’t seem to pin anything down, I’ve never had this happen before.” He stepped up onto the pavement and paused briefly to catch his thoughts. “Dibben, this is a shit of a case, even if I do say so myself and the sooner, we catch this bastard, the better.”

“Yes sir, I totally agree.” He continued walking waiting for Abberline to fall back into step with him.

“Mm, so glad you do Dibben, I’m glad you do. Now take me to the scene will you.”

Dibben hailed a cab. The journey across Whitechapel took about fifteen minutes. The streets were now getting busy with morning traders and early shoppers wanting to get the best of the wares on offer. Abberline looked out of the cab watching the comings and goings and wondered if the murderer was within the crowds of people, hunting for his next victim.

The cab came to a halt outside a townhouse with an adjacent alleyway, covered with a brick archway. Abberline stepped down onto the pavement and walked up to the Constable standing outside guarding the entrance.

"Good morning, Inspector." The officer looked rather peaky as he spoke.

"Good morning, Constable Baker, down here, is it?" Abberline turned to Dibben before making his way to the entrance to the alleyway. "Stay here would you and keep the locals out."

"Right, you are Sir." Dibbens turned away from them and placed his hands behind his back.

Baker didn't move.

Abberline frowned and turned on the Constable. "Baker, since when do you not accompany a senior officer to the scene of a murder?" He raised his eyebrows in question, as he barked at the Officer.

"Sir, there's no way I can go back to that room." Baker stood outside the door to the room, "my stomach is churning." He was tall, almost six and a half feet, with a broad chest and a police uniform that was crisp and well-pressed. His hair was black and slick with oil, shining in the harsh lights of the hallway. The sweet aroma of tobacco clung to him. "Sir, no human being should have to see the likes of that!" He threw a thumb over his shoulder.

"Good heavens man, pull yourself together and Baker show me where this has happened." Abberline stood aside to allow Baker to lead the way.

"I'm sorry Sir." Said a pasty-faced Baker, "I can't I'll lose my breakfast if I go back in there." He said as he gagged.

Constable Baker stood before Inspector Abberline, his posture rigid and tense Abberline's voice was hard like granite as he spoke. "If you don't get back down this corridor in the next five seconds, I will have you suspended for insubordination and make sure your colleagues know all about it. Do I make myself clear?"

Baker nodded quickly and averted his gaze. He turned on his heel and trudged down the hallway, Abberline followed closely behind. They arrived at a small courtyard with a door on the left. Baker stopped in front of the entrance.

"If you don't mind Sir, I'll wait outside if that's agreeable?" His pallor didn't look good again.

"Of course, wait here." Abberline stepped into the room and was immediately overcome with a sickening stench that assaulted his senses. "Good Lord!" He gagged loudly as he viewed the carnage before him before quickly retreating out into the alleyway. "I see exactly what you mean Constable. Has Doctor Sequeira been sent for?" His throat burned from the noxious odour as he dug around in his pockets for his handkerchief, wiping away the sweat dripping down his forehead and upper lip.

"He has Sir, but I don't think he'll be able to do much to help the girl now," Baker smirked at his comment.

"Don't be so insolent Baker, have more respect." Abberline's stomach rolled, and his mouth filled with saliva. "And what is that awful smell?"

"I've no idea, Sir, maybe the Doctor could enlighten us?" Asked an uncomfortable Baker as he saw the pallor of his senior officer, "Inspector, you, ok?"

"I…er, excuse me. Constable." Abberline walked to the back of the property, leaving Baker in the alley. He stood by an iron-barred drainpipe that hung from a wall, casually looked around at the unkempt yard and tried not to throw up. The foulness of what he had seen lingered inside his head like a rotten meal.

The girl lay flat on her back on the bed under the window, her face was unrecognisable as if she'd been beaten. Her legs drawn up but parted at the knees. She was partially clothed as her undergarments had been cut away, revealing the lower half of her torso. Two large flaps of skin lay on both sides of her cadaver on the bed. The lower part of her body was void of any organs, and her genitals had been cut away. A cut ran from her throat to her pubis. Her internal organs were lined up around the room like unclaimed luggage. Some of her flesh was missing; it had been wrapped up as a present for someone and placed on the table near the fireplace along with a gin bottle that had been left there. A broken walking cane lay next to it covered in gore.

Everywhere he looked a bit of the woman was placed or smeared. Written in, what he assumed to be her blood, upon the wall opposite the bed were the words *Alice Sprig.* The girl's name perhaps?

The scene proved to be too much, and he bent over a grate that sat under the conduit. Abberline heaved once as his mouth filled with spittle again and then he vomited.

He wiped his mouth with his handkerchief as he stood upright, checked that he hadn't splashed his coat or shoes, and then turned back to join Baker.

"Feel better Sir?" Baker raised an eyebrow.

Abberline didn't answer just threw Baker a glare. "Hopefully, Dr Sequeira should be joining us shortly." Abberline reached the door handle of the room behind him and without looking inside pulled it closed. "I think it's best that nobody sees that Baker, only myself or Sequeira should enter, do I make myself clear?"

Baker cleared his throat, "Yes Sir, shall I wait here Sir?" He stood with his back against the wall.

"You should, thank you." Abberline said as he made his way back to the street and Constable Dibben.

Abberline was glad to see an approaching Hansom Cab with the Doctor inside. The cab pulled over and Sequeira climbed out looking dishevelled and tired.

"Morning Fred, lead the way." He waited for Abberline to walk in front of him then followed.

"Aubrey, how are you?" Abberline sounded concerned as he glanced back at his friend.

"A rough night I'm afraid Fred, I didn't get much sleep." The Doctor rubbed the back of his neck as he spoke then cursed under his breath. "Lead the way, ole boy."

Abberline ignored the swearing, "It's just up here."

The two men walked down to the door, Abberline stood back to allow Sequeira to enter first. "Doctor, could you please enlighten me on that awful smell." Abberline replaced the handkerchief over his mouth again, as he hung back in the doorway.

The Doctor, who was yet to say anything, had knelt next to the bed examining the corpse. "Oh, that… that's faecal matter, Fred." He replied matter-of-factly as he reached into his medical bag and pulled out some forceps.

"Good lord, where from? I hope the sick bastard didn't defecate in here." Abberline grimaced as Sequeira used the tongs. He retrieved an object covered in gore from the girl's body cavity. Then pulled a rag from his bag and proceeded to clean off the item.

"No… I think it's from our lass here," he answered as he examined what he'd found. "It's because her lower bowel was perforated during the attack. Well, I'll be…" Sequeira turned to Abberline with the now clean object between his thumb and index finger.

The light through the window glinted briefly off its metal edge.

"Is that what I think it is Aubrey another one of those coins?" Abberline stepped forward to gain a better look at what the Doctor had between his fingers.

Abberline's heart raced as he saw the year etched into the coin - 1855. His stomach tightened and suddenly, he was filled with a sense of dread. He knew what this meant but was reluctant to accept it. He wished that the engraved number was different or that the coin wasn't real, but he knew all too well that it was. "Oh, my God, the perpetrator of this murder must be the same individual responsible for the other killings, given that coins have been left at each crime scene."

Aubrey nodded his head in agreement, "Certainly seems like it, Fred." He agreed as he dropped the silver disc into his pocket, then bent down as if looking for something from his bag.

"If you don't mind taking that with you and cleaning it up at the mortuary for me Aubrey, I'll collect it from you when we discuss the post-mortem." Abberline felt his stomach roll again. "Can I leave you for a moment ole chap, I need to get some air and give Dibben the name on the wall there and see if he could make some enquiries to see if it happens to be our victim?"

As Abberline stepped away, he noticed the Doctor hadn't moved an inch. His eyes were fixated on his medical kit and his forearms lay on his knees. "Aubrey?" Abberline called out, taking a few steps closer. He squinted, searching the Doctor's face for some sign of life as he furrowed his brows in concern.

"Huh… I'm sorry Fred, what did you say?" Sequeira lifted his head and rested tired eyes on Abberline.

"Aubrey, what on earth is wrong, this isn't like you, is everything okay?"

Dr. Sequeira let out a sigh and his gaze dropped to the floor again. His equipment bag sat open on the floor next to him, and he absently plucked a rag from it as he spoke. “Fred, Ida has been having some stomach trouble lately, so I suggested that she should go see a specialist. Unfortunately, my speciality is in the dead, not the living. Anyhow we had her looked at…” He swallowed hard. “…and we got the news yesterday that Ida has cancer.”

“Good god Aubrey, I’m so dreadfully sorry, is there anything I can do?” Abberline was momentarily frozen to the spot as he watched his friend, his face etched with genuine concern.

The Doctor shook his head, “Nothing, I’m afraid, absolutely nothing.” He pulled his hip flask from his inside jacket pocket, unscrewed the lid, and took a long drink.

Abberline reached out and gave Sequeira’s arm a reassuring pat, his eyes relaying everything to the Doctor. “I’m sorry I have to ask you to do this under the circumstances, but you are the one I trust to get me the answers that may help me to solve these cases.” He said as he watched the Doctor’s eyes fill with tears. “Would you rather I called a colleague, and you go home to be with her?” Asked Abberline.

Sequeira shook his head, screwing the lid back on his flask and pushing it into a pocket, “I have some time before the inevitable happens and I need to work for now. Ida has said she wants things to remain as normal as possible.” His rubbed a hand over his face, “There’s nothing I can do, damn it, and she’s the love of my life.” A single tear ran down his cheek and dripped off his chin.

“I’ll do what I can here Fred and bring you up to speed later, no need to stay with me.” Sequeira didn’t turn as he spoke just continued with the grim task in front of him.

“Oh, and Aubrey, if you need anything…” Abberline let the sentence hang in the air as he left the room.

Constable Baker was still outside the room as Abberline had ordered earlier. He stood poker straight as Fred came out.

“Baker, stay here until shift change over, no one goes in or out except for me or the Doctor there, understood?” Abberline instructed.

The constable nodded and looked sheepish after his previous reprimand. “Yes, Sir and Sir, I apologise for my earlier comment.”

Abberline nodded at the officer, “Apology noted and please ensure that your replacement at shift change knows my instructions.” He said as he walked back to the street to speak to Dibbens.

“Constable Dibbens, please find out if the name Alice Sprig is indeed the victim that is laying in that room, the name was written on a wall, sadly in her blood. Ask around and see if anyone may have seen her with anyone last night, then report back to me.” He looked up and down the street in the hope of seeing a passing cab, then changed his mind. “I’ll be at the station for the rest of the morning.”

The image of what he'd just witnessed was burned into his mind, tormenting him with the knowledge that it would revisit him in his dreams. Another woman had been slain, this time more viciously than the last. Who was capable of such heinous acts and found them to be perfectly acceptable? The coins left behind were a mysterious clue that seemed to imply some sort of date, but what could it mean? His instincts told him there was something more to uncover, but he wasn't sure where to start. Abberline trudged onwards, feeling the distance between him, and finding the killer growing ever wider. The biting cold wind brought him back to reality, almost mocking his efforts and taunting him because of the time he'd already wasted with no clues in sight. He tugged his coat tight around his neck, but it provided little solace; determination had made its home inside him, yet he felt a growing sense of despair as each step led him closer to police headquarters. The number of victims was rising and deep down he knew he wasn't able to do a damn thing about it.

Chapter Nine

After Abberline left the murder scene it took Dr Sequeira until lunchtime that day to finish the grim task of the examination of the room. He also had copious notes to go over when he had the next meeting with Abberline. Although his home life was still of great concern, the task, albeit unpleasant had helped to take his mind off of his darling wife. He'd had the remains of the girl sent to the mortuary and was still waiting for news as to who she could possibly be. Years of experience told him that believing the inscription on the wall of a girl's name wasn't to be taken as truthful, so he'd ask one of the constables to drop into the mortuary as soon as they could confirm it one way or another.

He felt for the owner of the lodging house as they had the job of repainting and scrubbing the floorboards of the room once the police were happy that they'd been as thorough as possible. He picked up his medical bag, checked that he'd removed all organic matter pertaining to the victim and stepped outside the room.

"Constable Baker, isn't it?"

"Yes, Doctor that's correct."

"The broken walking cane that was found in the room, did that go on the kart with the girl? I didn't see it leave and I wanted to be able to show Inspector Abberline as I think it's a significant piece of evidence as it has the top missing, also judging by the girl's facial injuries I'd hazard a guess and say it was used as a weapon." He looked about the alley to see if it'd been left by chance propped against the outside wall.

“I believe I saw the lad place it on the sheet covering the girl’s body Doctor, so I’d assume that’s where it’ll be, for you upon your return.” Baker rocked backwards and forwards on his heels trying to stretch out his tight calf muscles.

“Good, I need to ensure Inspector Abberline knows about it. Oh, and Constable can you see to it that I am notified as soon as possible as to the correct identity of the girl, I will of course need to have her formally identified by a member of her family or someone she is well acquainted with, at least.” He took a deep lungful of air and reached for his hip flask. Empty. “But that won't be a pleasant task for whoever does that job as her face is so badly mutilated. I’d really like to spare them the horror of that.”

“Certainly, I think it’s Constable Dibbens who has been given the job of finding out who she may be, but I’ll relay the message. Yes, not a nice task for her family, I certainly feel for them on that.” Baker agreed and now stood with his arms behind his back.

“Thank you.” He pushed the hip flask into his medical bag. “Right, I’ll be on my way. thank you again, Constable.” Sequeira said and walked back to the main street.

“Can I call you a cab, Doctor?”

“No, I’d like to take in some air, so the walk will be nice.” Without looking back Sequeira turned left and headed in the direction of the mortuary.

He took his time and ambled along, dropping in to refill his hip flask at his favourite shop, then buying the remainder of the bottle to keep in his office drawer. For medicinal purposes.

As Sequeira trudged through the streets, he could feel the warmth of the sun on his face but could not bring himself to enjoy it. He exchanged pleasantries with people he had known for years, though Ida only occupied his thoughts. He was all too aware that this was the time they had long dreaded - a time when there was nothing more, he could do to save her. His mind and heart in turmoil, Sequeira tried to keep up appearances, nodding and smiling in all the right places.

He pushed open the doors to the post-mortem examination room and walked over to the slab where his lab assistant had placed the dead girl. Samuel had been a good trainee and did as he was shown, keeping all shrouds over the deceased it hosted until Sequeira began the examination.

Sequeira glanced around the room, looking for the cane and then spotted it on the slab next to the girl's shrouded left side. Perfect, Abberline needs to see this.

He picked up the walking stick and took it over to the window so he could get a better look at the shaft. The top part had been badly splintered and Sequeira could see that the palm rest, be it silver or brass had been forced off. How?

Suddenly, the sunlight picked up a yellow strand caught in amongst the splintered wood, only about two inches in length. He trudged over to his instrument table and frantically searched for the tweezers he needed. When he found them, he took a deep breath and carefully manipulated the fibre free and placed it between a white cloth's folds, then placed it onto the table with the pincers on the top so it couldn't be mislaid. He cautiously pulled back the shroud that had been covering the girl's head, revealing her thick blond hair. In that moment all of Sequeira's fears bubbled to the surface. The cane was definitely used against this girl.

He went back to the walking stick that he had left over by the window and picked it up again. He turned it around in his fingers checking every splintered part of the wood. Sequeira moved his thumb to get a better grip and his eye fell on some partial lettering that had been carved into the wood, just under where the top of the cane would have been. He realised he was looking at the lower part of some lettering. Some initials? A name perhaps?

"Samuel, could you come in here for a minute please." He shouted. "I'd like you to take a look at this and see what you make of it." Sequeira didn't take his eyes off the cane as he called for his lab assistant. Moments later he heard the doors being pushed open.

"You called, Doctor, what can I help you with?" Samuel asked.

The lad was around sixteen years of age. Sequeira had taken him under his wing after he'd found him wandering the streets several years ago. The boy had been sick with Scarlet Fever and the Doctor, who had been working at the nearby infirmary took pity on him. Aubrey's medical connections helped as he was able to find the correct medicine to make him well. When Sequeira first took on the challenge of treating the erythrogenic toxin produced by the infection, the antitoxin was still in its early stages and untested. But he gambled anyway, and it worked—the boy lived.

"Ah…there you are, see this?" Sequeira turned the cane around so Samuel could see it better. "What'd you make of that, my lad?" He held the walking stick steady for the youngster to take a better look.

"Doc, it looks like some sort of writing, maybe a company name, person's name, definitely lettering, there are only a few partial letters left though." With his blue eyes, Samuel peered closer. "Mm… Doc, I reckon that could be someone's initials, maybe we could work out what they could possibly be by a process of elimination?" He stepped back and folded his arms.

"Do you think you could do that lad? I've got this…" Sequeira turned and looked at the slab.

"Well, I can certainly try for you Doc, might not be of much help but I will do my best." He took the cane from Sequeira, "leave it with me." He gave the Doc a lopsided smile.

“Brilliant.” Sequeira ruffled the boy’s red hair, “You’ve grown into a smart lad.” He slapped him on the back and returned to the slab, picked up and tied his apron and then pulled off the shroud.

Sequeira examined the body in detail, checking every square inch for any clue of who could have done this. All he wanted was something small, just that one little thing that could crack the case wide open.

His sustenance was in the form of liquid from his hip flask. It warmed his senses but did nothing to fill the hole he now felt in his stomach. His work helped to busy his mind, but when he paused to take a mouthful, it didn’t stop his mind wondering back to his wife. Deep down he knew he was losing her, and he had to begin to accept that that was inevitable.

He had just finished washing his hands and begun writing more notes when the doors swung open and Abberline joined him.

“Good afternoon, Aubrey, Samuel has brought me up to speed on the walking stick.” Abberline was already standing in front of him with the customary handkerchief across his nose and mouth. “Did you manage to clean up that coin for me too?” Came a muffled question.

“I did Fred, now where did I put that… ah yes here it is.” Sequeira picked up the piece from the sink, wiped it on the bloodied apron and handed it over to his friend. “Same year on it ole boy, 1855.” He walked around to the front of the slab, leant back against it, and folded his arms.

“Really, very interesting. So, my thinking is that the date the coins have been minted in,” Abberline began, his voice muffled from the handkerchief, “is relevant, something significant to the killer, either a birthday, an anniversary, that sort of thing.” Fred scratched his chin with his empty hand. “Any suggestions, Aubrey?” He waited patiently for Sequeira to answer.

The Doctor was still leaning against the slab as he mentally chewed over what he’d suggested. A few moments later, “I think that’s a strong possibility, Fred, what other reasons could there be?”

He watched as Abberline nodded in agreement, “I’m glad you agree, ole boy,” the Inspector said as he turned the coin over in his fingers, his face etched in thought. Finally, he asked, “So, what do you make of the cane, could it have been the murderers?” Abberline raised his eyebrows in question before slipping the coin into his coat pocket.

“Hard to tell, Fred, but there are remaining initials around what I’ve deduced to be the top where the silver or brass hand rest would have been, but the remnants of the lettering were destroyed when the two pieces were splintered.

Inspector Abberline gestured with his thumb over his shoulder in the direction of where Samuel had the shattered object. “Your theory on how this happened, Aubrey?” He asked.

Dr. Sequeira looked contemplative for a moment before raising his right arm and making a striking motion in the air, as if swinging a bat. "I think the killer used it to bludgeon their victim with enough force to snap it apart. Simple, but effective. Hopefully, if the initials can be worked out, Fred, then that'll help no end." He rubbed his eyes, "then if you can find the top, it'll be puzzle solved." He held his hands out to the side and shrugged. "Oh, before I forget, I've found this too." Sequeira turned and leaned over the slab to the instrument table and reached for the white rag containing the strand he'd found earlier. He opened up the cloth and handed it over to Abberline.

"What is this, a hair?" Abberline's hand dropped away from his face. "Where did you find it?" He moved over to the window to try and gain a better look at the rag and its contents.

Sequeira followed. "Yes, I think it is a hair and I found it caught up in the splintered part of the cane. It's fair too, and it came from our girl over there," He pointed his thumb over his shoulder in the direction of the slab. He scratched the afternoon shadow on his chin, then pulled his hip flask out of his apron pocket and took two good gulps.

"So, this implies to me that this cane was used on this girl and it's definitely not one of the other victims' hair, one was dark and the other a redhead, Aubrey," Abberline stated.

Sequeira nodded, "I did think the very same my friend. Any idea of her name yet?" He asked as he screwed the lid back on the container. "Was it Alice Sprig?"

Abberline placed the rag back on the instrument table and then took out his pocketbook and thumbed through the pages. "Ah, yes… yes, it is, Alice Sprig, worked in the local tavern the Dog and Duck at night, and looked after her ailing mother during the day whilst her father works as a blacksmith. Lived at the back of Ealing Lane with both parents and was in her early twenties. Needless to say, her parents are devastated and between you and I Aubrey, I wouldn't be surprised if this didn't finish her mother off. She's very frail and ailing with consumption."

Sequeira picked up the pages of notes he'd left on the side of the bench. "So, my earlier assumption that the name on the wall may not be true was wrong. Ah well, it's good that we've got her name now." He plucked up his pencil and scratched something on the paperwork before continuing, "Okay ole boy, let's go through what I've written to bring you up to date with my examination." As he moved, he kicked an old, bent, and rusty bucket, the contents of which had an interested blue bottle circling around. "You alright? You look awful my friend."

He observed Abberline, whose face was now as pale as whitewash and had his handkerchief back in place, pointing at the bucket. "Ah, sorry about that…listen if you need to bring up your lunch Fred, I suggest you go outside, no buckets to use in here, I'm afraid, they're for other organic material, if you get my drift." He pointed down to the bucket and grinned at the Inspector's discomfort.

Abberline waved a hand for Sequeira to carry on.

"As you wish ole boy." He glanced down at the pages whilst still leaning against the slab. "Most of it you're already aware of. However, I made a list of all the organs that this young lady is missing or rather had removed." He bent and picked up the bucket from earlier and dumped it in between Alice's feet.

He noticed Abberline's gag reflex had kicked in but ignored it.

"So, the girl or Alice had many of her internal organs removed from the waist down, including her outer organs, namely her genitals." He paused and glanced up at Abberline, his pallor hadn't improved. "I managed to locate most of these whilst at the room in which she was found, but there is one that I've still yet to find." He put down the pages on the area of the shroud that covered Alice's shins, then moved up to her head. He lifted back the cover and prized her jaw open. "See that, Fred?"

Abberline inclined his head just enough so he could see inside the girl's mouth. His eyes baulked.

"That's right Fred, you are seeing correctly. The poor girl is missing her tongue."

"Good Lord, what use is the girl's tongue to anyone?" Abberline heaved.

Sequeira ignored it. “I’ve absolutely no idea ole boy.” He shrugged, replaced the cover, and returned to his notes. “The main thing is that the girl was bludgeoned first, most likely to knock her out and then had her throat cut. She hadn’t been bound to the bed at all. If she had, she would have been heard screaming out and fighting back, if he’d done the lower extremities first, and he wanted her quiet. Probably the only thing that he was merciful about, to be honest, at least the poor girl was already dead before he did that to her.” He looked to gauge his colleague’s expression. “Shall I continue Fred?”

Abberline gagged again but nodded for him to continue.

“I’d say the person who did this to her and the others we’ve had the misfortune to be dealing with is experienced with a knife. He may be a butcher or even a surgeon,” Sequeira turned and lifted the lower end of the shroud but obscured the view underneath, “these cuts are precise and clean, there’s no tearing or ripping of her flesh at all.”

“Did she still have her uterus?” Came the muffled question from Abberline.

“Mm, yes, she did, but it had been significantly dissected. Quite odd actually, why he chose to do that, but then that may answer the mystery as to why these murders are happening.” Sequeira dropped the shroud and turned back round to face Abberline.

“If you have a theory, I’d love to hear it.” Abberline said.

Sequeira pinched the bridge of his nose, the lack of sleep was catching up with him. “Well, I think, and it’s only my theory, but this could be someone who has been quite liberated with their conquests, Fred, finds a sort of freedom in his killings.”

“Such as?”

“Maybe it makes him feel good, or he feels almost godlike, powerful, if that makes sense. I think he has a temper too and has a strong hatred for women, judging by the injuries sustained by the victims that I’ve examined. This person doesn’t just cut their throats, he disfigures them and then opens them up, almost as if cutting their throats isn’t degrading enough. He likes to belittle them and uses the local whores, maybe because he thinks they’re not going to be missed as he considers them to be the lowest people in society, but he also enjoys their company too, gets his pleasures then kills them. However, that doesn’t match with the killing of the show girl, that one I need to think through a while longer. Judging by her injuries, it’s definitely the same killer, but the reason as to why he chose her baffles me.” Sequeira put down the notes again and pushed his hands into the pocket of the apron. The feel of the hip flask prompted him to indulge.

“A Corinthian who is very loose in the haft, someone like that?”

Sequeira nodded "Yes, a man that frequents brothels regularly, of easy virtue and with very few morals, strong possibly Fred." He put the hip flask on the slab as he continued. "He may have certain tastes in the girls he chooses too, in other words, something in their appearance or features, that type of thing." Sequeira began to untie the cords of his apron. "You remember the other spate of murders a few years back in Greenwich?"

Fred nodded.

"Well, a colleague of mine worked out that the killer had certain preferences for the victims he chose, the man was caught and hanged, but was questioned about his motives before he went to the gallows. He plainly said they all reminded him of his mother who used to beat him."

"So, your point Aubrey?" Abberline asked a look of confusion flashed across his face.

"It could be there's only one reason why this man is continually killing whores, what that reason is, illudes me. Obviously, this is only my theory, it might be completely incorrect, but one thing that is correct is his dissection of the bodies as I said before." He threw the apron over the slab and walked over to where he kept his jacket. "Now, I'm off home, I want to be with Ida as much as I can and to catch up on some sleep. Is there anything else you need to know ole boy?" He pushed his arms through his coat sleeves and shrugged it on then began buttoning it up.

"No nothing else, thank you. Is Samuel capable enough to help the father of the victim when he does come in?" Abberline asked.

"Samuel is more than capable, and she doesn't need to be moved off of there," he gestured towards where the girl lay, "well, not until it's needed again, that is." He picked up his medical bag, finally clasping it shut. But not before a bottle of Laudanum had shifted forward in the bag, gleaming in the light. Sequeira held his breath, waiting for Abberline to question him. "It's for Ida, for her pain," he said hastily. Would Abberline see through his lies and realise his true intentions with this powerful opioid? He let out a sigh and felt a jolt of relief as the question didn't come, but it was soon followed by a wave of guilt and shame. Would he be able to keep his plans hidden? After all, the only other person that knew of his idea was Ida.

"Aubrey, I have no need to question any of your motives, you're a good man and you'll do whatever is necessary for her, I know that." Abberline stepped forward and placed a hand on his friend's shoulder. "Now, go home, try to get some rest. If I need anything more, I will drop a note to Samuel and if he can't give me the answers then it'll wait until you're back here." He gave a reassuring smile and followed him out of the building.

"Your information gives me hope for this case," Abberline said as he watched Sequeira walked a few steps away from him. The blonde hair, the initials, the type of injuries, the kind of person it could be ... it all helps a lot." He paused in thought. "It's a step closer to catching this bastard."

Despite his hesitance, Sequeira knew Fred was grateful for his help, he heard him let out a heavy sigh as he began to walk away.

Abberline called out to Sequeira. "It all truly helps Doc -- but is it enough?”

“That’s where you come in my friend.” He shouted back to him, “I’ll see you, Fred.”

Sequeira gave him a melancholic, fleeting glance, his mind in turmoil as he observed the evidence that kept building up. He knew it wasn't his job to catch whoever was responsible, and it pained him to think of what would become of those already affected. He prayed silently that it wasn't someone from the medical field, but his suspicions were that it was. His arm moved almost instinctively, as if to wave goodbye, and yet he stood there momentarily rooted in place, unable to face the path leading back to his beloved wife Ida.

Chapter Ten

Two days later Ruby was contacted by Elsie's lawyer. After a brief meeting at his office, she discovered that she was the sole beneficiary of Elsie's estate. Unbeknownst to Ruby, Elsie had purchased the apartment that she had been living in after the death of her wealthy parents. It had never occurred nor interested Ruby to know the finer details of her late lover's possessions, after all, it was the woman that she was in love with and not her worldly gains.

Ruby paused, her thoughts heavy with grief as she summoned up the strength to take charge of Elsie's final arrangements. She asked Isabel, Elsie's beloved maid of many years, to stay on at the apartment and help organize the dressing room after Elsie's departure. Ruby couldn't face packing up Elsie's clothes, it seemed to be too final. So, Ruby had Isabel leave them in place alongside her own. Ruby knew that Elsie would want a lavish funeral and wasted no time with the arrangements for the service. Though there were few attendees, Ruby wanted nothing less than for her lover to have every luxury in death as she had in life. She paid for an ornate oak coffin and visited a stonemason to have a marble headstone engraved with Elsie's favourite psalm.

Ruby visited the bank vault where Elsie had her jewellery stored, removed them, and then took them to a reputable jeweller in Mayfair to have them valued.

Aside from a Ruby drop pendant with matching earrings and bracelet, she sold the rest.

Donating a substantial amount of the proceeds to Dr Barnardo's, a new charity that helped orphaned children and one that Elsie had been interested in from its start. The rest was Ruby's and would be a nest egg, should the need ever arise. She was now an extremely wealthy woman.

Arthur was a constant presence during Ruby's days. He never tried to hinder her relationship with Elsie, instead gently telling her that he only wanted her to be happy. And despite the fact that she knew she could handle her life on her own, his warm support somehow made it easier for her to carry the hurt and sadness she felt deep in her heart.

She received a message from the theatre to clear out Elsie's belongings from her dressing room and after breakfast the following day she and Arthur made the trip together.

The morning was cold and damp with heavy black clouds above. How fitting for the mood. She watched as Arthur hailed a Hansom cab and then helped her inside, covering her from her lap down with the blanket on the seat. Afterwards, he climbed in beside her.

The touch of his hand in her gloved one was welcome, and she glanced across briefly thanking him for his comfort.

"No need to thank me, Rubes, what else would I do for the woman I'm in love with." He said, lifting her hand and kissing the fabric of her glove.

The rest of the journey was spent in silence as Ruby felt no need to talk. She didn't notice the rain starting to fall and the locals trying to stay dry whilst going about their business in the street.

Thirty minutes later the cab jolted to a stop outside the theatre. She climbed down to the cobbles, looking at the building as she did so.

"It doesn't look the same now Arty, it looks cold and uninviting." She waited as Arthur paid the cabbie not wanting to go in alone.

"It's just a building my love, nothing more." He offered his arm for her to put hers through.

"I know, but it seemed so much more when she was here, warmer somehow, does that make sense?" She lifted her skirt off the ground and avoided a large puddle as she walked towards the entrance.

"It does, the warmth has gone now she's no longer there. That's because Elsie was a very warm and caring person." He squeezed her arm with his and began to lead her up the stone steps. "This will be over in a jiffy, then we can go home." He opened the door for her and stood back to allow her to enter.

The main foyer was dark with only one small oil lamp to illuminate the lavish wallpaper, patterned with gold fleur de lis and on a blue background. Elsie had it made as a gesture to the management for their long-term engagement of her services. Several inexpensive paintings of different scenes from several plays were hung on the walls and the floor beneath their feet was freshly swept. Ruby used to like to hear her footsteps on the bare floorboards, but that day was different.

She slipped her arm from Arthur’s and walked towards one of the paintings that had a likeness of Elsie in the scene. A melodrama written by Henry Arthur Jones, *The Silver King* and Elsie had been cast as the female lead. It had received critical acclaim and played to record-breaking audiences, placed the theatre firmly on the map and the artwork had been commissioned shortly afterwards.

Ruby touched the likeness of Elsie with her gloved hand, and the now familiar ache returned in her chest.

Footsteps sounded from the other side of the foyer. Ruby instinctively stepped back from the picture and turned in the direction from which she’d heard the steps. Arthur had turned too but moved to Ruby’s side.

“Miss Myers, Mr Morris a pleasure as always.” A well-dressed man in his fifties was walking towards the pair. “So grateful you could come here today, such a terrible business. How are you coping? I know you and Miss Lancaster were as close as sisters.” He gushed.

Alistair Bennett was of average build and wore his signature blue suit. His hair was well oiled, combed back and cut above the ear. His oval face had a flush complexion and bloodshot eyes lacking empathy. He shifted awkwardly and twitched his nose three times, like a rabbit sensing danger.

Ruby felt Arthur's body tense up as soon as the other man entered the room. She nervously looped her arm through his in an attempt to reassure him, but it didn't seem to make any difference – he still eyed the man with contempt.

"Good morning, Mr Bennett. I must say I've been better." Ruby said, giving away very little. "Mr Morris and I are grateful to you for allowing us some time before clearing her dressing room, it wasn't something I could face before now." She looked up at Arthur, his expression unchanged.

"Of course, I totally understand." Bennett gestured for them to follow him. "Miss Lancaster was a valued member of our cast, and she will be truly missed." He glanced briefly behind as he walked, leading them to a door on the left side of the foyer. He turned the handle and pushed it open, then stepped aside holding it ajar so they could enter. "This way please." He took the lead again and walked down a dimly lit corridor in need of some restoration. Although narrow, the passage didn't feel oppressive but had a musty smell. Doors were on either side, some with names painted on the wood. Bennett stopped at the last door on the right, took out a key from his waistcoat pocket and unlocked it. Elsie's name had already been removed and he did a clumsy job of trying to hide it as he held it open for them.

"Too late Bennett," Arthur growled. "Truly missed will she, couldn't wait to get her name off the door." Arthur met Bennett's stare with cold, hard eyes.

"Mr Morris, this was done as a security measure, we didn't want anyone coming by and looting her dressing room." Although Bennett's nose was twitching more than usual, he stood his ground. "We've had it happen in the past and didn't want that happening again, especially to Miss Lancaster's belongings. I hope you understand my point?" He stepped away from the door and was now standing on the threshold. "I've also taken the liberty of providing you with some tea chests, I thought this would be something that you'd neglected to think of." He looked past Arthur and to Ruby instead.

"It's okay Arty, it's of no difference now. She's been gone three weeks her name would've had to be removed at some point. Thankfully though, it's several weeks without another murder." Ruby looked around the small, cluttered room, but didn't look in Bennett's direction.

"If you don't mind, I have some other business to attend to, if you should need me, I will be in my office. Bennett held his line of sight at Ruby, "Miss Myers you have my deepest condolences, and may I say once again that Miss Lancaster was a true talent." Bennett bowed from the neck, reached for the door handle, and closed it quietly behind him.

"Cretin," Arthur muttered under his breath.

Ruby glanced around the room, a flurry of emotions coursing through her veins. She knew she had to investigate Elsie's possessions to see if they might provide any clues as to who killed her. Taking a deep breath, Ruby made her way to Elsie's dressing table and her hands trembled as she started to comb through the scattered theatre makeup. Her heart raced as she opened the drawer beneath it, almost expecting something sinister to come out.

Arthur went to the rack of dresses on the other side of the room and began to take them down and fold them into a nearby trunk, embellished with Elsie's initials. "Rubes, I'll put all these dresses in here, I think that's what Elsie must have done when moving her things from different theatres." He continued to fold a green silk dress into the chest, then turned to Ruby. "Rubes, do you agree?"

Ruby searched desperately through the drawer, her hopes lifting as she frantically pushed her hand to the back. Finally, her fingers made contact with something cold and unfamiliar, and she carefully pulled it out. Ruby had found a letter, its wax seal broken, tucked away beneath forgotten trinkets. The writing was nearly illegible, but her eyes managed to scan the contents. Ruby's heart raced as she read. With each word, she could feel her nerves heighten and her stomach twist into knots.

Eight little whores, with no hope of heaven, Myers may save one, then they'll be seven. Seven little whores begging for a shilling. One stays in Henage Court, then there's a killing. Six little whores, glad to be alive, one sidles up to Jack, and then there are five. Four and whore rhyme aright, so do three and me. I'll set the town alight then there are two. Two little whores, shivering with fright. Seek a cosy doorway in the middle of the night. Jack's knife flashes, then there's but one, and the last one's the ripest for Jack's idea of fun.

Her hand dropped to her lap still clutching the piece of paper. "I think you should read this Arty." She held out the letter for him.

Arthur was silent for a moment. "Good god, did she ever show this to you?" Arthur threw the page onto the dressing table and knelt at Ruby's feet.

"Never, she never mentioned it. I know she used to have the odd fanatical fan, but she never became concerned about them at all." Ruby looked into Arthur's eyes, her hands still trembling. "It even mentions her home, Henage Court, do you think it was someone who had worked out the truth between me and her? We may have been seen together at some point. This place isn't very private, our conversations may've been overheard, or someone saw me visiting her apartment and staying overnight, putting two and two together? Or did the writer have intentions of going there to get to Elsie?" The questions hurtled from Ruby's mouth.

"Rubes, Rubes… calm down, I don't know Rubes, but we'll figure it out." Arthur put his hands on her shoulders, "but I'd not worry about your overnight visits, it's just a woman spending the night at her friend's home, nothing more. I don't want Abberline to know about this. It could lead me to the killer before the Inspector, which gives me the chance to deal with the madman our way. Leave this with me and I'll speak to my associates, there's bound to be one of them that knows something. Come on, we're not staying here, speak to Isabel and tell her to come and finish up today, I'll then have one of my lads come over and move the stuff back to the apartment. Once this is done, we can gather our thoughts and go from there." He opened the dressing room door.

Ruby stood, folded the note, and then slipped it inside her glove. "Arty, I want to speak with Bennett before we leave, and see if he knows anything about this letter." She walked towards the door.

"I can't see that cretin would know much, but if it's what you need to do, I understand." He waited until she was in the corridor then pulled the door closed behind them.

"The person who wrote it may have given it to him to give to Elsie." She wondered. Ruby fiercely pondered who had written the mysterious note and begged the question of whether it was secretly placed in Elsie's dressing room instead. Anxious thoughts raced through her mind as she tried desperately to make sense of what it all meant.

Ruby was deeply frustrated by Bennett’s lack of help. Every question she asked was answered with a minimal or dismissive response, and his body language suggested he wanted nothing more than for them to leave. Despite her deep-seated anger, Ruby still felt a strange connection to the theatre and a desire to come back one day. She quickly made her way out, but not before taking in the sights and smells of what had once been one of her favourite places.

The heavens had opened up and a steady rainfall was now pattering on the cobblestone streets below. Ruby and Arthur were out on the road and Arthur had hailed a Hansom cab. She watched as the cab stopped in front of them and Arthur opened the door for her.

"We must divert the journey back to Henage Court to speak with Isabel first," said Arthur, climbing in after her. "Then I'll take you back to the townhouse." He closed the door, and the cab took off into the wet street.

As they travelled through the city, Ruby looked out the window and noticed how peculiar the atmosphere had become. The whole city seemed to be enshrouded in a grey, misty fog and the rain was falling harder now. The only sound was the occasional rumble of thunder in the distance. She felt a little uneasy at the thought of what this portended.

The cab pulled up in front of Henage Court and Arthur helped her out into the rain. He gave her his umbrella, then walked up to the door to talk to Isabel while she waited in the cab. After a few minutes, Arthur returned, and they drove off again into the deluge.

Arthur dropped Ruby off in front of the townhouse before continuing on to contact some of his associates. Ruby watched him go, standing there in the rain, feeling a deep sadness for what the future might hold. She hugged herself for warmth and went inside, the rain still pattering down around her.

The note felt cold in Ruby's glove, and she was relieved to remove it and put it in her bureau for safekeeping when she got home.

Rose had built up a nice fire in the hearth of her parlour, but it wasn't enough to banish the chill that she felt. What did the letter mean? How did the writer know so much about Elsie's life? Above all, who was the writer?

Ruby's heart raced in her chest, and she felt unsteady on the floor beneath her. Her hands trembled and her mouth felt dry as cotton wool. She was desperately aware of someone else knowing every intimate detail about her life, and it seemed to make the room close in on her. Arthur sat beside her, saying nothing but radiating a reassuring presence. She stared into the orange and yellow flames that crackled in the fireplace, trying to subdue the anxiety racing through her mind and the heaviness in her belly.

A knock at the parlour door startled her.

"Come".

Rose came into the room. "Miss Ruby, I just wondered if you'd like some tea and a slice of freshly baked bread with some butter?"

"Tea would be lovely Rose, but I can't stomach the bread and butter right now, thank you." Ruby gave Rose a weak smile.

"Are you all, right?"

Ruby gave a small nod. "Thank you for the tea, Rose." With that, she turned back to watching the flames in the hearth, rested her head against the back of the chair, closing her eyes.

****

The painted wooden sign hanging outside of the bar looked faded and worn. The Neptune was an old establishment named after the mythical sea deity.

This old saloon had seen better days, like a beach that had been beaten by storm after storm and now lay broken and forgotten, washed up on the shore. Arthur closed his eyes and saw surf crashing in white-tipped waves upon rocks. The thick oak door creaked loudly as Arthur pushed it open and entered his bar. The green interior was dark and smelled of stale sweat and tobacco smoke. Some of the alcohol on sale was windowpane clear and tasted like a swipe of thin and bitter lemon peel, like the kiss of a tart and masterful woman. Arthur leaned on the bar and sniffed in the rapturous smells of strong booze.

The gin smelled of juniper and the rum syrupy and bold, while the whiskey rocked a baby on a cradle. This place was his kingdom. The tavern was dark, wooden, and warm. A fire casts light from the hearth and over the long oak bar, the only piece of furniture the room is lined with. Underfoot are bare floorboards covered in sawdust.

Oil lamps were burning low in the hostelry. A cosy sanctuary from the bitter cold, the wind and frost outside. As the fire roared to Arthur's left the other patrons were huddled around it, their backs to him. The smell of unwashed bodies and sour mouths wafted in Arthur's direction. He wrinkled his nose, but the smell was nothing compared to the way his mouth watered at the thought of his single malt.

His long-serving barman, Eddie was thin and had a large nose. His face was clean-shaven and hard like an ogre and his eyes were like almonds. He stood wiping out glasses with a dirty rag and smiled at Arthur as he saw him approach. Instinctively he uncorked a bottle of whiskey and continued to pour him a glass.

"Good day boss, a large one?" Eddie had the bottle poised to pour.

"Please, Eddie." Arthur rested his forearms on the bar and waited for the glass to be passed to him. "I need this today." He said as he took it and downed the amber liquid in one.

"Bad news?" Eddie had picked up the rag and started wiping out another glass.

"Humm, I guess you could say that I'm looking for the lad; I need him to deliver a message to a few of the boys."

"He's out back stacking crates." Eddie nodded in the direction of the back door behind the bar.

“When he’s done tell him to come see me, I’ll be upstairs in my office.” Arthur gestured for a refill then took the glass with him to the stairs on the far right of the bar. “Check with me first before letting anyone upstairs, I’m seriously not in the mood for any needy folk today,” Arthur said as he began to climb the stairs.

“Right, you are boss. I’ll get George on to it for you once he’s done in the yard.”

Arthur opened the door to the office, which was of average size. A desk sat over by a window, giving a view of the street below. He liked to see the punters coming and going, as he always needed to be prepared for any eventuality. Paperwork was piled up in several places in the room and filed on several small shelves. Two armchairs faced the desk and on the left of the room, a small fireplace played host to a well-lit fire. The room felt stuffy, so Arthur crossed to the window and slid it open a few inches to allow some airflow. He sat down in his chair and glanced quickly at the fresh correspondence that Eddie had left over the past few days. Nothing important.

Arthur's interest piqued as he watched an imposing figure weave through the busy throng of people. He was well dressed, and his sharp gaze scanned each stall and shop, his expression impossible to discern from this distance. Arthur held his position, not wanting to be seen as the stranger stood still for what seemed like an eternity. Then his eyes locked onto the building of the pub as though he was looking for something. Just when Arthur thought he'd confront him, a copper approached the bloke from behind, startling him. The officer said a few words, the male just smiled and nodded. Then constable walked away, but the man remained standing there like a sentinel.

Arthur's vision suddenly blurred as the man approached, his deep gaze penetrating Arthur like daggers. The stranger thought himself untouchable, unbuttoning his coat and revealing a sliver of steel glinting in the daylight. Fury bubbled inside Arthur's chest, and he felt a sinister rage stirring. This was going too far - who the fuck did this man think he was?

Before Arthur could even process what he was doing, he had jumped to his feet and raced down the stairs, his legs barely able to keep up with his racing mind. His heart pounded against his ribcage like an enraged animal trying to escape its cage as he burst through the door and frantically searched for any sign of his watcher. But in that moment, it seemed the stranger had vanished without a trace.

"Have you seen a bloke of say five foot eight, looked dapper?" He asked one of the nearby traders.

"Sorry Mr Morris, I was serving punters." The seller dropped some apples into a basket for a woman he was serving. "If I do, should I come get you?" He said as he nodded his thanks to the woman and then gave Arthur his full attention.

"Cheers, Bob, if you do there be a drink in it for you." Arthur patted his shoulder in thanks and headed back inside, but he couldn't shake the feeling that something bad was going to happen.

George sat on the stairs waiting for Arthur. "Mr Morris." The lad removed his cap and pushed it into a pocket in his trousers as he stood up. "You wanted to see me?"

"Yes George, come with me." Arthur gestured for him to follow.

Arthur opened the door to the office and sat down in one of the chairs in front of the desk. "Right George, I need you to get a message to Billy Mills, tell him I need to see him urgently and ask him to bring some of the lads with him too, understand?"

"Yes sir, Billy Mills can I do anything else whilst I'm out Mr Morris?" George stood just inside the doorway, now holding his cap in his hands. "I've done the jobs Eddie asked of me." The child looked eager to please.

"Good lad George, here, get yourself some chocolate limes." He said flicking a coin over to the boy.

"Fanks, Mr Morris, Sir." He said as he left the room.

Arthur smiled to himself, stood up, picked up his glass and crossed to a small table laden with a decanter and glasses, for a refill. Arthur took a long drink of the amber liquid, his mind still full of the mysterious figure outside. Who was he? Did they have some connection in the past? No, if that were true, Arthur would have recognized him instantly. What could he have wanted, and why had he been watching the pub so intently? Arthur's face reddened as his frustration grew. He felt his chest tighten and a nauseating dread swirl in the pit of his stomach. The longer he pondered these unanswered questions, the more it ate away at him. He despised not knowing the truth when other people were involved.

Arthur knew he had to be careful as he asked around about the bloke. Too many questions and he would send alarm bells ringing and potentially put himself, and whomever he was asking, in danger. He wasn't sure whom to trust, outside of his associates, but had to take the risk if he wanted to get any information.

Arthur was down in the bar and had several more whiskeys as Billy Mills strolled into the bar. Standing at six feet four and broad-shouldered, Mills was a big bear of a man, gruff, with a swaggering gait. With his sharp wit and unswerving loyalty, he had gained the respect of even the most hardened criminals. Arthur had no qualms entrusting him with his life; confident that his friend would do whatever it took to protect him and anyone close to him. A round, bald head balanced upon a thick neck with cauliflower ears, a misshapen nose and small beady eyes, Billy wasn't an attractive man, but women loved his gentle nature with the female sex. Men, on the other hand, feared him and for good reason, Billy Mills had an animalistic temper and thought nothing of snapping the neck of any man that threatened him or anyone he loved.

"Arthur, you asked to see me." He strode up to the bar, covering the floor in four strides, and slapped Arthur on the back. "How yah doin govna?" Billy signalled to Eddie for a beer.

"Good to see yah Bill, could be better." Arthur drained his glass.

"I guessed as much, what'd need?" Billy took a long swill from the fresh pint Eddie had served him. "Some heads to roll?"

"Had some killings recently, no secret I know, but these are a bit too close to home. Ruby's friend Elsie has been one of the victims, not to mention several others that Rubes has known from her past." Arthur turned the empty glass around on the bar, "I need you and some of the boys to ask around and see if they can find anything out." He glanced at his friend, then back down at the empty glass.

"You think Ruby could be a mark?" Billy asked between gulps.

"Hope not, but I'd rather be aware, at least I can keep her and the girls at the townhouse safe if it comes to it. I want a couple of very capable lads to watch her place twenty-four hours a day until this mess is sorted. Oh, and nothing, and I mean nothing goes any further than between you and the boys you've chosen to help. Is that understood?"

"No problem, can I ask why?" Billy leant on the bar with his forearms, still holding his tankard.

"Coppers have asked for a temporary alliance but I'm not happy about working with the pigs, as we know some of them are corrupt bastards, nothing like us lot, Bill, we're straightforward, have easy rules, these fuckers are a different kettle of fish." He waited as Eddie topped up his glass, then took a glug.

“Sounds like a shit arrangement if you don’t mind me saying and I can’t see why we need to do it. I hate the filth and they’ve done fuck all for us, just making out that they’re upholding the law when in fact they’re working it to suit themselves.” Billy’s face screwed up and a look of distaste flashed across his face. He took a long swill of his drink before he spoke. “Look you know me Art, I’m happy to work on the same page with you on virtually everything we do, but I’ve got to be honest, this arrangement stinks and I can see a lot of the other boys saying the same.”

Arthur nodded his head in agreement. “I know what you’re saying Bill, but couldn’t this be worked in our favour, get a bit closer to rooting out some of the real awkward bastards?” Arthur pursed his lips in thought.

“Why don’t you let me do a bit of digging myself, I’ve got some associates that have some of the pigs in their pockets.” He turned, still leaning with his elbow on the bar, tankard in his free hand. “Give me some names and I’ll look into it for you, discreet like.” He downed the last of his drink, “but that doesn’t mean I’m happy about this so called agreement, Art.” He said as he put the empty tankard down on the counter.

Arthur fixed Bill with a determined gaze and lifted his arm, palm facing up. "You need to trust me on this one, Bill," he said, “look, we don’t need to work with them per se, just let them think we are.”

Billy raised his eyebrows at the suggestion, a crease furrowing his brow. His lips parted to form an O-shape as he inhaled sharply. He then slowly nodded his head and bared his teeth in a malevolent smile, as he digested Arthur's suggestion. "Now that idea may be more to the lads' liking, and we could make it very beneficial to us." He lifted a finger to get Eddie's attention and slid the tankard across the bar.

Arthur grinned at his friend's comment, "Abberline is one, although he seems pleasant enough, I've worked him out. I think he's what you see is what you get, so to speak, but he's still a pig. Royal, on the other hand, complete wanker." Arthur jerked his hand back and forward. "Rubes seems to think that she knows him from somewhere but can't work out where from. He was a complete arsehole to her at the station when she was there the other morning and wanted none of it. Frankly, it wouldn't surprise me if he's got something to do with these murders. Anyhow, she told him straight and then left. It's that prick I want to know more about, more so than Abberline."

"Art, I get it, you're doing your best for Ruby, but surely there must be a better way than what you're suggesting?" He questioned and subconsciously swilled his ale around in the tankard.

"Look, I know it's a crazy idea," Arthur put his finger to his temple and circled it around, "but that Royal is a crooked bastard, that much we already know, Bill, and he's been breathing down my neck for years, one way or another. He told Rubes it'd be good if she went to the gallows! If I can get to that piece of shit through Abberline then so be it."

“All right Art,” Billy put his tankard down and raised both hands in the air palms up, “I’ll speak to the others, but they ain’t gonna like it none. This ain’t like you my friend, is there more to this than you’re telling me?”

Arthur kept his eyes down on his drink, brow furrowed. “I’m worried this is something to do with Ruby as I said.”

He lifted his eyes and locked them on Billy.

Billy held his gaze, momentarily stunned, “You’re serious, aren’t you?”

Arthur nodded, “I’ve got a feeling that someone is after her. A letter was found in Elsie’s dressing room when we were there clearing out her things earlier, it mentioned Ruby, and how I read it, the person that wrote it could be the one committing these murders and if so, has intentions of eventually coming for her.” Arthur paused to gauge Billy’s reaction. “Plus, some bastard was stood outside this gaff earlier eyeing the place up, then the fucker had the neck to show me he was carrying. If that wasn’t a threat, then nothing is.”

“Did you manage to get hold of the prick?” Billy asked as he took another swill.”

“No,” Arthur shook his head, “Fucker had vanished by the time I got outside.” He looked down at his glass as Eddie topped it up. “Thanks Ed.” He said.

Billy belched before he asked, “So, you’re concerned that this cocky bastard is something to do with all this as well? And suggesting that the murders of these women could be someone who knows Ruby?” Billy looked to the floor with a thoughtful expression on his face.

“Yep, on both questions, Bill. Look, all the girls that have been done over she knows,” Arthur paused, “I’ll be completely honest mate,” he said quietly so that only Billy could hear, “I can’t lose her. I love the bones of the girl, I need to keep her safe if anything happens to her…” He let the sentence hang in the air, then took a swill of his drink, “I’ll kill any man that does anything to hurt her.” He straightened up and faced his friend, the rest of his whiskey left untouched.

“Leave it with me, Arthur, nothing will happen to her, I’ll help you to make sure of that. I know several capable lads and everything we’ve discussed here stays with me.” He squeezed one of Arthur’s shoulders and gave him a nod.

“I know I can trust you, Bill, without a doubt. Thanks, let me know as soon as you do. Right, I need to go, if you want me, I’ll be at the townhouse.” He put out a hand and the two men shook hands. “Oh, one more thing, that geezer that was watching the pub earlier today, he was about five feet eight, dressed in expensive threads, black hair, try and find out about him too.”

“Sure will.”

“Chcers Bill, speak soon. Eddie, I’m off I’ll nip back in a day or so.” Arthur headed for the door.

“No problem, Mr Morris,” Eddie said to his bosses retreating back.

“Oh, give Mr Mills as many drinks as he wants, on the house, he’s thirsty today.” Arthur instructed over his shoulder. “He’s some business to sort out later.” He said as he pulled open the door and headed in the direction of the townhouse.

Chapter Eleven

He was happy, he knew that he'd seen him at the pub, which was his intention. Now he made his way to the brothel. He knocked on the door of the townhouse, and whilst he waited, he noted how clean the steps were and how well-polished the brass knocker. After a few moments, the door opened and a young girl of maybe thirteen or fourteen stood there.

"Can I help you, Sir?"

"I hope I'm at the right place, is it run by," he pulled a piece of paper from his lapel pocket and pretended to read from it, "a Miss Ruby Myers?" He asked then pushed the paper back into his coat.

"It is, Sir, could you wait here for a moment?" The girl pushed the door closed.

He could hear her walking away, several moments later the sound of approaching footsteps and the door swung open. A woman in her late forties stood in front of him, dressed in a light blue dress and with an apron tied around her waist.

"Yes, Sir, how can I be of help?" The smile she gave him lit up her eyes.

"Good day, Madam. I've been told by some associates that this is the place to visit for some female companionship, and run by a Miss Ruby Myers?" He gave her his best grin.

"Yes, Sir that is correct, do you have a calling card?" The woman wiped her hands in her apron.

"I apologise, I don't. I used the last one the other morning." He oozed charm.

The woman smoothed down her hair. “Just a moment, Sir, Miss Myers would prefer not to accept gentlemen that have no calling card. Let me just see if I can speak with her.” She closed the door.

Christ, this is a hard place to get into, a brothel filled with whores, and they want a fucking calling card. He clenched his jaw and balled his fists, breathing deeply at the same time. Minutes ticked by. Then what seemed like an eternity the door re-opened and a stunning red-headed woman in her twenties opened the door.

“You asked to see me.” Her deep blue eyes looked him up and down.

“I apologise, Miss, I was looking for a Miss Ruby Myers, I’m told that this is the place for clean female company?” He gave a small bow from the neck.

“Return tonight with a calling card and your entry may be considered. Payment upfront, no relationships with any of the girls, and all male visitors must be clean and wear a French letter. No mistreatment of the girls or you will be removed, their choices must be respected. Are there any questions?” She stared hard, her mouth set in a thin line.

“Thank you for the enlightening, Miss Myers, is there any restriction as to the times I can come in?” He was still trying to break through her hard exterior, but the charm wasn’t the way to go. So, she was a woman that couldn’t easily be taken in with such tactics as charisma.

“No restriction, but no overnight stays unless it’s been prearranged with one of the girls and paid for in advance.” Her façade didn’t change.

"Very fair Miss. I will return later this evening and bring a calling card, as per your request." He bowed from the neck again and began to descend the steps.

"How did you hear of our establishment?" She stood at the door with it partially closed not taking her eyes off him.

"Oh, an associate from an inn I frequent, I believe it's called The Nags Head, have you heard of it?" He questioned from the cobbles.

"Yes, I know of it." With that, she shut the door.

A hot rage surged through him, fuelled by the knowledge of the hoops he'd have to jump through just to satisfy his carnal urges. His teeth ground together, threatening to shatter as he envisioned the steps, he would have to take to obtain a whore. But he was resolved - nothing would stand in his way.

He stalked ahead on the cobblestones with purpose, each step punctuated by a seething fury that threatened to consume him whole, but nothing as simple as obtaining a calling card would stop him enjoying the next ritual. Deep in his loins the familiar tingle began, and he smiled to himself. Not long now Miss Myers, not long now.

Chapter Twelve

Sequeira's apprentice, Samuel sat for hours trying to decipher the partially carved lettering on the cane, and finally, he was ninety-nine per cent sure he'd worked it out. His stomach growled telling him he'd missed his lunch. He went to the hook on the back of the door, lifted down his overcoat and pushed his arms into it and started to make his way out into the early evening air. Traders were now packing up for the night, but Sam was lucky as his favourite stall was still open.

"Good evening, Mrs Wilkins, so glad you're still here, I wondered if I could have some of the broth, that's if there's enough." He rubbed his hands together and then blew into his palms.

"Missed your lunch again?" Mrs Wilkins tutted but smiled at the boy all the same. "Isn't good for your stomach yah know, three square is so important." She ladled some broth into a chipped bowl and then handed him two thick slices of bread and butter. "Just give me enough for the broth, the bread and butter are on the house." She handed him the bowl.

Samuel took a mouthful straight from the bowl, "thanks, Mrs Wilkins, as always, it's delicious."

The boy shovelled heaps of food into his mouth, barely chewing before he swallowed. She smiled and gently placed her hand on the back of his neck. "There, there, take it easy now," she said in a warm voice. She began gathering the crockery from her stall, wiping them clean with a dirty rage before shifting them to the cloth bag.

"I'm in a bit of a hurry, I need to see my govna about something I've just found out for him." Sam mopped the rest of the broth up with the bread and butter and wiped his mouth with his sleeve.

"Nothing can be that important than to rush yah food." Mrs Wilkins said as she took the bowl and wiped it clean with a rag.

"This won't keep, I needs to see me boss, smartish." Samuel handed her a coin, "Thanks again Mrs Wilkins, see you tomorrow."

Fifteen minutes later, he approached Sequeira's home. His knuckles rapped against the hard wooden door, echoing in the silence of the neighbourhood. He shifted his weight impatiently as he waited for a response, and eventually, the door creaked open. There stood an exhausted looking Sequeira, with bags under his eyes and hair unkempt.

"Ah, Sam, good evening. What is so urgent that you needed to come here?" Sequeira beckoned the boy indoors and led him through to the kitchen. The room was untidy and looked like it hadn't been cleaned for several days. "Excuse the mess, not had time and our maid has taken to her bed with a heavy cold." He sat in a chair at the table and indicated to Sam to do the same.

"I'm sorry to call at this hour boss, but I've managed to work out the lettering carved into the cane." He sat down in a chair opposite. "Taken a while, but I'm sure I've got it now."

Sequeira took a swig from a dirty glass on the table in front of him. "Continue," he said, as he swilled the amber-coloured liquid around in the tumbler.

Sam pulled the chair in closer, pulled out some paper from his pockets and began showing Sequeira exactly what he'd found.

"Samuel, are you quite sure that's the letters that are missing?" Sequeira was finding it hard to concentrate on what the boy was telling him. He refilled his glass.

"Sure Doc, it can't be any others, I've gone over and over it, I'm sure that's it." Sam stabbed a finger at a piece of paper in front of the Doctor, his eyes full of triumph.

"So, in your opinion, the letters are someone's initials, definitely not a business?" The Doctor took a swill.

"Absolutely not, my friend, who works with this kind of craft daily, told me that businesses typically engrave in block letters, while individuals use italics like the ones here. He also said the ebony indicates a wealthy punter as that sort of wood is expensive. The initials were carved into the shaft rather than having the hand rest engraved, which could have been difficult due to its unusual shape. But on the other hand, and due to fashion trends at the moment, it's not common place to etch details into the hand rest of a personal walking cane." Sam folded his arms across his chest.

"Well, Sam, I'm very impressed. Excellent job. I'll get onto Abberline in the morning and tell him what you've found out. Now if you don't mind, I need to go to my bed." Sequira stood up and staggered backwards. "Oops, misjudged the booze tonight," he chuckled under his breath. "Right lad, I'll see you out and see you bright and early tomorrow." He moved on unsteady legs to the front door as Sam followed him.

"Thanks Doc, I'll see you in the morning, oh and you should probably give this to Abberline in the morning." I thrust the crumpled piece of paper with my notes into his hands, then strode off down the path.

Sequeira's voice followed him as he stood by the door. He could still feel his gaze on his back. "Just a moment Sam, come here." He called, "The name down here," he pointed down at the scrawl of black ink with a shaky finger, "I've heard it before, but I can't recall from where from."

Chapter Thirteen

Ruby rose earlier than usual the next morning. The same horror of a snake slithering through her bedsheets and constricting around her, threatening to choke the life out of her, woke her up yet again. In her dream, she looked down and saw the muscular coils digging into the flesh on either side of her rib cage. The forked tongue flickered over cruel lips, like flames licking at dry kindling. The monstrous reptile tightened its grip and Ruby was wrenched from a deep sleep by black claws clutching at her throat.

She found herself pacing the bedroom in the early hours as Arthur slept soundly. She went down to the kitchen around six, where Rose was building a fire in the aga.

"Morning Miss Ruby, you're up and about earlier than usual," Rose said. "Can I get you a cup of tea when I've got the stove going?"

"That'd be great Rose, thank you. I'll go and sit in my parlour so as not to get in your way." Ruby said, as she closed the kitchen door behind her.

The parlour was unusually warm due to the early morning, late autumn sun coming in through the window. She sat at her bureaux and pulled out the letter. Re-reading the note did not provide any more information than before, so she decided to abandon her search for answers and returned it back to its hiding spot. Should she mention this to Abberline? If so, what good could it do? Would it make any difference as to how long it would take to apprehend the killer? She hated it that they had an allegiance with the constabulary and even though there'd been several meetings with the Inspector over the past few weeks, which Royal refused to attend, nothing had come to fruition. Not to mention Arthur putting out feelers with his associates. Usually, Arthur's acquaintances came back with some information. There'd been some titbits on Royal and his love of one of the local brothels, but that'd had been all. Maybe that could be used as leverage? Strange how everywhere was so quiet.

A while later Rose bought her some breakfast and some tea. Ruby was surprised that she had an appetite and happily devoured the meal, much to Rose's delight.

At nine o'clock, a note from Abberline arrived and requested a meeting with her and Arthur to discuss developments. He would arrive at noon.

True to his note Abberline arrived on time. Arthur and Ruby were sat in the parlour.

“Good day to you both. I hope you don’t mind I’ve asked Dr Sequeira to join us today, he should be along in a few minutes. He’s been the one responsible for bringing these details to my attention.” Abberline looked pleased with himself. “May I?” He pointed to a chair tucked under the table. “I took the liberty of letting your Housekeeper know that another guest should be joining us,” he said as he sat down.

“Well Inspector, I hope he arrives soon as we have other business to attend to, we need to see some associates shortly that may have further information for us too.” Ruby lied.

Arthur’s jaw clenched as he stood and took his pipe down from the mantlepiece. “Miss Myers and I can’t spend too much time waiting for information to be dropped into our laps, we do better, we call it the underworld grapevine.” He added sarcastically as he picked up a worn leather pouch, opened it and began to fill the bowl of his pipe.

“Yes, I can only apologise about the lack of information regarding this case, all the constables have their eyes peeled whilst out on the beat, sadly, the killer eludes us at every step.” Inspector Abberline licked his lips, shifted in his seat, and reached for the small leather-bound notebook he kept in his inner pocket. He ran a thumb along its spine, opened it up, and began skimming intently through the pages.

Briefly, the tension was broken as Rose showed in Sequeira. Ruby noticed that he looked tired and unkempt. Could it be sleepless nights due to the rising body count?

“Aubrey, thank you for coming.” Abberline stood up and shook his hand.

“Fred.” He turned to Ruby and Arthur. “Good morning, Miss Myers, Mr Morris, I do hope this information is of some importance, I have my assistant to thank for this.” He sat in the chair Arthur had pulled out for him and took out the piece of paper that Samuel had left with him the night before.

“Dr Sequeira we’ve been made aware of the coins that have been left at the scenes of all these murders, so if that’s what you’ve come to tell us I’m afraid you’re wasting your time,” Ruby said in a tight voice. She glanced across at Arthur and rolled her eyes.

“This may crack the case open," Sequeira said, smoothing the paper on his thigh. He looked between Arthur and Ruby. "A cane was left at the scene, with a missing silver or brass top that had a strand of blonde hair lodged in its shattered wood, which has been confirmed as the recent victim. So -”

Ruby cut him off, “We weren’t made aware of this, how long ago did this come to light?” Her nostrils flared and her eyes narrowed as she looked between the two men.

“Miss Myers, I can assure you this has only recently been bought to our attention; I will explain more once he’s done.” Abberline nodded at her. “Aubrey, please continue.”

“After the discovery of the fibre, it was pure luck that whilst I had the cane held up to the light, I happened to catch a glimpse of what was left of some letters carved into the wood. Only partial ones but letters all the same. My assistant has spent hours trying to decipher what the letters are. After a process of elimination, his conclusion is that the letters are initials, and they are R.H.C.B.”

“So, you are of the assumption that the person who owns the cane has those initials?” Reiterated Arthur as he took a deep pull on his pipe.

Sequeira leaned forward, elbows resting on the armrests before his hands intertwined. He eyed Arthur and Abberline before continuing, “Absolutely, Mr Morris."

Sequeira cleared his throat. "I’ve looked at the damage to the girl’s head and face and judging by the injuries, I believe that the cane is what was used to subdue the latest victim?" His gaze flicked over to Abberline whose pen froze mid-sentence as he looked up in recognition.

“Yes, I’m still trying to understand the ferocity of this person’s attack,” he shook his head before returning his attention back to his notebook.

"The wood this cane is made from is particularly strong," Sequeira continued. "And not easily broken. It’s been used to strike her down with a lot of force and multiple times—hence why it's so broken."

“Why does a person need to do such a violent thing?” Ruby asked quietly.

He looked across to Arthur, "Mr Morris, such information is quite distressing, and I'd rather spare your good lady the horror." He cleared his throat searched his pockets and pulled out a hip flask.

"It's quite alright Doctor," Arthur said as he watched him take a deep swig. "Miss Myers isn't that fragile that she can't hear the details, you may continue."

The Doctor nodded in Arthur's direction and then turned his eyes on Ruby. Well, Miss Myers, I think he's a very angry individual, for one, for two, my theory is that he's a deep hatred for women and three," he counted off on his fingers, "he enjoys immensely what he's doing it isn't just that he's getting revenge with each one of the victims, he also seeks ah…ah…" He paused for a second, "please excuse the terminology here Miss Myers… a sexual release in his actions." Sequeira shifted uncomfortably in his seat before clearing his throat.

Ruby's eyebrows shot up as the doctor spoke. She tilted her head, peering at him intently through narrowed eyes. "Please continue." she confirmed in a low voice.

Sequeira sat back in the chair, "However, since my last meeting with Inspector Abberline, I re-examined the woman's wounds and did check the top of the head of the victim and I found two places, here and here," Sequeira indicated the areas on his head, "where there are some compression injuries of around two and a half inches in width. Something that could possibly cause blunt force trauma, the size of which, may be that of a round hand rest or one of that particular diameter, but it's hard to tell without comparing it to the top, which as we know is missing."

Ruby swallowed and pursed her lips together, "I see, thank you." She said as her hand lightly touched her throat.

"I apologise again, Miss Myers, it isn't a pleasant thing to discuss." Sequeira glanced across at Abberline who was still scribbling in his notebook, then turned his attention back to Ruby.

"My assistant agreed to try and decipher the letters, mainly through a process of elimination and some help from a friend who happens to work in a place that makes walking canes. The information he gained from him was very useful, and he's fairly confident those initials are correct." He took an impromptu swill from his hip flask. "So far, that is everything that I've discovered and nothing further to tell you at the moment." He looked over at Abberline, "Fred, I hate to be rude, but I need to attend to Ida, my visit was only intended to be brief."

"Mmm," Abberline looked up at the mention of his name. "Of course, Aubrey."

“Miss Myers, Mr Morris, it was a pleasure, but I’m needed somewhere, if there’s anything else that comes to light, I will let you know.” He said as he stood up and made his way to the door. “I’ll see myself out.”

“Thanks again, Aubrey.” Abberline stood up, “I’ll be in touch.”

Sequeira nodded at his friend, then was gone.

“I do apologise if the Doctor seemed curt at any point, I’m afraid he’s going through a lot at this present time,” Abberline said.

“It’s information that we need Inspector, and that is exactly what he gave us.” Ruby kept her eyes narrowed at the man; her lips drawn in a thin straight line.

Arthur broke the tension, “So Inspector, have you any idea as to whom these initials belong to?” He placed his pipe in an ashtray and walked over to the bureaux. “Can you repeat them to me please?” He picked up a pencil and scratched them onto some paper as the Inspector read them to him again.

“I’m afraid these initials do allude me somewhat, Mr Morris,” Inspector Abberline added, “but hopefully sharing them with you two will help.” He said as he stood up. “Now if there’s nothing else?” He looked between the two of them.

“One moment Inspector,” Ruby said, “as you’ve shared information with us, I feel it is only correct to do the same.” Ruby stood and crossed to the bureaux, her steps measured and purposeful. She reached into the writing desk and retrieved the letter, her hands trembling as she handed it over to Abberline.

He unfolded the page and scanned the words, his face growing paler with each line he read.

Arthur and Ruby watched him in anticipation; she perched on the edge of her chair, her lips clamped shut as she held her breath.

Abberline exhaled sharply and his eyes moved from one to the other. “Good Lord…I… Miss Myers, this is frightening,” he said slowly, tapping a finger against the letter's edge. “It mentions Miss Lancaster’s place of residence and suggests that there’ll be eight victims, but what’s standing out to me too is the name Jack—a newspaper covering the murders has given the killer this name: Jack the Ripper.”

Fear flickered in Ruby’s blue eyes and her porcelain skin seemed to pale and a deep crease marred her forehead as she spoke, her voice heavy with worry. "As I feared then," she said. "A name – but that is all. No clues about his appearance or whereabouts. Just a constant taunt." Her hands were painfully clenched in her lap, so tight the knuckles shone waxen against her skin.

Inspector Abberline leaned across to Ruby, his voice soft and reassuring. "I know this man is very illusive and takes great pleasure in taunting the law and I find it so infuriating, but please try to believe me that I will do everything in my power to stop him.” He placed a gentle hand on her shoulder as she looked up at him. "I know it doesn't seem that way, but with your help," he looked between the two of them, “hopefully it’ll be sooner rather than later.” He said, letting the sentence drift off into the stillness of the room.

The tension hung heavy in the air each of them lost in thought about what had happened and what was yet to come.

As Abberline turned to leave, he paused at the door and looked back at her once more. "Thank you for sharing that with me, we'll get him" he said firmly again, as he pushed the letter along with his notebook back into his jacket pocket. "Hopefully these dreadful events will soon be bought to a close. Good day to you both." He said as he made his way into the corridor.

The sound of the front door echoed down the hallway into the parlour, and Arthur turned to her.

"Do you think it was a good idea giving him the letter Rubes?" He questioned as a look of concern flashed across his face.

"Can't do any harm," she replied as she returned his concerned expression, "And it'll be more use to him than us." Ruby's eyes lit up with excitement as she spoke. A sly grin spread across her face "The thing is Arty, I know something he doesn't know." She said as she held Arthur's stare, "I know whose initials they are."

Arthur cocked an eyebrow and smiled. "Really? You do seem pretty smug there Rubes. So, tell me, who does it belong to?" His voice carried a hint of satisfaction, as if he already knew the answer.

She nodded slowly, the same self-satisfied smile on her face. "If I'm right about this," she said, standing from her chair and beginning to make her way across the room, "then Abberline will need to know, but only if I'm correct. Plus," she held up her finger," if it's the person I think it is then this could put someone right where I want them." She paused near the parlour door, her gaze resting on Arthur as she continued, "Get your coat, Arthur Morris. You and I need to pay someone a visit."

****

The house stood back from the road with a large, overgrown front garden. The black iron, eight-foot railings that enclosed the forepart of the property looked like a garrison of soldiers keeping guard. Green ivy had covered nearly all of the front of the house, hooking its vines deep inside the brickwork, seemingly choking any chance of life out of its walls.

Fortunately for Ruby and Arthur the tall wrought iron gate wasn't locked, and Arthur was able to slide the bolt with little effort. The path was hidden under dense weeds and snaked up to the front door.

"Christ Rubes, this place is depressing." Arthur looked around at the garden. "Seems they need a gardener too."

Ruby hesitated in front of the dispiriting mansion, as she curled her fingers around the ornate brass bell pull. The tinkling echoed throughout the house yet felt muffled by the thick walls. Her eyes scanned the windows for signs of movement until finally, after much anticipation, the large black door creaked open, and an elderly woman came into view.

"Can I help you?" She eyed the pair with dull green eyes, letting the door bear her weight.

"Yes Madam, I'm truly sorry to bother you, but we were wondering if we could perhaps talk with the lady of the house, Mrs Mildred Byford?" Ruby turned to Arthur, "this is my companion Arthur Morris, and I'm Ruby Myers."

The woman was frail, her breathing laboured, and her thin grey hair hung about her face in tendrils. She coughed into a handkerchief before managing to croak out "I've heard of you two from somewhere before." She took a few steps back and gestured at the doorway with a trembling arm. "P-p-please, do come in. I'll see if Mrs Byford is around… Give me some time, though! I'm not as spry as I used to be."

The hall opened up inside with a large staircase in the centre. Two double doors were on each side and dark wood panelling lined the walls, with the floor covered in black and white marble tiles. The old lady, whom Ruby could now see was bent over with a hump on the right side of her back, had disappeared into the one of the left.

Arthur's face softened as he moved close to her ear and spoke in a low, gentle tone. “Rubes, you can see the frailty in that woman’s eyes, a gust of wind and she’d be blown over. She needs someone to take care of her.” He paused for a moment, his eyes full of empathy.

Ruby looked up at him and couldn’t help a smile, “that’s why I love you, Arthur Morris.”

A few moments later and the old lady shuffled into the hallway. “Mrs Byford will see you, please come this way.”

The two followed her back into the room on the left and found their host sitting in a large armchair covered with a thick patchwork quilt. The chair was positioned right next to a wide fireplace with a fire burning in its hearth.

The rest of the room was sparsely furnished, a large, buttoned back, leather sofa sat on the right, facing Mrs Byford. The shelves that once played host to books and ornaments were virtually bare, aside from the odd volume or statue placed here and there. The large windows on the left of the room were void of drapes and the interior of the glass was dusty and held several cobwebs. On the mantlepiece above the fireplace sat a single ornate oil lamp, the only illumination for the large room.

“So, Miss Myers and companion, what do I owe the pleasure?” She asked.

Ruby noticed a pallor had settled over the usually jovial Mrs Byford. Her usual shrill voice was now brittle and croaky and her pinched face pale. She looked to be in poor health.

“Mrs Byford, this isn’t a pleasure for us,” said Ruby, “we have some questions for you and if you want to keep your late husband’s antics quiet then you’d best give us some answers.” Ruby crossed to the sofa and perched herself on its edge.

Arthur didn’t move from where he stood.

Ruby sat across from Byford in the dimly lit living room. She watched as Byford rubbed her eyes with a wrinkled, bony hand, and took a deep breath before speaking. "I can assure you," she said with a crackle of tiredness in her voice, "I've no fight left in me. It's long gone." She paused to cough into a small, floral-patterned handkerchief before continuing. "Running this house, trying to make ends meet, my husband's abandonment of me and then his death have all taken their toll, as well as my poor health."

Ruby nodded in acknowledgement and tried to find sympathy as she listened to Byford's heart-wrenching story. The air around them felt heavy with sadness--a palpable weight that could be felt on the skin.

“I do sympathise Mrs Byford,” Ruby said in a tone that belied her words. She cleared her throat as she glanced around the room, feeling uncomfortable with the coldness of her voice. “But we've some questions so if you'd be good enough to answer them, then we can be on our way.”

Mrs. Byford gave a tight-lipped smile, her weak green eyes boring into Ruby. “Do you know Miss Myers, I’ve never actually had a problem with you or your establishment.”

Ruby snorted in disbelief. “Well, if you don’t mind me saying Mrs Byford, you had a very funny way of showing it. Every chance you got wasn’t wasted on being nice to me, quite the opposite.” Her nostrils flared and her fists clenched at her sides as she remembered the ridicule and mocking, she endured from the woman.

“My problem is deeply rooted with my late husband,” Byford began cautiously. “I’ve just been extremely angry, and I suppose the closest thing that I could vent my anger on was you.”

Ruby's eyes narrowed as she processed the words, her chest rising and falling slowly as she waited for Byford to continue. “And why would that be, I’ve actually done you no harm.” Ruby straightened her back and placed her hands in her lap. “Prey, continue, I’m all ears.”

“As you know he frequented your establishment on a regular basis, I pretended not to know, but a wife knows because they know the man they’re married to.” Byford began to gasp, desperately trying to catch her breath.

Arthur picked up the glass of water on the table next to her chair, but she waved it away.

“Thank you, Mr Morris, but it doesn’t help.” Byford looked amused at his shock at her using his name and his mouth hung open.

“Don’t be surprised Mr Morris, I know who you are too and know more about the pair of you than you realise,” she teased, “but also my housekeeper did tell me your name when you arrived.” She gave a breathy laugh before continuing. “It is true what you said to me that day in Mrs Miller’s, he did have certain tastes, and sadly not tastes I could accommodate.” She looked away watching the flames of the fire.

Suddenly to Ruby, she looked vulnerable, not the bitter, shrew-like, woman whom she’d first assumed her to be. “Is this an apology Mrs Byford?” Ruby's asked, her heart felt heavy for Mrs Byford, and she wished that she could take away her pain. As much as she wanted to offer support and comfort, she knew nothing she said would make anything better. Ruby felt a pang of guilt for not reaching out sooner to try and understand what Mrs Byford was going through. “Mrs Byford, I’m so sorry for your loss…” She trailed off, unsure how to continue.

A single tear slipped down her face and Arthur stepped forward and handed the woman his handkerchief, offering a gesture of sympathy where words had failed.

"Thank you, Mr Morris." She dabbed her face with the corner of the hanky. "Nothing can be said or done, of that, I'm sure. When he finally left me for Scarlet, it wasn't much of a surprise, we'd hardly spoken in years, but the legacy he left me with is far less forgiving. Clifford had always maintained he would keep me safe as long I excepted his other dalliances. I agreed, as long as he was discreet and kept our name out of the mud. After all, being a member of parliament comes with a lot of responsibility and if his colleagues got wind of his other extramarital affairs, well, you could imagine." Byford lifted her glass a took a sip of water. "The wrinkles that cover my face are deep and sorrowful. I had become bitter without realizing it, the bitterness has finally taken its toll. The pain of the mistakes my husband made weighs heavily on my heart, like a boulder too big for me to carry. I looked at you Miss Myers, so strong and confident, and I became jealous, I wished that I could have been stronger and stood up for myself and refused the treatment that Clifford thought acceptable. I realise I wanted you to feel the burden I carried, even though I knew it was wrong of me. I've tried to push this pain onto you, and it's something I can never forgive myself for. Please accept my heartfelt apology." She paused briefly and looked straight at Ruby.

Ruby continued to listen, trying her best to keep her face impassive as she did so.

“I knew his true intentions," Byford said. He had moved Scarlet into lodgings so he could visit her discreetly, then moved in with her permanently, claiming love. But she wanted only his money. He agreed to pay me enough to live on and keep the house staff, until he died eighteen months later. He left the house to me and the rest of his estate to Scarlet. The only other thing he left me with is sickness. She looked back at the fire."

“Oh, such as?”

“His love of Dollymops has been the bain of my life, Miss Myers.” She paused and took another sip of water, “The Right Honourable Clifford Byford left me with Cupid’s disease and this god-forsaken house, which is all. So, again you are correct when you implied, he wasn’t The Right Honourable after all.” She dabbed her eyes again with the handkerchief.

Ruby was at a loss for words. She had been wrong about Mrs Byford; the woman before her was nothing like the hard-nosed, interfering person she had imagined, and the apology was sincere. Ruby felt guilty for what Mrs Byford had gone through - if only she had known sooner! Could Ruby have seen what was happening with Scarlet? Possibly not, but she could at least have tried. Every emotion imaginable whirled around inside of her; guilt, pity, confusion, regret. Yet, nothing seemed to fit together. She glanced over at Arthur, who merely shrugged.

Ruby reached across and took the woman’s hand. “Let me help you, so your last days are comfortable and worry-free.”

"I can't allow that Miss Myers, thank you for your kind offer, I fear that I am far from deserving after the way I've treated you these past months." She squeezed Ruby's hand, then turned to Arthur, "I've always respected her, not that I'd ever had let her know. I just took my pain out on the wrong person, and for that," She looked back to Ruby, "I'm truly sorry."

"Mrs Byford, I feel somewhat responsible for your situation. Scarlet said she was clean when she worked at my establishment. Nonetheless, it might have been another bordello that made your husband sick but sadly we'll never know for sure. So, please, let me help you get the care you need."

"I couldn't possibly impose; I don't feel I deserve it, Miss Myers." Byford's eyes had filled with tears.

"Miss Myers won't take no for an answer, she's too stubborn." Arthur said through a small chuckle, He looked over at Ruby, reached across, and kissed her gloved hand.

"Please just let me help, it's the least I can do." Ruby pleaded.

"Let me think it through, I must admit, having this house full of staff again, with regular visitors, would be lovely and hosting bridge games once more would be wonderful." Suddenly the woman looked younger, and some colour had returned to her cheeks.

"Think it through, then please get a message to me to let me know," Ruby said.

“Of course, I will and thank you.” For the first time since Ruby and Arthur arrived, the woman's face lit up with a warm smile before continuing, “When you both got here you said you have some questions for me?” She gestured for Arthur to take a seat next to Ruby.

“Ah, yes, if you’re sure you’re up to it?” Arthur asked as he settled into his seat.

Mrs Byford tucked the quilt further up her body and reached for her glass with an alabaster hand.

“Mrs Byford, do you still have your husband’s cane in the house?”

The old woman gasped softly and shook her head slowly. “Why no Miss Myers, he took the cane when he left, can I ask how you know of it?”

“It was found by a doctor, whilst he attended a recent death,” Arthur answered gravely.

Mrs Byford’s eyes widened with interest. Her hand flew to her chest, and she exhaled sharply. “Oh, good lord, that’s awful…” she said, voice hushed. She took a sip from her glass and coughed gently into the handkerchief. “Such a terrible thing to have happened.” She paused in thought, fingers tapping lightly against her lips.

“The cane was lovely. It was made of black ebony with a silver top and had been given to him by his colleagues in parliament as a sign of respect for his service.” Her eyes flicked between Arthur and Ruby.

Arthur's eyebrows arched in surprise. "Did they carve the initials into the shaft?"

She smiled fondly but shook her head. "It was my idea. I asked a carpenter to etch his initials just below the handrest so that no one else could ever claim it as their own." She licked her lips, "But how did this walking stick end up in a room with a different woman if it wasn't Scarlet?" Her forehead creased in confusion.

"That's exactly what we're trying to establish, Mrs Byford." Ruby added, "Do you think that maybe it was stolen or possibly she may have sold the cane once your husband died?"

"It's possible," she agreed, "and that she sold his belongings after he died, which is why it ended up where it did," Byford said with a sigh. "Clifford had bought her gifts, but during a heated financial discussion, he let slip that he'd showered her with gifts. I always thought she was after his money, not him. He was convinced she loved him, but only it's only Scarlet knows the truth." She made a sour face, dabbed her mouth, and looked away.

"Well, I think we need to pay Scarlet a little visit." Arthur said. "I'll get Billy to put out some feelers, see if anyone may know of her whereabouts."

Mrs Byford looked thoughtful for a moment, "That's most likely the only way you'll know for sure. I do hate to seem rude, but I'm very tired now and like very much to rest."

Ruby stood up, "Of course, Mrs Byford, and thank you for your time today, it was very… enlightening." She smiled warmly at the woman, who tried momentarily to stand.

“It’s okay Mrs Byford, Miss Myers and I will see ourselves out,” Said Arthur, “I think it would be quicker if we did.” He grinned as he made his way to the doors.

“Of that Mr Morris, you are correct.” Mrs Byford gave a tired giggle. “I’ll be in touch very shortly.”

As Ruby and Arthur made their way down the serpent-like path they digested everything Mrs Byford had said to them.

Arthur's grip tightened on the gate as he turned to Ruby, his expression tight and urgent. “We need to talk to Scarlet immediately. She may be our only hope in finding out where the cane maybe.” He pushed the gate closed a little too harshly, sending a loud, metallic clang echoing through the air. “As I said inside, I’ll get Billy to get a message around that we're looking for her.”

Ruby's strides were long and determined as she linked her arm with Arthur’s. She could feel the tendons of his arm tense beneath her grip and noticed that her own fingers had dug into his flesh as though trying to channel Ruby's drive through him. There were a lot of questions that needed answers and she was determined to get them no matter how long it took. Scarlet was out there somewhere, and it wouldn’t be long before they found her.

Chapter Fourteen

He found it simple to obtain the calling card. He slipped it into his lapel pocket and made his way to the townhouse. The night was surprisingly mild, and many locals had taken the opportunity to go out for an evening stroll. He ambled along, greeting people as he went. Tonight, was special and there was no need to rush it.

Forty-five minutes later he arrived at the townhouse. That evening, it looked more inviting than his visit earlier in the morning. The outside of the building now seemed to shine with an inner light; the polished knocker glowed like a pulse and stood out amongst the white steps and dark wood of the door. It was plain but elegant; practical yet innocent. A beacon for all to see. A touch of hypocrisy for the brothel. Did it appear this way because of his plan? Distant church bells chimed as if to taunt him, to say "come and be saved". The wind howled through an alleyway at the end of the street and knocked over a pile of large wooden tea chests and whistled through an open door in an opposing house. He used the brass knocker, stood back and waited.

The woman from his last visit opened the door.

“Hello ‘gain, Sir.” She smiled coyly.

He noticed her reaction to him and inwardly smirked.

“Good evening, Madam, my card.” He pulled out the card and handed it to her with a dramatic flourish.

"My Sir, we are in good spirits." She glanced at the writing, "Mr Witherington-Smythe welcome." She stood back and held the door so he could enter.

"You are so kind Madam, and may I say you look particularly lovely this evening." He handed her his hat, gloves and overcoat then watched her hang them on the stand just behind her. "Tell me, would Miss Myers be here this evening?"

The woman smoothed her hair down. "I'm sorry, but Miss Myers is not in residence this evening, but you are welcome to leave a message."

"It's of no consequence, I'll see her another time." He gave her his best smile. Perfect.

"If you'd like to come this way." She led him down to a room on the right of the hallway.

The space was tastefully decorated, with a deep red wallpaper on the walls with a gold floral pattern running through it. A large, patterned rug lay in the middle of the room and covered most of the floorboards. He sat on one of the three ornate sofas each had a walnut side table at the end. The ticking of the coals from the fireplace sounded like a parent tutting at a defiant child. Its heart burned orange and red-blue flames licked the back of the hearth. A subtle smell of soot hung in the air. On the mantlepiece above placed at each end were two brass oil lamps and a small, glass, chandelier hung from the ceiling. To the left of the hearthside another walnut side table hosted a bottle of whiskey and some glasses.

"Sir, if you'd be so kind as to wait here, I will send you some girls that would like to entertain you this evening. You of course are aware of the house rules and the payment required?"

"But of course." He reached into his pocket and pulled out some coins, "Will this be enough, my good lady?"

She glanced at the money in her hand, "You require an overnight stay?" her head tilted to one side, "this is enough for one night, Sir." She dropped the coins into her apron pocket.

He said nothing, just nodded.

"One moment Sir, I will be back, whilst you wait, please help yourself to the house whiskey, it is complimentary." She indicated to the bottle and the glasses on the nearby table.

"Thank you, I will." He watched her leave and sat motionless for a moment before reaching for the bottle of whiskey, pouring out its rich, spicy nectar into a glass tumbler. The tantalizing smell of alcohol, spice and heat wafted through the air like an aphrodisiac. His eyes fixed absentmindedly on the window as he took a sip of the golden liquid, feeling its warmth spread across his entire body. It was the familiar anticipation that returned to his groin as his hand trembled around the glass. He smiled to himself as thoughts of his earlier rituals returned to his mind. Adrenalin surged through him, yes, they'd all been perfect, but tonight would be the best one yet. He drained his drink quickly, rising to get himself another refill, she had already returned with three companions. The excitement was palpable as he stepped forward.

"Sir, these are the girls that would like to entertain you this evening. This is Molly, Connie and Jane."

"Nice to meet you, Sir." The three girls greeted in unison.

He looked all the girls up and down, One, was buxom, with a pinched waist, and wiry red hair. The other two were more petite, one blonde, one dark-haired.

His gaze methodically scanned the three whores before him, all of them vying for his attention. The one with the coarse ginger hair, had a sad and crooked smile that failed to reach her eyes, and a disfiguring, jagged scar from her bottom lip down her chin. Her ample bosom didn't impress him in the slightest. The blonde was far better proportioned with a perfect set of surprisingly white teeth and flushed cheeks. In comparison, the last girl's dark hair, pockmarked face, and curve less figure made her look more boyish than womanly. But his eyes were drawn back to the blonde; he knew she was going to be the one.

"What's you name my dear?" He asked her as his eyes traced down her body.

"Jane, Sir." She answered with an alluring, provocative smile.

"Why I think I'd like to have Jane's company this evening. Maybe next time ladies." He winked at the other two. "Thank you, Madam, you've been most helpful."

Jane stood swinging her hips and batting her eyelashes. "My pleasure, Sir. Please follow me."

Jane tightly grasped his hand and guided him up the stairs, past a corridor with a window that beckoned at its end. The walls were panelled halfway up, while the rest were washed in white with flickering oil lamps illuminating every few feet. Five doorways lined the walls on each side, four of which emitted low moans and grunts emanating from within. Jane paused at the fifth door and released his hand before twisting the doorknob and slipping inside. His palms trembled as adrenaline surged through his veins and his heart thundered with anticipation. Not long to wait.

"Now, Sir, I understand you've paid for my company for the entire night?" She pulled on a ribbon holding together a see through pink negligée. She let it slip to the floor.

"You are a fine specimen, Jane. Now, I'd like you to know my name." He said as he turned the key in the lock. "After all, I like all my rituals to hear my name at least once."

He began to undress and folded his clothes on a nearby chair.

She dropped her bodice and looked at him, her eyes flashing. He felt the electricity in the air as he let his britches slip to the floor and responded with a deep chuckle.

He looked over her body hungrily, barely able to contain himself, before finally throwing his head back and inhaling deeply. “Jane,” he said, his voice thick with lechery, “I am Rupert Constantine, so nice to make your acquaintance.” He lunged towards her. Grabbed her around the throat with a vice-like grip. His fingers dug into her skin as he forced her back onto the bed.

She gasped in terror, her ragged breaths falling hot on his arm.

"Jane," he said darkly in her ear, "today is your lucky day, you have the honour of being part of my ritual."

Chapter Fifteen

Arthur and Ruby stayed at Henage Court that night. They needed time alone. Mrs Byford's confession and subsequent apology had left Ruby confused. Why had she let Scarlet and Mr Byford continue with their affair? They ate a light meal before taking evening drinks in the sitting room.

"I do hope we get some information on Scarlet soon, Arty" Ruby sipped her wine, then looked over at Arthur. "I hate the waiting, it makes me restless."

He sighed and scrubbed a hand against his face. "I know and me too, I think our next move is to inform Abberline about our findings. It looks as if he's our best bet for quick action. He can have the police look into pawn shops and question local vendors. Billy needs to spread the word on the streets too—see if anyone knows of any robberies that involve this cane." He took a swill of his brandy, let out a long, slow breath as he lent down and began to unlace his shoes.

"Are you okay, Arty?" Ruby asked, her voice warring between concern and worry. Arthur pulled off his Loake Loafers and settled back. "Mmm… yes, I think so. Just a bit tired," he replied, although the tension across his forehead negated that statement. "To be honest, Rubes, I'll be glad when all this is over," he said as he reached over, taking her hand in his own.

|Ruby sat for a while enjoying the closeness then stood and walked over to the window. The street was quiet, and the streetlamps let out the familiar watery glow. “I’ve given him the letter, but should I tell Abberline that I know the initials on the cane too.” She glanced across at Arthur, “What do you think?”

He rubbed his chin, frowning as he did so then Arthur put his glass down and lent forward, put his elbows on his knees and rested his chin on his fists. “As much as it pains me to say it Rubes, you should.”

Ruby folded her arms and continued to watch the street outside. A well-dressed man was walking alone down the cobbles, and it prompted a thought to come into her mind. “That fella you mentioned that was watching the pub, any news on him?” She asked over her shoulder.

“It's like I'm hitting a brick wall. Normally, I'd have some useful leads from my sources by now, but nothing. It's never been like this before. And I don't like it when strangers start hovering around my pub," Arthur said with a troubled frown as he stood and joined Ruby at the window. He put his arms around her and kissed her neck.

Ruby turned to face him and put her arms around his waist. “I’ll tell Abberline, hopefully it’ll get us closer to bringing our own justice on the bastard that killed my girls and Elsie. Then it’ll be me to be the one to pluck out his eyes.” She rested her head on his chest.

He rubbed both her arms, "that is not something I want my lady doin, understand?" Arthur stood back and held her at arm's length. "It's a man's job that and my girl, you aint that sort, but I'll allow you a bit of torture if the mood takes you." He grinned at her.

"OH, for the love of god, Arty, you can't keep protecting me." She said with a teasing smile, her heart bursting.

"I know you want to make an example of him, I do too, but let's catch the bastard first, how we deal with him can be decided later." Arthur pulled her back into a hug as he spoke. "Now, let's get some sleep and then in the morning we can decide when to meet with Abberline."

Ruby slept badly, plagued again by the usual nightmare. It pulled her from her sleep several times. She'd drift back off, only to be woken by the same dream repeating itself. It was early when she rose, washed, and dressed and waited in the sitting room for Arthur to wake. She felt drained, desperate for a good night's sleep, as Isabel, Elsie's maid, arrived sometime after seven and began preparing breakfast for the two of them.

"Good morning, Miss Ruby, I'll have breakfast ready shortly." Isabel disappeared into the kitchen before she could reply.

A bleary-eyed Arthur appeared in the doorway. "Morning Rubes, how's my girl?" He said as he kissed the top of her head.

"Morning, tired. The same dream woke me several times last night." She rubbed her face with her hands. "I'm desperate just to sleep all night." Ruby yawned and lent her head on the back of the chair.

Arthur's hands trembled as he quickly pulled on his trousers and buttoned his shirt, then sat down heavily to lace up his shoes. "Again? You should have woken me, it may've helped." Arthur worry flickered in his eyes. "Maybe we should talk with a doctor and get a sleeping draft, just so you can get a good rest." He suggested.

"I think that's a good idea, I don't like to wake you, Arty, there's no point two of us being tired, I'll turn in early tonight and hopefully that'll help." Ruby put on a bright smile as she inhaled deeply. The comforting aroma of bacon and eggs escaped from the kitchen, reminding her of how hungry she was. She stood up and adjusted her thick plaid robe before walking to the door with purposeful strides. Although she tried to keep her thoughts light, they quickly drifted back to the previous night's nightmare. Ruby shook her head and focused on the comfort food awaiting her.

Arthur cautiously steered the conversation away from the unbearable topic and praised her choice of keeping Elsie's maid, Isabel. "She said she was an excellent cook," he added as they both entered the kitchen.

The tantalizing scent of the breakfast and freshly brewed coffee wafted through the air. A feast for two sat upon the kitchen table – plates of bacon and sausages, a large earthenware dish of scrambled eggs steamed nearby, stacks of buttery slices of bread. Isabel had also made a steaming pot of tea, tucked underneath a woollen cosy.

Ruby smiled appreciatively at Isabel as she took a seat at the table. "This all looks delicious, thank you Isabel."

"I wasn't sure if either of you like one or the other," Isabel explained, gesturing to the two cups of freshly poured steaming liquid, "so I made coffee as well." She smiled widely as she watched Arthur fill his plate.

Arthur congratulated Isabel with a nod as he viciously pierced a sausage link on his plate and quickly opened his mouth to stuff it in. He chewed noisily, swallowed, and reached for a slice of bacon balanced atop his fork before snatching a piece of buttered toast from the neighbouring plate with his free hand. "C'mon Rubes tuck in." He said with his mouth full.

Ruby watched with amusement as Arthur wolfed down his breakfast, while Isabel hovered nervously at the edge of the table. "Isabel," Ruby said gently, motioning to the chair across from her. "Please join us and eat too. There is more than enough for everyone."

Isabel nodded, hesitantly pulled out a seat, and served herself before taking a tentative bite. Ruby smiled warmly as Isabel took her first mouthful, seemingly enjoying the breakfast for the first time.

A frantic knock at the front door interrupted breakfast. Arthur opened it to Polly breathing heavily and her hair sticking to her face and forehead, her eyes wide.

"I'm sorry Mr Morris, Sir. Rose has sent me, she said your both needed back at the townhouse, she says that something terrible has happened." Polly said between breaths.

"Okay, Polly, calm down, I'm sure it's nothing that can't be sorted easily. Come in and have a glass of milk whilst we finish breakfast then we'll go together." Arthur stood back and pointed in the direction of the kitchen.

"No… time… Mr… Morris, Rose said it's really urgent."

Ruby's heart began to race as she hurried down the corridor, her feet pounding on the marble tiles. When she reached the front door, she was struck by a single glance at Polly's frightened expression. "What the hell is going on here?" Ruby gasped, her voice echoing through the hallways. She took a step closer, searching for answers in Polly's wide eyes. "My god, what has happened? What has made you so scared?" she whispered, feeling her chest tighten with dread.

“She says that Rose has asked us to come back to the townhouse urgently, something bad has happened.” Arthur went into the living room and came back out with his jacket. “Polly, go and call down a cab, me and Miss Myers are right behind you.” He said as he slipped his arms into his jacket and shrugged it on. “Rubes, I don’t like the sound of this, something must be really off if Rose has sent Polly.”

Ruby's mind felt like it was freezing up, numbed by the dread of knowing that something horrible must have happened. Every step closer to the townhouse dragged like an eternity of torture, and the knot in her stomach twisted tighter with every breath. Could it be Rose who was in trouble? She'd sent Polly instead of going herself, so that couldn't be it. Her stomach sank at the thought, the possibility of one of her girls getting beaten by a punter felt too close, making her throat tight with fear.

As Arthur helped Ruby down, rose rushed onto the cobbles.

“Miss Ruby, oh thank the lord you’re back, something awful has happened, and I never thought in a month of Sundays it would happen within these walls.” She grabbed Ruby with trembling hands.

"We need to call the coppers urgently Miss Ruby!" Rose snapped, her voice brittle with emotion.

"Tell me what’s happened first," Ruby replied softly, her heart pounding in her chest as she tried to quell the rising panic. "Please, Rose-"

Rose cut her off abruptly, shaking her head slowly in despair. "It's Jane...she's gone..." The rest of her words died away and there was only an oppressive silence that hung heavy in the air.

"Jane… gone… gone where?" Ruby frowned.

"She's not gone away, Miss, she's dead…" Rose watched Ruby's expression as she said the sentence. "Upstairs…"

Ruby dropped her hands to her side, she said nothing. Her mouth felt dry and her hands clammy. The colour drained from her face. She looked up the stairs and then at Arthur. "Arthur, take Rose into the kitchen and get Polly to put the kettle on then she can go and get the police. I'll go and check on Jane." She looked back at Rose. "When did you realise something was wrong?"

"This morning Miss, she hadn't come down for her usual cup of tea or for her breakfast. I thought it was strange, so I went up and knocked her door." Rose answered as she began to cry again.

"I'll be there in a minute Rubes, once I've got Rose settled." Arthur added as he led Rose into the scullery.

Ruby climbed the stairs two at a time and took a deep breath as she made her way down the corridor to Jane's room. She paused at the door, her hand tightened on the knob, her knuckles whitened as she hesitated. As she contemplated what was hidden inside, her heart raced, and her stomach churned. Taking a deep breath, she cautiously opened it.

Jane lay on her back, devoid of clothing. The bed linen was soaked in red, and a deep gash ran from ear to ear across her throat. Milky blue eyes stared lifelessly up to the ceiling. Her mouth gaped open as if she were trying to cry out as she was dying. One fist was clasping desperately at the cotton sheet underneath her, the other fist held onto the bedstead above her head. Her legs were drawn up and parted, her modesty heartlessly taken from her in her dying moments.

Ruby averted her eyes noticing her nightdress laying on a crumpled heap on the floor beside the bed. Her stomach clenched as she staggered towards it. She picked it up and even though she was appalled at the sight before her, she placed the garment across Jane's lower extremities. The young woman lay there, torn, and bloody like a sacrificial lamb.

It was pure evil, the kind that consumes and devours everything in its path. Her mind screamed with the realization that the devil has unleashed his fingers of terror and they were now clenched tight around her heart. The smell of copper flooded her nose as the bile in her throat rose inexorably. She swallowed it down with an iron will, its sour taste coating her tongue like a film of poison. With her hand clamped over her mouth, Ruby stumbled towards the window, desperate for fresh air. She thrust it open and just managed to get her head out before she vomited violently. The acidic bile splattered onto the ground below as Ruby wept for the girl laying in the room and for the life that had been lost.

The rest of the area was untouched. All of Jane's meagre belongings were still in place. Ruby checked the hiding place she had where she kept her money. Still there.

Her foot kicked something on the floor as she crossed the room to where Jane lay. Ruby glanced down as Arthur entered. She bent down and picked it up.

Arthur's shock rooted him to the ground as he beheld the unspeakable horror before him. "This is a travesty," he hissed through gritted teeth.

Ruby could see the rage consume him, as it appeared to be thrumming through every vein in his body. His eyes widened until they bordered on madness, focused solely on Ruby. "What the hell-?" Arthur roared in a voice that shook the very walls of the room. "Who could do this and be so evil to a woman?" He screamed out.

Ruby clenched her fist around a small, cold, silver box. Her knuckles turned white with each turn of the hexagonal shape, as if the simple act could somehow quiet Arthur's anger. But when she opened her palm and presented him with what she'd found, the reflection in his eyes was that of pure rage. "Arthur," she said gently, "I've found this on the floor." She held out her hand and opened her fingers so he could see what she had resting on her palm. It was engraved with a picture of a big, gothic building, not dissimilar to a church. She frowned slightly, tilting her head in thought. "Arthur, is this a pill box or snuff box?" She asked as she handed it to him.

The sound of her voice seemed to flick a switch in Arthur's head and Ruby could see him beginning to calm down. After several moments he reached out and began to turn it over in his hand. "It's something like that," he managed to say, "it has small hinges, see?" He pointed at two small hinges on the other side of it and above the engraving. He pushed his fingernail into the small, thin seam and prized the lid off. The strong smell of cloves permeated the air, and a dark, yellowish, brown powder lay inside.

He wet the tip of his pinkie finger with his tongue and then dabbed it into the powder, then sucked the digit clean. After a few seconds, "Snuff." Arthur snapped the lid back on and handed the box back to Ruby, "It's a snuff box Rubes."

"Jane didn't use snuff, at least I don't think she did." She glanced down at the woman laying before her.

"Rubes, this box is some serious coin, there's no way any of her usual punters could afford this." Arthur gave the box back to Ruby, tapping on the lid as he did so. "This is stuff of money." He rubbed his thumb and index finger together to reinforce his theory.

"The engraved picture on there Arty, is it a church or something like that?" She raised her eyebrows in question. "Christ, you don't think this was clergy do you a man of the cloth?" She glanced down at the object in her hand, "Here keep hold of this please." She passed it back to Arthur, wiping her hands down her dress afterwards as if it were dirty and bloody too.

"Nah, would've thought so, although anything is possible. When Rose calms down, we'll speak to her find out who Jane entertained last night."

A thought came into Ruby's mind. "I need to check something Arty," Ruby said, as her stomach rolled again, she took a deep breath to try and quell the nausea. She turned her head away as she slid her hand underneath Jane's head and felt around blindly.

"Bloody hell, Rubes, let me do that." Arthur exclaimed. "There's no need for you to do something so horrible, let me." He stepped forward in an attempt to move Ruby aside, but she stood her ground.

"It's ok," she said as she pulled her hand back, although bloody, it was empty. She checked under the rest of her body. "Jane was my friend, which hasn't changed now she's dead, Arty, the poor girl can't help all this." She waved her hand over her.

What she was looking for wasn't there. No coin.

Was this a random killing?

Arthur watched her closely, questions written all across his face.

Ruby beckoned to him to follow as she left the room and then shut the door behind them. The other girls were now out of their rooms.

"Ladies, go downstairs and wait in the front drawing room, I will be in to talk to you all in a while. Close the door behind you. Today, we're not trading." Ruby took hold of Arthur's hand and put her mouth up to his ear. "Arty, there's no coin…"

"Do you think this is just a coincidence?" He handed her his handkerchief. "Your hands, you need to wipe your hands, Rubes."

Ruby took a deep breath and let it out slowly. Too many things had happened in too short a time, and she was feeling the pressure of it all bearing down on her.

With a shudder, Ruby glanced down at her palms. Jane's blood was smeared across them, like an abstract painting of intricate swirls and curves. Some stray hair had caught underneath her fingernail, and Ruby stopped for a minute as she felt an overwhelming sadness come over her.

She took the handkerchief and began to wipe her hands. "I'd like to think this was coincidence," she said, more to herself than anyone else. "But somehow, I think this is connected. The letter, I remember something about one being saved by me, but it's definitely not this Jane. Perhaps he had Martha in mind, Arty couldn't get to her so went for Jane instead. This could be what it meant the note meant, but I expected there to be a coin, just like the others." Ruby took a deep breath and steeled herself.

They were interrupted by the arrival of a Constable. He took one glance into the room and said he'd need to have Inspector Abberline or Inspector Royal present. He went back downstairs and stood on the steps of the townhouse and blew his whistle.

An hour later Abberline arrived, followed by Inspector Royal. Ruby was sat in the kitchen trying to comfort Rose.

"I'm sorry this has happened in your establishment, Miss Myers. Can I be shown to the room where the victim is please?" Abberline asked.

"I'm not, it was only a matter of time." Royal stood in the kitchen doorway, his shoulders back and a smug look on his face. "It's part of the job, you entertain a lot of men, for a while the inevitable illudes you, until, one day, it'll be your turn." He cleared his throat and glanced around the kitchen at everyone. No one looked in his direction.

"Please Bernard, could you at least wait until we are elsewhere before you begin with your philosophy of life." Abberline glared in his direction. "I'm sorry, Miss Myers, please, could someone show me where she is?"

"Polly, stay here with Rose while we take him upstairs." Ruby commanded, her voice shaking with anger.

Arthur silently gestured for Abberline to follow him up the stairs, Ruby close behind them both.

Abberline turned his head away in shame. "I am so sorry for my partner's outrageous behaviour."

"I wouldn't expect any better from someone like him!" Arthur spat as he strode up the stairs, not meeting Abberline's gaze. When they reached the top of the stairs, Ruby stepped onto the threshold and watched as Arthur brought the Inspector into the room.

Abberline gasped, bringing a handkerchief to his mouth in shock. "My word... Who did this?" he murmured in horror through cotton. "The poor girl. Was this how you found her this morning?" Abberline's voice was clipped and intense as he glanced across at Ruby who stood stock-still with her arms tightly folded in the doorway.

She shook her head, unable to speak. Her mouth had dried up. She licked her lips to moisten them before speaking. "I'm sorry..."

"It's okay my dear girl," Abberline soothed, although his eyes were blazing with rage. "This is an abominable thing to have happened here on your own premises."

"He pulled her legs up and then apart," she said in a whisper, her heart pounding in horror as tears streamed down her cheeks. "I... the nightdress, I put it there. Please excuse me." Ruby stumbled back to the top of the stairs, struggling to contain her suppressed emotions that now overwhelmed her.

Ruby's face filled with concern when she entered the kitchen, as she watched Rose slowly shuffle towards the table. She noticed sweat beading on Rose's forehead, and her hands were shaking as she clasped Polly's cup of tea. Her long grey hair was dishevelled and her usually bright eyes were dull.

Royal stood watching in the corner but said nothing as Abberline and Arthur came back into the room. They both eyed Rose with concern.

Ruby took a calming breath and ran her fingers through her hair before slowly walking up to Rose. "My dear Rose, it's been such a difficult morning for you - why don't you take some time off in your room? I'm sure you could use some rest. I'll bring you another cup of sweet tea soon," Ruby said, smiling warmly and placing a gentle hand on Rose's shoulder before watching her leave the room.

Inspector Abberline waited until Rose had shut the door to her bedroom before addressing Ruby and Arthur. He pulled the leather notebook from his pocket and licked the end of a pencil, ready to take notes. “Miss Myers, I’ve asked Constable Jenkins to bring a doctor and a wagon for the young woman. Are the other young ladies present in the house? May I speak with them?”

Arthur shrugged at Ruby's questioning glance before innately answering, “No harm can come from it.”

Abberline nodded in agreement before turning towards Royal, who had thankfully kept quiet. “Yes, I will need to question them as they may have seen something that could help us understand what occurred here last night. I would like to speak to Rose when she is feeling better .” He said, “Bernard, will you sit in with me too you may think of something I don’t.” He frowned as he waited for his colleague to speak.

“If you so wish, Fred.” Royal agreed half-heartedly. “Although I can’t see what light a few whores can shed on the situation. They were all flat on their backs when it happened.” He chuckled at his own comment before sidling out of the room, then stopped and waited for Abberline to follow.

Arthur's nostrils flared; his fists clenched at his side. Ruby moved quickly to stand in front of him and placed her hands on his forearms, running her thumbs along his skin soothingly. “Shh, Arty,” she whispered gently. His gaze was fierce, and Ruby felt the tension radiating from him in waves. She stood up on her tiptoes and pressed a gentle kiss to his warm cheek. “He's not worth it. His time will come."

Ruby turned to Abberline, who appeared pink up to his earlobes. "I apologize sincerely once again for my colleague’s totally unacceptable remark," he mumbled, shifting awkwardly from foot to foot. "He will of course be reprimanded as soon as I've concluded things here."

"Polly," Ruby said softly, glancing over her shoulder at the girl waiting in the doorway, "could you show the Inspectors into the front sitting room please?"

"Of course, Miss Ruby," Polly answered hurriedly before disappearing down the hallway.

She turned back to Arthur. “Stay in here whilst I speak with Rose, if Royal comes back into the kitchen wanting to speak to her too…” Ruby headed towards the corridor at the back of the kitchen. She glanced over her shoulder at Arthur. “Arty?”

“It’s fine Rubes, go on, I’ll make sure he doesn’t go snooping.” He pulled a chair out from under the kitchen table and sat down.

Ruby made her way to Rose's bedroom, knocked, and entered then closed the door behind her. "Rose, who was the last person to spend time with Jane? I know she had a punter with her when I left, was it him?" She sat down on the bed next to Rose and put an arm around her shoulders.

"No Miss, there was another caller after. The man who came before, without a calling card, remember?" She answered with a look of total exhaustion.

"What him, did he have one this time?"

"Yes Miss, I left it in the tin in the kitchen, with the others."

"His name Rose, can you recall his name?"

Rose thought for a few seconds, "yes it was Mr Joseph Witherington-Smythe, it said he sold perfumes, paid for a night too."

"Well done." She gave Rose and squeeze. "This wasn't your fault; you did everything that you could. Just promise me one thing, you'll say nothing to Abberline or Royal, not until I've spoken with Arthur." She stood up, "I'll have Polly bring you some more tea, now get some rest, I'll check on you later."

When Ruby had got back to the kitchen, she was pleased to see that Royal wasn't there. She sent Polly with a cup of tea to Rose and then she shut the door behind her. Arthur still sat at the kitchen table.

"Where's Royal and Abberline?"

"They're still in the front sitting room with the other girls." Arthur turned as he spoke, Ruby noticed that he looked tired and pale.

“Are you alright Arty?” She crossed the room, stood behind him and put her arms around his neck.

Arthur placed his head on her chest. “Me, I’m okay, just tired is all.” He reached out and pulled out the chair next to him.

“Thanks.” She sank into it. “Arty, I need to tell you this before one of the coppers comes back, a bloke called the other day, without a calling card, I sent him packin’ thought nothin’ else of it.”

Arthur listened closely, as she continued.

“Well, he came back last night, was the last one to see Jane. Had a calling card this time, a Joseph Witherington-Smythe by all accounts, said he sold perfumes.”

Arthur’s jaw hung open for a moment, “Rubes, are you sure that’s the name?”

“Yes, why?”

“The chap I knew by that name died, some six months back. He used to run stuff for me up north to some other associates. The perfume business was just a front.” A vein in Arthur’s neck pulsed and he frowned. “What’d he look like, did Rose say?”

“Dark hair, around five foot eight, moustache and a mole on his cheek.” She searched Arthur’s face.

Arthur slammed his chair back, face twisted with rage. He roughly grabbed Ruby's hands and squeezed them tightly, his own fingers trembling in fury. His grip tightened so much they felt like iron vice clamped around her wrists. Ruby could feel the heat of his hatred radiating across her skin. "Sounds like the same bloke watching the pub and the bastard has taken someone else's name too. We have to get to him before the pigs," he said urgently. "Whatever you do, don't let him set foot in this place again. Don't let any of your girls turn tricks until we take care of this." He squeezed her hands as if to give her strength for whatever was to come. His gaze bored into hers with the intensity of desperation. "I promise you nothing else is going to happen here, Rubes. Lock both doors and windows at all times and don't open them for anybody, only me and Billy. Got it?"

"Of course, I understand Arty, but none of this makes any sense. Why would this bloke target me or the girls, plus there's no coin up there, not like the others?" Ruby stood up and went to the tin where all the calling cards were kept. She flicked through four on the top before she came to the one, she wanted. "Here it is, Arty, this is the one he gave Rose." She handed it to Arthur.

He glanced at the front of the card before turning it over, then froze.

"What is it Arty, what have you seen?" Ruby watched as Arthur raised his eyes to hers and then handed the card back to her.

"Look on the back Rubes."

Ruby turned it over and scribbled on the back were the words, *to find a penny*. Ruby's mouth dried up, her legs felt like rubber. "Arthur," She said. "It looks like the same handwriting as the letter."

"Christ, Rubes." For a moment Arthur looked stunned. Then, "That bastard has been in my girl's place, not only threatened her safety but killed someone in her home too." Arthur started to pace backwards and forwards. "I'll kill the bastard; he'll wish the coppers have him once I've shown him what happens when he messes wiv me girl." His face was bright red, a vein in his neck pulsed, his hands were clenched into fists. "Who the fuck does he think he is, playing games like this with my girl."

Ruby watched silently, her heart thumping in time with his rage as he struggled to contain himself. She knew better than to intervene, but she could feel the wild, untamed energy radiating off him like fire. When his tirade had died down, Ruby stepped forward and embraced him tightly. "Arty, I know you won't give up until this is fixed," she murmured into his chest. "But, if it's me he wants, then surely letting him think that he can have me would work for the better?" She looked up at him the question flashed across her face. "It may stop him killing any more girls." Ruby added.

"You are absolutely insane if you think I'm going to let this happen, Rubes!" He stepped back from her; his eyes narrowed in anger as he took her in. His whole body was tense, and his jaw clenched with rage. "No way am I letting you use yourself as bait!" His voice rose to a feverish pitch and his wild eyes daring her to challenge him.

The sun shone beams through the window, catching on something metallic on the table in the window.

Ruby crossed the room to see what it was. Her heart nearly stopped in her chest when she realised what lay in front of her. She picked it up with trembling hands and handed it to Arthur.

He took it from her and turned it around in his fingers and looked at it closely.

Arthur was holding a coin dated 1855.

Chapter Sixteen

Abberline waited outside of Jane's room until the corpse was taken away. He sent Royal into the front sitting room to help out with the body's removal, but Abberline had no choice but to make him leave when he came back in. Apparently, Royal had made a scene, assaulting one of the girls and using insulting language toward them all. Abberline knew this would not sit well with Miss Myers and Mr Morris, and Royal had essentially sealed his own fate. Not only that, but gossip at the station also indicated that Royal might have been exploiting his rank for personal gain. Deep down, Abberline still didn't quite want to believe it. First things first though; there was more pressing work at hand before any other concerns were addressed.

He knocked on Miss Myers' parlour door and waited. Arthur threw the door open, red faced and sweating.

"Mr Morris, what on earth has happened, can I be of any assistance?" He kept his tone light so as not to appear condescending.

"You'd better come in, there's some things that you need to be made aware of." Arthur stood back to allow him to enter.

Miss Myers was sat in her usual chair. She looked straight at him, "Inspector, there you are. Please, take a seat."

Arthur continued to pace backwards and forwards.

Abberline kept his eyes on Ruby. He hoped he had finally made headway with the pair gaining mutual respect for each other. Not to mention possibly being made privy to some things that would otherwise have gone unmentioned. Should he mention Royal's indiscretions earlier?

"Inspector," Ruby began, "Firstly, do you have the letter I gave to you?"

Abberline nodded, "Yes, it's here." He said patting his pockets down.

Ruby held out her hand, "Here, I think you should look at this, we always ask for one from punters if they are new to our establishment."

Abberline took the card and read the front of it. "It's a calling card Miss Myers, can I enquire as to why you require one from some of your clientele?"

"We ask for one to ensure that the girls are safe above everything else, but" she raised her finger, "if they've announced their presence in the local area then we can establish his position within society and also his reputation and we find it a very useful way of recalling any new punter that frequents these premises." Ruby sat with her back straight and her hands placed in her lap and watched Abberline intently. "I've found that this is a good way to keep some punters in line, if we've been given one bearing his personal details then most of the time, they respect our rules here. It worked well, until…" she let the sentence trail off.

“It was given to Rose last night when a punter visited, the same man that went up to Jane’s room and the last one to be with her.” Arthur had stopped pacing and had reached for his pipe. “Turn it over, Abberline.” Arthur said in a clipped tone from behind Ruby.

He flipped the card in his fingers. The scrawl on the back screamed out to him, he pulled out the letter and compared the two. “Good lord, Miss Myers, Mr Morris, they are of the same hand.” Abberline’s mind whirred. “Have you spoken to the man who is the owner of this card?” Abberline looked between the two.

“That’ll be difficult, that fella died some six months ago, he happened to be one of my associates.” Arthur dropped the coin and snuff box into his hand. “That, was on the table over there,” he said, “and that we found earlier on the floor by the bed.” He rested his index finger on the silver lid as Abberline held it in his hand.

“I assume this box wasn’t owned by the girl?”

“Not as far as I’m aware.” Ruby answered. “The etching on the surface gave me the impression that it is of a church or cathedral.”

Abberline held it closer so he could see the etching, “Mmm, interesting. I see what you mean Miss Myers and expensive.” He agreed as he examined the gothic style building on its lid.

“The coin bears the same date as all the others found with the other victims, Inspector.” Ruby pointed out. “I think the man responsible for this letter, the calling card, this coin and the owner of this snuff box could possibly be one of the same.” She placed her hands in her lap and glanced over at Arthur, who had now stopped pacing.

Arthur stood with his hands in his pockets. “We also now know what this bastard looks like.”

Inspector Abberline's eyes widened as he heard the news. His face broke out into a wide grin, and he clapped his hands together. "This is wonderful! We may finally have the lead we've been looking for!" He paced back and forth, barely able to contain his excitement. Arthur recounted to him the description, his hand worked quickly across the pages of his notebook as he scratched down the information. “How long have you known all this?” He stood up, folded his glasses, dropped the coin and the silver box into his trouser pocket and slipped the note and calling card in between the pages of his notebook.

“Only worked it out this morning.” Arthur said as he folded his arms but still stood his ground.

“Well, I feel it’s only correct that I now share some details with you.” said Abberline.

“You’ve hidden information from us,” Ruby cut in. “I must say that this so-called alliance isn’t working too well is it.” She glanced at Arthur his face was set like stone.

Abberline raised his hand, “Miss Myers, Mr Morris,” he said without taking his eyes off Ruby, “this information isn’t pleasant, and I really didn’t want to distress you any further.”

“You could’ve warned me Inspector,” Arthur spat, his eyes flashing with anger. His voice rose in volume and each word struck like a hammer against the walls of the room. "What are you trying to do - keep us in the dark?” He concluded, his stare burning into the Inspector's face.

“Yes, I could’ve Mr Morris, and I can only apologise, but we’ve both been guilty of the same thing, the letter for instance...” He looked across at Arthur, whilst the statement floated precariously in the air between the two men.

Arthur watched Abberline’s expression then pursed his lips together. “Abberline, let’s just make sure that all fresh information is made known to both parties, shall we? Wrangling over minor details isn’t going to get us any closer to getting this bastard off the streets, but if it happens again, then this allegiance ends.” He said gruffly and walked to the chair next to Ruby’s and sat down.

Abberline nodded, “I agree and thank you Mr Morris. Now, I must warn you Miss Myers, these details aren’t pleasant.” He looked back at Arthur for approval before continuing.

“Rubes?” Arthur tipped his head in her direction as he asked her but kept his eyes on Abberline.

“It’s okay Arty.” Ruby swallowed and inhaled deeply. “Please continue, Inspector.”

Abberline propped his eyeglasses on the end of his nose, looked down at his notebook and flicked through the pages, "Some of the girls had body parts missing, namely internal organs." He paused and looked over his spectacles at the pair then continued, "which as of yet we've never been able to find. Miss Myers, it saddens me greatly to let you know that Miss Lancaster had foetal matter on her person." Abberline's eyes softened as he relayed the information to her.

"Yes, I recall you telling me that Elsie was pregnant?" Ruby's eyes filled with fresh tears.

"That's what the Doctor first assumed, yes. However, it was later discovered that she was sadly unable to bear children. Unfortunately, Miss Lancaster was born without ovaries and therefore couldn't produce eggs." Abberline paused, his words hanging in the air as Ruby's face contorted with heartache.

Arthur slowly reached for her hand, squeezing it in reassurance and offering an unspoken promise of support.

Finally, Abberline continued in a low voice, "There is more, Miss Myers, if you feel you're able?" He glanced at Arthur then back to Rub, his gaze full of empathy.

"Please continue, Inspector, I need to know everything about Elsie." Ruby wiped away a tear.

"As yet, we are unable to pinpoint as to why the foetal matter was on Elsie's… ah, body." Abberline's felt his ears turn red, and he cleared his throat before continuing. "We know that the organic material was, as the doctor said, freshly deposited, but as yet we can't determine the original source, or rather the donor of said material. If I'm to be entirely honest, this has me rather baffled." He looked down to his notebook and began flicking through the pages again.

"Rubes?" Arthur asked.

Ruby made no comment, her posture stiffened.

Arthur spoke first, "So, why would this sick son-of-a-bitch do something like that to a woman, let alone, have that sort of material in his possession?" Arthur let go of Ruby's hand, stood up and began pacing again. "I think Miss Myers has heard enough, don't you?" He flicked the comment in Abberline's direction as he paced.

"It's okay Arty, please continue Inspector."

“As you so wish Miss Myers.” Abberline sat down again. He looked up at Arthur. “In answer to your question Mr. Morris, I’m afraid that is something that can only be answered by the cretin who is doing this.” Abberline bit his lip and rubbed the back of his neck. “I will be quite candid with you both, I’m very uncertain about a lot of the things that have come to light since I was assigned to this case, and I am desperate to get the justice that each of these poor girls deserves.” He shook his head before continuing, “to me they are women and none of them deserved a demise like they had.” His eyes were wet and dull, and he blinked slowly, “at the moment I do feel that I’m letting them all down and the longer this continues…” He pinched his lips together and looked between the two of them, “the more innocent women are going to die.”

Arthur stood with his fists tight, fingernails biting into his palms.

Ruby held up her hand to stop Inspector Abberline's words. Her face was drawn with emotion, and she slowly stood up from her chair. She walked a few steps towards the fireplace, folding her arms across her chest while her eyes burned into him. Arthur sat in confusion, unsure of what was about to happen. "Inspector, your compassion is refreshing it is so comforting to hear such kind words about these women.” She paused for a moment deep in thought. “I feel that I have your confidence," Ruby said as she steadied her voice. "Would this be the case?"

"Miss Myers, I know I may be an officer of the law, but I'm nothing if not discreet. You have my confidence of that I can guarantee." Abberline swallowed and pursed his lips. "Please, Miss Myers, you can tell me, it may have some bearing on the case."

"This will certainly not have any bearing on the case Inspector, this is something that I feel you may need to know, just in case it could be of use."

Arthur looked on with uncertainty, his discomfort palpable in the room.

"Inspector… Elsie wasn't just my friend…" She paused, "Elsie was my lover." Ruby bit her lip and clasped her hands together in front of her. "I know that this may be deemed immoral or even abhorrent in today's society and could even cause me some severe problems within my business contacts, but as I said I feel I can trust you with this information and can't help but feel that this may have some relevance. I'm wondering if this person was also a fan of Elsie's, the note in her drawer for instance." she glanced around the room as she spoke. "Had he seen or heard us there when I'd visited her in her dressing room?"

Abberline noticed her nervousness, but his face remained impassive.

Arthur watched Abberline closely.

"I see," Abberline said as he wrote some more notes." Miss Myers, I already knew that." Abberline's eyes didn't betray him as he looked up from his notes and continued. "When I first came here to deliver the devasting news of her murder, you flushed."

Ruby shook her head. "I'm afraid I don't understand."

"Your face flushed at the mention of her name, a reaction that is common when people are either infatuated or in love with another." Abberline gave a soft smile. "I've known from the beginning and I'm the only person except of course for Mr. Morris that is aware of this." Abberline stood up. "I'm a great believer in watching people, the body's natural reactions give quite a lot of information about a person, especially when they are unaware of it." He tilted his head and kept his tone gentle. "Miss Myers, I'm neither your judge nor a gossip, therefore what is discussed between the three of us, will stay within the three of us." He stood up.

Ruby's face had taken on a new expression. One of respect? Abberline was sure it was, and he would keep her secret as promised. "Now, please excuse me, I'm needed at the mortuary and Mr Morris, with you permission I'd like to arrange an officer to stand outside."

"Inspector Abberline, although your intentions are good, I don't think that'll be necessary. I will be with Miss Myers, day and night and I've already got several of my associates doing exactly that but thank you." For the first time Arthur stood up and offered his hand to shake Abberline's.

The Inspector returned the gesture. A sign of newfound admiration from this man.

"Well, an officer will need to be present upstairs for now, at least until we are happy to release the room back to you." He patted his pockets to ensure he had everything. "Ah, just one more thing." Abberline said. "Sadly, I am loathe to tell you this, but as we agreed to be completely open with each other I feel I have little choice." He paused and pulled in a nervous breath before continuing, "I need to apologise on behalf of my colleague Inspector Royal. He wasn't pleasant to you, or your girls and it gives me no pleasure to inform you that he indeed slapped one of the women and was incredibly rude to the others. I did ask him to leave the premises as soon as I became aware of his actions." He crossed to and opened the parlour door.

"Did he now?" Ruby spoke through her teeth. "Thank you for the information, needless to say, he won't be dealt with by just you, Inspector." Her eyes were cold as she looked between him and Arthur.

Arthur's stance was wide, and he held his chin high. "Thank you for telling us, Inspector." Arthur swallowed hard as he shook his head.

Abberline dropped his notebook. Bent and picked it up. "I didn't hear that last statement." He gave a quick smile that didn't reach his eyes. "May I ask that we put our heads together in the next day or so and see if we could, possibly, devise a plan to bring this cretin to us?" He looked between the two.

"I'm sure we can certainly arrange something, Inspector." Arthur looked at Ruby and nodded. "Rubes?"

"I agree with Arthur, Inspector. Of course." For the first time Ruby smiled at Abberline.

"Excellent, I'll wait to hear from you, I'll show myself out."

Abberline trudged down the steps of the townhouse, a feeling of dread in his gut. The promise of an alliance with Miss Myers and Mr Morris held great potential. He knew that working with them, he had an opportunity to find the one responsible for all these murders. But he also realized this could come at a tremendous cost – possibly even his own career.

He wanted to work with these people, but did they really trust him? Could he rely on their allegiance beyond bringing the monster to justice? He felt he could now.

Abberline's mind raced through all the clues – letter, calling card and snuff box - desperately trying to understand what connected them all. As he walked along the cobbles, he re-lived every crime scene. He felt powerless and was aware that failure was not an option.

Miss Myers' confession had surprised him, yet he kept his judgement silent. In his two decades as a police officer, he had gotten used to counting on people's trust in him whenever delicate matters were revealed.

Abberline stumbled through the city, his feet dragging and his fatigue weighing heavy on him. He had been ready to give up on this case, but he knew too much was at stake to quit. His exhaustion was pulling him home to the comfort of his wife's embrace, but a voice in the back of his mind kept telling him that another life could be lost if he didn't continue working. He wanted so badly to turn away from the station and go home, but he kept pushing forward. With every step, his tension and despair grew deeper. The Inspector was a deeply concerned man.

Chapter Seventeen

It was in the early hours that the bad tempered and abusive Captain Oliver Smythe left the brothel. He had taken pleasure in violently assaulting a whore while she was performing her services and all due to his excessive consumption of the cheap house whiskey. It wasn't his usual place to call upon, thanks to Miss Myers kicking him to the gutter. But there are lots of places where his money could be spent.

The ladies of the establishment could spot him from a distance; his small, stout frame, overly oiled hair, and loud voice were unmistakable. As he strutted in, every woman held her breath. Each hoping to avoid being subject to his twisted sexual preferences, crude jokes, and innuendos. Still, it was better to tough it out than risk expulsion and being left destitute should they decide not to follow his orders.

The house Madam would approach him with trepidation, politely asking that he remain respectful towards her girls. Yet, each time she did so, he refused to acknowledge her pleas - his eyes glinting with satisfaction at the knowledge that he held power over them all.

As he sat down at one of the tables, he glanced around with a smug grin on his face. The other patrons avoided making eye contact with him, for fear of being dragged into his twisted world. They could see his coldness creep under every woman's skin like snake venom.

He casually dropped two shillings into Violet's hand as if they were molten lava, the coins clinked together as if to mock her. She breathed deeply on her cigarette and watched as he buttoned his coat and adjusted his hat. He had paid well for his time, but she knew it was never enough money to make up for the humiliation she felt every time he visited.

A chill settled in around her as he walked away without a backward glance, and she pulled her thin red shawl close, trying to ward off the icy feeling that lingered long after each of his visits.

Smythe adjusted his collar to keep the wind from chilling his neck, but it didn't help much. He was thankful he was wearing a long overcoat, which he had picked up in Paris, it had kept him warm on the walk from the office to the brothel.

The gas lamps provided a weak and yellow light, even they knew they were at the end of their service. The flickering of each flame moved up the metal pole holding the lamplight, the metal and glass covering the flame were cracked in a spiderweb of fissures.

As he marched through the night air, his thoughts kept returning to the hushed conversation he had with a doctor at the men's club. Though few words were spoken, Smythe noticed the physician's eyebrows rise in delight several times in response to his words.

Was he intrigued by the salacious talk of what could be found on Pickett Street? Regardless, Smythe knew that if the Doctor liked what was being offered, he would certainly be crossing Smythe's palm with silver. And if not, then Smythe now knew he'd have somewhere to gain some extra funds should it become necessary to keep quiet about this doctor's questionable tastes.

He could smell his own unwashed body coupled with fresh horse manure and rotting food. A few minutes later the pungent stench of piss and excrement reverberated from an alley that ran adjacent to the main high street. It was also littered with rubbish, but he knew it would be the perfect place to relieve himself without being seen.

He propped his new cane against the wooden fence and unbuttoned his trousers.

Something brushed against his foot.

He froze, his eyes straining to see.

It brushed against his foot again.

Instinctively he kicked out.

Whatever it was squeaked in pain as his foot made contact, and then it scuttled deeper into the darkness, sending a bottle skimming across the alley as it went.

Smythe waited a few seconds.

The fingers of unease began to stroke his spine, just as a woman caressed the man she loved.

Instinct told him he wasn't alone.

A movement in the shadows rattled a dustbin in a corner to his left.

"Who's there?" He said shakily.

Smythe picked up his cane and threw it in the direction of where the noise came from. A cat howled as it was hit square in the face.

Moving into view, the stripy feline hissed at Smythe and darted from the seclusion of the bin into the dimly lit street.

The gloom crept further forward.

"Go away with you." Smythe shouted, "Fucking strays."

He paused for a moment just to check he was alone.

Nothing.

Relief washed over him like a warm bath.

The urge to relieve himself reminded him why he was there.

Smythe retrieved his cane then moved back down the alley and propped his stick against the fence again.

His cold fingers fumbled with his trouser buttons. "For fucks sake, what the devil-"

Footsteps behind him came quickly.

Before he could turn his face smashed into the wall in front of him.

For a moment he saw stars. Then came the metallic taste of blood as his ichor ran into his mouth from his nose.

"Oi, yah bastard, I've no money, it's all gone at the brothel up the street." He tried to turn.

He felt a cold, steel grip clamp around his throat as he was yanked backwards. His left arm was wrenched up in the air and he could feel a burly forearm crushing his throat. His assailant's hot breath steamed his ear as they tightened their hold. His heart raced and he thrashed about in an attempt to free himself, but the iron grip only tightened.

Who was holding him?

The smell in the alleyway started to sour the whiskey that sat in his stomach and Smythe felt the urge to gag. “I say, ease off a bit.” He pleaded.

His assailant loosened his grip enough to turn him to face him.

Smythe looked into cold blue eyes. Realisation crept over him like an oil slick.

“My god, you, how the fu-”

“Shut the fuck up.” His attacker interrupted.

Although the night was cold, a bead of sweat slid down Smythe’s temple.

“How’d you find me?” Smythe moaned as the warm sensation of his urine ran down his legs into his new, handmade shoes.

“Don’t flatter yourself, you’re not that hard to find.” The blue eyes looked back at him, devoid of emotion.

“What’d want?” Smythe whimpered.

“Didn’t I tell you to be discreet.” The face in front of him tightened.

“But I was.” His legs began to tremble.

“So, gobbing off at the men’s club is discreet, is it?”

“I’ve said nothing to anyone about the place we go to, I swear.” Smythe croaked.

“Well, you beat that whore because you couldn’t get to her kid, is that discreet?”

“How the fuck do you know about that?” Smythe’s mind spun and his mouth dry.

“Word travels fast in Whitechapel, especially when it comes to dickheads like yourself. You should know that I make it my business to know exactly what happens around here.”

Smythe noticed spittle had gathered at the corners of the mouth in front of him.

"Look, I'd had too much whiskey, it does that to me." Smythe laughed nervously. "Makes me want to slap em."

"That's as maybe, but now we've got the local pigs sniffing around the other place too." He pulled his lips back and bared his teeth. "Now why would they be doing that?"

"I-I- I've no idea, not said a word to anyone." Smyth felt the urge to pee again.

"What, you never told that Doctor bloke that runs the orphanages or didn't even hint about the fact that you enjoy them younger?"

Smythe frowned, "I've no idea who you mean, what Doctor?"

"You fucking ole prick, you've no idea have you, in the men's club the other night you were talking to a Doctor, Doctor Bernardo." He snapped.

"Smythe's eyes bulked, "Him, no he's not that fella, he just works at the local hospital that's all." He stammered.

"That's where you're wrong, that Doctor runs children's homes and you were stupid enough, to tell him of the place on Pickett Street, now the pigs are sniffing around. Do you know how much money that place is making me? How much you could cost me if that place is raided?" He sneered.

Smythe's face contorted in fear as the truth dawned on him. His whiskey-filled bladder let out a hot stream of the brown liquid, as he frantically pleaded with God, "How could I have known that this loathsome creature had anything to do with children? You can't pin this one on me!"

"You're nothing but a pathetic old fool, a total waste of space in this world. A filthy, disgusting pervert."

"Wh-what do you mean? All I did was to let him about the services offered at your bordello! How does that make me a pervert?" Smythe felt a searing pain as the steel barrel of a gun pressed hard against his skin. "Please, don't—"

A macabre laugh filled the alleyway and Smythe's heart tightened in fear.

A deafening bang shattered the silence and with it all of Smythe's hopes for survival.

****

The killer heard the sounds of animalistic screams echoed through the air, a dog howled further down the street. The noise of anguish being torn from its throat as a thick blanket of gunpowder filled the alley.

He watched as Captain Smythe stood rooted to the spot, his eyes wide with fear as he felt the hot trickle of blood coating his skin in a crimson river.

His body dropped like a rotten fruit, hitting the ground with a sickening thud, and leaving something akin to tar flowing out from his skull.

The murderer stepped forward, a twisted smirk playing across his face as he let out a malicious laugh before crouching down to spit on the captain's corpse.

With one final contemptuous glance, the assassin threw away his weapon and disappeared like gun smoke into the shadows, leaving nothing behind but death.

Chapter Eighteen

Doctor Thomas John Barnardo hadn't had much sleep and it wasn't due to patient calls. He'd been to the gentlemen's club the previous evening and been chatting to a very inebriated Captain Smythe. Barnardo had never liked him and did everything he could to avoid the odious man, but last night he wasn't so lucky.

He'd been sat in his usual chair reading the Daily Tribune and Smythe had dropped into a chair next to him and the man reeked of whiskey and stale pee. Wonderful.

Barnardo was a tolerant man, and it was unusual for him not to like his fellow human beings, but for this man he'd made an exception. The rumour mill at the club wasn't favourable to Smythe and although Barnardo knew that you couldn't believe everything you heard about a person, deep down he knew that some of it was true. That and the fact that Smythe was exceptionally indiscreet at the best of times, but when drunk, everyone heard about his regular visits to the local brothels and his treatment of the women.

He sat slumped at the kitchen table, his hands clutching a hot mug of oolong tea. He stared at the swirling steam, lost in thought. His plate of half-eaten toast was pushed to one side, and he glanced aimlessly at the day's headline which read: '*Another murder of a woman in Whitechapel*'.

The previous night had been unpleasant, not just because of the man's company, that could be tolerated. It was what the man had said to him.

“You must try and eat something Thomas, you can’t go out without eating at least a little.” Came the concerned voice of his wife Sarah.

“I know, love, but I cannot disregard what has been told to me.” Barnardo shook his head and stroked one of his long, wiry sideburns. “What I've heard is truly distressing.” He pushed himself off the chair and donned his jacket that had been draped over the back rest.

Sarah’s face had a soft roundness to it, her lips narrow, and her small nose curved slightly upwards. Her eyes were a warm, deep brown that hint at a kind and caring personality and matched her hair. “My dear, you can’t save everyone, although I know you’d love to. Sometimes there are some things that are out of your hands.” Sarah rose from her chair and moved round to where he was stood. “Is there anything I can do to ease your burden? Usually, you talk to me about everything that troubles you.” She looked up into his eyes as she slipped her arms around his waist. “I hate seeing you like this.” Sarah said with affection as she put her head on his chest.

“I just wish I hadn’t been privy to what that odious man had said to me last night. My thinking is to speak with the police, so I’ll go along and discuss it with someone there this morning.” He hugged Sarah to him, looked at her with soft hazel eyes, then kissed her gently.

"Thank you, my darling, what would I do without you." He smiled softly before making his way into the hallway. "I'll be home as soon as I can, could you get Constance to keep a meal for me please?" He pulled on his overcoat, checked his appearance in the hall mirror, ran his fingers through his short dark hair, then picked up his medical bag and stepped out into the dull day.

He reached the main street and hailed a cab, the streets were busy so the journey to the station took longer than anticipated. Barnardo fidgeted as his mind felt like it was full of treacle and his fingers fiddled with a loose button on his overcoat. How had the goings on at the Pickett Street brothel escaped his attention before now?

The cabbie pulled up a short walk from the station. "Sorry, Sir, the road is blocked with an upturned cart." He shouted.

"Not a problem, the walk will do me good." Barnardo stepped down to the cobbles and reached up to the cabbie to pay his fare. "Keep the change my good man." He broke into a quick stride as he made his way up the street.

"Cheers govna, and a good day to you." The cabbie said as he tipped his cap.

Barnardo walked up the steps to the station and strode into the front office.

A Constable was sat behind the counter scratching down some notes with a badly chewed pencil. He didn't look up.

Barnardo shifted his weight from one foot to the other, nervously tapping his toe on the dusty floorboards. He inhaled deeply and cleared his throat in an effort to break the officer's concentration. His face grew hot, and he quickly glanced away from the glossy bald spot at the top of the dark-haired man's head.

Nothing.

He knocked on the countertop.

The Constable raised his index finger.

"My good man, I've been stood here for several minutes and-"

The Officer cut him off, "As you can see, I'm rather busy," He remarked with a face like iron. "I will be with you in a moment, please take a seat over there," He pointed to a single wooden chair against the wall behind Barnardo, "and once I'm finished here, I'll be able to deal with your inquiry." He said in an uncompromising fashion then cast his dull, green eyes back to the desk.

Barnardo, took a deep breath through flared nostrils, raised an eyebrow, and then took his five foot six inch frame to the indicated chair.

Some twenty minutes later the Constable stood up. "Right, how can I help you?" He had his hands clasped together on top of the counter.

Barnardo chose to swallow his frustration, stood up and slowly crossed the room.

The Constable gave a fake smile, "I take it your inquiry is urgent?" He said in a decidedly unwelcome manner.

"Officer, I need to report an establishment that has been brought to my attention." Barnardo straightened his tie. "Frankly, it is of a very delicate nature, so I'd better speak with one of your superiors."

"Well, firstly I need to know exactly what has been brought to your attention," he said with a hint of sarcasm, "before I notify my superiors," He bent down under the counter and pulled out a wad of paper. "Fill this in and then we'll talk further." The Officer handed him a sheet from the wad and the chewed pencil.

Barnardo stepped forward, squared his shoulders, and fixed the officer with a hard stare. "Officer," he said through gritted teeth, "What is your namc?"

"Constable Gubbins." He answered with ill-concealed exasperation.

"Well Officer Gubbins, it is very clear to me that you have little regard for your job or the reason as to why I'm here this morning, would I be correct?" Barnardo ignored the chewed pencil in front of him and reached into his inside pocket and pulled out his own.

Gubbins stiffened with smouldering disapproval at the question. "Sir, firstly, I am the only officer in this department today, secondly, all my colleagues are out on the streets trying to catch a madman, and three," he pulled in a sharp breath before continuing, "my superiors are out at another murder which occurred last night, so in answer to your question Mr?" He raised his eyebrows and fixed Barnardo with a questioning stare.

“Doctor, Doctor Thomas Barnardo.” He answered but didn’t look up from the form he was now filling in.

“So, Doctor Barnardo, you’ll have to excuse me if I’m not too concerned about the reason as to why you’re here this morning.” The Constable waited for a reply, when it didn’t come, he looked down at the form that Barnardo was completing.

Barnardo replied to the Constable with fake tolerance, "Not a problem. Just give this to them and I'll wait for contact." He threw Gubbins a grimace of reproach as he headed for the exit, flicking his goodbye over his shoulder without looking back.

With each step, Barnardo felt the anger and disgust of how he’d just been treated. He couldn’t believe it - not only was a brothel in his city, but one that was exploiting children! His determination to seek justice grew with every breath as he trudged towards his office – but at the same time, he feared what they would do if he tried to pursue the matter. It was irrelevant how much he wanted to do something, he also knew that each step was pushing him closer to a confrontation that could have dangerous consequences. After all people that are prepared to do such heinous acts are people that should be feared. But what really bothered him was that the Constable on duty hadn’t attempted to call him back to the station, even after he’d read the paperwork, he’d just filled in.

Barnardo climbed the steps to his first-floor offices on Rippling Road, knowing that he'd a pile of paperwork to work through but the intention to get it finished evaded him. He sat at his desk in his office that had gradually, over the years, become overwhelmed with files and documentation. The children's homes he'd run over the past decade had a surprising amount of red tape and official forms to contend with.

He rose from his chair and poked the fire in the hearth situated behind him. The log hissed at him like a discontented cat as the flames jumped back into life. The coal bucket on his left had been freshly filled that morning, so he picked up the tongs and began to rebuild the fire. His mind kept replaying the conversation of the previous night and his gut twisted. How could any man treat another human being in such a way? He straightened up and glanced around his office. Files and paperwork lay scattered everywhere. It was time to have some of it filed away and clear some space. Maybe it would help to clear his mind somewhat?

"Mrs Keaton," he called, "Could you come in here for a moment please?"

Seconds later and the door to the office swung open and his middle-aged secretary appeared clasping her notebook and pencil.

"Yes Doctor, what do you need?" Her salt and pepper hair was neatly tucked into a bun, without a strand out of place. Her wide features were hosting a small, round pair of spectacles that were perched on the end of her petite nose. Her dark, green eyes were filled with curiosity as she crossed to one of the chairs sat in front on the desk and sat down, flicked open her notebook and poised her pencil.

"Firstly, I think it's time to file some of this paperwork." He watched her trying to gauge her reaction.

"Oh, thank the lord, I've been wanting to get this room sorted for some time now." She placed her notebook and pencil in her lap and rested her hands on top of them. "When should I begin, Doctor?"

"Whenever you like, I need to sort out a rather delicate situation, so I'll be out of the office for most of the day." He walked to the coat stand and picked up his jacket and punched his arms into it. "Do you know, Mrs Keaton, I paid a visit to the local constabulary this morning to inform them of something I heard last night at the gentlemen's club and the officer that I spoke with wasn't the least bit interested, shocking." Bernardo could feel his frustration rising again as he shook his head. He tried to ignore it as he buttoned his jacket.

"Did you attempt to tell the Constable exactly what it was?" She asked.

“He point blank refused to listen, gave me a form to fill in, and that was that.” He reached for his overcoat. “I’m really at a loss as to what to do next.” He patted himself down to make sure he had everything and then realised that he’d left his gloves and spectacles on the desk.

“Could the police be of use though?” Mrs Keaton queried, with an expression of complete astonishment.

The question stopped Barnardo in his tracks. “What do you mean, Mrs Keaton?” He blinked rapidly.

“Well, is it something that affects the homes for instance?”

“Not directly, no, but it could do I suppose.” He began slowly buttoning his overcoat as he digested what his secretary had just said.

“Please don’t think me talking out of turn, Doctor.” She displayed a slight trace of a wince as she spoke.

“Go on.” He said pushing his hands into his gloves.

Keaton handed a paper to Barnardo from a stack on his desk. "Maybe talking to people who recently donated might help," she suggested. "I've also heard rumours of police corruption, but it's hard to know what is true and what isn't. Keep that in mind if you do talk to them about what I assume is a delicate matter." Her voice grew quiet.

Barnardo scanned the page in his hand. “I think you could have a very valid point and yes it isn’t pleasant, so I’ll spare you the details.” He passed the piece of paper back to her, picked up his spectacles and headed for the door. “I know it’s not customary to visit unannounced, but I think this is the exception.” He hastened to add as he made his way down the staircase and out into the street.

Half an hour later he arrived at Miss Myers’ townhouse. A woman was washing down the steps outside and was on her hands and knees scrubbing as he approached. He cleared his throat before speaking so as not to startle her.

“Good morning, Madam, I’m looking to speak with Miss Ruby Myers?” He reached into his top overcoat pocket and handed her his calling card.

Rose stood up and wiped her hands on her apron before taking it from Barnardo. “Well good morning, Sir.” She greeted before she read the details in front of her. “Doctor Barnardo, a pleasure to meet you, please would you like to step into the hallway, it’s rather cold this morning.” Rose led him up the steps and once in the hallway, shut the door.

“I hope I don’t appear rude by visiting unannounced but there is a matter I wanted to discuss with Miss Myers which is of a rather urgent and delicate nature.” He unbuttoned his overcoat and slipped it off his arms, pulled off his gloves and handed them to Rose.

"I'm not sure Miss Myers has time to see you this morning, Doctor, although I do know that she is very impressed by the work that you do for the children of the city." Rose hung his coat up and pushed the gloves into one of the pockets. "Please, just one moment and I'll see if she can spare a moment or two." Rose walked down a long corridor and then disappeared into a door on the left.

Bernardo fidgeted with the hem of his suit jacket, using his thumb to remove invisible flecks of lint. He then turned to the coat brush on the stand and methodically worked it over his lapels and trouser legs, as if cleaning down his attire would also cleanse away his nervousness. A minute later Rose reappeared.

"Dr. Bernardo, if you'd like to come this way." She invited.

He gave Rose a warm smile and followed her down the corridor. Rose knocked on the same door and stepped back so he could enter.

"Miss Ruby, Doctor Bernardo to see you." She said as she closed the door behind her.

"Thank you Rose, Doctor Bernardo, so lovely to meet you."

A beautiful red-headed woman stood up from a chair placed in front of the fireplace. She wore a pale blue dress, draped gracefully over her slender figure, and her blue eyes sparkled in the firelight. She held out her hand to Bernardo, who felt his cheeks flush as he shook it, speechless in her presence. "Ah... Miss Myers, a pleasure," he finally managed to reply.

“Please do take a seat, I’m sorry but Mr Morris isn’t here to meet you with me, he’s out sorting some other business.” She watched him sit down and then fixed her eyes on him.

Bernardo suddenly felt rather awkward and fidgeted in his chair before his eyes met hers. He cleared his throat. “Excuse me… not a problem I will look forward to meeting Mr Morris at a later date.” He threw her his best charismatic smile, whilst brushing down his trousers as he crossed his legs.

“Could I offer you some refreshment?” She asked.

“No thank you.” He said, his voice wavering slightly as he gave a forced, awkward laugh and shifted uncomfortably.

If she noticed he was uneasy she didn’t say anything, just tilted her head to one side. “So, how can I help you today, doctor?”

The question fired up his brain again and he remembered why he was there. “Well, it’s of a rather delicate nature and also something I loathe to speak of to a lady, such as yourself, but as you’ve been one of our most generous donors to our cause I felt that it might be, not only beneficial but also it would lift the burden somewhat.” He said candidly.

“Well, they do say a problem shared is a problem halved Doctor, so please continue.” She frowned slightly, but she looked at him with soft eyes waiting for him to resume.

The Doctor pulled in a deep breath before he spoke, his features hardened, and he drew his lips into a thin line before speaking. “Miss Myers, I was at the gentlemen’s club last night and a rather vile, drunken man approached me.”

“Thank you for trusting me Doctor Barnardo, I’m listening.” She straightened her head but didn’t take her eyes off him.

“Um…,” he cleared his throat again and felt his neck flush, “Miss Myers, what I have to tell you is of the most abhorrent and disgraceful behaviour and it breaks my heart to inform you that it is some of the abandoned children of this city that it is happening to, let alone the women too.” He looked down at his hands as he placed them on top of on his thigh. He swallowed and felt his stomach flip, “Miss Myers, there is a brothel on Pickett Street…”

“Yes, I’m aware of the establishment, it’s a bordello if I’m not mistaken.” Miss Myers interjected. “Nothing unusual about that, Doctor.”

“Well… ah… no,” He crossed his legs, “but this place is where not only do the women get beaten, but they have children, most under the age of twelve being, ah… um… used, for want of a better expression, by the men that frequent the establishment.” He felt his shoulders slump with a heavy realization as he made the confession. His eyes widened and his nostrils flared as he waited for Miss Myers’ reaction.

As the truth registered in her mind, her slender hand clasped to her chest. Her jaw dropped and her mouth gaped open, unable to find words to express her shock. She stumbled away from him towards the window; letting out strange choking noises as tears started streaming down her face. She leant on a chair to supported herself.

Barnardo sat frozen in his seat, not knowing what to say to calm her. Finally, after what seemed like hours, she turned back to him.

Her hand trembled as she spoke, the words spilling out in a jumble of indignation and disgust. The lilt of her Cockney accent crept back into her speech, a clear sign of rising anger. "This is despicable, utterly shameful, and cruel! It sickens me to my core!" "And who was it that told you this information?" She looked out of the window, not turning as she questioned him, her arms bent at the elbows and her hands now clasped in front on her.

"The man in question was a Captain Oliver Smythe, an odious specimen of a man, someone I always try to avoid, but I was unfortunate last night." He waited for her to speak.

"I know the man you're talking of, Doctor, I've had the misfortune to have him visit one of the girls here and she received a nasty beating when she refused him her fourteen-year-old daughter. He actually thought it acceptable to have her daughter service him whilst under my roof. Needless to say, he received a good lathering for raising a hand to one of the ladies." Miss Myers turned and crossed to a bureau on her left and pulled out a small, rectangular tin. She popped the lid and flicked through the contents, paused about halfway through and drew out a card. "Yes, this is the cretin." She handed it to Barnardo.

Barnardo glanced down at the details in front of him. "Yes, this is him." He confirmed as he handed it back to her.

Miss Myers dropped it onto the small table next to her chair and sat down before she continued. "Doctor, that man is quite the deviant and I had great pleasure in dragging his disgusting carcass down my front steps. That was after I threatened to force his face into a pile of horse dung. That was several weeks ago, needless to say he hasn't been back." She sat forward placed her elbows on her knees, and her chin on her fists as she watched Barnardo's expression.

Barnardo's face drained of colour, and he nervously fidgeted with his tie. He cleared his throat before managing to ask, "Uh… so you are familiar with this man Miss Myers? Please forgive me, you don't seem to be the type of woman who would stoop to such a level; You are so-" He cut himself off, unable to complete the thought.

"Doctor Barnardo, I will save you embarrassment by informing you that I'm not the average woman." Miss Myers interrupted, "My establishment is a place of safety for the girls that choose to work here and they are to be respected by every customer that comes through that big black door." She pointed behind her as she spoke. "I will not tolerate anyone, and I mean anyone, treating the girls here poorly." Her cheeks flushed with anger.

Barnardo held up his hand apologetically, "Please Miss Myers, I meant no disrespect to you, I was just taken by surprise." He smiled weakly at her.

"So, Smythe actually told you about the goings on at Pickett Road Bordello?" Miss Myers questioned.

"Sadly, yes, he did, even told me that a lot of upper-class men are visitors there, even goaded me to ask him for their names. I think he was trying to prove a point by being able to tell me who these other men were. Like I'd want to be associated with such cretins." Anger flashed briefly across Barnardo's face.

They were interrupted by the parlour door being flung open and Arthur walked in.

"It's okay Doctor Barnardo, this is Arthur Morris." Miss Myers introduced.

"Nice to meet you, Doctor Barnardo." Said Morris extending his hand. "I've heard very good things about you, so your visit is an unexpected pleasure." Morris looked down at Miss Myers. "I'm sorry to interrupt Rubes, but I've heard some news that may be of some interest." He gave a wonky grin, and a look of excitement crossed his face.

"Can't it wait Arty?" queried Miss Myers, "I'm having quite the discussion with the Doctor."

"Well, I think this will be of some interest, but yes, please continue, I do apologise Doctor." Mr Morris conceded then sat down in the seat at the table.

"So, Doctor what is it that I can do to help regarding Smythe?" Miss Myers asked.

"Well-"

"You're talking about Smythe?" Mr Morris interrupted.

"Indeed, we are Mr Morris, just to bring you up to speed, I was told by him that some rather unpleasant things are happening at the Pickett Road Bordello-"

"I'll stop you there, Doctor," Morris was holding up his hand. "I've been made aware of the goings on within that establishment and it's not pleasant to hear either, I've been working with some of the lads to try and find a way as to how we could close it down."

The Doctor looked between the two of them.

"I'd already mentioned that we are aware of the place, but what is it that you know Arty?" Miss Myers turned in her seat to look at him. "Do you know that it involves children?" She a look of disgust settled on her face before she turned back to the Barnardo.

Mr Morris nodded. "Sadly yes." He folded his arms and glanced at the back of Miss Myers' head and then at the Barnardo. "This may seem like I'm going off the point, but I think what I've heard this morning will be rather relevant."

Miss Myers' head snapped round, and Barnardo sat up straight in his chair.

“There’s been another murder, not far from the bordello you’ve just mentioned Doctor and the person that’d been killed is your man, Captain Oliver Smythe. Shot, apparently, in an alleyway.” Mr Morris continued. He looked pleased with himself as he laced his fingers behind his head and sat back in the chair. “Nothing he didn’t deserve, by all accounts, and one less pervert on the streets.” He concluded smugly.

“Good lord, Smythe has been murdered,” exclaimed Barnardo. “What on earth…” he let the sentence hang in the air as he tried to gather his thoughts.

Miss Myers had raised her eyebrows and Barnardo could tell she was actually surprised at what Mr Morris had just told them.

“Well, that’s unexpected news this morning.” Miss Myers added.

“It is that Rubes,” Mr Morris pinched the bridge of his nose. “Doctor, do you know of any other of the men that may frequent that place?” He asked.

Bernardo noticed that he looked tired. “It just so happens I do Mr Morris, Smythe did say some names of one or two others that are also using the place.” A cold shiver ran down his spine and he trembled. “It makes me feel utterly disgusted that there are repulsive human beings like that in the world, something must be done and, as you said Mr Morris, this place needs to be shut down?” He stared down at the floor, his heart raced with the horrible truth he had learned. Despite the atrocities which had taken place in the bordello, people still continued to go there, not showing a hint of regret or remorse. How could they be so callous? He wanted to yell and scream at them for their selfishness, yet he was frozen in place, unable to act on his anger.

"So," Mr Morris suddenly said, "Would you like our help sorting out this mess at Pickett Street, Doctor?" He clapped his hand on his thigh as he stood up and crossed to the table where the whiskey decanter was.

The question felt like he'd swallowed a calming tincture. "Thank you, but my answer is no." He said and gave a polite smile.

"Not a problem, Doctor." Mr Morris replied and poured some of the amber liquid into a glass, raising the crystal container in a gesture of asking if the doctor would like to partake.

He politely declined.

Mr Morris downed the drink in one, placed the glass on the table and held out his hand. "It's been a pleasure meeting you Doctor, even under such horrible circumstances," Arthur said.

Barnardo rose from the chair and the two men shared a handshake.

"And it was a privilege meeting you both and I feel relieved having told you both what I know." The doctor bowed from the neck, "Miss Myers," then he looked again at Mr Morris, and nodded. "Now I'll be on my way, thank you both for your hospitability and I look forward to speaking to you again." He made his way to the parlour door.

Mr Morris followed, "I'll show you out."

Barnardo stopped at the coat stand and shrugged on his coat, “Thanks again for your time, Mr Morris.” He said as he did up the buttons and then slid on his gloves.

“Most welcome.” Mr Morris opened the front door and stood aside.

“Good day to you.” Bernardo said as he descended the steps.

Bernardo trudged down steps of the townhouse, his head bowed and his long coat flapping in the evening breeze. When he eventually stepped out onto the pavement, he felt relief coursing through him. He knew that with help from Mr Morris and Miss Myers, he could finally gather enough evidence to put an end to the bordello's immoral practices. He made a mental note to visit some other donors who might be willing to act on the situation - the more people involved, the quicker it would be solved. With a newfound determination in his stride, Bernardo continued with the new belief that the Pickett Street brothel would soon be a thing of the past, sooner rather than later.

Chapter Nineteen

The body of Smythe had been placed on a cart, shrouded in cloth, and taken away from the alleyway. Inspector Royal stood and looked at the area trying to gain an idea of what exactly took place. The only evidence was the small pistol that had been used to separate the deceased from the living. He turned around in an attempt to see if Abberline was still nearby.

"Fred, come take a look at this," he called out. Royal had picked up the pistol. He waited for Abberline to get closer before he continued. "See here, it has inlaid mother of pearl, so I think this is a Deringer, known as the women's handbag pistol." He held his hand out towards Abberline, "Take a look."

Abberline took the gun from him and turned it around in his hands. "You think a woman did this, Bernard?" He raised his eyebrows at Royal and looked unconvinced as he handed it back to him.

"Not necessarily, no, but I'm sure it's a woman's pistol, and the pretty inlay got me to that conclusion, I think the person who originally owned this had a lot of money," he lifted his hand and rubbed his finger and thumb together, "guns aren't cheap, especially one with a nice inlaid handle, that's pricey too." He pushed his hands into his coat pockets and rocked backwards on his heels.

"Well, that's the only clue from this mess Bernard, thankfully it appears that it's not the work of that bloody madman." Abberline looked behind Royal. "Ah, good lad, Samuel thank you."

Samuel had come back from the morgue with a bucket of water and a broom and had begun to wash down the mess off the wall and slosh down the ground where Smythe had been found.

"Well, there is that I suppose," commented Royal, "but the paperwork we've had to deal with, because of this madman, is a bloody nuisance frankly," he glanced at Abberline, "the woman were all fallen women, and in my opinion, not worth the ink." He frowned, his restless feet shuffling and dragging as he slowly kicked at the dirt and stone of the side street. Without a word, he turned away from his colleague and made his way up to the main street, eager for something interesting to break the monotony. "I'll be back at the station if you want me, Fred." Then walked out onto the road as he slipped the pistol into his pocket.

The previous evening had left him feeling quite light-hearted that day and his spirits were such that he decided to stop at a cake stall and buy himself an iced bun. His thoughts were of the night before and he'd had the pleasure of the company of a very nice young woman, unbeknownst to his wife Penny. Melissa, the young woman in question, had been most obliging and with a little extra coaxing and an extra few pennies, she had serviced him on her knees. He smiled to himself as he ambled back to his office and had eaten his food before he'd arrived.

The reception was quiet as most of the Constables were out on duty, except for Gubbins. Royal wasn't in the mood for talking, so he nodded to the officer and made his way to his office.

He walked into the room, his old overcoat brushing against the ancient wood of the walls. He removed it and felt the weight of the gun still in one of the pockets. Leaving it where it was, he hung it from an antique coat stand near the door and moved towards his desk. On top lay several envelopes – one with his name scrawled across it – and a small oblong box bound with string. His fingers peeled away the wax seal covering each envelope before setting them aside in a neat pile. He then picked up the package, his letter opener made light work of the tightly tied string and he took off the lid. The contents were hidden by thick brown paper but resting on the top was a neatly written card with a message. *Whoever watches his mouth and tongue keeps himself from trouble.*

Royal read the card several times trying to work out exactly what this could mean. After several moments he put the card to one side and decided to see what was in the box. As he moved the package closer, he noticed a familiar aroma of copper and an acidic smell. His hair on the back of his neck prickled. The brown paper covering the article within had been folded neatly. He pulled back each piece gently and then sat back in disbelief. The article that lay before him was a decomposing human tongue.

Chapter Twenty

Ruby finished off the last of the bread and butter on her plate and swilled down the coffee. She felt her energy level spike as she pushed back her chair and stood up.

"Thank you Rose, I feel better for some breakfast and a good sleep." She smiled at her housekeeper as she passed her the cup and plate. "It seems to have been a while since I slept through the night without dreaming. Now, I need to go if I'm to be on time at Mrs Byford's."

"I'll fetch your coat for you." Rose walked out into the hallway and took it down off the stand. "What time did her note say for you to arrive?" She asked.

"Eleven. I never thought that Mrs Byford and I would ever become allies, Rose, but I'm glad we have, it makes things so much better." Ruby said as she pushed her arms into her coat and began buttoning it up.

"I totally agree Miss Ruby, it certainly does." Rose stood back and watched her as she readied herself for her outing.

"Right, now Arthur has already gone out this morning, he had some business to attend to, so would you please be kind enough to change the linens on my bed." She picked up her gloves and pulled them on. "It's also the day that Martha moves out too, so her room will need a good airing and a clean." She looked sadly at Rose. "I wish she'd reconsider, I've a bad feeling about this, you know how Martha doesn't think of the possible repercussions before she makes any decisions.

She's so hasty at times and at the moment with that killer on the loose…." She let the sentence trail off and picked up her velvet reticule and slid it over her wrist, the coins inside clinked as she did so.

"There's nothing you can do if the girl won't listen, Miss, we both know that it's not a good idea, but Martha has always been headstrong and Jane's death has affected her pretty badly, they were close friends you know." Rose reached for the clothes brush from the stand and had begun to remove the dust and fluff off the back of Ruby's coat.

"Yes, I do understand Rose, but somehow this feels all wrong." Ruby let out a sigh, "anyhow, she can always come back if she so chooses." She waited for Rose to finish then walked towards the front door. "I'll see you in a while." She said as she opened it and descended the steps into the street.

The morning was crisp and bright, and the low winter sun had begun to burn off the frost that had settled on the nearby railings and the cobbles under her feet. The local stall holders were happily filling the baskets of their customers. The familiar smells of the market tickled Ruby's senses as she made her way down the street and even though the retailers and customers were happily going about their daily lives her heart didn't feel any lighter.

She walked to the end of the road and looked left and right in the hope of flagging down a cab. About a hundred yards away she noticed a cabbie dropping a fare, she raised her arm to catch his attention.

"Ealing Avenue please cabbie," she said as he pulled the cab over to where she stood.

“Right, you are Miss.”

Ruby climbed in and pulled the rug on the seat over her knees.

The journey took around thirty minutes, and she arrived on time. She was just raising the door knocker when the lady that had greeted her previously opened the door.

“Good morning, Miss Myers, do come in, I know Mrs Byford is expecting you.”

“Thank you.” Ruby nodded and smiled warmly and as she followed her.

The room had improved a little since Ruby’s last visit and some small items of furniture were now in the room and new, velvet drapes hung at the windows. Mrs Byford was sat in the same chair but was now dressed in a dark green silk dress, her sharp cheeks had a glow from the fire, and she fixed Ruby with bright eyes as she entered the room.

“Miss Myers, so lovely to see you again. Thank you, Mary,” she said to the old lady behind her, “bring a tray of tea, would you?” She indicated to the chair opposite for Ruby to sit down. “Please, do make yourself comfortable.”

Ruby crossed to the chair and sat down. “May I say you are looking so much better than the last time I saw you, Mrs Byford?” She smoothed imaginary creases from her dress as she spoke to deflect her feeling of trepidation as to why she had been asked to visit.

“Why thank you, Miss Myers, I do feel better. There are days when I have to rest as I have some flare-ups, but sadly, this is all part of my condition.” She said.

"Anyhow, let's not dwell on something so depressing. I've not called you here to discuss my ailments." She said dismissively. Byford took a deep breath before continuing. "Now, I've much nicer things to discuss with you." She clasped her hands in her lap and plastered a wide grin across her face.

"Of course, I apologise, I didn't mean to pry about your health," Ruby said with a look of humiliation on her face.

Mrs Byford shook her head and waved her index finger, "Now, now, no harm done, I thank you for your concern. Miss Myers, I have given your proposal a lot of thought and although I feel I don't deserve any help from you, I would graciously like to accept your offer, which is of course if the kind gesture is still available?"

"Of course, I never go back on my word Mrs Byford. I would be delighted." Ruby felt her heart swell with pleasure, she always felt great happiness and satisfaction at helping others any other way she could.

The two women smiled at each other.

"Well, I feel it's only correct that I share with you the plans I've made." Mrs Byford took a sip of water from a glass on the table next to her before continuing. "I've recently become quite friendly with a Doctor Bennardo, have you had the pleasure dear?"

"Yes, I have, he helps orphaned children," Ruby replied.

"Ah, good, well I've decided that I'm going to open the house to some unfortunate children as Doctor Bennardo is desperately looking for another place for the children to stay." She paused and raised her glass to her lips again, "and this house hasn't ever had any children within its walls." Mrs Byford took a mouthful of the liquid.

"What a wonderful idea." Ruby agreed. "It'll bring you so much joy having children here."

"Ah, won't it be a beautiful thing?" Mrs Byford smiled, her eyes twinkling in anticipation. "At last, this house will be full of love and light again. All these children are going to have a home that is their own - safe and sound." She crossed her hands over her lap, looking around the large room with pride.

Ruby's gaze softened as Mrs Byford's face lit up with sheer joy. The transformation from the hardened, callous woman to a giddy one was beautiful to behold. But Ruby's mind wandered back to the unfortunate children living at the Pickett Street brothel who would never know such blissful contentment, comfort and safety.

"I will draw up the paperwork for Dr Bennardo shortly with my lawyer and set the wheels in motion, I'd like to have everything in place within the month. Do you think that is a possibility, Miss Myers?" Byford's gaze met hers, and her eyes gleamed with determination as a plan began to form in her mind. Her lips curved into a confident smirk, and she took a deep breath before she spoke, "I'm rather excited and I don't mind admitting it." She said as Mary came into the room with their tray of tea.

"I see no reason why that can't be possible, I will have the funds arranged for you by tomorrow afternoon," Ruby said.

"My dear, that is most excellent, I cannot thank you enough." She glanced around the room. "This will be the first room that will be organised, I'm not sure as yet what the use will be, but I've considered it to be either to be for schooling or a room for board games and such like." She held her chin with her index finger and thumb in thought, "or should the library be a better room for schooling?" Byford pondered for a moment. "I'm sorry my dear," she said as she returned her attention back to Ruby.

"It all sounds perfect, I'm sure the children that stay here will be very happy, after all a happy childhood is so very nurturing," Ruby added. "I've no family you see," she found herself admitting. "They died whilst I was small, perished in a fire." Ruby surprised herself with the admission. Why did she talk of her family? It'd been such a long time, but it felt so good to be remembering them, but the sadness she'd felt for years now still clouded her heart.

Mrs Byford's next gesture took Ruby by surprise as the woman reached forward and took Ruby's hand. "It isn't easy when one loses all the people that they care about so deeply." She eyed Ruby sympathetically.

Ruby's eyes widened as she spoke of her family, and Mrs. Byford interjected kindly, "That I can understand, my dear; I can tell it hurts you so." She leaned back in her chair, resting her forearms on the armrests.

Ruby was thankful for the change of conversation as Mrs. Byford began to speak of her younger sister Penelope and her husband. She described him as controlling and having dalliances, almost spitting out the words with contempt. Her brother had two boys who he bought up by himself after his wife passed away while they were very young.

Mrs. Byford's face lit up with pride as she told a story about her two nephews, one living in France managing an art school and Rupert living nearby and dropping in to see his aunt when he can. Both have become eligible bachelors, and Mrs. Byford couldn't seem to contain the delight that beamed through her words.

Ruby said nothing, just smiled and nodded politely.

"My sister's husband works for the local constabulary, so you'd think he'd be a gentleman of complete integrity and treat my sister better." Byford sat poker straight her face had taken on a pinched look.

Ruby's ears pricked up, "Does he?" She had to ask the next question. "Would I know him, Mrs Byford?"

"I would have thought so my dear, he worked at H division when he began his career, but now runs the local station, his name is Inspector Bernard Royal." Ruby's jaw fell slack. Unbelievable. Her hand trembled slightly, and her blood had run cold at the mention of his name. A shiver ran up her spine, making the fine hair on the back of her neck stand on end.

"Are you alright my dear, you look a little shocked?"

"Ah… um… no I'm fine, just didn't expect that." She gave Byford a weak smile.

“It isn’t something I tend to divulge if I’m honest, I do so loathe the man, but I cannot interfere with my sister’s choices, as much as I like to. Do you know, for her birthday one year, he bought her a gun?” She exclaimed, “A gun I tell you, what on earth would she do with a gun?” She looked incredulous as she relayed her story to Ruby.

Ruby raised her eyebrows, “Really? Not a gift to give a lady.”

“I should think not,” her voice shrill with disbelief, “he said it was a lady’s gun, it could fit in her bag, not that she’d carry it anyhow.” She blinked rapidly before continuing, “Oh, what was the name of the thing?” She looked over at the fireplace as she tried to find the name that was eluding her.

“Would it be a Deringer Mrs Byford?” Ruby suggested.

“That’s it, a Derringer,” she looked pleased that she finally had the name for the weapon, “he said it’s dainty enough to fit into the small palm of a woman.”

Ruby's eyebrows knit together as she made a silent vow to tell Arthur every bit of information she had just learned. It would be worth paying money to see the expression on Arthur's face when he heard the news about the odd gift.

Her imagination painted a picture of Inspector Royal, stripped of his power, dragged away in handcuffs to be locked up like the criminal he was.

The thought sent chills down her spine and gave her a satisfying sense of justice. What could Royal possibly have been thinking when he bought his wife that gun? Was this the evidence they needed to finally begin to bring him down?

Ruby took a final delicate sip from her cup and set it down with a clink on the saucer. A self-satisfied smirk emerged onto her face as she listened to Mrs. Byford chatter on. With every agreeing nod, Ruby's anticipation grew, as she knew this would be an evening full of surprises.

Chapter Twenty-One

Abberline took the steps into the station two at a time and strode up to the front desk. "Constable, put that newspaper down, get your feet off the table and do some work." He barked to the officer with his feet up on his desk reading the daily news, then strode straight past him. Abberline knocked Royal's door and entered without waiting for permission.

"Bernard." Abberline sat down in the chair in front of Royal's desk.

Royal slowly raised his eyes from the box in front of him at Abberline's entrance, meeting his gaze with an appalled expression. Abberline felt the tension in the room and saw the other man's knuckles whiten as he gripped the edge of his desk. The clock seemed to tick slower and louder filling the oppressive silence until Abberline finally spoke first.

"Good grief man, cat got your tongue?" Abberline placed his elbows on his knees and rested his chin on his fists.

Royal pushed the box across the desk at Abberline, "You've no idea how near you are with that comment Fred, take a look at that, some joker sent it to me along with this," he flicked the card at Fred then stood up, pushed his hands into his trouser pockets and crossed to the window.

Abberline leant forward and held the box with a thumb and index finger, tipping it towards his face so he could see the contents. The sight of what was within made him wretch and he placed the lid back on then sat back and covered his mouth with his free hand. "Good god Bernard, have you any idea who may have sent this?" Abberline asked as he scanned the writing on the card.

"I'm afraid I have no idea, Fred." Royal rocked backwards and forwards on his heels. "Whomever it is must be a very sick individual." He turned to face Abberline. "My question is who the hell does it belong to?" He wiped his hand over his mouth and then returned to his chair.

"I think I may know, Bernard, give me a moment." Abberline stood up and opened the office door. "Could a Constable come here please?" He called.

A moment later an awkward-looking officer with frizzy black hair and pock-marked skin came into view.

"Can I help you, Inspector?" He asked as he walked towards Abberline.

"You certainly can, I need you to go and get Dr Sequira and bring him to me here as quickly as possible and tell him it's urgent, go on off you go, and be quick there's a good lad." He didn't wait to see the Constable leave as he turned his attention back to Royal. "Bernard, I have a theory as to whom this belongs to," he pointed to the box, "I think it's from one of the recent victims, Doctor Sequeira said that one of the women was missing hers. Pass me the card again, I want to check something."

Royal pushed it back towards him, “There’s no signature or any indication who may have written it.” He sat back in his chair and laced his fat fingers behind his head and watched Abberline.

Abberline pulled out his notebook from his inside jacket pocket and extracted the letter and calling card that he’d placed inside its pages earlier. He placed both side by side on the desk, then added the one that came with the parcel and stood over them scrutinising the penmanship. His brow furrowed and he chewed his bottom lip absentmindedly as he concentrated on the lettering in front of him. Several moments later he spoke.

“By God, Bernard I do believe we have a match.” He confirmed.

Royal stood up from his chair, the wooden legs scraping across the floorboards as he did so. He leant across the desk to get an even better view of the bold lettering in front of Abberline. His face became a mask of intense concentration as he studied the wording, “So, the bastard that is slicing up whores has now taken to writing fucking messages too…” He paused for a moment, and exhaled slowly, shaking his head in disbelief.

Abberline noticed that his face was deep red and that he’d begun to sweat again. “It’s all right Bernard, this means that we’ve only one perpetrator.”

“That’s as maybe Fred, but why the hell would they send something like that to me, it makes no sense whatsoever.” Royal narrowed his eyes and bit his bottom lip.

"It's clearly a way of gaining our attention, taunting us, Bernard. He is trying to tell us that he has control and that we can't stop him. We have to consider that this sick bastard is beyond the realms of your usual murder suspect. This man is articulate, intelligent, a family man and someone who can blend into any social situation, basically hiding in plain sight."

"Good god, Fred, what on earth makes you think all this? This prick is, without a doubt, sick in the head," Royal stabbed a finger at his temple, "and he'll stick out like a sore thumb. Articulate, intelligent, hide in plain sight, I've never heard so much bullshit in all my life." He spat as he pushed the parcel nearer to Abberline and shaking his head in disgust.

Abberline pointed to the box, "Well, that's my opinion Bernard, I don't give a shit if you like it or not, you'll see." He replied bluntly then turned his attention back to the package in front of him. "What's in that box will be confirmed by Doctor Sequira as belonging to one of the women he's murdered." He rubbed both hands over his thighs, even though the room was warm, he felt a chill. "Bernard, you do need to try a calm down, I've noticed that you're extremely edgy of late." He eyed his colleague and tried to work out what he could be thinking. "I've known you a long time but over the past few weeks you've not been yourself."

Royal stalked to the fireplace, gripping the poker in his hand like a weapon. "I'm bone-weary from this case," he snarled. "The Commissioner breathing down my neck makes it worse, going on about catching this bastard, when all he's doing is cleaning up and getting some scum off the streets for us." With barely contained rage, he jabbed at the log with the poker, sending sparks flying. "Plus, I'm sure as shit not happy about working with Myers and her twisted empire. Haven't you considered that it could be Myers and her cronies? She's got the money for a gun, it's a known fact that she and that Morris bloke has a lot of clout within their network…" he paused momentarily to slow his breathing. "Seriously, Fred, you know it could be her bumping off these whores because they've pissed her off somehow. Is it just me that is looking at the bigger picture? Christ, it could even have been her that sent this parcel just to rattle me. Had you considered that Fred huh?" He gave one final jab at the log before dropping the poker on the hearth.

"Bernard, I do know that Miss Myers and Mr Morris want this madman caught as much as we do, and-"

A knock at the door interrupted them.

"Come." Royal barked.

The dark frizzy haired constable entered. "Inspectors I've got the Doctor for you as requested." He stood back and Dr Sequira entered the room.

“Thank you, Constable,” Abberline said, “Aubrey, good to see you,” he stood up and shook the man’s hand, “apologies for the urgency, but I think this may be of interest to you.” He stabbed a finger at the box on the desk.

“Fred, Bernard.” The doctor acknowledged both men before crossing to the desk, “So what do we have here?” He asked as he picked the box up and removed the lid. After gently peeling back the paper within, Sequeira’s eyebrows shot up in surprise as he tipped the box to gain a view of the entire contents. “Good lord, well gentlemen, I do believe I know whom this belongs to,” he looked between both men before continuing, “the girl in the mortuary, Fred, remember?” He raised his eyebrows in question.

“Yes, sadly I do Aubrey, can you be sure it’s hers?” Abberline felt his stomach churn with the reminder.

“Well, I’d have to check it against the body still at the morgue, but she was the only one of the victims missing one. One things for sure, it is human.” He tipped the box again to see the organ more clearly, then picked it up between his thumb and index finger, crossed to the window and turned it around studying it closely, he then dropped the tongue back into the box and turned round to face the two men.

Before they could continue someone ran down the corridor outside and stopped abruptly at the door, an urgent knock followed.

“Yes, yes, what on earth-” Royal complained as he crossed to the room and yanked it open.

Constable Dibbens stood on the threshold, panting, and sweating profusely. “I’m sorry for the interruption Sir, but you’re needed urgently over at Drury Lane.” Dibbens did his best to slow his breathing and swallowed hard.

Abberline met Royal at the door. With one glance at Dibbens his gut instinct told him what was coming next.

“Inspectors, I’m sorry to say, there’s been another murder.

Chapter Twenty-Two

The woman's body was at the top end of the alley. Abberline stood at her feet trying hard to keep his lunch down. She lay on her back with her legs drawn up and her knees parted enough so that her lower extremities were visible. The dress she was wearing was pulled up to her thighs and both the bodice and skirt were shredded. Her arms were at her sides, palms up and her head positioned to the left. A deep gash ran from ear to ear, the depth of which had almost decapitated her. Crosses had been gouged across her eyelids and finished on her upper cheeks and the end of her nose was missing. The mouth gaped wide with her tongue protruding from the orifice, and she was devoid of her lips.

To save time Sequeira had accompanied the two Inspectors. He knelt beside the body of a young woman, his face grave. He carefully tucked her skirts beneath her knees before beginning his examination. "The poor girl deserves some dignity," he muttered as a solemn reminder to himself.

Royal stood further back down the alley giving two constables instructions. Abberline could hear his tone and noticed his lack of interest or compassion for the girl on the ground.

"Is there a coin in situ, Aubrey?" Abberline asked as he bought his attention back to the cadaver. He then pulled out his handkerchief and covered his mouth.

Sequeira checked the external areas of the body. "Nothing on the ground around her Fred, it may be completely separate from the ongoing case, possibly a lovers tiff or a pissed-off punter."

"It doesn't feel right Aubrey," Abberline began, "I've got a strong feeling that this is connected to the others." He glanced around to see if he could see anything pertaining to the scene around them. Nothing. His stomach knotted and he frowned as he pressed his lips together in a thin straight line. "Bernard, what'd you think?" Abberline raised his voice enough to gain his colleague's attention.

Royal ambled over, "Yes Fred,"

His demeanour aggravated Abberline and he felt the now familiar frustration with his colleague bubbling up within him. He struggled to keep his voice from shaking and clenched his free hand as stepped closer to Royal, He glared over the handkerchief at him. "What's your opinion? Do you think this is connected to the other cases?" His brow was furrowed in scrutiny as he asked the question.

"The only difference is the savagery she was subjected to." Royal conceded, "the injuries have been taken to a whole new level beyond all recognition - from slashing her throat almost to the point of decapitation. At least one good thing comes from this mess," he pointed at the girl, "it's another whore off these streets." Royal expression hardened in agreement with his own dark musings.

Sequeira's head snapped up from what he was doing, his eyes narrowed, and his face contorted as it took on an expression of fierce distaste. "Good God, man, she's still a human being and no woman, man or child deserves a demise such as this, have some respect for the poor girl, how the hell do you know that she was a whore, there's nothing to suggest that she was." He shot a look at Fred.

Abberline's mouth dropped open in amazement as he heard the doctor's sudden outburst. He remained speechless, his eyes darting back and forth between the two men, trying to read the subtle nuances of Royal's reaction.

Detective Sequeira groaned in exasperation at Royal's comment, but it had no effect on the smug look on his face.

"She was a whore, plain and simple," Royal declared. "No lady would be walking down an alley in the dead of night, not like that. I've been on this job long enough to know what kind of trouble these hussies can get into." He crossed his arms, as if daring anyone present to challenge him.

The Doctor didn't respond; he just stared silently back at Royal, his expression stony. Sequeira stood up, his body stiffened, "how the hell do you know that it happened last night, I'm the Doctor here Royal, not you." He fired the words at Royal as if they were flaming arrows, "For fucks sake you're such an arrogant bastard." He spat.

Royal didn't flinch, "As if I care about your opinion of me, Doctor." He countered.

"This girl was a daughter, sister or niece, possibly a mother too, it's irrelevant what she did when she was alive, she was an innocent person with a life which she had the right to continue living." Sequeira was breathing rapidly as he spoke, and his words landed like bricks at Royal's feet as he looked over to Abberline. "If you'll excuse me, Fred, I will take this girl to the mortuary where I can continue my examination, I can't work with this imbecile," he pointed his chin in Royal's vicinity, "around me. I'll see you there in a while." Without looking in Royal's direction Scqueira walked back to the main street.

Abberline turned to Royal, "What were you thinking, Bernard?" He shook his head and folded his arms over his chest. "You never used to be like this back in the early days, what's changed?"

"I've grown up, Fred is what, not so gullible anymore. The streets we protect are rife with crime, and that includes the likes of her," he glanced briefly at the corpse, "when I last checked, Fred, prostitution was still a crime. So, forgive me if I don't agree with the romantic ideas of the Doctor. Fred, I'm a copper and coppers enforce the law, so, to me, when one more whore ends up dead, in my opinion, it does us a favour. She can't tout her trade and we don't get any more paperwork because of it."

Abberline said nothing, just shook his head. Then, "I never thought I'd hear something like that come out of your mouth Bernard and to be honest it saddens me. I need to go to the mortuary, not my favourite place, but right now I'd rather be there than stood down this alleyway with you."

Abberline began to walk past his colleague, but Royal stepped in his way.

"Fred, I'm not the only one on the force to feel like this. Low pay, long hours and piles of paperwork take their toll, morale is low, lower than it's ever been, and you need to wake up and take a look around you. The constables that parole these streets are fed up and are sick of being treated like shit, they've no respect from the locals, and some of our colleagues have even started to fight back."

Abberline looked at Royal, he was right about the pay, hours, and paperwork, but, to Abberline it was always part of the job.

"That look tells me you know I'm right, don't you Fred?" Royal asked as his eyes drilled into Fred's.

"To a point Bernard, yes, bu-"

"There's no buts about it, Fred, these boys are the law," Royal interrupted," and the law is what they are enforcing, they want respect, and they'll get that by whatever methods they see fit, the civilians around here need to understand that. If that means being heavy-handed with some of the scum, then so be it. If a person commits a crime, he or she is a criminal and will be dealt with accordingly."

Fred had heard enough and turned to leave, but Royal grabbed Abberline's arm as he walked past him.

"Fred," he said quietly, "we all deserve decent pay, the meagre amount that we receive doesn't cut it and frankly, there are many methods to subsidise our income and that can be done in many ways." He winked at him and kept his voice to a whisper, "It's the way it needs to be, we do a hard job, and I don't see why we shouldn't reap the benefits if you get my drift."

Abberline's face went ashen as his stomach plummeted to his feet. His mouth dry, he stammered, "What…what else are you privy to, Bernard?" He couldn't meet the other man's gaze and found himself instinctively trying to back away. He shook his arm free from Bernard's grip and started taking long, hurried strides back to the street.

“Things are changing, Fred and you can either be part of that or not, but it’s pointless trying to stop the inevitable,” Royal shouted. “The police are taking over and there’s nothing you can do about it, my friend.”

“I’m not your friend Royal,” Abberline muttered as he turned left out of the alleyway and headed in the direction of the mortuary.

Abberline quickened his pace as he walked towards Doctor Sequeira’s practice, his thoughts consumed with the news Royal had shared. His fears were confirmed and now he was faced with an unpleasant truth and a difficult mission. He felt resigned to help bring down the other crooked officers, even though it pained him to do so. The world seemed to grow heavier on his shoulders as he thought of the darkness ahead. It was no wonder that Miss Myers, Mr Morris, and associates didn’t trust the police, how could they when they knew that there was so much corruption? While a part of him welcomed the challenge, another begged him to turn away from it all.

Sequeira briefly looked up from what he was writing as Abberline entered the morgue. The other gurneys were now vacant of any guests and the only one was the woman from the alleyway up on the slab.

The light in the room was poor and the oil lamp placed near the woman’s head cast a warm, orange glow across the tired doctor's face. Abberline had noticed over the past few weeks that his friend looked thinner than usual, his features were drawn and his eyes sunken with dark circles.

“Firstly, Aubrey, was it that girl’s tongue that was sent to Royal? Abberline asked.

“Yes, it was Her’s Fred. I thought so, but just wanted to confirm it for myself, so there was no mistake.” He smiled weakly at Abberline.

“Great job, my friend, now what else do you have for me?” Abberline asked timidly from under his handkerchief. Although he knew he’d not been the reason for the Doctor’s earlier outburst, he still didn’t want to cause him any further stress.

Sequeira stopped what he was writing, put his notes down and stepped around the front of the slab. He leaned back against it and folded his arms before he spoke. “Fred,” He began. “Firstly, we’ve managed to find out where she lived, and I also found this.” He held his finger in the air as he walked around to the sink at the back of the room. He put his hand into the water, removed the object he wanted and walked over to Fred. “This is what I found…, here.” He dropped a coin into Abberline’s outstretched hand. “Same date as all the others.” He stood back to let Abberline process what he’d just been given.

“Where did you find it? We know it wasn’t at the scene, we looked.” Abberline slid the coin into his pocket.

“Well, it was at the scene indirectly,” Aubrey said as he walked over to the slab.

“Really, where?” Abberline frowned.

“It was inside her, Fred, that’s why we couldn’t find it.” He arched an eyebrow as he picked up his notes.

"Was it concealed in her chest or stomach?" Abberline made an unusual step closer to the slab. "No, not in either of those, Fred… Sorry to be so explicit ole boy, I found it inserted into her vagina." Aubrey winced with evident embarrassment at his colleague's lack of understanding.

Horrified, Abberline gaped in silent disbelief.

Now three coins both bearing the same date.

It was Sequeira that broke the silence.

"Also, Fred, we've found out her name."

This caught Abberline's attention, "How so?"

"One of the boys that loaded her onto the cart knew her, apparently he'd paid for her services a few days back." He glanced down at his notes, "Ah, here it is, her name is Martha, don't know her surname as he wasn't told it."

Inspector Abberline's face went white with disbelief. He stepped back. Momentarily he removed the handkerchief from his mouth and his hand clasped his forehead as he tried to take it in. "I've got to talk to Ms Myers," he mumbled. "there was a Martha living at the townhouse – I'm hoping it's a coincidental name. It looks like Royal wasn't too far off the mark, she could've been touting for business." Abberline shifted uneasily on his feet, his stomach churning with dread. "Any other news for me, Aubrey?" He asked as he put the handkerchief back in place.

"Well, this time all her internal organs were left intact, he'd sliced open her belly though." Sequeira scratched his chin, "I think he was interrupted somehow, so didn't get the chance. That's why he didn't disturb her below the waist," He said tactfully, "but displayed her with her knees apart to still take her dignity." The doctor cleared his throat and then reached for his hip flask located on the slab near Martha's head.

"That's along with where he put the coin too." He took a swill and then screwed the lid back on. "He's a sick son of a bitch, Fred and there's no getting away from that, in my opinion, he has a real hatred for prostitutes or even women in general." He took his place back in front of the gurney. "After carefully examining her and removing the object, I can confirm that this woman has given birth at least once before. Sadly, this may indicate that she was a mother - assuming the child survived."

"Good lord, Aubrey, when the hell is this all going to stop?" Abberline's stomach twisted, and his jaw took on a hard line. "What will this bastard stoop to? I wil-"

The last comment hung in the air as the door to the mortuary swung violently open and Royal strode in.

"Ah, Fred, right where you'd said you'd be," he threw a glance at Sequeira, "don't worry yourself I'm here for the organ grinder, not the monkey."

Sequeira scowled at Royal with silent consternation then walked round the back of the gurney and continued writing.

"Bernard," Abberline barked, "I really don't appreciate you being so rude to our colleague, this man is an important part of this investigation, and his knowledge is invaluable." He turned to Sequeira, "Aubrey, I apologise on behalf of my colleague." Abberline then returned an angry scowl back to Royal, "Now, let's discuss whatever it is you want to talk to me about outside."

Royal spun on his heels as Abberline grabbed his elbow and directed him to the exit. "I say, Fred, no need for the heavy handed attitude, I was only trying to get a point across, bring him down a peg or two."

The two men stepped into a small courtyard, Abberline made sure that they weren't overheard.

Royal stood and smirked at him.

Abberline chose to ignore it, "Now, what the hell are you here for?" He snapped.

Royal took a moment before answering, then, "I wanted to question that bitch Myers about the shooting last night. As I said, Fred, the gun at the scene was a woman's, she's got money and it wouldn't surprise me if she killed the bloke. Anyhow, I went to the whorehouse, but she wasn't in, gone to see an acquaintance apparently, so I thought the next place should be the pub that her bloke owns, thought she might be there."

“So, did you want me to accompany you?” Abberline knew exactly what Royal wanted him to do, but in light of the recently obtained knowledge he wasn’t going to give him an easy time.

“Well, you have a rapport with the man, and… um…” He stammered; the smirk had evaporated from Royal’s face.

It was Abberline’s turn to smirk, “Why, I do believe you’re scared Bernard, now why would that be I wonder?” Abberline took pleasure as he watched Royal squirm.

“I wouldn’t say scared, Fred, just uneasy.” His colleague averted his eyes and kicked uncomfortably at the ground as he spoke.

Abberline knew he was lying but didn’t care to pursue the subject. “I’ll come with you but will do all the talking. Mr Morris and I have an understanding and mutual respect for each other that has taken some time to build. Plus, I’ve other questions to ask him, besides that about the gun. If I didn’t know any better Bernard, I’d say you were trying to pin that on Miss Myers.” Abberline commented as he looked down his nose at Royal, then turned and walked away. He didn’t wait for Royal to answer or to follow, his footsteps behind him told him he was.

****

The pub only had a few drinkers in, and the owner was nowhere in sight. The barman was wiping glasses out with a dirty rag and Abberline noticed the look of concern from him as they crossed the space between the door and the bar. Fred realised that Royal stayed two steps behind him as he approached. Coward.

"Good day to you, I wondered if Mr Morris may be here?" Abberline asked as he turned and surveyed the room.

"Who's asking?" The barman questioned but didn't stop what he was doing.

"I'm Inspector Abberline and this," he turned and indicated to Royal, "is Inspector Royal and you, my good man, are?"

"Eddie, I'll just go see, he may have left already." He put the glass on a shelf behind him and then threw the rag down on the countertop. "Wait here." He said abruptly.

Abberline watched him walk across to some stairs then turned his attention to the room. The punters had gone very quiet and just eyed the pair of them with suspicion but continued with their drinks. Fred smiled as he scanned the bar, Royal just stood with his back to drinkers and said nothing.

Moments later Eddie reappeared and beckoned to Abberline. "He said it was ok for you to go up but he," the barkeep stabbed a finger at Royal, "stays down here."

Abberline glanced at Bernard, whose pallor had changed for the worst. He walked past him towards the stairs. "Not a problem, would you be so kind as to serve him a whiskey whilst he waits, it looks like he needs one." He didn't look back at Royal.

"Ah, Fred, I'm on d…d…duty." He heard him stammer.

"Since when's that bothered you, Bernard?" Abberline threw the comment over his shoulder as he walked up the stairs.

He heard Royal mutter something but didn't catch what it was.

At the top of the stairs was an office with half wooden and half glass walls, the door was ajar and Abberline could see Morris sitting behind his desk, facing the window on the right side of the room his fingers laced behind his head. He looked like he was deep in thought. He caught sight of Fred from the corner of his eye and turned towards him.

"Inspector Abberline, to what do I owe the privilege?" Morris said as he sat forward and then stood up. "I'm afraid Miss Myers isn't here, if it were her you wanted to speak with."

"Mr Morris," Fred extended his hand, "good of you to see me," he looked at the button-back leather chair to his right, "May I?" He asked.

Morris nodded and waited for him to sit down. "So, if it's not Miss Myers you wish to see then why are you here?" he crossed towards a small oak table to his right placed against the wall and laden with a decanter and glasses. He gestured towards the amber liquid within and raised his eyebrows in question.

“Not for me thank you.” Abberline reached into his pocket and pulled out his notebook.

Mr Morris filled his glass then returned to his seat and after a swill he placed the drink in front of him on the desk. “You didn’t answer my question, Inspector.”

“Mm.., Oh yes, I apologise. Inspector Royal did call on Miss Myers earlier, but she wasn’t available, that’s why we’re here. I’ve got a couple of questions I’d like to ask.” He said as he looked at Morris and placed his spectacles on the end of his nose. “There’s been some developments.”

“Oh really, such as?” Arthur turned the glass around in front of him his face impassive.

“A man was found dead down an alleyway last night, he’d been shot. Further enquiries have given us the name Captain Oliver Smythe,” Abberline watched Morris’ face for any reaction. Nothing. “Next to the body a small pistol was found, a weapon that would be ideal for a lady to carry. It fits nicely into a small hand.” He paused as he looked down at his notebook, “A Deringer I believe, and inlaid in the grip with mother of pearl.”

Mr Morris didn’t react, just sat back, and laced his fingers behind his head again. “So, you think I may know something about this death, do you?” He looked down his nose at Abberline his chin was tilted in the air.

Abberline noticed Morris used the word, death not murder. “He was shot at close range,” Abberline continued, “the pistol pushed up under his chin, like so.” He placed his index finger under his chin to demonstrate his point.

Morris folded his arms before speaking, "Inspector, why are you telling me this? I can assure you this was nothing to do with me or Miss Myers for that matter." His jaw clenched.

"I'm sorry, I should've made myself clearer. Mr Morris, there is some suspicion from my colleagues at the station that it was Miss Myers' pistol and that she committed the murder."

Morris' body tensed and Abberline could see a vein in his neck begin to throb.

Abberline knew he was on shaky ground. "I myself don't believe it was her, even though she would've had just cause." He said.

"Oh, and what cause is that Inspector?" Morris narrowed his eyes, his body remained tense.

"I've had it on good authority that the victim used to frequent a lot of establishments such as the one Miss Myers owns, and I've also had it on good authority that he recently visited Miss Myers' establishment and gave one of the girls a severe beating."

Arthur sprung from his seat, his face contorted and deep red. Abberline dropped his notebook and recoiled in shock at his sudden movement.

"Mr Morris, please just hear what I've got to say." Abberline said as he raised his hand, "I'm not here accusing her of anything, I just need to get to the bottom of this, believe me, I'm doing everything I can to keep her name out of it."

Arthur slowly walked across the room, avoiding making eye contact with Inspector Abberline. He stopped at the window and folded his arms behind his back. His voice was low as he said, "Miss Myers has never owned a pistol. She doesn't believe in weapons of any sort," he turned to face Abberline with an expression of admiration. "Miss Myers is a remarkable woman and certainly doesn't need one."

"Why do you say she is exceptional, Mr Morris, aren't all women?" Abberline asked, as he kept eye contact while he waited for a reply.

"Yes, they are, but she is exceptional because she knows how to defend herself, so therefore, she wouldn't need a weapon." A look of pride flashed across Morris' face as he retook his scat. "How do you know about the beating at the townhouse? It was never reported to the police. In fact, Ruby dealt with Smythe on the night in question." Mr Morris reached across the desk and retrieved a pipe and a small rectangular tin.

"One of the constables from the station happened to be visiting one of the other ladies on the night it happened and recognised him," Abberline cleared his throat and felt his ears turn red, "when he was being moved from the alley."

Mr Morris had his pipe in his hand and was filling its bowl with tobacco from the tin. "What a constable that frequents a bordello? Really? Well, that is a surprise, Inspector." His voice edged with mockery.

Abberline looked into the man's eyes with a measure of caution but kept his voice neutral. He sensed danger lurking in the air and didn't want to further agitate the situation, so chose not to pursue the comment. “It appears so, Mr Morris.” He said in agreement. “Well, that aside, there is something else that I needed to bring to your attention.”

Morris looked up from his pipe but said nothing as he put it in between his teeth, then looked about for matches.

Abberline took it as a cue to continue. “Sadly, last night there was also another murder. A woman, found in an alley off Drury Lane, mutilated like all the others and it appears to be the same person responsible.” He paused to gauge Morris’ reaction.

Morris had located matches and had taken a long pull on his pipe. “Name?” He asked with the pipe still between his teeth.

Abberline's eyes flew through the pages of his notebook, "Ahh, here we are, but no surname as yet" he muttered; the silence that followed was deafening as he realized the weight of their task to inform her next of kin.

Mr Morris interrupted his thoughts by clearing his throat, “You were going to tell me her name, Inspector.”

“Ah yes, apologies… Martha, her name is Martha, Mr Morris.”

Morris' face suddenly contorted in recognition. "Seriously… oh, for fucks sake," he cursed loudly, his cigarette smoke curling round his head like a ghostly embrace. "When in god's name will this ever stop, I do hope that woman in the mortuary is not the Martha that Miss Myers knows. That one has just moved out of the bordello." He took another long pull on his pipe. "If it is I dread to think how she'll take the news, it was bad enough with all the others." He shook his head in disbelief.

"When did she move out, Mr Morris?" Abberline asked.

"A week or so back with her daughter." Morris took another pull on his pipe then realised it had gone out.

"She has a daughter?" Abberline asked with raised eyebrows.

"Her name's Polly, she's about twelve or thirteen I think, nice kid." He picked up the matches again and pulled one from the box.

"Well, the Doctor has said that the deceased is a mother, but that could be any number of women in this area." Abberline scratched his head and frowned.

Morris struck the match and sucked on his pipe until the tobacco caught.

"Mr Morris, would you come down to the mortuary to confirm if it is her? Someone has already said that it is, but I'd like another person to confirm this for me, any idea of her surname?"

Morris shook his head and turned his mouth down in an expression of denial. “I don’t but whether Miss Myers does… to be honest I’d rather not upset Miss Myers any further, maybe I should ask Rose instead, she may know.”

“And the identification?” Abberline queried.

Before Morris could answer their attention was drawn to a commotion happening in the bar. Raised voices could be heard coming from two men, along with scuffling of feet and ascending thumps on the stairs.

Moments later Royal stumbled through the office door followed closely by Eddie.

Eddie glared in Royal’s direction, “Mr Morris, I do apologise, I did tell him that he shouldn’t be up here and to stay in the bar, he’s been knocking it back too, must have had four or five.”

Morris waved his hand at Eddie, “Not your fault Ed, go on, go back downstairs, I’ll deal with this.”

“Right, you are Mr Morris.” Replied the breathless barman as he made his way to the stairs without closing the door behind him.

Abberline looked across at Royal, “Bernard, what the hell do you think you’re doing? Good god, man, I said one whiskey.”

Royal belched, which fired alcohol-saturated breath directly in Abberline’s direction.

“Christ, you wreak, how the hell can you throw down four or five whiskeys in the short time I’ve been up here?” Abberline stood and tried to get Royal in the chair opposite him.

Royal shook him off, swearing under his breath in the process. Then he turned his attention on Morris. "You, you piece of shit, sat in your ivory tower." He belched again, "you don't deserve to be here, you'd be best off swinging from a rope," he slurred, "go on, do us coppers a big favour and put a noose around that neck of yours, save us the trouble." Royal stood in front of the desk with a look like he'd had the misfortune to have stepped in something unpleasant on the pavement.

Inspector Abberline stood up, his face the colour of glowing embers and his nostrils flared like an angry dragon. "For Fucks sake, Bernard," he shouted.

Abberline's outburst briefly took the wind from Royal's sails, but not for long enough, as he just stood in front of them and returned to the same expression as before.

Abberline's temper had taken over and he yelled, "Shut the hell up," Abberline continued, "I've had quite enough of your infernal rudeness, and I strongly suggest that you get back downstairs and sober the fuck up!" He stood behind Royal and grabbed both his arms in a desperate attempt to guide him back towards the bar. "Mr Morris, I'll have him out of your way in no time at all." Through his anger he did his best to give him his best reassuring smile. "I can only apologise."

Morris was on his feet, his eyes narrowed and had taken on a look harder than granite. He shot his gaze over to Abberline. "Get him out of here." He hissed. "That bastard never sets foot in this bar again." Morris balled his fists and the same vein in his neck stood proud.

"Oh, fuck off Morris, like I care about coming in this shit hole, I wouldn't line your pockets with my hard-earned cash anyhow, I've not paid for the booze I've had, and I won't be either." Royal's words slurred again.

"Bernard, I said, that's enough, get back down to the bar, right now." Abberline pushed in front of Royal and shielded him as best he could.

"Get him out of my sight and out of my bar before I rip his head off." Morris pushed the words through gritted teeth.

Abberline had managed to get him over to the doorway, but it wasn't quick enough.

"You don't scare me, Morris, you're just another prick that's a boil on the backside of society." Royal's face was crimson as the words fell like hand grenades. "I know that you and that whore are the ones responsible for these murders and it's only because of him," he slapped a hand on Abberline's arm, "that you and her haven't been brought before a judge, it's the likes of you t-"

At break-neck speed Morris grabbed Royal by the lapels of his coat. Royal's eyes widened in horror.

Abberline was thrown to the floor. He was taken aback by the strength that Morris had and all he could do was watch from his place on the floorboards.

Morris' biceps bulged under his shirt. He pushed Royal backwards out of the door.

Royal's arms were flailing around as he tried to grab any part of Morris.

The two men were at the top of the stairs.

Morris was inches away from Royal's face, his eyes ablaze with fury. "No-one belittles me or my girl in here!" he growled, every syllable like a thunderclap. "The last person who tried never made it out of this pub alive."

Royal looked as though the air had been sucked from the room as Morris' threat reverberated around him. His heels were now off the edge of the top step.

Still holding his lapels Morris extended his arms so that Royal was tilted backwards.

"Go on you bastard, finish it," Royal yelled, then he began to back pedal. "Please Mr Morris, I'm just a sad old man who's overstepped the boundaries, I shouldn't have insulted your woman… and I use the law for my own ends, I beg of you, d… d…don't do it…" He stammered, his eyes wide and his body shook.

Morris' eyes were narrow and cold, and his arms trembled. Suddenly he looked deadly calm, he dropped his chin down but kept his eyes on Royal. "I love nothing better than to see you bounce down those stairs, trust me when I say, it'd be my utmost pleasure. But you, you piece of shit, you're not worth going to the gallows for." He replied as he began to slowly pull him back.

Abberline stood up, "Oh thank g-"

But Royal couldn't help himself, "Ha… see you can't do it can you," he goaded, "You're not capable are you, not brave enough, you can't even stand up to that bitch of yours and show her who's boss and what a real man is made of."

"Bernard, for fuck's sake shut up." Abberline bellowed.

Royal's eyes baulked again, and his mouth gaped in horror as Morris let go of his lapels.

Chapter Twenty-Three

Ruby settled back in the cab. The afternoon was chilly, and a cool breeze whistled around the hood of the Hanson. Her morning meeting with Mrs Byford had gone extremely well and she welcomed the lightness in her chest coupled with the urgency to tell Arthur everything that had happened.

The horse pulled the carriage along at a steady pace. Ruby watched a small group of children as they played on the side of the street. A woman stood by and roasted chestnuts in an iron skillet. The nutty smell reached Ruby's nostrils, her mouth watered, and her stomach growled to remind her that it was lunchtime. Further down the street, a stall holder sold seasonal vegetables, an array of cabbages, potatoes, parsnips, and carrots. She made a mental note to ask Rose to top up the kitchen provisions.

The church bell chimed twice as she left the sights and sounds of the market behind her and arrived outside the townhouse. As she paid the driver, she was surprised to see Rose standing on the doorstep.

"Rose?" Ruby asked, her brow furrowing with concern.

"You have a visitor, Miss," Rose replied as she followed Ruby up the hallway and took her coat from her shoulders.

An uncomfortable knot of curiosity formed in Ruby's stomach as she wondered who the guest could be. She opened the door to the kitchen to find Polly sitting at the table.

"Polly, what a lovely surprise." Ruby greeted the girl with a broad smile, "How's your mother?"

Polly didn't answer instead she rose from her seat and flung her arms around Ruby's waist and let out a sob.

"Polly, what on earth is the matter?" Ruby pulled another chair out from under the table and ushered Polly into it, then took a seat in one next to her. "Tell me, child, what on earth is making you cry so?" Ruby said gently.

"I'm sorry Miss, it's just that I love this place and you so much, everything was good here, my little room and Rose's cooking," the girl wiped her eyes with the cuff of her sleeve, "Miss Ruby, my mum's gone missing, she's not been seen for two days and I've no idea where to start looking. Mum's friend Paulette isn't too fond of me, and when mum aint about she's quite nasty. So, when she didn't come home two nights back it made Paulette mad because she didn't get her rent off mum, so no money and no gin." Her fingers played with a stray thread on her dress, "it got worse on the second night," she continued, "so I told her that this is where I'd be, I hope you don't mind?" She gave a rapid series of blinks, before wiping her nose on her sleeve, then looked up at Ruby.

Ruby felt a heaviness in her chest as she listened to the small child's sad story. Tears welled up in her eyes, and she was momentarily speechless. "Polly, you did the right thing, you'll stay here until we can find your mother and I will see if I can talk her into coming back here, for a while anyhow, at least until she can find somewhere more suitable than Paulette's." She put her arms around the girl and pulled her into a hug. "Don't you worry now, everything will be all right, have you eaten?"

Polly shook her head.

Ruby noticed that she looked pale. "Well, I'm sure Rose would be more than happy to get you something to eat, wouldn't you Rose?" She glanced across at her housekeeper who had already begun to bring out a joint of boiled ham and a fresh loaf from the pantry.

"Leave it with me, Miss Ruby, we'll get this girl fed in no time." She wrapped an arm around Polly's shoulders and gave her a squeeze before returning to the pantry for more food.

"There now, all will be well, mark my words." Ruby gave the girl a wink. "I'll have one of those sandwiches too, please Rose." She requested as she threw a cheeky grin in Rose's direction, "Well one more mouth won't be too much trouble, will it now?"

Rose glared in mock outrage at Ruby, then clicked her tongue. "Well, I'll just have to see if there's enough to go around then, won't I?" She teased.

Over lunch, the atmosphere was light between the three of them and Ruby took pleasure in seeing Polly relax in her familiar surroundings. Even though she had deep concern for Martha's whereabouts she didn't let that show in an effort to shield Polly. The girl had been through enough.

They were just clearing the table when someone knocked on the front door. Polly rushed out of the room and down the hallway. Ruby silently hoped that it may be the girl's mother at the door. Polly returned with a note in her hand addressed to Ruby.

Polly's face fell; hope had shone in her eyes for a moment, but quickly evaporated when she realized that it wasn't her mother at the door. Ruby watched as the child's shoulders drooped in sadness, and her heart ached for the little girl.

"The boy who bought it is waiting for a reply, Miss," Polly said as she sat back down. Her shoulders drooped again as she did so.

"It's an invitation from Doctor Barnardo," Ruby said, "he'd like me to go for dinner this evening." She put the letter down on the kitchen table.

"It's short notice." Rose had a large mixing bowl on the kitchen table and was pouring milk into it.

“I agree Rose, but I will go along, there are some things that I’d like to talk with him about. Polly, go tell the lad I’d be delighted, and I’ll be along at the time requested and make sure he remembers to thank the Doctor too for his kind invitation.” She called as Polly went back to the front door. “That’s a surprise, Rose,” Ruby said, “I’d been told that the Doctor rarely had dinner guests, so it must be important.” Was it to do with the business at Pickett Street and the children there?

****

A carriage arrived promptly that evening. From the top of the townhouse steps Ruby could see another person inside and assumed it was Barnardo. She walked down to the cobbles and the driver jumped down beside her opening the carriage door, allowing her to climb in. Once inside her heart sank, as she realised it wasn’t the Doctor.

“Who are you?” She asked as her body stiffened. The man appeared unusually tall, although he was sitting. He wore a dark brown tweed suit, a crumpled white shirt and a bow tie fastened at his throat. His hair was swept back on top and combed behind the ears. The skin covering his body was dry, with red, loose, scaley patches. The shoulders of his jacket were peppered with, what Ruby assumed to be, dry skin. The man kept his hands firmly on his thighs, and Ruby noticed that the middle and ring fingers on his left hand were missing. The rest were long and bony with long dirty nails.

“Miss Myers, glad to meet your acquaintance,” he dipped his chin before continuing.

Ruby noticed some of the dry skin fall into his lap with the movement of his head.

"I'm Bullstrode Doctor Barnardo's assistant, he asked me to accompany you on the carriage trip." His green eyes glistened as the lamplight hit them, but they showed no warmth.

"Why did Barnardo send you instead of accompanying me himself?" Ruby demanded, her mistrust evident in her voice. She reached for the door handle, ready to run away from the man and his deceitful promises.

"Miss Myers!" Bullstrode barked, interjecting before she could get away. He gave her a sly smile that sent chills up her spine. "The Doctor will meet us there shortly, I assure you. So just relax and enjoy the ride."

Ruby's body tensed as she pulled a rug over herself, silently screaming inside as she wished she had gone against her better judgement and ran while she had the chance.

They'd been travelling for about two or three minutes when he reached into his pocket. Ruby watched as he pulled a clear glass bottle from his pocket and carefully poured some of the contents onto the handkerchief. Its pleasant, sweet odour hit her nostrils like a punch, and she realized what it was.

Chloroform.

Billy had spoken with her about this stuff before. "You never know when this knowledge will come in useful Miss Ruby." He'd said.

Though every cell in her body screamed for her to run, she stayed motionless, as if glued to the spot, her eyes wide with fear as her chaperone lunged at her. She wanted to scream out, to raise the alarm, but her throat was dry, and her breath had left her body.

He held the drenched handkerchief and lunged at her, his expression unfathomable.

She pushed off the rug and threw herself at the door of the carriage and tugged furiously at the handle. It was jammed.

Before she could turn, he was on her back, an arm around her neck.

She bucked and clawed behind her in an attempt to catch his face.

A knee pushed into her back shoving her closer to the floor of the carriage.

Ruby drove her elbow into his ribs.

Bullstrode let out a groan as the air rushed from his lungs, but his hold tightened.

Her mind whirred.

She had to fight back.

She threw her head back to break his nose. A crack from the cartilage as it broke and a cry from Bullstrode confirmed she was successful.

He forced her onto her side with the full weight of his body. His nose bled, drops of warmth dripping down her cheek as he pressed his cheek against hers. She bucked and tried to escape, but it was no use – he had her pinned.

He threw his leg around her waist, trapping her in a tight grip that grew increasingly tighter. Her heart raced, pounding through the fear that had taken hold of her mind as she unleashed all her energy in one fierce bite on his wrist.

Desperately, she snapped with her teeth and felt the thick flesh yield beneath her hold. He yelled out in pain, yet he still didn't let go.

"You are a fucking bitch!" He breathed harshly into her ear.

Ruby refused to surrender; she had no intention of giving up without a fight. She contorted to reach back and claw desperately towards where she guessed his face should be. But before she could connect, he clamped the handkerchief over her mouth and nose, smothering any words she spoke or screamed under its fabric.

The chloroform worked quickly on Ruby's senses - already, the oily darkness began to set in. She was fuelled only by the desire to survive, she wriggled and kicked viciously until his hand came down with a sharp crack across her face.

She tried to gasp for air, desperately trying to fight back, her limbs weakening. No matter how hard she tried the vapours were too powerful - they slowly paralysed her senses.

As if possessed by some inner strength, Ruby thrashed and kicked with every last ounce of strength left in her body until finally, everything went black.

Chapter Twenty-Four

Abberline grabbed Royal's arm with both hands and tugged him towards him. With the momentum he swung his body onto the top step, and Bernard followed close behind. When they were all on the top step Bernard fell to the floorboards and cursed loudly. Fred bent and placed his hands on his knees and rubbed them up and down in slow circles as he tried to catch his breath. The creak of the wood beneath his feet filled the silence.

Morris looked at Abberline and then at Royal, who had regained some composure, before saying, "I need another drink." He returned to his office and stood pouring himself another whiskey. His face impassive.

Abberline walked up to Morris' desk, "what the hell were you thinking?" He didn't wait for him to answer, "You could have killed him." He turned to see if Royal had moved off the step. He hadn't.

Bernard sat with his back against the banister, sweat ran down his face as he continued to tremble.

Abberline returned his attention to Morris who had sat down in his seat. "Well?"

Morris just shrugged and then folded his arms.

Fred shook his head and walked out to the stairs. "C'mon Bernard stand up." He watched his colleague stand. "You need to go back to the station and sober up, in fact, I'd advise you to buy some strong coffee first. I'll be along shortly to discuss what has transpired here today." Abberline said.

"I'll have that bastard at the end of a rope, you mark my words." Royal spat as he balanced on unsteady legs.

Abberline turned, "Get back to the fucking station now, Royal, I won't say it again." He shouted, his eyes cold and flinty, as his nostrils flared again.

Royal didn't argue just returned a hard stare, then walked down the stairs.

Moments later Abberline heard the door of the pub open and then close. He let out a sigh as his shoulders sagged, before sitting down in the same chair he'd occupied before.

Morris surveyed him with hooded eyes. "I wanted him dead." He said, his voice monotone.

"Mr Morris, I'm not going to sit back whilst you pick off my colleagues one by one. Firstly, I'd need to arrest you for murder, secondly, there's more to Inspector Bernard Royal than you're aware." Abberline held Morris' stare as he spoke. "Thirdly, I need you to help me bring this mess to a conclusion and you can't do that from inside a jail cell."

"More to him than I'm aware," Morris repeated, "he's bent, isn't he? Well, then it's no different to most of the coppers in this city." Morris looked directly at Abberline then shrugged again. "Known fact." He concluded.

"I hope that you aren't insinuating that I am like most of these coppers?" Abberline asked.

"If the cap fits." Morris drained his glass and stood up for a refill. "What, you expect me to tiptoe around you after what I've done?" He said as he poured himself another, "Not going to happen, that piece of shit has been on my case for years and if he'd broken his neck that would've solved a lot of problems for me." Morris stood by the oak table with one hand in his pocket and the glass in the other.

Abberline contemplated his next move. Should he know about Royal? Would it help? He bit his bottom lip in thought. Until "Mr Morris, there are many things I'm aware of and one of those things is corrupt officers. You may like to think that I'm one of those, but underneath you know that to be untrue. You're angry because I saved his sorry arse and, in the process, I saved you from going to the gallows. Don't worry, he will be dealt with along with the other cretins that pollute the force, but my main concern right now is to catch the bastard that is roaming the streets. I know right deep in my marrow that you and Miss Myers have absolutely nothing to do with these murders and if it costs me my career, I will see to it that you are both kept out of it. However," he paused and looked at Morris over his glasses, "until such times that we are able to catch this madman I'm asking you to continue to help me and trust me to deal with Royal as I see fit once this situation has been brought to its conclusion."

Morris downed his drink and then put the empty glass down on the table. He stood with his feet planted wide and his arms folded. "Inspector Abberline, how many times do you think I've heard that, one copper outing another?" He let the question float without an answer, "too many, and frankly I've no reason to trust you any more than I trust any other copper," he perched himself on the edge of his desk before continuing, "That said, I have to admit I like you and although it troubles me, I do trust you and I also believe that what you're saying you mean it, but if you're playing me Abberline I won't hesitate to do exactly what I deem necessary to protect me and Miss Myers."

"Mr Morris," Abberline began, "as I said before you have my word and that is all I can offer you. Now, if you'll excuse me, I've one angry, drunk Inspector to deal with. Oh, just one more thing I should share with you, Inspector Royal had a human tongue sent to him via the post."

Morris frowned.

Abberline raised his hand, "It's already been identified by Doctor Sequeira as the one missing from one of the victims. It had a card with it saying," Abberline glanced down at his notebook and flipped a page, "*Whoever watches his mouth and tongue keeps himself from trouble.* Lord alone only knows who sent it and what it means, but my gut instinct is telling me one thing and one thing only and is that is that it isn't good." Abberline pushed his notebook back into his coat pocket and slid his glasses into the inside of his jacket.

"Or it could be from the murderer, some sort of sick game." Morris rubbed his chin in thought.

"Anything is possible Mr Morris, but sadly, one way or another Royal's time in the force is numbered. Thank you for your time today, I can only apologise on behalf of my colleague for his behaviour, but I'm thankful that he didn't end up down the bottom of the stairs as the outcome would've been entirely different." He walked to the door, "I'll be in touch."

Abberline descended the stairs, his heart heavy, and his mind felt like he had a thousand bees buzzing around in it. Tired. Dog tired. Sleep seemed like a luxury he could ill afford right now, but something had to give, and he had no intention of letting either situation resolve itself. "Hang in there it'll all be concluded soon," he muttered to himself as he trudged down the street in the direction of the station.

Chapter Twenty-Five

Arthur sat in his office contemplating. The correspondence he'd received that day went unread. He'd eaten a small late lunch not because he was hungry, but to soak up the whiskey. Now he needed to see Ruby.

He stretched, stood, picked up his empty plate and went down the stairs.

Eddie was in his usual place. The pub had filled up and he was busy serving punters. "You off Mr Morris?" Eddie passed a tankard to a slightly inebriated man and picked up the coin that the fella had pushed across the counter.

Arthur nodded in reply, left his plate on the bar then made his way outside. The night had drawn in quickly and a frost was already visible on the cobbles. He quickened his pace and nodded politely at the people he passed.

Half an hour later he arrived at the townhouse. He walked up the steps and knocked on the door.

Rose let him in, "Miss Ruby isn't here Mr Morris, she was asked to dinner by Doctor Bernardo, earlier today." She said as he followed her through the hallway and into the kitchen.

"Lucky Doctor Bernardo, then," Arthur said as he picked up the newspaper from the table and sat down in an armchair near the fire. "I'll be here for the night anyhow Rose." He said absentmindedly as he read the top story on the front page.

The back door opened, and Polly came in, her face sallow.

A cold blast of air hit Arthur's ankles and he glanced up from the paper. "Hello Polly, nice to see you." He remembered his previous conversation with Abberline as he asked the next question. "How's mum?"

"Hello Mr Morris, my mum has gone missing, it's been a few days since I've spoken with her. You haven't, have you?" Polly looked hopeful as she asked the question.

Rose glanced across at the child with a frown on her face. "Miss Ruby says she can stay here until her mum shows up Mr Morris."

"Well, that's very nice of Miss Ruby. I'm afraid I've not Polly," Arthur said, his voice heavy with worry. He shifted in his seat and rubbed his temples before his eyes locked with Rose's and gave her a discreet shake of the head.

Rose's hand flew to her chest and her face went pale.

"Try not to worry yourself, now off to bed with you, get some rest, you look like you need an early night." Arthur said to the girl, who nodded before slowly walking down the corridor at the back of the kitchen and shutting the door to her room.

Taking a deep breath, Arthur turned to Rose.

"Do you know something, Mr Morris?" Rose asked in a quiet voice from where she sat at the table. She nervously clasped her hands in front of her. "Is it bad news?"

“I don't know for sure Rose, but a body was found in Drury Lane and the suspicion is that it could be Martha, but Abberline won't jump to conclusions yet." He gestured anxiously toward the folded newspaper on his lap before continuing. "He asked me to go and confirm if it was, but it went out of my head. An unpleasant task, but I'll go along to the mortuary in the morning."

Rose gasped at his words and clasped her hand over her mouth. "Oh, good lord," she murmured in distress. "The poor child, I do hope it's not her; it would devastate the girl."

“That’s if it is her, and there’s no confirmation that it is.” Arthur pinched the bridge of his nose. “It’s been a long day Rose, I’m going to turn in too." He stood up and threw the newspaper onto the table, “I was going to wait up for Miss Ruby but I’m dead on my feet.” He walked to the kitchen door. “I’ll see you in the morning and we won’t say anything to Polly just in case it isn’t her mother.”

“Whatever you say, Mr Morris, good night to you. I’ll get Polly her coco then I’m off to bed myself.”

“Good night, Rose.”

He made his way to the bedroom, sat down in the chair next to the fireplace and slipped off his shoes. Once under the covers, he lay on his back staring at the ceiling, his mind whirred, and his stomach knotted, something didn’t feel right. Arthur tossed and turned until he finally fell into a restless sleep.

Just after midnight he turned over and realised that Ruby's side of the bed was empty. Concerned he rose, slipped on some trousers, and made his way into the kitchen to see if she were there. She wasn't. Strange.

The kitchen felt icy and the embers in the fireplace glowed with a sickly light. He grasped a small log, almost too tightly in his hands before throwing it on with force. Sparks flew as the flames spat and hissed before erupting into an almighty roar that filled the room with both welcome heat and a sweltering tension.

A crashing sound filtered through to Arthur from the hallway, reverberating down the corridor like an explosion of thunder. His heart raced and he froze in place, trying desperately to listen for anything more. But all was still again.

He inched forward cautiously until he reached the stairs and checked the front sitting room for any signs of activity. Nothing. When he turned back towards the kitchen, something caught his eye on the mat by the front door. He bent and fumbled with shaking hands, unfolding a note and some rolled-up material.

Back in the kitchen he lit the oil lamp on the table and unrolled the cloth. His blood ran cold.

Ruby's evening glove.

Arthur's hands trembled as he picked up the note and brought it nearer to the light. The handwriting was untidy, but legible.

Mr Morris, We hav yur girl. Ewe want her to live then call off the pigs. Will send word wiv moor instructions.

He pounded his fist against Rose's bedroom door, crushing the paper in his fist. "Rose, wake up NOW!" His voice echoed through the house as he waited for a response. Finally, he heard movement from her room followed by a faint groan. His heart raced and his fists clenched tightly as he paced the kitchen waiting for Rose to join him. An acidic taste filled his mouth making him feel nauseous. He swallowed hard in an effort to quell the uneasiness that crept up into his throat as he tried to comprehend what had happened. Beads of sweat trickled down his face and his entire body felt heavy and cold.

Arthur slammed the note back down on the table and he whirled around as he heard a shuffling of feet, desperately hoping it was Ruby. “Rose, we need to do something.” He grabbed her upper arms tightly, his words tumbling out in a rush. “Somebody took Ruby, Rose! Someone has her, look at the note!” His arm pointed wildly towards the table.

Rose blinked stupidly as Arthur's news hit her over the head like a pan. With trepidation, she stepped forward to inspect the glove also laying on the tabletop. "Mr Morris, what is this... Is this one of Miss Ruby's evening gloves?" She glanced between him and the table nervously.

Arthur snatched up the note and shoved it into Rose's hands roughly. "R… read it," he spluttered breathlessly. He furrowed his brows and began to pace, raking his fingers through his hair.

Her eyes skated quickly over the paper before gasping in surprise, "Oh my god!" She threw the note back down and began to frantically walk back up the hallway. "We must inform the police immediately! Get Inspector Abberline here- we can't just stand here doing nothing!" She paused for a moment and then spun on her heels towards her room. "I'll get dressed." With that, she disappeared within its walls.

Arthur's heart pounded so loud he can feel it in his ears. His Ruby, taken - he couldn't bear the thought of her being hurt.

Rose, once dressed, wanted to go to Abberline's house herself, but Arthur refused. "I need you here Rose." He said, but Arthur was finding it hard to focus. "Rose, I need to find her. Now." He stormed out of the room and headed to Ruby's parlour.

Arthur frantically rummaged through Ruby's parlour, every creak of the floorboards heightening his racing pulse. Every tiny movement appeared amplified which ricocheted off the walls like an invisible prison. With bated breath, he finally stumbled upon the invitation from earlier and snatched it up, determined to compare the writing to the one on the kitchen table. His hands trembled uncontrollably as he forced himself back into the main hallway - this wasn't a game anymore, this was life or death for Ruby.

Carefully scrutinizing both documents, he noticed a stark difference between the two; the first was written with finesse, each letter formed properly, and words spelled correctly, contrasting sharply with the sloppily scrawled second piece. “Fuck,” he cursed, “they’re not the same. Look Rose.”

Rose stepped up beside him and looked down at the table. “They’re very different, Mr Morris.” She agreed.

"Rose," Arthur mutters darkly, "we're running out of time.”

“So, do you think that Dr Barnardo has something to do with this, Mr Morris?” Rose asked.

Arthur’s lip curled, and he nodded his head.

“But why would Barnardo chase after Miss Myers? All she did was donate some money.” Rose voiced her confusion.

“There was more to the conversation than that, Rose." Arthur snapped.

Arthur stared off into the distance, preparing himself for whatever lay ahead. His mind raced with questions- so many questions- and he knew it would take more than just a cup of tea to find the answers. He returned to the bedroom and threw on the rest of his clothes and then marched down the hallway. "I need the boys and a lot of tea if we're going to get to the bottom of this.” He said as he shrugged on his coat.

The night sky loomed dark and menacing, like a portent of all the horror in store for Arthur. The icy cold air bit at his skin, every breath he exhaled hanging in the still ether like a casket lid being nailed shut. His feet sank into the freezing blanket of frost that coated the cobbles, each step a reminder of the pain and suffering Ruby must be enduring. In his mind's eye he saw her struggling against unspeakable acts, the thought too unbearable to contemplate in full.

He finally reached Billy's door and pounded it with desperate fists. Moments later it was flung open, and his dozy-looking friend stood on the threshold.

"Fuck Arthur, I thought I was being raided again." Billy rubbed a hand over his face doing his best to shake off the last dregs of slumber. "Jeez man, you look like death warmed up, what's happened, you'd better come in." He stepped aside and allowed Arthur inside.

Arthur slammed the front door behind him and stalked into Billy's living room, his breathing staccato and harsh with barely contained rage. He spat out a string of words with venomous intent, "It's business time! I need to call in some favours from our associates that only money can buy - and there'll be a hefty reward waiting for whoever gets me those bastards." His words were an unstoppable avalanche of sound.

"Whoa, Arthur - take a step back," Billy threw up his hands defensively, "What the fu-"

Arthur didn't give him time to finish, "It's Ruby, some bastard has got Ruby."

Chapter Twenty-Six

Penny Royal glanced furtively around her as she hurried down the street, a single envelope clutched tightly in her hand. She had been afraid to leave the house for weeks, terrified of what Bernard might do if he discovered that she had gone out. Even now, she couldn't help but look over her shoulder every few steps, imagining his wrath should he encounter her here. As she approached the pillar box and dropped the letter inside, a wave of relief swept over her. Soon Mildred Byford would receive it, along with the one for Miss Myers; this time tomorrow the deed would be done.

As she hurried towards home, Penny remembered the looming presence that awaited her. Her heart sank at the thought of his coldness and austere instruction. Intimacy was expected of her, but if any emotion showed on her part, there would be consequences - an arm raised or a belt thrown in anger, followed by intense pain and silence. Despite wanting to cry out with every strike, she never did; not knowing if it could mean the difference between life and death.

Penny stepped inside the house, her heart racing with fear and anticipation. She had to keep herself safe, so she would slide her spare key back under her mattress before her husband would find it.

Her feet stumbled over the black and white checkerboard tiles of the hallway, as she charged up to the top floor. Each tile reminded her of a painful memories- ones that was inflicted by him, and each of them could never be forgotten.

She knew the consequences if she were to stray and venture outside alone, but here she was, unlawfully climbing the stairs of a place she had sworn never to leave. As her feet pounded against each tread board, her heart raced faster with each step, pushing her forward.

She could hear the sound of his voice echoing throughout the walls, a faint whisper that reverberated through her mind. He was everywhere. A haunting presence that she could feel deep in her bones. Each bruise had now run so deep it tainted the marrow. She craved constant slumber as this was the only place, he couldn't get to her. Her solace was now in her dreams, her only place of safety.

When she reached the last step, Penny paused outside a heavy wooden door, struggling to breathe as her stomach churned. Taking a deep breath, she opened it and immediately felt a wave of relief come over her – this was where all her pain ended. This was where he allowed her to have privacy to recover from his beatings or when she needed a break from looking at his face. But despite that feeling of relief, Penny couldn't help but also feel conflicted knowing he had given her this space.

The room was tiny but welcoming. A single bed was pushed against one wall and a small bureau sat in the corner with various family photos atop it. But not one of their wedding day. The wooden floor was bare, except for a small rug beside the bed that had been crafted from some of the fabric of her wedding gown. It was now as trampled as she had been for all these years.

The faded yellow wallpaper, tinged with a hint of floral pattern clung desperately to the walls. Plans for the nursery were as just as worn-out as the décor. Yet she felt an odd sense of comfort as she stared at it. Thoughts of the children that could've made this house a home filled her heart with both sorrow and joy. She felt comforted in knowing that these unborn souls would always be a part of her life, yet also haunted by the possibility of what might have been.

Her body was a graveyard of unborn infants, a bleak reminder of her failure to carry them to term. She had lost count of the number of times she had become pregnant, only for the child to be ripped away from her by another beating. A part of her heart ached with the loss, but another side was filled with an unexplainable relief that she wouldn't have to share them with him. In the end, it was easier to grieve alone than for them to suffer at his hands. They were safer this way.

On her bed lay an old, tattered pillow that Penny had kept from her childhood. It was here that she would spend her days; here that she could cry without fear of interruption from him or anyone else.

But as comforting as this room was to Penny, it wasn't enough. After all these years of abuse from him, she knew it was time for her to escape his grasp once and for all. The final straw had been discovering his unspoken past. She spent many nights planning her getaway, down to the last detail.

Letters written to her sister and Miss Myers explaining everything would be his demise. He didn't think she knew about the other women, but he underestimated how much Penny did know. She lay in wait when he had guests for dinner, skulking through the shadows and lurking outside the study. When his guests left, she silently crept in and started searching through his papers until she found something damning.

When her suspicions were confirmed, she teetered between trying to ignore them or confronting him. As the night went on and the more, he drank, she felt emboldened and finally decided to take a chance. She apprehensively asked him about his secrets, pressing further when he gave her vague answers. At last, she had uncovered his past from the depths of a deep, dark heart.

Disgusting, vile man, soon everyone would know the depravity her husband was willing to sink to for his own pleasure. She would not be here to see his world implode, and with enough courage and careful planning, she knew she would finally be free.

After bathing she reached for her best dress, the one with the shorter sleeves that he never let her wear. Penny's fingers trembled as she pulled the frilly, lace garment over her head. She felt a surge of repulsion as she remembered the shredded tatters of what remained of her wedding gown lying discarded on the bed in Bernard's chamber. She changed the bed linen but left off the over-blankets. Stark white sheets would be fine.

Reaching over to the bedside table, she grasped the small glass bottle filled with laudanum - a potion she had saved for months from doctor visits and feigned ailments. With one swift motion, Penny lifted it to her lips and finished the contents in a single gulp. A warm wave of comfort and freedom washed through her body as a gentle smile spread across her face for the first time in years.

As her eyelids began to droop, she lay down on the bed. The white cotton smooth and cool against her skin. She let out a sigh as she closed her eyes, feeling like a new mother who needs the comfort of sleep after giving birth. "I'll be there soon my darlings," she said as she settled herself.

Penny knew that soon she would be somewhere far away - a place where Bernard could no longer haunt her, a place he would never go, a place to be with her lost children.

That place for her was eternal paradise.

Chapter Twenty-Seven

Arthur and his fourteen cohorts were gathered around the worn wooden table in the kitchen townhouse, their faces a mix of grim determination and anxiety. Rose scurried about madly, keeping the group sustained with tea and hastily made sandwiches. As soon as news broke that one of their own had been taken, they all converged like a storm. Rage ran through the cracks of the old townhouse walls where they had chosen to plot their revenge.

Billy had worked quickly to spread the word through the seedy underworld of locals that a generous reward was being offered for any information about Ruby's whereabouts. He was Arthur's trusted ally and could sense when Arthur needed time alone to grapple with his overwhelming fear. He could feel Billy watching closely from the shadows, keeping the other associates away from him. Arthur tried to make sure none of the other associates would notice his desperate attempts to feign strength, but Billy saw the brokenness that lurked beneath his hardened exterior.

Arthur knew if he showed any signs of weakness or vulnerability around his cohorts, it would soon be used against him in an attempt to unsettle him further. So, he forced himself to put on a brave face, toughing out the hours that dragged by. The ticking of the clock stretched out the dwindling chances of finding her alive.

The usually bustling underworld network had gone silent. No one had even a whisper of where Ruby might be. All that was heard were the distant echoes of voices and occasional gunshots, ringing from the city streets below. Time dragged on endlessly, each day feeling longer than the last as desperation began to set in.

Arthur returned to the pub silently hoping that he would hear something amongst the regulars. He stood at the bar drinking his third whiskey of the day when one of the local wagtails approached him.

"No punters out tonight, Daisy?" He asked. "Look, I'm not in the mood to be talking to anyone. Come see me tomorrow if it's a loan you're in need of." Arthur didn't turn in her direction, just rotated the half-full glass around in his fingers as he lent on the wooden surface.

"I have some urgent news for you, Mr Morris," Daisy said in a tone laden with concern that made Arthur stand upright and focus his attention on her. A curtain of long, dark hair obscured one side of her face. A stronghold of disfigurement, the marks having been left by a street fight that had happened three years before. The other side, however, showed the rest of her delicate features. Clove-scented breath filled the air as she spoke, her blue eyes trained on the ground beneath their feet. "Rumours about your girl are floating around town. We can't talk here; let's go out back."

Arthur nodded and headed towards the rear of the pub. He tugged aside a heavy velvet curtain to reveal a dimly lit room. As the patrons jeered and cheered him on, Arthur simply glanced towards the ceiling and declared, "There's only one girl for me, lads - you all know that!" Then he stepped through the curtain with Daisy close behind him.

With a steady yet determined hand, Arthur reached out and grabbed a glass of clear liquid from Eddie, who had predetermined Arthur's thoughts and followed them both into the room. "Thanks, Eddie." He said as he looked at it and then at Daisy. His voice was like steel as he uttered the question, "Talk to me Daisy, what've you heard?"

Without hesitation, Daisy seized the glass. She brought it close to her mouth and took a long, hard gulp. Her gaze still locked with Arthur's, she watched in silence as Eddie backed out of the room. She downed it in one then handed the glass back to Arthur.

"What's the price for what you know?" He asked irritation evident in his voice.

She kept her head low, too ashamed to face him. "Sorry to press you, Mr Morris, but..." Her body quivered, wrestling with discomfort as she shuffled from one foot to the other.

"If you give me the information, I need then I can waive your loan, chuck in enough gin and a wad of cash to make it worth your while." Arthur watched as her features hardened at his response.

"That much just to help get your lady back? You must really care about her?" Daisy risked a glance up in an attempt to read his expression.

Arthur leaned forward, desperation lacing his words. “Daisy, just start talking.”

“I was servicing a couple of punters last night in an alley just down Caldwell Street. We were stood quite a way back so that we couldn’t be seen by their ladies. The two blokes were pretty out of it, I know that because one had problems finishing you see.” She glanced up quickly and then looked away again, the terror radiating from her pale face palpable.

“Yes, yes, I get the picture, Daisy, then what happened?” Arthur folded his arms across his chest and chewed the inside of his cheek.

“Well, his mate was having his turn when two other blokes stepped into the alleyway, I could just about see that one was a really tall fella, they didn’t realise we were there as we were quite a way down.”

“I’ll stop you there, Daisy, what'd these fellas look like, you say one was really tall, what about the other?”

“I couldn't really see them too well to be honest Mr Morris, the alley was dark, and I was down on my knees for the second bloke, but I could hear them talking. One of them called the other Bullstrode or something, he didn’t say as much at first, but his deep gravelly voice filled me with dread as he warned if Miss Myers plays up anymore then he’d plant one on her and it would be better if they kept her out of it...whatever it is.”

Arthur's heart pounded as he ruminated on the potential consequences of their actions. He felt his own terror mounting with each passing second. All Arthur could focus on was the thought of what might be happening to his beloved Ruby.

“Did they happen to mention where Miss Myers is being held?” Arthur stormed over to the curtain and pulled it back. “Eddie give me a drink.”

"No, they didn't say where she was," Daisy answered quickly, her lips white from where she gnawed them. "But they did say that she was in some derelict building outside town. Could be anywhere." Her voice trailed off and she rubbed her lip, her eyes narrowing as she thought. "I did hear the tall one use the other's first name. Barney? Bobby? Something like that."

Arthur leaned forward; his drink suspended in mid-air. "Bernard?" he said carefully.

Daisy bit her lip and nodded slowly, her expression twisting in concentration. Her hands trembled as she clasped them together, the skin around her knuckles going white as she spoke. "I think so Mr Morris, but my memory's a bit foggy on the details." She glanced up at him quickly, her face betraying a mixture of determination for more money and fear in her eyes.

“Ok, Daisy, I’ll add a little more cash if you tell me everything,” Arthur wiped his mouth with the back of his hand then drained his glass, “and?” He asked as his eyes bore down on the girl.

“Yes, sir, it was Bernard, but he didn’t use a last name, although he did say he’d be at the pigsty if needed.”

“Don’t need one, I know who the bastard is. Thank you, Daisy, I’ll settle up with you in a day or so, I need to get this problem sorted first.”

“I’ll be back a day after tomorrow, Mr Morris.” She said as she walked towards the velvet curtain, “and Mr Morris?”

“Yes, Daisy.”

“I do hope you get her home safe and well.” The woman said as she disappeared back into the bar.

“So do I,” Arthur said to himself as he rushed to the back door.

Arthur gathered together his most trusted contacts in the cellar of the pub. With plans in place and urgency pushing them on, he and his fourteen associates hurriedly loaded up into two carts. The team was made up of some of the most formidable figures in their network, and their speed did not waver; when it came to one of their own, they operated with conscience-clearing speed. They now had an idea where Ruby had been taken, and they were determined to get to her before the person or persons holding her did their worse. Each derelict building would be searched, and it didn’t matter how long it would take, they’d tear each place apart until they found her.

The night was icy and tense, the impending storm of violence hung thickly in the air. One by one, the gang members armed themselves with lead pipes, bats, and knives. One by one they stepped forward into the dim glow of a single gas lamp, if there were more captors, they still wouldn’t be a match for this aggressive show of force.

The darkness of the street felt oppressive and heavy, a tangible reminder that something was coming. The air seemed to crackle with anticipation as Arthur clenched and unclenched his fists. He would get justice for what had been done to his girl no matter what it took.

"Arthur?" Billy's voice cut through the night like thunder, jolting Arthur out of his thoughts as Billy reached out and slapped a comforting hand on Arthur's shoulder. "She'll be alright mate," he said, reassurance rang in his voice. "We'll have her free afore you can say lightning, I promise."

Arthur nodded slowly, determination written all over his face. The hardened lines of his face softened, just a little. Billy was dependable; he always had been, and right now Arthur needed nothing more than to trust in him. He knew that if Billy said they'd do it, then they'd do it. He said nothing just scoured the streets for any signs of life. The only movement coming from the occasional gust of wind that snaked through the city like a wraith.

"Arthur, I've been thinking about the derelict buildings nearest to town, there's an old slaughterhouse, a disused dairy and an abandoned farm that might be worth checking first." Billy's voice boomed out into the night. "If there's no luck with those, then we'll put our heads together and think of some others."

Arthur nodded solemnly, "Thanks Billy." He said blinking slowly.

The ground trembled beneath the cartwheels as they rounded a sharp left turn in the road. In the distance, the towering brick building loomed like a monster, its flaked white paint resembling scales. On top of it sat a roof with broken tiles scattered across it, reminding them of a gaping mouth filled with missing teeth.

Billy and Arthur leapt down from the wagon bringing the convoy to a halt with a raise of Billy's clenched fist. They moved quickly now, gathering the group of rebels around them with a whisper in the darkness. "This is the old slaughterhouse; they may have Miss Ruby hidden inside. Me and Billy are going to sneak in through this gap in the hedge here, take a look around and to see what we're up against, if she's here then we'll be back for you guys. Got it?" Arthur's eyes darted between each member of the gang, daring anyone to question his decision as he spoke. They nodded agreement; some mumbled a quiet 'ok Arthur' as he and Billy sprinted away.

The two men forced their way through the thicket, the foliage clawing at their clothes like a raving madman desperate to trap them in its grip. They cowered against the brick wall of the building, scurrying along until they reached its end. Arthur peered out cautiously to take in his surroundings - an open courtyard with several old stables, their doors left wide open as if beckoning them inside. All that could be heard was the muffled sound of wind whistling through the stark silence.

The walls of the main slaughterhouse were stained brown from the blood of livestock, the floors grey from the ashes of the coal furnaces that once burned day and night. The stench of the abattoir was absent, overgrown with the subtle scents of drying blood and impending death. The wood in the rafters creaked and groaned as if protesting the pain, it was forced to bear as the wind blew around the outside of the building.

Arthur snapped his fingers sharply and gestured for Billy to go in the other direction so they could explore each side. In a flash they ran off into separate directions, frantically searching each building before reuniting back at the hedge and re-joining the rest of the group.

Solomon Hardy, a man of medium height with an eye patch covering a missing eye, stood across from Arthur. Despite their opposing views on the way the network should be run, they had developed an unspoken respect for each other over the past decade. Solomon had always been loyal to Arthur and supported him whenever he needed it. He had also made it clear in the early days that he was interested in Ruby, though when he realised, she wanted Arthur, he stepped back and admired her silently from afar. "Well?" Solomon asked, his face void of expression.

Arthur shook his head, "Nothing mate."

"Where next Bill?" Solomon asked.

"There's a disused dairy 'bout a mile or so down the road, most of the place was burnt down in a fire, but there's a couple of buildings that could still be used. We'll check there next."

The ruined farm was built from thick stone, cracks had appeared through the weight of time and rubble was scattered around like breadcrumbs. Several wooden beams protruded from the upper portions. The roof, a tangle of collapsed beams and spires, which sagged in the middle. Outside the building tall grasses, overrun by weeds. The wreckage of the wooden fence lead to a small pond most likely used to water the cattle.

A single window stared out at the front of the building like a cyclops and stopped three feet from the ground. A shingle hung over the opening, its rusting nails threatening to pull away at any moment.

Although the fire had been a long time extinguished, Arthur could still smell the smoke in the air and taste the charcoal on his tongue.

Empty.

He trudged back to the group, his mind now sluggish with fatigue. They had to keep searching. In the sky was a half-moon tracing a crescent against a charcoal sky, not quite eclipsed, but Arthur wasn't sure if it was an optical illusion, or a trick of the wind. He was so cold and could see the air, like a crystal curtain, jagged icy needles, all frozen in place, no movement, no sound. It was as if mother nature understood what was happening.

"We need to keep searching, now!" he growled, his voice seething with urgency as he desperately tried to shake off the tiredness. "It'll be daylight soon and it'll be harder to surprise them."

With a single powerful leap, he grabbed onto the edge of the wagon seat and effortlessly hoisted himself up. He barked orders like a raptor, "C'mon then...let's go!"

Billy snapped the reins and the cart lurched forward in an instant.

About four miles from town, they followed a dirt road with overhanging tree branches and weeds that lined the edge of the road. In the dim moonlight, they pulled up to an old farmhouse with shutters hanging lopsidedly from its windows and the smell of mouldy thatch heavy in the air. Arthur's chest tightened as he felt anticipation rising inside him. He felt a surge of relief when he noticed some light coming from one of the windows. This had to be the place.

As the posse descended from the carts, they moved like ghosts in the night, taking care not to make a sound. They had hidden their horses and wagons far away from the target, so they could approach with the element of surprise. Arthur and Billy were leading the charge, their hearts pounding with anticipation as adrenaline surged through their veins. They spread out among the group, some guarding the entrances while others would go inside.

Arthur gripped a lead pipe tightly in his hand, ready for whatever lay ahead. His eyes scanned the shadows for any sign of movement as he prepared himself for what was sure to be a vicious fight. "Get some of thc lads to check the perimeter of the building, I want to make sure there's no others." He watched Billy take three of the group with him and kept low to the ground until he came back.

"All clear Arthur, there are no others around." Billy reported.

The group crept forward, crouching low so they wouldn't be seen. Arthur snuck a quick glance up at the window, and he could see Ruby slumped on a chair in the corner of the room, her hands and feet were bound. Arthur's temper spiked, he ground his teeth and his knuckles whitened as he gripped the lead pipe tighter. Desperation to get to his girl burned inside him, like acid on his skin.

At a table in the centre were three men, their playing cards scattered across the wood. Several empty bottles and three glasses filled with an amber liquid surrounded them – likely whiskey from the smell that wafted out from the crack in the window. There were three that sat at the only table, the room was dark and smoke-filled, only the candles lighting the area. They all had grimy hands and tattered clothes, two had grey beards, and one was clean-shaven, but neither looked overly tall. They all shared the same eyes empty of all hope and care. The one without facial hair had a scar on his left cheek. As Arthur looked up, he saw he was also missing an ear. This shouldn't be too hard.

Arthur clenched his jaw, surveying the door. It was aged and strained, nearly broken in two. His raised a fist to the group, counted down from three with his fingers and then charged.

The door shattered open, emitting a deep groan as it flew off its rusty hinges. The three people inside jumped from their table in surprise, but the group had them outnumbered four to one.

"What the fu-" the man with the scar and missing ear shouted.

"Run," one of the others yelled.

One of the captors stepped forward and raised his fist, but before he could make a move, Billy swung a lead pipe at him with lightning speed. The man screamed as it collided with his forearm and shattered the bone, with a sickening crunch. "Shut up you prick," Billy seethed. "That's nothing to what's coming."

The smaller of the trio lunged at Ruby, grabbing her violently from the chair and pressing her against him. Arthur could see a cold glint in his eyes and a cruel smirk on his lips as he jammed a homemade shank against her neck. Ruby's body trembled with every panicked breath she took, unable to move or open her eyes.

“Don't even think of it!” Arthur growled through gritted teeth. “If you harm one hair on her head, I will make you regret the day you were born!”

The man started to drag Ruby towards the door, his voice laced with a thick menace. “You have your warning, gangster prick. Get out of my way now and let me go before I carve a flute out of your whore's throat!"

Amid the turmoil, the man holding Ruby didn't notice another of the posse approach from behind.

Arthur kept his eyes trained on Ruby, giving no clue of what he knew would happen next.

The man screamed in torture as his back arched sharply, stiffly releasing his grip on Ruby. His wild eyes grew wider until the horrifying sound of his voice abruptly stopped, and he crumpled to the ground with a sickening thud, an axe protruding from between his shoulder blades. His attacker behind him moved quickly, catching Ruby before she could hit the floor and pulling her close to his chest.

Arthur sprinted towards her; she hadn't moved an inch with the commotion. He could only hope she was still alive. With his heart pounding, he touched her gently, like a feather falling on a millpond. Relief flooded through him when she stirred in response to his touch and opened her eyes slightly with a weak smile upon seeing him. “I'm so glad it's you," she whispered before she closed her eyes again.

“Take them out to the carts, I want them alive!” Arthur shouted to the others sternly. "They'll all pay for this, our way." He tucked his hands underneath Ruby's fragile body and lifted her into his arms, with purposeful strides he headed out the door, while the other lads stepped aside to let him pass.

He climbed into the cart holding her to him and lay her down covering her with his coat. Arthur's expression hardened - he'd never seen her like this. He approached one of the men, who was sat with the two others in the first wagon, lunged forward and grabbed him by the ear, snarling in rage.

“Tell me what you’ve given her, and you'll keep your ear, for now.”

The man spat defiantly right in Arthur's face.

Billy stepped forward, eyes blazing with anger.

“That was a stupid thing to do,” Arthur glanced in Billy’s direction as he wiped his face with the back of his hand, “Billy, his ear.”

The man thrashed and writhed against his bindings, but it was to no avail. In one swift stroke, Billy brandished a gleaming blade from his pocket and cut off the man's ear with a single slice before dropping it into the man's lap. The man screamed in agony and terror as he surveyed the grisly sight of severed flesh resting on his thighs. "You're one sick son of a bitch! What kind of monster would do such a thing?" he roared.

Arthur drew even closer and bared his teeth in fury. "'What have you given her? I asked once, but you didn't answer then. So, tell me or I'll take the other ear," he growled. The man's clothes were covered with blood from the wound, but still, his eyes were cold and defiant. "Go to hell you gangster prick and your whore!" he spat in contempt.

Arthur had heard enough, took the blade from Billy, yanked the man's head back and forced the blade up under his chin. As Arthur pulled the blade free, the man's eyes rolled up into his head and his body slid sideways in the cart, he gargled for a few seconds then was still.

The two other men backed away, trembling as their round eyes peered at Arthur in fear. "Please Mister, let me go, I didn't want anything to do with this anyhow." One begged.

Arthur took a step in his direction, and the man flinched instinctively, trying to escape his grasp. It was futile.

"I'll ask you then, what've you given her?" Arthur queried, gripping onto the blade so tightly that his knuckles started to turn white. Just as he was about to lunge forward, the man quickly responded.

“Cocaine, Mister, she kicked up such a fuss that we figured it would be wiser to give her something to keep her quiet.” He averted his gaze from Arthur's intimidating presence.

“Wiser for who? You or her?” Arthur wiped the blade on a spot of the dead man's garments that was still untainted with blood. “How much?” The knife travelled back and forth between his hands as he manipulated the weapon in the hope of getting an answer out of him.

The man cleared his throat before continuing. “Just enough to keep her asleep, not enough to yah know, kill her.” He glanced back at the other man sitting motionlessly in the corner of the cart, who shook his head at him, snarling with disapproval. “Coward.”

Arthur bared his teeth and dragged the long blade against the man's face, carving another deep gash along the other side of his face. He screamed in agony as his blood spilled down his features, staining his shirt, and dripping onto the wooden boards of the cart.

“You vicious bastard.” He screamed as he bought his hand to the gaping wound.

Arthur looked at him and grinned, “You have a matching pair now, and that’s taster of what will be happening to you. Keep quiet and I’ll leave your tongue in your head.”

He turned and nodded at Billy. “I’ll follow behind with Ruby. If they become too awkward do what you need to do for compliance. I want to know who they’re working for before you kill them.”

Billy nodded, “Not a problem, they’ll talk with our methods of persuasion.” He swung himself up into the front of the wagon.

Arthur climbed into the other and sat up beside Ruby. He stroked her cheek gently as her eyes flickered open again, “I know who did this.” She said breathlessly as the carts pulled away.

Chapter Twenty-Eight

Ruby woke up with her body stiff and sore. She slowly opened her eyes to find Arthur sitting in a chair near the fireplace, reading a newspaper. He glanced in her direction at the sound of her stirring.

"Well hello sleepyhead, so good of you to join us at last," he said softly as he stood up and walked to the side of her bed. "How're feeling?" His voice was gentle and full of concern as he took a seat next to her.

She groaned, feeling like she'd been drugged or slept for days on end. Her mouth felt dry, and her head ached like something had broken inside it. She reached out weakly and took his hand.

"It's so nice to be home, how many days was I out?" As she gingerly touched her forehead with the other hand.

Arthur stood, looking down at her with worry in his eyes. "Lay back and rest," he urged softly. "I'll get Rose to bring you some tea and food, build your strength up." A small smile curved one corner of his lips as he hesitantly added, "Rubes... I'm so glad you're okay." He muttered almost to himself. "I couldn't imagine ever losing you." He gave her one final concerned glance before heading out the door, saying, "Back in a bit".

She lay on the bed, her thoughts tumbling around her head in a jumble of confusion. She felt the soreness and saw the bruises on her wrists and ankles from where they had been bound. What had she done to deserve being taken captive?

The bedroom door opened again, and Arthur reappeared, followed by Rose carrying a laden tray.

"Oh, Miss Ruby I'm so glad you're home and safe," Rose said as she placed the platter on the bed next to her and removed the cloth covering it with a dramatic flourish.

"T-dah, a nice big plate to fill your boots." Rose smiled at her, "it's so good to have you back, I've missed you." She headed towards the door, "I'll pop back later for the tray, now eat up." Rose said as she shut it quietly behind her.

Ruby's mouth began to water at the sight and recognizable aroma of bacon and eggs - just what she needed right now.

Arthur sat in the old, worn chair next to the fireplace and pored over the newspaper as Ruby quietly ate her breakfast. After sipping two cups of steaming tea and gulping down several glasses of cool boiled water, the throbbing in her head started to dull. When she felt steady on her feet again, she stood up, washed, and changed into her favourite red dress.

"You look like beautiful, Rubes," Arthur said from behind his paper. "How's that headache?"

"Almost gone now, Arty." She smiled at him gratefully and turned around so he could help button up the back of her dress.

"I suspect I've got several days' worth of correspondence to look through in the parlour." She said as he finished fastening the last button on her clothes.

Arthur turned her to face him his grave expression spoke volumes as he put his hands gently but firmly around her waist. “Ruby, you’ve not said much about what happened, is there something you’re afraid to tell me?” His eyes were full of worry, searching hers for an answer he didn't want to hear.

She could feel her heart pounding in her chest, and she wrapped her arms around his neck, pulling him close. “All they did was make me sleep Arty.” She brushed a gentle kiss against his lips. “I don’t really understand why they did it though, what was the purpose behind it? Very odd, but I do know that all of it was down to Royal, I made out I was asleep and overheard them.”

He took a deep breath and stepped back from their embrace before pushing his hands into his trouser pockets. “Yes, was told that it was him too, should we tell Abberline?”

“The note didn’t say much just call off the pigs and they’d be in touch with more instructions, but I didn’t wait. I called in some favours from the lads and before I knew it, they found you at some abandoned farm and we were on our way to get you out." He paused momentarily before continuing, "Billy is working his magic to get more out of them, no doubt he’ll be in touch later to let me know what he’s discovered."

Ruby smiled at the mention of Billy; loyal and dependable to Arthur since they first met. She opened the bedroom door and headed for the parlour.

Ruby entered the sitting room, feeling the warmth radiating from the freshly lit fire in the hearth. She noticed a cluster of letters on the table and went to the bureaux to read through them. Most were mundane—invoices and invitations to luncheons—nothing important.

Just as she was pushing the letters into her draws, a knock at the door broke her concentration. “Come in,” Ruby said, turning towards the entrance. Rose appeared, her eyes sad and her face drawn with worry. “I’m sorry to disturb you Miss Ruby, but Mr Morris didn’t tell you that we have Polly staying with us at the moment. Martha is missing, hasn't been seen for four days now. Polly is very upset and none of us know why she would just disappear like this. It's not like her at all."

Ruby felt her stomach knot as she looked into Rose's eyes. “I agree it is unlike her. Did you tell Mr Morris?” She asked as she gave the bureaux draw a sharp tug, slamming it closed with more force than necessary.

“I did and he said that Inspector Abberline told him of a woman found dead in an alley at Drury Lane, apparently she shared the same name, but Abberline didn’t want to jump to any conclusions until he knew for sure, so he’d asked Mr Morris to go along to give a positive identification, but then you were taken…” Her voice faded away into silence, leaving the air heavy with unspoken worries.

Ruby's heart skipped a beat as her forehead furrowed in alarm. She desperately tried to keep her voice even as she answered, "Okay Rose, leave it with me and I'll see Inspector Abberline and see if I can go and get the identification done - hopefully it’s not her." Quickly, she pushed the invitation back into her bureaux “That’ll have to wait,” she said, before a loud pounding on the front door reverberated down the hallway.

“Ok, I’m coming, no need to bang the door off the hinges,” shouted Rose as she left the room.

Ruby could hear a familiar voice resonate through to the parlour, and she felt her heart quickening with every step as it drew nearer. When Rose appeared in the doorway, Ruby was taken aback by the look of dread that had enveloped her face. “Ah, Miss Ruby, I’ve Mrs Byford here to see you.”

Ruby swallowed hard before finding her manners again. “Please, do come in Mrs Byford, this is an unexpected pleasure.” She rose to her feet as the woman entered and gestured for her to sit.

The air in the room was so still and thick with tension that Mrs Byford's gaze seemed to hang in the air. She shifted her focus away from Rose, her brow furrowed and voice barely above a whisper as she turned to Ruby. “Good morning, Miss Myers, I do apologise for the unannounced visit, but I'm afraid this is rather urgent.”

Ruby could feel her chest tightening; she understood all too well the meaning behind Mrs Byford's words. She reluctantly nodded before calling for Rose to bring tea and ordering her to close the door behind her when she left.

Mrs Byford waited until the door had been shut before allowing a flood of tears to stream down her cheeks.

Ruby's heart plummeted as she saw Mrs Byford standing, dressed in a dark shroud. “Mrs Byford! What is the matter?” Ruby cried out, shocked at the woman’s tears. She grabbed her gloved hands and implored desperately, “What could possibly be so awful that you resort to such sorrow?” Yet as she spoke, the edges of Ruby's vision blurred at her friend’s anguish until she too was fighting tears.

Mrs Byford reached into her pocket and pulled out a crumpled piece of paper, trembling fingers handing it to Ruby. As Ruby read its contents, horror swept over her face. “Is this... Mrs Byford, is this a suicide letter written by your sister?!” She shook her head in disbelief, desperately searching for hope in this wretched situation. “Surely there must be some way of getting her away from Royal?”

But the look on Mrs Byford's stricken face told Ruby everything that words did not need to say. In a moment, Ruby realised with a jolt - it was too late. She silently rose and moved to sit next to Mrs Byford in solemn solidarity.

Mrs. Byford's face contorted in anguish as she sobbed into her black, lace-edged handkerchief. “My brother-in-law arrived this morn’, to tell me how he found my poor sister had taken an overdose of laudanum that day. He discovered her in her finest gown, cold and unmoving like a china doll.

I decided not to tell him about the letter she had written; it wouldn't have changed anything, as it only contained her reasons for thinking this was the only solution." She sniffed back tears as she held the crumpled paper close. "It's a shame, I should have seen this coming. Poor Penny, her life cut short in such a cruel way!" A flood of tears threatened to spill as she paused for breath, her voice trembling. "Oddly though, she left this for you, Miss Myers - I don't know what it contains, but I had to make sure you got it immediately." Her eyes were wide and desperate, filled with the anguish of an unforgivable tragedy as she handed Ruby an envelope sealed with wax.

Chapter Twenty-Nine

Abberline trudged slowly down the street, his head bowed, and shoulders slumped, each step feeling heavier than the one before. The December sun had begun to dip below the horizon, and he knew Emma would be waiting at home with a steaming hot meal that she had probably spent all day preparing. He could almost feel the warmth of the fire in his living room as he thought of slipping into a hot tin bath after dinner. He dragged his feet up the path, and as he approached the entrance to his house, it was still no clearer what the answers were that he had been looking for all day. When in hell would he get a break in this infernal case? Why was Captain Smythe murdered? How deep does the corruption in the force run?

Abberline mechanically cut his food into precise, tiny squares and shovelled each one into his mouth while doing his best to ignore the sound of Emma's voice as it filled the room. He could sense her gaze burning holes in the side of his face, and he knew she was trying to get him to talk but he had made a promise early on in their marriage that he would never discuss his job with her, for fear of exposing her to the dark truths of his police duties. He felt guilty for zoning out and not hearing what she said, so he glanced up at her sheepishly and asked "I'm sorry, dear. What did you say?"

Emma studied Fred's tired eyes, his slumped shoulders, and the way he pushed around a few peas on his plate. "Bad day?" she asked.

He nodded slowly, avoiding her gaze. He spoke as if the weight of the world was on his shoulders. His voice was low and cracked with exhaustion, like he had been talking for hours. "Yes, I'm afraid so," he said, shaking his head. "It's not a pleasant place to be right now... so many secrets have come out about so many people that it's overwhelming, where to even begin?"

Emma changed the subject and began telling Abberline the gossip she'd heard at the market that morning.

Abberline knew it was her way of trying to keep his mind of his job.

She lowered her voice as if someone might be listening in. "There's some talk around the area about a brothel on Pickett Street, Fred," she began. Her words seemed to lift him from his low mood, and Fred leaned forward with an alertness in his eyes as he waited for her to continue. "I overheard two women talking at the market this morning. Quite unpleasant goings on apparently."

Fred took a sip of his tea, and Emma shifted in her chair. “What sort of unpleasant things?” Fred's voice was low, but it carried the weight of concern.

Emma nervously bit her lip, her eyes shifting from Abberline and back to the table. She shifted uncomfortably in her chair and let out a soft sigh before reaching up to brush the remnants of her meal into her palm. The crumbs settled deep in her hand before she delicately tossed them onto her now-empty plate.

Fred waited patiently for her to speak.

Emma cleared her throat. "I know you can't believe gossip, but I thought I'd mention it to you, maybe you could look into it, and then if it's just gossip, no harm done." Her eyes welled up with tears as she continued. "The rumour is that it's not just women that work at that place, but children also." She covered her mouth with her hand as if she was about to vomit.

Fred's frown deepened as he listened intently to Emma, the silence in the room was thick with unspoken words.

A cold wave of dread washed over him as he recalled the furtive whispers and averted gazes when he asked about Captain Smythe at the gentleman's club. His instincts had been correct—that a sinister secret was lurking in the shadows. He felt his heart thud against his chest as beads of perspiration trickled down his forehead. Emma's words echoed in his head, confirming the hearsay that Smythe had been frequenting a nearby brothel, and suddenly everything began to make sense. His gut instinct kicked in telling him Smythe's demise was no mere coincidence.

Fred's eyes sparkled with excitement at Emma's words, finally an answer to one of the questions was beginning to show itself. There had to be a connection to Smythe's demise, but where and why? He sprung to his feet with newfound energy. He grabbed the dark woolen winter coat from the back of the chair, pulling it on as he jogged for the door.

With a glowing gaze he planted a sweet kiss on her forehead before tucking a strand of hair behind her ear.

“Oh Emma, you’re a mine of information and you’ve helped answer some questions that had been troubling me. I have to follow this up right now - I promise I’ll be home soon. Don’t wait up for me.” His lips met hers in one last, chaste kiss before he darted out the door.

Inspector Abberline charged through the cobbled streets of London, a chill wind nipping at his heels. The full moon hung in the night sky, casting its pale light across the frost-coated paths beneath him. He moved with remarkable speed, every nerve tingling as if driven by some unseen force towards Miss Myers’ townhouse. Yet the streets were strangely deserted for this late hour, and he wondered what sinister activities may be unfolding out of sight.

He paused in front of the imposing ebony door, his heart racing as he lifted the heavy iron knocker. His breath fogged around his face in the chill air as he rapped on the door three times.

Chapter Thirty

Ruby bowed her head and attempted to keep back the tears. Even the pleasant scent of Mrs Byford's floral perfume had vanished from the parlour, replaced with a heavy blanket of sorrow that Ruby felt like she was almost being crushed by. Mrs Byford was determined to take care of her sister's arrangements quickly, mistrusting her brother in law to give his wife the sendoff that she so deserved.

Arthur sat motionless, staring into space. His entrance had put a pause on opening Penny Royal's letter, which was now sitting untouched on the table. He had just returned from his meeting with Billy but had made a detour to the mortuary before coming here. Arthur had to assist in identifying Martha's body – the murdered girl they were all so desperately hoping wasn't her. Now they had to confront the reality of breaking this news to Martha's daughter Polly. "I must regrettably tell you that the body lying there is Martha." He'd said and might as well have been delivering a death sentence, as his words were heavy with gravity and weighed like chains dragging her spirit to the ground. The coldness of what he said unfiltered could not be softened, no matter how much effort he put into cushioning the blow.

Ruby's hands flew to her cheeks and her pupils dilated in shock as she looked at Arthur unable to fathom the news he had just delivered. Tears blurred in her eyes, and the sorrow of their situation overwhelmed her. "Why Martha? What about poor Polly?" Her voice cracked as she spoke, and her breath caught in her throat. She leaned forward and covered her face with her hands, muffling what little words were left. With a tremor in her voice she asked, "Arty, was she killed by the same person? Tell me."

Arthur took out his pipe, filling it with tobacco as he sat back in his chair. He reached for the box of matches on the side table and slowly struck one against its edge. He lit the bowl and puffed on the stem before responding. "That I don't know Rubes but put it this way: she was carved up pretty bad. So, I suspect it's a very strong possibility."

The silence was dense and oppressive as Arthur puffed on his pipe, the blue-grey smoke swirling through the air. Ruby's gaze was caught by the flames of the fire, her thoughts and fears spinning out in her head.

“We need to bring Rose in on this Arty, after all she’ll be with Polly most of the time as it is, and I think we should tell Polly all together."

“I think that’s a good idea.” Arthur agreed. “No time like the present.”

They called Rose down from changing bed linens. She gasped and covered her mouth as the news sunk in. “Deep down I had a feeling it was Martha,” she said as she sank heavily in one of the chairs.

They called Polly into the room, her shoulders shook, and her cries filled the parlour as Arthur spoke as gently as he could. Rose wrapped her frail body in a warm embrace, but no phrase of comfort or kind gesture could take away the pain that had drawn tears from this child's eyes: she had just been told her mother was gone.

Ruby's chin jutted out and her eyes burned with defiance. Her thin frame seemed to swell as she spoke, her voice full of authority. “Polly, you shall remain living in this townhouse under our care.” She planted her hands firmly on her hips and the room fell silent in response.

Polly nervously lifted her gaze to meet the kind eyes of her new guardian. She tried to steady her voice, “Miss Ruby, thank you so much. I know my ma would be so very grateful.”

Ruby opened her arms, and Polly stumbled into them. The girl's eyes were wide with uncertainty, and her hands clung tightly to Ruby's dress. Ruby held her close, feeling the warmth of Polly's body against hers, and whispered in her ear. "You're safe now, darling. No one will ever hurt you." She took a deep breath, thinking of Polly's mother, who had once been her friend. "Your mother and I had a good relationship," she said softly, "and I so wanted her to stay here. But she thought it was the best thing to do." She paused, swallowing hard. "I can't be your mother, Polly, and I wouldn't try. But I will do my very best for you and for her memory." Ruby stroked the child's hair, her fingers brushed lightly against her soft cheeks. She leaned in, pressing a gentle kiss to Polly’s forehead.

“I promise I will make sure your mother has the best resting place and that you will be able to visit her when you need to. It won’t be easy for you now, but with time and love from us all, it will get better.” As she spoke, a single tear rolled down Polly’s cheek. She nodded silently and managed to whisper a quiet “thank you” between sobs.

"Come on Polly, love, how about you help me make your favourite for tonight? We've got a nice stew and I thought you'd like a rhubarb crumble for afters?" Rose suggested. "It may help to take your mind off things a little."

Polly nodded, wiping away the tears from her face with the back of her hand. "Ok, Rose, I'll do my best to help but I may not want a dinner this evening."

"Now, don't you go worrying about that, see how you feel later," Rose advised as she began bustled out of the room. "C'mon now child, let's get busy."

Arthur and Ruby followed to the kitchen and lingered with Polly and Rose, not wanting to abandon the girl when she was so troubled. Ruby noticed how Rose had taken it upon herself to involve Polly in the dinner preparations, attempting to keep her distracted from what was going on inside her head. Although Ruby was trying her hardest to comfort Polly, the sadness present in the kitchen simply could not be escaped. Her chest felt heavy for Polly, as she knew too well what the girl was feeling.

Finally, it was Arthur who suggested they return to the parlour. "What did Mrs Byford want?" He asked, curiosity sparking in his eyes as he lowered himself into his chair.

She turned her attention back to him, her mind slowly came into focus again. "Oh, um… it was about her sister, Royal's wife, apparently she has passed away." She looked off into the space between them, uncertainty in her voice. "By her own hand from what Mrs Byford has said. She left me a letter too, although I'm at a loss at to why she'd send it to me."

Arthur took the pipe from his mouth and stared at her in surprise. "Mrs Royal sent you a letter?" he said incredulously. "Have you read it?" He struck another match and relit his pipe.

Arthur and Ruby had barely taken their seats when three solid knocks echoed through the parlour.

Rose opened the front door, inviting the visitor in. Soon a light tap at the sitting room door announced the Inspector's arrival.

Ruby stood, her body stiff with apprehension. Please Lord, not more bad news? She attempted to mask her surprise with an expression of disinterest as she offered Abberline a seat. Arthur followed her gesture and extended an offer of whiskey, which Abberline politely declined with a subtle shake of his head.

The couple settled back into their chairs as Abberline sat down across from them.

His eyes darted between Ruby and Arthur as he cleared his throat. "I apologize for arriving unannounced, however, I have new developments to discuss with you both," he spoke cautiously as if he himself was uncertain that it could be true.

Ruby clasped her hands together in her lap and asked if he would like tea. When he politely declined, she asked, "How can we help you?"

He shifted his weight in the leather chair, a faint squeak echoing across the quiet room. His eyes darted around the room, then back to his hands folding on his lap. "Since the incident at the pub... Mr

Morris," he began haltingly, each word carefully selected. He paused, biting his lower lip before continuing. "I've been somewhat concerned it may hinder our..." He trailed off briefly as if searching for the right word. "Allegiance." His sharp exhale betrayed his concern before he quickly masked it with a practiced air of indifference. A crease appeared between his eyebrows before he tilted his head slightly, studying Arthur's reaction. "I do so hope I'm wrong?" he asked.

Ruby looked questionably at Arthur, her face a mask of confusion and concern. "Something you need to tell me Arty?" She asked.

Arthur sighed and adjusted his hand-woven tweed waistcoat before settling back in the armchair. He cleared his throat before speaking, carefully choosing his words to tell the story without revealing too much. "Firstly, we'd discussed that at the time in question Inspector Abberline," he pulled out his pipe again hoping for a brief distraction, "and I'll tell you more later Rubes, other things happened that are more important right now. Inspector, would you please tell us why you're here?" Arthur enquired.

The Inspector cleared his throat and nodded. "I'm so sorry for the loss of your friend Martha, Miss Myers an-"

Ruby interrupted him and said softly "Thank you, Inspector." She adjusted her posture, pushing back against the tall armchair. "Now why the visit at such a late hour?" She asked as she noticed Arthur had frozen with his pipe in his mouth.

Inspector Abberline locked eyes with her. “Miss Myers, would you happen to know Martha’s surname at all?” His already chewed pencil was poised for notcs if needed.

“Smith, I think that’s the name she gave me when she came here," Ruby said, shooting a suspicious glance at Arthur. What hadn’t he told her? He still hadn't lit his pipe. “Her daughter is with us now and will stay with us for as long as she needs - although Martha never mentioned any other family in her life."

Inspector Abberline underlined the surname twice before changing the subject. He paused, shoulders hunched, and brows knitted in concern. His gaze moved to the windowpane as he exhaled slowly and shifted the conversation to the recent shooting of Captain Smythe. "The investigation of this case has become even darker," he said grimly.

“How can it be any darker?” Ruby sneered in disgust; her face twisted into a fearsome scowl. “It's already dark enough with all the innocent women who have been mercilessly murdered!” Her voice was louder now, anger threatening to consume her.

Abberline held up his hand as if trying to stop a wall from falling, “Well, after further enquiries, it sickens me to say that a Captain Smythe frequented a brothel on Pickett Street and at said brothel it wasn’t just women that worked there, but…” he shifted in his seat again.

Ruby noticed that his hand holding the pencil trembled slightly. “Please continue Inspector.” She urged.

"Also, children." Abberline licked his lips then bit the top one.

"Actually Inspector, we'd already been made aware of this, but my capture prevented us from talking with you." Ruby added sternly.

"Capture? I had no idea, I'm all ears, Miss Myers, pray continue." Abberline shifted his poise and sat back.

"Dr Barnardo came here to see me one day last week. He'd had concerns about Smythe as he'd had the displeasure at the gentlemen's club that he frequented." Ruby began.

"Yes, I'm also aware of the club." Abberline agreed.

"Smythe was drunk when he approached the Doctor and told him about the bordello. Then Bernardo went to the constabulary, but the constable showed little interest." Ruby informed him.

Abberline's face darkened with that piece of information. Why would the officer on duty be so off hand regarding something so despicable? He kept the question to himself as he said, "Is that so?"

"So, after thinking it through, he approached me as I'd just recently given a substantial donation, hoping that if he involved several of the donors it may gain some notoriety at the station. Needless to say, someone took steps to ensure Smythe's silence." Ruby concluded.

"Well that much is certainly clear, Miss Myers." Abberline politely agreed again. Tell me, did Bernardo happen to mention the constable's name?"

"No, he didn't, and I didn't ask to be honest. It was during that conversation when Arthur came here and told us about Smythe's demise." Ruby said.

"I see." Abberline scribbled something down. "I did mention to Mr Morris that the weapon in question was a small pistol called a Deringer and that it's generally used by a woman as it can fit into a petite hand." He raised questioning eyes at Ruby.

"Before you ask, Inspector, I don't own any type of weapon especially that of a Deringer. I don't and never will agree with being armed." She sat poker straight, her face impassive. Ruby gingerly touched her temple as if what she was about to say actually hurt, "Inspector, I received an invitation from Dr Bernardo to have dinner with him, this I assumed was to discuss some details regarding the children's homes, however, it wasn't Dr Barnardo, I was taken prisoner by three goons." She unconsciously rubbed her wrists as if feeling the residual effects of being bound. "Thankfully our network of associates was able to find me within a few days and bring me home.

We are currently trying to get them to confirm who they work for; although we have found out who is responsible, one was called Bullstrode, the other, Inspector Abberline, is your friend Royal." She paused waiting to see Abberline's reaction.

Abberline's eyes widened in disbelief, his lips pursed together as he raised a hand to scratch his temple. "Good Lord, what the hell was Royal playing at?" He jumped out of his seat, mouth agape, and began stomping around the room. He glared at the woman before him with a flinty gaze, fists clenched tightly as he asked his question. His face flushed red with frustration and rage. "Miss Myers, are you certain that this recent abduction is the work of Inspector Royal?"

“It has been confirmed by someone who overheard him and Bullstrode talking in an alleyway, and I heard one of the goons mention his name, they thought I was asleep at the time.” Ruby’s voice wavered on the last word, and she shuddered even though the room was warm.

Inspector Abberline’s face was still flushed with anger as he glared at Arthur and Miss Myers. “Mr Morris, Miss Myers,” the Inspector began, his voice low with disapproval, “why on earth didn’t you send word to me? I could have helped somehow, that is at least my job.”

“We were told not to involve the police, Inspector, which is ironic.” Arthur held Abberline’s stare, “It wasn’t anything personal, I just wanted to get Miss Myers home as quickly as I could.”

Ruby’s eyes were cast to the floor, and she noticed Mrs Byford’s black lace handkerchief near the chair Arthur was sitting in. “Inspector, you are aware that Mrs Byford is Inspector Royal’s sister-in-law?” She asked.

“Mrs Byford?... I must admit I’ve never met the woman” Abberline scratched his chin in thought.

"Mrs Byford was married to a member of parliament, Inspector the late Clifford Byford and she told me about her sister and his poor treatment of her, sadly she called here recently to inform me of Mrs Royal's passing and to give me this letter from her," Ruby turned towards the table without leaving her seat, reached across and lifted the sealed envelope to show Abberline, "although I'm not sure why she felt the need to write to me?" She paused at her own question and dropped the letter back on the table, "so, she'd also said he'd bought his wife a gun once for her birthday, the handle inlaid with mother of pearl."

Abberline's face drained, his shoulders slumped, and he looked down to his lap. "Oh, dear god Bernard," He raised his hand to his cheek and closed his eyes, then moments later rubbed the back of his neck the stood up. "It may have been his wife's but that doesn't mean he committed the murder." Abberline began to pace, then paused for a moment, "The letter Miss Myers, would you permit me to read it?" He asked as he continued to walk the room in thought.

"I've not read it myself yet, but I can't see what harm it'll do when I have. I said to Arthur that I know Inspector Royal from somewhere but can't work out how." Ruby said, as she stood up to poke the fire in an attempt to defuse the tension in the room, then turned her back to it and stood with her arms folded.

Abberline continued pacing.

"All I know is that as soon as I saw him, I felt that I knew him, he was familiar to me, but I've no idea how." Ruby looked at Abberline with confusion in her eyes, "you see, I'm usually really good with names and faces and remember people from way, way back, but him, I keep drawing a blank." She let out a sigh, "it'll come to me eventually." She said dismissively, as she perched herself on the arm of Arthur's chair.

A knock on the door of the parlour distracted them and Rose stood in the doorway, "excuse me Miss Ruby, Mr Morris, I've got Billy here to see Mr. Morris, says it's urgent."

Arthur stood up, "thank you Rose, I'll see him out in the kitchen." He followed Rose out of the room.

Ruby could hear the two men greet each other, then their voices faded as they went into the kitchen.

"It gives Mr Morris and me no pleasure knowing that Inspector Royal could be the killer, Inspector Abberline." Ruby watched his face for a reaction.

"It gives me no pleasure either, Miss Myers, I can assure you." Abberline's face suddenly looked drawn and sad. "There is no excuse for corruption within the force and when we get to the bottom of this mess, Royal is in a whole lot of trouble." Abberline frowned, "it also bothers me that he hasn't told anyone at the station about the loss of Mrs Royal." Abberline's frown deepened. "But, why on earth has he not told anyone at the station?" He shook his head in disbelief.

"As I said previously, Inspector, Mrs Byford informed me that the marriage wasn't a happy one and that Mrs Royal was badly treated by him, this wasn't a loving relationship by all accounts." Ruby concluded.

The pair was interrupted by Arthur coming back into the room. He looked straight at Ruby as he spoke, "Billy got it out of one of the men and again it's been confirmed they've confirmed it's Inspector Royal."

Abberline slammed himself into the chair, fury radiating off of him in waves. His furious eyes were locked on a point beyond the room, rage colouring his features with disgust and contempt. "This is too much," he seethed, his hands balling into white-knuckled fists. "How can he consider himself an upstanding, law-abiding citizen when he's blatantly exploiting his power for personal gain and corruption? God alone knows what else he's up to. I wonder what else he's hidden from me over the years as my colleague and I dread to think what Mrs Royal has put in that letter to you Miss Myers." He covered his eyes with his hand as if trying to shield himself from any other grim revelations.

Ruby didn't respond as she picked up the letter from the table and crossed to her bureaux. She lifted up her letter opener and sliced through the top of the envelope. Her fingers trembled as she pulled the paper from the inside. The air thickened around them, as she read through its contents, and no one spoke.

Moments later, she dropped the letter onto the table and turned to look at both the men, her face ashen and her eyes filled with tears. “I…I’ve… remembered where I know him from,” she stammered. She pulled out a chair and sat down, just as her knees buckled from under her. “My god, Arty...” Was all she could say as she buried her face in her hands.

Chapter Thirty-One

Royal pushed open the door of the undertaker, the evening sky illuminated by the gas lamps. He paused for a moment to take a deep breath; he could feel a weightlifting off his shoulders as he stepped out. His shoes scuffed lightly on the pavement as he strode forward, letting a hint of a smile play across his lips. For the first time in years, Royal felt truly free and alive.

He thought back to all the times she filled his house with oppressive silence and gloom. The only thing he might miss was the rough treatment he'd often given her – an airing of frustration after one too many of her tearful looks. He almost felt guilty for the joy that bubbled up inside him at the thought of her absence - but only almost.

Despite the initial relief, he couldn't help feeling a dull pain in the hollow of his chest. He wished he'd been so much harder on her. Such a weak, fragile and dull woman she'd been. He should've taken more time to antagonise her before every beating rather than reacting so quickly to her moods. The ridicule may have strengthened her inner fibre. How he would miss the cruel hold he knew he'd had over her.

Royal couldn't help but feel that Penny had had the last word, and for once, her actions had beaten him. But it was too late now. The die had been cast, and the only thing left to do was accept what was to come. He recalled the noise that echoed in the empty house as he swung shut the front door, like a signal of the new life that awaited him.

He slowed his pace and glanced at his reflection in a shop window. My, what a fine figure of a man. He licked a finger and ran it over an eyebrow. How would any woman want to leave him? The thought was just too ridiculous.

His eyes glinted with satisfaction as he remembered the arrangements for the funeral he'd just made: the dark and weathered pine coffin, the absence of floral arrangements or eulogies, and the lack of a wake. He had already taken measures to ensure that his wife's secret stash of money wouldn't be wasted on superfluous details — it belonged to him now, a result of her dedication and months of careful saving.

He watched her covertly as she saved every penny yet pretended that she was doing nothing of the sort. He made it impossible for her to make a clean break, making her life so difficult that he was sure someone else would never get the chance to love her. He waited patiently, knowing his grip on her would eventually be too much and she would snap. Finally, she did.

He strutted down the pockmarked cobbles towards Pickett Street. The evening air was filled with a variety of smells, each one more intoxicating than the last. He had her money in his pocket, not that he needed it at the brothel. Why would he when the bordello belonged to him?

The business he'd started as a small venture years back had now become quite profitable, thanks to his savvy dealings. Unfortunately, the same could not be said for his ability to erase Smythe and his overactive mouth from existence - until finally, late one night, he pulled out a Derringer pistol - a gift for his wife - and blasted away at Smythe's head. In the aftermath, Royal had hoped that police would assume it was Myers who had done the deed; as if the Derringer wasn't enough of a giveaway, he had also made sure to give Abberline a hefty hint regarding the murderer's gender. But alas, no such luck. With a wry smile, Royal knew there'd be another opportunity to put an end to her.

His mind drifted back the other night and the girl he'd met at the bordello; she had said her name was Melissa, with wavy brown hair and dark eyes that seemed to peer into his soul. She'd been with him all that night and was the tender age of thirteen years old. With anticipation, he quickened his step.

The gas lamp outside the brothel flickered in the moonlight, beckoning him like an old friend. As he stepped inside, his nostrils were filled with cigar smoke and the cloying scent of perfume. The red shredded paper clung to the walls like wilted vines, as if it had been drained of all its vitality from witnessing decades of debauchery within the building The tatters were so thin and frail that they seemed to shimmer in the scant light that filtered through the half-closed shutters. They rustled faintly at every shift of air, creaking as though they were trying to escape their own shame.

It was clear that this house had been home to too many secrets and sins to count.

His ears were assaulted by a cacophony of feminine giggles and masculine growls from upstairs rooms. He nodded to the Madame as he passed, his eyes already searching the room. Sure enough, there she was, sitting at a corner table with six other children.

He didn't hesitate. He took Melissa by the wrist as tears streamed down her face, he turned to the Madame and said, "Bring me two more in an hour, I’ll be in the same room as before." His voice had a commanding tone as he pulled the girl into the corridor.

The Madame gave a slight nod in response, her face expressionless as she silently glided away. Melissa, her arm still in his grip, looked pleadingly into his eyes. He stepped closer, so close that he could feel her warm breath on his skin. He dropped his voice to a whisper, "Don’t you cry my dear, tonight will be wonderful."

He led her through the winding corridors and up the stairs. When they arrived at the room, he opened the door and stepped aside as he shoved her inside. His eyes traced every inch of her as he swung the door shut, then turned the key in the lock.

Chapter Thirty-Two

Arthur snatched the letter from the table from where Ruby had dropped it. She howled in anguish after reading its contents and then bolted from the room. He quickly skimmed over page before thrusting it into Abberline's hands.

"You need to see this Inspector." Arthur's voice was cold, emotionless as he sunk into the chair that Ruby had vacated mere moments ago. His fingers pinched his nose as his eyes squeezed shut, a million thoughts racing through his mind. He could hear Abberline gasp behind him.

"Am I thinking what you are Inspector?" Arthur opened his eyes to catch sight of a rather ghostly looking Abberline.

"Oh God...What...I don't even know how to respond to this. Was the poor woman out of her mind?" Abberline cursed as he braced against the back of a chair, gripping tightly onto the letter.

Arthur sat rigidly in his seat, unable to move. His eyes darkened like a worn-out storm cloud, while his jaw tightened as he spoke. "I can feel it deep in my gut," he said. He slammed his fist on the armrest and shot up from the chair, pointing his finger at the pages Abberline was holding. "That woman was speaking the truth about Royal's past and there's more in there that must be revealed!"

He watched Abberline's knuckles whiten as he gripped the letter tightly in his hand. Arthur's heart thumped painfully against his chest as he stared ahead and clenched his jaw in frustration.

Abberline suddenly spoke, “Unfortunately, I must admit, I have the same feeling about this as well." He moved around to the front of the chair and proceeded to slump into it, letting out a sigh of despair. His head rested on the backrest, and he closed his eyes, still tightly holding the letter in his right hand resting on his lap. “I am completely horrified," he spoke with a heavy voice, not opening his eyes. “I would’ve never expected such corruption within the force, it makes me sick to my stomach.”

Arthur shook his head at Abberline’s naivety. “It’s worse than you thought,” he yelled out. “This goes beyond your garden-variety bribery and collusion, this corruption has gone on for years! It runs deeper than anything you’ve seen previously.” He said with a sneer as he started to pace around like a caged animal. “The bloke is a fucking hypocrite, plain and simple.” His pacing increased as his anger mounted, and he strode across the room searching the air for an answer.

“Mr Morris, Mrs Royal has been completely candid in these pages, but sadly, there’s nothing conclusive!” Abberline flipped through the papers, frustration flashing across his face.

"Inspector, we must not overlook the fact she’s confirmed that her husband is corrupt, and definitely not the person that you believed him to be, morally or otherwise. Mrs Royal has provided you with information about his past and with very little digging I’m fairly sure that it’ll help uncover everything else he’s involved in," Arthur pointed out. His attention was then diverted to Ruby as she entered the room, her steps hesitant and unsteady.

Her eyes were red-rimmed, and her complexion was ashen; it was as if the life had been drained from her. Arthur felt a wavc of compassion pass through him, and he stood up and stepped forward to offer his support, lightly resting a hand on Ruby's shoulder. "Are you alright, my love? Would you like anything?"

"A brandy would be perfect," she spoke in a quiet and insecure voice. The trembling in her hands revealed how much inner turmoil she was facing.

Arthur looked into her eyes with determination and said firmly, "We'll get this bastard Ruby, I promise, I swear, Rubes, I will make sure this man pays for what he's done." Arthur's voice rose in anger and his grip on her hands tightened until she winced; he let go immediately. He looked around the parlour, the fire crackled in the grate and the shadows of night danced across the walls.

Abberline cleared his throat, "I need to find Royal and get some answers from him, I think it's better if I question him before you Mr Morris?" He said.

Arthur's jaw tightened and his eyes looked like they were made of granite as he gave a stiff nod.

Abberline looked at Ruby, "Miss Myers, I'm truly sorry this has bought you so much distress, and I will do my utmost to bring this nightmare to a conclusion, of that I promise, I'll see myself out." He said as he opened the parlour door then closed it quietly behind him.

Arthur waited until he knew Abberline had left the building before turning back to Ruby. His voice was heavy with emotion as he knelt down in front of her, “I will kill this bastard if that’s what it takes.”

Ruby leaned in so close to Arthur that he could feel her breath on his neck. With a fierceness that matched her gaze, she uttered the words "I know you will and that's why I love you." She sat back, but the fire in her eyes continued to smoulder. "We need to find Royal before Abberline does," she suggested, "get him to a place where we can deal with him our way." Her expression shifted from one of love to one of revenge as her jaw jutted out and her lips contorted into a cruel grin. “Get Billy and a few of the other lads onto it, there’ll always be someone that wants to rat out a pig, especially one like Royal.”

"That's my girl," he whispered as he planted a gentle kiss on her forehead, "the Ruby I know is coming out to play again." He stood up and made his way into the kitchen. "Billy is still in the kitchen," he announced, “I asked him to wait until Abberline left.” He called out, "Bill, it's time for us to fight dirty with that pig Royal."

Billy grinned as Arthur entered the room and took a seat at the kitchen table. In a voice brimming with malice, he exclaimed "At last! That's the best news I've heard in a long time. Let the fun begin!”

Chapter Thirty-Three

He stalked through the darkness, his pulse thrumming in anticipation as he watched the three of them in her parlour. The gas lamp within barely kept away the shadows, just enough to outline the silhouettes of the figures inside. The wooden fence was a fortress, like a battalion of knights ready to shield their queen from any danger lurking outside its walls. His eyes were drawn to the scene before him with the knowledge he would be the one to seal her fate.

He glanced up and down the alley ensuring that nobody saw him, then took out a worn leather pouch and started rolling a cigarette. The sweet images of what he would do to her kept flitting across his mind, bringing an insidious smile to his face as he shuddered with delight. Not much longer my sweet Miss Myers, not much longer now.

He'd wait until the two men left, then sneak into her house through the back entrance. The housekeeper wouldn't stand a chance against him; one swift slice and she'd be gone.

Where would Miss Myers be? Would she be in her parlour or better still, her bedroom? It didn't matter one way or another; either place would be ideal. Of course, he had to make sure she stayed quiet so no one would discover their secret rendezvous. It was important for the ritual that they weren't disturbed.

He'd savour every moment, removing each piece of clothing with agonising slowness and drinking in the sight of her nude body bathed in soft lamplight. Her neck, slender and elegant; her breasts curved invitingly - He wanted to witness her fear first hand as she writhed beneath him while he made her completely his own. The bindings cutting into her smooth porcelain skin as she attempted to free herself.

Oh yes, Miss Myers would tremble with fear, realizing her fate as the final sacrificial offering. The whores were dull and dispensable, but she offered something more: a challenge. With predatory anticipation he stalks her like prey, eager to savour every moment of her destruction. Her lover's face will surely contort in shock and horror when at last he finds her, ravaged and broken beyond recognition.

He grasped his pocket watch with trembling fingers, and flicked it open, its face briefly illuminated by the glowing tip of his cigarette. He cursed in surprise as he saw the time. How could it have flown so fast? The hour dictated his next move: a cheap whore it would be and disposed of into the Thames to make her harder to find. That’s if the fish didn't devour her first. Well at least she’d be useful for something in the end.

His city was plagued with despair and darkness, and he had every intention of making sure Miss Myers felt both. He’d return tomorrow and the day after, every twenty four hours until he had his way.

Until then, he'd be patient and watch. But he'd get to her, there was no doubt about that. He flicked the end of his cigarette onto the dirt of the alleyway and without glancing back walked into the street, heading in the direction of one more whore.

Chapter Thirty-Four

Ruby's eyes were full of determination as she gripped the edges of the cart. With a deep breath, she pulled herself up beside Arthur. He looked at her in surprise, but she refused to be left behind.

The streets were cloaked in darkness with nothing more than occasional gas lamps providing a dim light that illuminated the walls, emphasizing the looming demise of Bernard Royal. An overcast moon hung low in the sky, casting a faint gleam across their path as they continued on their mission. The underworld hummed with news of Royal's whereabouts, and it didn't take long for the network to spring into action. In a matter of minutes, they knew exactly where he was and what he was up to. The speed at which information travelled gave them an edge that could be lethal.

A sharp chill bit her skin, but Ruby barely noticed as she adjusted her coat and took one last look at her associates. Each face held unwavering determination, as well as an unspoken promise of loyalty and protection. Arthur's gaze was particularly fierce, his expression clear in its resolve; whatever awaited him at the end of this journey would not go unanswered.

The creaking of the carts and horses echoed in the dark alleyway as they stopped under a concrete viaduct near the end of Pickett Street. The group was engulfed in blackness, Ruby watched as each man made out the whitewashed walls of the brothel several doors up – a beacon of cleanliness and a majestic appearance, a sharp contrast to the filth that was taking place inside.

One by one, they took their chance and knocked on the door to enter, until only Ruby and Arthur remained in the shadows of the archway. Knowing glances were exchanged between them in the oppressive silence, and not a word needed to be said for Ruby to know it was time to move forward.

She could feel Arthur's determination and readiness for what was about to happen radiating like a fire in his chest, as he prepared himself for what was to come. Ruby was aware that she was safe, but a feeling of dread filled her stomach with knots and anxiety built on her shoulders. All the associates had instructions to leave Royal in situ and leave him to her and Arthur. Even though she knew that Royal had to answer for what he had done, now that she knew how he was familiar to her, it did nothing to calm her inner turmoil. Arthur held her hand and the two walked towards the door and knocked.

The inside of the three-storey house the walls were papered a bright red and the shutters a faded mustard yellow. Under their feet were bare floorboards. A run-down building with cheap posters plastered to the dank, flaky stucco, and a flickering red lantern.

In a room to their right, several women were dressed in delicate undergarments and laid on their backs on filthy beds, their mouths agape and silent, waiting for a man to have his way with their bodies. The room was devoid of privacy curtains. Music from a piano could be heard from another room on the ground floor. A poor attempt at trying to drown out the moans and cries of paying guests.

A staircase was at the end of the long hallway and several of Arthur's associates had gone upstairs ready to overtake the rest of the building. Most of the women and children had been rounded up so they can move them out, some of whom talked in French.

Ruby recognized none of them, but their faces were painted with fear and abuse - black eyes, split lips, and bruises. The children stayed huddled together, drawing closer as she approached.

"What do you want, miss?" An older boy stepped forward, speaking with a strong French accent, and trying to protect the younger ones from her presence. His voice trembled with barely concealed terror. "No one here would be of use to you or your monsieur there." He pointed at Arthur.

Ruby's voice caught in her throat she had to swallow to be able to reply, "We're here to get all of you out. We'll take you somewhere safe." She reached out to stroke the boy's hair but withdrew her hand when he flinched in fear.

"It's okay," Ruby soothed. "Where are you from? There's some of the ladies speaking in your language too." Ruby asked as she glanced around at some of the other women.

"Paris, Madam, we were taken from our beds whilst we slept, our parents killed as they dragged us from our home." Tears began to fall down the boy's cheeks at the memory. "Then they took us to a boat and then here."

He wept as he looked up at the strangers in the doorway. His voice shook as he asked, pleadingly, “Are they here to help us too?” One of the children began wailing uncontrollably, and the older boy held her close.

Ruby turned towards Arthur with a determined look on her face. "It's time to get these kids out of here. I'm going to check the other rooms in case anyone else is hiding there." Without another word, she moved towards the door.

Billy grappled with a woman, her curse words flying out at him like bullets. Her raven-black hair hung in limp strands around her face, which was weathered and wrinkled from a lifetime of hard living and heavy drinking. An angry red scar marred its surface, arching up from her chin to just below her icy green eyes.

Ruby stepped forward and faced the woman, her own gaze coolly challenging. "Who are you?" Ruby asked, the air charged with tension as the woman fell suddenly silent. "Do you service the punters too?” The woman shook her head. “No, then you’re the madam?” Ruby searched her face as she waited for an answer.

“I ain't telling you nothin’.” The woman pursed her lips together in defiance.

Billy increased his grip on her upper arm.

“Oi, shovel hands, that hurts.” The woman looked up and glared at Billy.

“Tell the lady what she wants to know, or else I break it.” His eyes locked with hers then tightened the same fingers again.

The woman pulled in an agonising breath, “All right, ow, fucks sake, yes, I’m the Madam.”

“Just as I thought," Ruby replied flatly. “Get this piece of shit outta here! But don't take your eyes off her for a second. I’m not convinced that she is the brothel keeper, so I’ll question her later." Ruby snarled, venom dripping from her voice. The woman retaliated by spitting on the floor, but Ruby still stood tall and unshaken.

"Royal been found yet?" She inquired coldly, scanning the faces of the other lads for an answer.

"She said he’s on the top floor room apparently," one of them replied and pointed at the madam, “takes it every time just in case the place gets raided by the filth, ironic or what.” he said feigning amusement. "She only told us ‘cus we threatened to cut out her tongue.” He grinned at Ruby, “Arthur doesn't want anyone going in just yet, said to wait until the others were taken somewhere safe."

Ruby's lips pressed themselves together in a thin line as she solemnly nodded her head. Her eyes softened with understanding, he’s trying to protect any kids that may be in the room with him, she thought to herself as she started to walk away. "I'm gonna check the other rooms and make sure no one was left behind," she said softly, her voice cracking on the last syllable, "especially kids."

Within moments, the house was left with a mere handful of lads keeping watch. The men accompanying the women were allowed to go free, while those in rooms with children were forcefully loaded into carts awaiting beneath the viaduct. Some heavy consequences would be reaped afterwards.

"Nobody enters or leaves," Arthur commanded. "Royal is going nowhere if he gets down here." He turned towards Ruby and spoke with malicious glee, "Ready to have a little tête-à-tête with Royal? Let's end this now, Rubes!" Taking her hand, he proceeded to march up the stairs. "Billy, come with us."

"Arty, some of those people weren't English, what the hell has been going on?" She eyed Arthur waiting for him to answer.

"I think our friend, Royal has been bringing people over from overseas, all of which to use here, but how long it's been going on is anyone's guess." He looked back at Ruby as they climbed. "Don't worry love, it stops tonight, and we'll get all the answers out of him that we need."

Ruby's heart pounded in her chest as she quickly followed Arthur up the steps, anger coursing through her veins and as he flung open the door her breath hitched in her throat.

As the door slammed open, Ruby noticed Royal hiding under the bed. Three children huddled in a corner on the opposite side of the room, their frightened eyes darting around wildly.

"What the fuck do you think you're doing?" He shouted, as Arthur grabbed him by his hair, and dragged him out from under the bed and across the floor.

Ruby strode over to the children and quickly wrapped her arms around the eldest girl with dark hair, whispering comforting words into her ear.

"Come now," she said urgently, "See that big man there, he's Billy he's here to take you downstairs and out of this place. Nothing will ever harm you again, I promise." She gestured to Billy standing in the doorway who gave a reassuring nod, then she handed the girl a blanket from the bedroom floor.

The girl turned to the other two younger children and grabbed their hands before leading them towards Billy. They left without looking back, leaving Royal with Ruby and Arthur.

Bernard gaped in silent horror as Ruby locked the door.

Ruby stared viciously at Royal, her eyes narrowed in disgust as she watched him kneeling before her. He was half-dressed and his pale belly bulged out from the waistband of his underwear.

She took a chair from nearby and positioned it mere inches away from him, then settled into it with a predatory grace. Leaning forward, she entwined her forearms over her crossed legs, studying him coldly like a snake watching its prey.

"I have a letter here from your wife, Royal." She spoke calmly as she tilted her head and waved the crumbled envelope in the air, before securing it back inside the sleeve of her dress.

"My wife? What is this about?" Royal asked her his face contorted with fear.

Before Ruby could answer Arthur drove a powerful punch to his jaw, sending Royal crashing sideways, temporarily stunned. Arthur then grabbed him by the hair and dragged him back into position on his knees.

“What you gonna do, just beat me to death?” he asked, his face already swollen from Arthur's blow.

“Not just yet, but don't worry, there will be plenty more of that later - first, I've got some questions for you.” Her voice was icy and her face steely as she expertly pulled a long, sharp dagger out of the inside of her left boot. “You really sicken me, Royal. A hypocrite, a copper, a woman-beater – and if all that wasn't enough evil running through your veins, you're also a pervert." Ruby's lip curled in disdain as she spat out the last words.

“I am no such thing! I'm merely a disciplinarian - unlike those who use children out of pleasure; my method is merely to punish them when they do wrong.” Royal looked smugly up at Ruby.

Ruby's eyes flashed with a fierce intensity as she shook her head in disbelief. "Such bullshit, so taking children to your bed and doing unspeakable things is discipline?” Her stomach twisted in anger.

“Of course, what else would it be?” Royal asked.

“What it is, you bastard is wrong.” Ruby said, “You’re a complete hypocrite, call yourself a copper? Well tonight, it’s my turn to be a walking contradiction," she hissed, "normally I keep my hands free from weapons, but tonight...tonight I brought a blade to teach you the difference between right and wrong. My way of justice is for all your evil deeds, past and present, which also includes the time before you changed your name to Bernard Royal." She paused for a moment.

Royal answered with an arrogant smirk, mocking her words. "I’ve no idea what you’re implying.” He sneered at her with a fleeting glimpse of bravado. His arrogance was short-lived, as she swiftly shifted her weight forward and delivered a brutal kick to his face with a force that threatened to break his bones. Arthur held him still by his hair as rivers of blood streamed down from his broken nose.

"Now listen up," Ruby growled. She pinned him with an icy glare as Royal wiped away the blood dripping down his chin. "I'll be doing the talking - you just sit back and listen."

Ruby strode towards the window on the far side of the room. She spun around with a fire in her eyes, searing him in place as she spoke. “Mrs Royal informed me in her letter that you used to own a grocer's shop didn't you Bernard, under the name of Bernard Williams?”

Royal didn’t flinch, “So, what of it?” He goaded, “Not a crime changing my surname.”

“Shut up.” Ruby snapped, “One day a child came along, not me, another local and stole some bread from you, didn't they?” Her voice was steel, cutting through the air like a whip as she held him captive with her stare.

Royal raised his chin a notch as her questions grew more intense. He crossed his arms in front of him for emphasis and leaned back slightly, never breaking eye contact, or letting his arrogance waver.

"Well, you decided to teach that child some discipline of your own, didn't you?", She spat venomously.

Royal nodded gruffly, his chin jutting out in a defiant gesture. “Yes, the child was a thief, and that is wrong,” he spat, the words dripping with judgment.

His shoulders rose and fell in anger despite the gravity of his statement, as if his abhorrent actions were somehow acceptable that it was nothing but an ordinary affair, yet Ruby and Arthur could feel the utter shock in the air.

Ruby glared at him, "What you weren't aware of is that someone walked into the shop whilst this was taking place and saw what you were doing and that someone had just started working for you. Shall I go on?"

“Please, continue, I’m sure you’ll be telling me anyway.” Royal’s arrogance was followed by another punch from Arthur.

Ruby pulled in a deep breath, hoping to slow her heart hammering away under her rib cage, “Who was it, Royal?” She lunged at the man on his knees before her, not giving him time to answer. Her fingers extended as she clawed a deep four-fingered gouge on the left side of his face.

Royal yelped in pain as she drew back and settled herself on the chair again.

“I’ll tell you, shall I? You evil piece of shit… That person was my father, George Myers.”

The atmosphere in the room crackled with electricity as it strangled the air and crushed Ruby's chest. The feeling was so potent that Ruby thought she was going to suffocate. Her gaze blazed through Royal as she screamed out her truth. "Yes, that's right! He was my father!" A single tear seared down her cheek before she angrily wiped it away with a force so great it felt like shards of glass were slicing up her skin.

Arthur glanced at her in silent concern but there was no stopping Ruby now.

"My dad tried to do what any decent person would and go to the police," Her voice echoed around the walls as the fury inside of her boiled like a volcano ready to erupt at any second. "Which any person would have done after seeing a child being raped, but you weren't gonna let that happen, were you? Not when it threatened your status and reputation." She loomed over him, demanding an answer as the fire in her eyes blazed brighter than ever before.

Royal's jaw clenched as he stared defiantly at his accuser. He shook his head slowly and said, “No and do you know why – it wasn’t rape, the child needed discipline. I told your father exactly that, but he refused to listen.” His voice held a note of pride as he finished.

“My father was a hundred times more a man than you’ll ever be, you sick bastard.” Ruby's harsh words rattled in the air like heavy thunderclaps; she silently hoped her accusation cut through Royal like a sharpened blade. "You didn't just kill him in the shop, no... you took him home to his wife and kids, then beat them, raped my mother, my brother and sister.

Then you set fire to their home! All because you wanted to keep your reputation and gain a seat in parliament, not to mention one day becoming a judge! Is that how you'd dish out the discipline when you sat in your bench chair? No, I think it's because you actually enjoyed what you did and still do." Ruby's voice shook with sorrow as tears streamed down her cheeks. Her rage had reached its boiling point as she reminded Royal that if it weren't for her being locked away in the cellar as a punishment, she too would have been a victim that night and consumed by the raging flames.

Ruby's voice came out low and menacing, oozing hate. "You've known all along who I am, haven't you?" She didn't give him time to answer, she didn't care to hear it. "You destroyed my childhood, stole my family away from me and forced me to grow up in a workhouse just so you would be able to keep your business and reputation." Ruby felt her tears streaming down her face, yet she didn't budge - instead the anger evident in her eyes grew more intense as she leaned in close and hissed: "But that's not all, is it? You used to come to that workhouse and prey on the helpless children living there until the woman running it saw your disgusting behaviour. She threw you out, but the dread you caused lingered on like a dark cloud. Back then I tried to run away every time I saw you coming. Recently, your voice has been familiar too - but I never realised who you actually were because the trauma of that night has taken away some of the horror from my memory. In Mrs Royal's letter, I finally got my answer; she had spilt your secrets, opening my eyes to your true nature and your true identity and then everything began to make sense and the holes in my memory were filled, and then I remembered, I remembered it all." Ruby dropped her head while still keeping eye contact, "You're pure evil Royal, plain and simple.

Royal's mouth hung agape as his face blanched with shock. His hands now trembled and his pulse in his neck quickened as he processed the words that had just been spoken.

The air in the room was heavy with resentment, like a foul fog that clung to Ruby's skin. In her hand, she clenched the knife, her knuckles white from the strain of her grip. Her blood sang for revenge, and she wanted to plunge the blade into his eye but that would be too simple and too merciful. She needed to know if he was responsible for the deaths of all those innocent girls, so she could make him pay for his crimes in full. After all he was capable of, surely the answer would lie with him.

She gritted her teeth, fury boiling beneath her thin veil of civility. "Bernard, did you kill those girls? Or do you know who did?"

Royal's jaw quivered slightly as he glanced away, avoiding Ruby's gaze. He tried his best to maintain a stoic expression, yet his eyes had already begun to betray the truth—he didn't have an answer. His shoulders hunched forward as he breathed out a quiet "No, I didn't and no I don't."

“Oh, I think you do, so I should tell me, or your prize possessions won't survive the night!” She pressed the blade against his groin, pushing down until it rested against one of his testicles.

Royal's scream echoed off the walls as he shook with fear. Tears streamed down his face as sweat soaked his skin. "I swear I don’t know, but I do have a hunch who it may be!"

Ruby twisted the blade slightly to emphasize her point. "If you don't tell me - fast - I'm not going to stop at threats! Next time, I'll draw blood."

He shook his head vehemently. "Please believe me! The person in question visits here often, they’re from the upper classes of society," he said, his voice breaking with terror. "They have certain… tastes.” He said rapidly. “Listen, I kept a notebook downstairs; it was my retirement plan, a way of getting money for my silence, it’s yours, just let me go."

"Not likely," Arthur interjected mockingly. "The book… it’s blackmail in other words."

“No, no!” Royal stammered, his eyes wide and wild. His lips quivered with fear as he tried to force a smile. “It’s just... keeping me sweet so I don't speak up." He laughed nervously, but it only served to ignite Ruby's rage.

"Yes, blackmail," Arthur corrected coldly. "Fucking prick."

“If you are deceiving us, it won’t be just your nuts you’re lose.” Ruby sprang up, pushing her foot onto the chair as she slid the blade back into her boot. “Does it also have all the names of the women and children you’ve brought here against their will too?”

Royal’s jaw hung slackly at the question. “Ah, n…no, it doesn’t, the plan wasn’t to keep them here long, we… I-” He stammered.

But Ruby noticed his slip, “We, who?” She interrupted.

His face paled as he realised, she’d noticed, “It’s just me with some contacts in France, my wife’s nephew, he lives there, that’s all.” He broke eye contact and looked to the floor. “He needed the money, his business isn’t working well, so…”

“Unbelievable,” Ruby seethed, “so, is there anything else I should know? And where is the book, if you won’t say two of your crown jewels will be bouncing across this floor.” She sneered through gritted teeth.

“I have!” Royal exclaimed desperately. “I’ve told you all I know, I’m telling the truth,” He gasped, quivering under Arthur’s grip.

“Where is it hidden?” Arthur growled, yanking harder on Royal’s hair.

“It's locked in a cabinet down in the main drawing room, and the keys to it are in my waistcoat pocket,” Royal stuttered, pointing over at his clothes.

"Get dressed," Arthur snarled as he dragged Royal to his feet. "Billy’ll take him to the wagon with the others and then we can search for that book; let's see if any names leap out at us."

Ruby's eyes remained trained on the floor as she followed Arthur, her hands still trembled, and her heart continued to race. He held a squealing Royal with one arm as they descended the stairs, their footfalls echoing off the walls.

Ruby's heart was heavy from all she had just heard. To think of all the people he had hurt, and all that he would have kept on doing if they hadn't stopped him. He had committed countless atrocities and Ruby couldn't make sense of his cruelty. Despite what Mrs Royal had already told her, nothing could prepare Ruby for this truth. He was a real monster, and his words cut deep inside her soul like a knife. She thought of her parents and siblings that were taken too soon; nothing could bring them back.

With sadness overwhelming her heart, Ruby let out a solemn oath: "I promise he'll get what he deserves," she said, her gaze upwards towards the heavens as if seeking approval from her loved ones. She could only hope that they could hear her pledge of justice - even if, sadly, it had come far too late for them.

Ruby and Arthur raced through the rooms, ripping up the carpets and emptying drawers in search of the notebook. They worked with a feverish intensity until Ruby accidentally brushed against a panel on the wall. Ruby felt a tingle on the back of her neck as she noticed the unmistakable sound of something unlocking. A spark of anticipation flickered in her chest and her heart pounded. She pushed at the panel to reveal a small compartment of which was hosting an ancient wooden box. Arthur pulled it out with shaking hands and examined it to find that it was locked shut. No matter how hard they tried, none of the keys Royal had given them worked.

In a desperate attempt, Ruby used her hairpin to unlock the chest. After many failed attempts it suddenly rendered with a click, the lock gave way. Inside lay a well-thumbed notebook, promising answers to any questions they may have had. Finally, they'd found it.

Ruby and Arthur decided to regroup at the pub, after calling at Doctor Barnardo's to drop off the women and children. The two wagons rocked side to side in the faint light of the gas lamps as they made their way. It wouldn't be long before they would be extinguished.

The captives were bound with rope and shoved into the back of the second cart. Some trembled with fear, others silently wept as they realized their imminent fate at the hands of the associates. All around them, shadows moved quickly and quietly, judging eyes ever watchful of who had been up to no good.

Ruby and Arthur trudged up the gravel path to Dr Barnardo's clinic. Ruby pounded on the door until his light came on and she heard a muffled voice inside. Barnardo stood frozen on the porch, taken aback by the unexpected visitors. They rushed in, pushing past him and into the warmth of the house. Their breath fogged in the cold night air, and their faces were stung red from the chill.

Ruby guided the women and children inside, into the dimly lit hallway. The place smelled of carbolic soap and medicinal herbs.

A solitary painting of a man in clinical dress is hung on the whitewashed wall with no caption or decoration around it. The name on the plaque read John Michaelis Barnardo. The doctor's father perhaps? Heavy brocade curtains hung over the doorways leading off from the long hallway and muted moonlight filtered through a small window in the front door and played over the group of people as they gingerly stepped across the floorboards underfoot.

Ruby explained everything to Barnardo, and he then welcomed them with warmth and compassion. The women and children clung tightly together, their eyes wide with fear as they absorbed their surroundings.

Dr Barnardo ushered them into his office where he could examine each one in turn. After assessing their needs, he gave them blankets, warm clothes, and showed them to the bathhouse where they could wash away a little of the sorrow that hung around them like a fog.

Later, when they were settled in a safe space and had enjoyed a hot meal, Ruby spoke with the doctor. She sighed as she settled onto the couch next to Dr Barnardo. "What can we do to help these people?" She asked, her voice filled with concern.

Dr Bernardo steepled his fingers, rested his elbows on his desk and said, "We need to make sure they have a safe place to stay and that they're well-fed. But firstly, we must try our best to reunite them with their loved ones."

Ruby Myers had seen the toll of poverty, the unspoken grief, the unmet needs. But this, this was something different, and it had taken a toll on her too.

She followed the doctor into the hospital ward, where the group of people sat, exhausted from the journey. Most were now wearing the donated old clothes, but their faces were lined with worry. Ruby gazed at the scene before her, and her chest tightened as a lump rose in her throat.

"Let's start with finding their loved ones first," she said. “Do you think they’ll recover from this?” She looked across at Barnardo, her heart heavy after what she’d witnessed.

The doctor nodded. "It's hard to know for sure, Miss Myers, but being here is a good thing. I can make sure they get any help they need. Hopefully, the right care and being reunited with their loved ones will help a lot." He looked at Ruby his eyes full of concern.

Ruby felt a wave of relief wash over her. Thank you," she said, giving him a small smile, “I know they’re grateful for your help.

The doctor returned her smile and patted her shoulder lightly. "You're welcome," he said. "Now go and get some rest, you look exhausted."

Back in the cart, Ruby cradled the black notebook close to her chest like a treasure. She scanned through the endless list of names etched on each page - Clifford Byford, Captain Smythe… Some of them were familiar, and she thought of all the wealth Royal would’ve acquired from these people who frequented his brothel. Suddenly, the black notebook felt heavier than before.

Arthur noticed her distress and reached out to take her gloved hand in his own. He kissed her fingers gently before looking into her eyes with concern. "Are you alright, my girl?" he asked softly. She nodded and tucked the book into her pocket, then looked up at him. In that moment, she could feel some of the weight lift off her shoulders.

"I feel different," she said as she squeezed his hand. "After reading that letter from Mrs Royal, so many things I didn't remember came flooding back, and I've never cried like that before, but it's helped because I've let out all the anger and grief from losing my family, and the resentment over the upbringing in the workhouse, that's gone too." She looked away as the wagons came to a stop outside the pub. The horses sniffed each other with their broad noses, puffing clouds of warm air into the cold winter dawn as they climbed down.

Arthur's mouth tightened into a thin line as he surveyed the trembling men in the cart. He sighed in resignation and turned to Billy. "Put them down in the cellar, until we can find somewhere else less obvious."

Billy flashed a cruel smile, his sinister eyes glinting in the early dawn light. "Can't we start teaching them a lesson now?"

A man sobbed openly while another soiled his trousers, the others, including Royal sat with mouths hanging in a terrified gape.

Billy just laughed. “Christ anyone would think I’m the devil incarnate! What’s the matter ladies, cat got your tongues, oh no that comes later my cat loves the odd tongue for his supper now and then.” He winked at Arthur.

Arthur sniggered at Billy's taunting before clapping him on the back. “Now, now Bill it’s not nice to insult the local pond life, aye… Thanks for tonight mate.”

“No problem, Art, anytime, she alright?” He asked pointing his chin in Ruby’s direction.

“Yeah, she’ll be alright, nothing that sleep, and a good rest won’t solve.” Arthur answered as he walked over to join Ruby.

Billy gave a nod of understanding before turning his attention back to the cart. He motioned towards Stan who had just let slid the bolt back from the door at the end. “C'mon Stan, me ole mate, let’s unload the ladies shall we.”

Ruby opened the creaky door of the pub and stepped into the musty atmosphere. The edges of morning peeked in through the windows, but the only occupants were a few discarded whiskey bottles and dirty beer glasses. A faint smell of cigarettes lingered, mixing with the sweat-stained air.

Ruby made her way to the stairs, her movements loud in the emptiness of the place. She stopped at Arthur’s desk and slumped into one of its chairs, exhaustion streaming from every pore. She took a deep breath and prepared herself for what was to come.

Arthur shuffled into the room, two steaming cups of tea in his hands. He passed one to her with a tired smile. "Sugar, nice and hot, just how we like it." She smiled back and he leaned in for a kiss before settling down in the chair opposite her.

She wrapped her hands around the warm mug before taking a sip. The sweet liquid felt comforting on her tongue, like wrapping herself up in a favoured blanket. "Mmm, that's good." She sat back and closed her eyes momentarily enjoying the peace.

"Let's hope tonight will be the end of it all, Rubes." Arthur took a swig from his own tea before placing it onto the desk. "Once the others finish getting our guests settled, then we can sit down and see what answers that book can give us."

The pages in Ruby's pocket felt like a big carbuncle needing to be lanced. She pulled it out and handed it to Arthur. "Here, you hold onto it for now."

Arthur examined the book in his hands, flipping through each page with a growing sense of curiosity. He pointed out names of people in Parliament and local aristocracy, with a letter "C" next to those who had taken advantage of children. His face grew pale as he spoke, "Bloody hell, Rubes, this could be like molten lead in the hands of the coppers, this could bring down most of parliament and some of the gentry too."

Ruby's stomach sank at the thought. She looked into her teacup and spoke absentmindedly. "I know I run a brothel, but I couldn't imagine letting any of the girls be treated in such a way. All of the ladies at the townhouse have medical care, respectful punters too. I don't take money from them; it's the punters that pay me beforehand as well as paying the girls for their time. The girls' money is theirs, plain and simple."

Arthur gave Ruby's hand a reassuring squeeze. "Rubes," he said, "they'll always be someone that disagrees with whatever you do. The truth is all that matters, you and the girls have an understanding that works for both sides, anyone else should keep their noses out." He rose to his feet, gesturing for her to follow him downstairs.

"Just a moment Arty," She reached out and grasped his hand tightly in hers. "The list of names, some with upper-class titles and wealth," she sighed before setting down her cup of tea on the desk, and turned to him, her voice laced with worry. "Who is going to believe us over these people?" The question hung between them as she waited for an answer.

"I'd already thought of that, my love. I'll be handing this over to Abberline once we've got what we need from it. He at least will make sure the information will be used in the correct way and bring down some of the cretins." He looked at her with certainty in his eyes. "You trust him enough to do that?" She asked as she stood up.

"I wouldn't of before all this mess, but now I've seen how this copper works and it may surprise you, I can honestly say I think he will." Arthur smiled at her, "c'mon my girl, stop your fretting. Let's nip down to the cellar and see how Billy is getting on." Arthur stretched lazily and then walked towards the door.

A smirk spread across Ruby's lips as she spoke to Arthur. "I think I'll wait in the bar, if that's all the same to you?" She followed Arthur out of the office and down the stairs. "Do you think he knows more than he's telling?" She watched as he approached the steps to the cellar.

Arthur's fingers moved thoughtfully over the wood, running along the scuffed paint and warped planks of the cellar door. "Knowing Royal, I wouldn't be surprised. It could be that he's worked with someone else, not just Bullstrode either, or that he has put two and two together and has actually worked it out for himself. He did say that the killer does frequent his brothel, so…" With a deep breath, Arthur pressed down on the iron handle but didn't go through the door. "My theory is that Bullstrode is involved in this somehow, he'd be perfect as he's been working for Barnardo. He must have other contacts in London who are in on it. It's not something that can be run alone. Whoever else was involved, they have contacts, supplies, lads at port cities, and certainly someone like Bullstrode who had been working for Barnardo would be perfect to help transport the victims. That aside, we shouldn't forget that there's still a murderer on the loose and it's important that we catch the bastard that's roaming the streets." He rolled up his sleeves and pushed the door open it creaked loudly in protest.

"I think I'll come with you, I'm interested to know what he's got to say for himself." Ruby crossed the room and followed Arthur down the cellar steps "How's it going, anyone spill yet, Bill?"

Inside, Ruby could see several huddled forms in the dim light of the small room. Several whimpered quietly as Arthur stepped into the dank air of captivity.

Billy's eyes darted up, locked on to the man before him. "Well, this one won't be saying anything anytime soon, mate," he said coldly. His fingers ran along the man's jawline in three quick strokes, and then he pointed to his face. "He's dead, that last punch must've been too much." Billy signalled to one of the other lads who stood at the back of the room, who stepped forward and cut the man's bindings with practised efficiency. The body slumped heavily to the floor after Billy gave a one-handed tug to the dead man's shoulder.

Arthur nodded, his fists and jaw tight. With a single sideways glance at Arthur, Billy turned his attention to Royal in the corner. Billy bared chipped teeth in a menacing smile and chuckled. His left hand was smeared with dark red stains, which he used to gesture roughly in Royal's direction as he spoke in a low voice. "How 'bout you? I think it's time for me to have a little play time with our Inspector here." He advanced slowly on Royal, who cowered back into the shadows. The man reached out and grabbed Royal by the hair, yanking him up from the floor. "Get up, prick," Billy snarled as he pulled Royal toward the awaiting chair across the room. "It's ok Art, I've got this, if he tells me anything…" he said his voice was cold and menacing, reverberating off the walls that were still stained with the blood of previous prisoners.

Arthur bared his teeth and clenched his fists. His voice was tight with anger as he said, “Thanks, mate. If he coughs about the bastard who’s killing all these girls that is something I need to know urgently. I also want to know why he kidnapped Ruby too.” He shot Royal a venomous look, “just thank your lucky stars that it’s not me doing the asking, Royal, I’m not as gentle as our Billy here, plus I’ve a notebook to go through.” He watched Royal squirm in his seat before taking Ruby’s hand in his and leading her to the door. “C’mon Rubes, love, let’s go and get another cuppa.”

As they climbed the steps back up to the bar Ruby could hear the screams from Royal as Billy began his interrogation.

Once they were back in the pub Arthur collected the notebook from his office. The pair settled themselves at the largest table in the pub and waited for the other associates to join them.

The door creaked open, and Solomon entered accompanied by two towering bodyguards. He scanned the room, with his one eye, a silence following him like a dense fog. When his gaze found Arthur and Miss Ruby, a smile softened his face. “Arthur, Miss Ruby,” he said politely and then shook Arthur’s hand before settling himself comfortably into a chair.

He nodded towards the men at his back. “Thanks, lads, it's fine—wait outside.” His voice was casual, yet firm, like soft velvet brushed with steel.

Ruby caught Arthur's raised eyebrow as he watched his acquaintance relax into the seat. Solomon answered without Arthur asking the question. "Turf war over my district, that's why I'm playing it careful with the lads." His one eye settled on Arthur, and he pointed a thumb over his shoulder. "I'm surprised you haven't been informed," he asked in an even tone.

Arthur stood and crossed to the bar, gesturing to the bottle of whiskey he'd brought out earlier. "I heard something on the grapevine but figured if you wanted me involved, you'd ask… you always had my back Sol, so it works both ways, drink?" Arthur grabbed two tumblers and carefully filled them each with a generous pour of the amber liquid, before handing one to Solomon.

"Thanks Arthur," Solomon said and then proceeded to take a long, slow sip. He rolled the booze around in his mouth and smiled approvingly. "Single malt, huh? You always did know how to pick the good stuff." With that, he took another swig and lounged back, resting his half-empty glass on his thigh.

Arthur nodded his thanks at the compliment as his eyes looked up to the door as several of the others arrived.

Half an hour later and everyone was assembled. "Thanks for coming lads," Arthur began as he looked around the table at each of men sitting there. "We've still got a few people downstairs," He pointed down at the table, "with Billy," Several of the men sniggered at the mention of Billy's name. "Yep, Billy is playing host to our guests," Arthur continued.

"More like Angel of death, Arthur." A man with a chubby face tittered as he looked around at the other men chuckling at his comment.

Ruby couldn't help but smile herself, everyone was well aware of Billy's interrogation techniques.

"Yes, thank you, Richie." Arthur said with a grin, "We need to plough through these names," he picked up the black leather-bound pages and waved it in the air before continuing. "We all know what this book is about, and we need to go through it with a fine-toothed, and anything we're not sure of, I'm sure our friend Royal will be more than obliging with any missing details, once we've got anything useful that could lead us to the murderer then Abberline can have it. That's after we've had a good head start so we can get to him first, that is." He said dropped it back onto the table in front of him and sat down. "Each of us will take a few pages each and we'll go from there."

The room was silent, with only the sound of pages turning and pencils scribbling on paper, as the group searched through the book. They worked diligently and stringent notes were taken. Time seemed to pass slowly, but eventually they had all the information they needed.

Ruby scanned the list of punters, fury radiating from her and the others as they thought of the hurt these men had caused. Determined to get justice, each chose a name to start with. Once tracked down and questioned, they would be dealt with by the associates. But Ruby felt something was missing; none of the names seemed like those of a murderer.

She ran her fingers along the back cover and paused when she noticed a small gap near the spine. With a curious glance around the room, Ruby slipped in her pinkie finger and managed to pry open a hidden pocket. Inside, she found a neatly folded piece of paper.

"Arthur," Ruby called out, "look here! We missed this - it was inside this pocket on the inside back cover."

"Well done, Rubes," Arthur said with admiration as he watched her carefully unfold the page.

Ruby stood stunned as two of the names jumped out at her as she looked at the paper, she handed it to Arthur.

“You’ve got to be kidding me,” Arthur exclaimed, “Mrs Byford is on this page and Royal has the address of the local cemetery and I think this,” He pointed to the writing in front of them, “could this be where he’s having Mrs Royal buried. He looked at Ruby and back at the page in disbelief. “This doesn’t make any sense, Mrs Byford? Why would she be down here and why hide that in the back of the book?”

“But her nephew’s name and her husband’s is down there too.” Ruby looked incredulous as realisation dropped like a stone, this one, Rupert Constantine, and that one Clifford Byford.” Ruby ran her finger under the names, “The nephew lives in France, and owns an art school, her husband on the other hand is dead.”

Arthur's face tightened, "Well, Royal did say that the nephew was his contact in France. So, I think we need to speak with Mrs Byford, she could possibly have some involvement in all this after all." He called over his shoulder as he climbed the stairs to the office, "I'll grab our coats, make sure the cart is ready."

Ruby made for the door, "Billy," she called as she pulled it open, "leave the horse and cart, me and Arthur need to go and visit Mrs Byford." She said as she hoped that Mrs Byford wasn't involved with Royal's cruel enterprise.

Chapter Thirty-Five

The pair raced through the town, the streets silent and eerie as they charged towards Byford's house. The horses snorted frantically under the strain of their wild speed, pouring sweat as they skidded up to its doorstep.

Without hesitation, they both began pounding on the door until a terrified young maid wearing her nightgown opened it sluggishly. Mrs Byford had obviously retired the older woman.

"What do you want?!" She demanded, rage burning away the sleep haze in her eyes.

They didn't wait for an invitation and pushed their way into the hall like a hurricane.

"You can't just barge in like this! What-"

"Clara! Get back to bed now!" Mrs Byford silenced her with a sharp look. She waited until Clara was out of sight before turning her attention to them. "Well? Speak quickly, Miss Myers, Mr Morris, why are you here at this hour?" Her tone had taken on a hard edge as she gestured towards the living room. "I do so hate being roused from my slumber."

The room was dark and oppressive with heavy drapes closing out any possibility of light entering. The furniture was made of solid wood and matched the darkness that permeated the air. A stark difference to last time Ruby had been in there.

Mrs Byford strode over to her chair, but only stood behind it expectantly, her gaze never leaving the two figures standing in front of her.

Neither moved from their spot.

"As you both remain standing, I assume your visit is not one of joy. So?" she said with a silent challenge in her voice.

Ruby's questions swelled within her chest and threatened to explode as she glared at the woman in front of them. Her words stumbled over each other, desperate to be free from her throat. "Mrs Byford, we have evidence that Inspector Royal has been trafficking women and children into London and forcing them to work in the Pickett Street Brothel. Working alongside your nephew."

The blood drained from the woman's face and her knees trembled beneath her. She clung to the back of a chair before slowly sinking into it.

Ruby's eyes flared with rage as her jaw clenched tightly in fury. "Are you part of this too?" she demanded through gritted teeth. Arthur stood silently, the air crackling with anticipation and suspense around them.

Mrs Byford finally broke the silence, lifting one finger slowly but refusing to look at either of them. "Now," she began in a low voice, her gaze still straight ahead, "I have something to say too." She paused for a moment before finally turning her face towards them both.

A deep wave of nausea swept over Ruby as molten anger surged through her veins. Her lips curled back in a snarl as she shouted, "Is that all you have to say? Is this what my money has paid for?" Her hand flew up to grasp Arthur's reassuringly tight on her shoulder, though the calm he tried to impart was lost in a storm of rage.

Mrs. Byford's eyes blazed, and her cheeks flushed red as she spoke. She took a deep, shuddering breath before continuing. "Let me be crystal clear," she said, enunciating each word with purpose. "I wouldn't dream of partaking in something so vile. As for my nephew, I merely write him a letter once a month—it's hardly scandalous. Where on earth did you get this outrageous notion from?" Her raspy breathing punctuated her desperate plea for answers. She gestured wildly to emphasize the severity of her words.

"Earlier, Royal confirmed that he has been bringing women and children here from France to use in the brothel in Pickett Street. Look," Arthur handed her the piece of paper to the woman, "see here, your nephew's name is Rupert Constantine, that's him, isn't it? And this one, your husband?" He stepped back giving Mrs Byford space to digest what he'd just shown her.

"That's the name my nephew uses when he signs his artwork, yes, but that is not his given name." She looked between the two and blinked slowly as she read the name of the graveyard. "My husband as you are aware Miss Myers is no longer with us and the cemetery on the other hand is most likely where my so-called brother-in-law will lay my sister to rest, my father has a plot there for all of us to be interred when the time comes." She stood up and crossed to the fireplace.

Ruby thought she saw a tear trickle down her face.

“Listen,” she said as she turned her eyes on them, “You’ve got this all wrong, I am definitely not bringing people over for them to work in a brothel, yes my nephew lives in France, but as I said, he writes to me every month and I him, but that is as far as the contact goes.” Her breathing was shallow as she tried to get her words out. “I can’t believe that you think I’m involved, we are friends after all, Miss Myers? You think that because my nephew’s artistic name, my husband’s and my own are in a black book that my brother-in-law wrote proves that the three of us are involved in his dirty dealings? A man, may I add, that is the most despicable, cruel, vile human being?” Mrs Byford held their gaze with a challenging look on her face.

The two stood in silencc as Mrs Byford's voice trembled with emotion. She spoke urgently, her words hanging like a noose around them. "I can't imagine why my nephew would be involved in something so vile, the idea sickens me.” She repeated as she handed the page back to Arthur, “and how can my husband when he’s lying in the very cemetery written on that paper?”

“I don’t understand why Royal felt the need to write the name of his resting place on here.” Ruby countered, pointing down at the page Arthur still held in his hand.

Byford gave a weak shrug of the shoulders, “I’ve no idea either, Miss Myers.”

"Mrs Byford, Royal has said that your nephew mentioned that his business isn’t doing so well, and he needed the money," Arthur added.

Her gaze darted to the ceiling as if seeking guidance. “I don’t understand, my nephew has said nothing of this to me. All this is utterly ridiculous, and I don’t want to continue with this conversation any further, now," She spoke firmly as she rose with righteous fury. "It appears that there is nothing more for us to discuss at this time. I’m desperately dismayed that you could think such a thing of me, now I’m going back to bed. Miss Myers, Mr Morris, kindly show yourselves out of my house." Mrs Byford walked towards the door, her long nightgown trailing behind her like a scolded dog. “Miss Myers, my lawyer will be in touch regarding the money you’ve loaned me, I will endeavour to find a way to repay you,” she said over her shoulder. “Good day to you both.”

Ruby thought she heard the woman sob as she watched in dismay as Mrs Byford left the room. Her mind in turmoil as she tried to work out exactly what the conversation had achieved. Apart from the fact that her friendship with Mrs Byford had just gone up in flames, it was painfully obvious, nothing.

Chapter Thirty-Six

Ruby hooked her arm through Arthur's after she climbed down from the cab, and they walked towards Abberline's home. After several hours of sleep and a hot meal, they felt refreshed and sent word to inform him of their visit.

The Inspector opened the door and led them into his parlour. After polite introductions, Emma went into the kitchen to make them all tea.

"So," Inspector Abberline began, "I take it you have some news for me?" He asked indicating for the pair to take a seat.

The sitting room was modestly plain, with few decorations to be seen. A small side table held a vase of roses surrounded by books, the floorboards scratched and marked with a few rag rugs thrown over it. A desk covered in papers, with a candle sending out thin streams of light from its wick, sat in the top left corner of the room. The fire crackled away in the hearth and the delicate scent of rose petals did nothing to dilute the smell of soot. The soft candlelight from the wall sconces above the fireplace cast dancing shadows across Abberline's face, emphasizing his weary expression as he sat in his armchair.

Arthur's face was flat and expressionless as he began to explain. "Inspector, we've been told by Royal that he's been involved in smuggling women and children from France with the intention of exploiting them in his own brothel on Pickett Street. Furthermore, he owns the establishment."

Inspector Abberline shook his head, disbelief colouring his words. “Oh, good lord.” He said and covered his face with one hand, “What the hell... for how long?” He glanced back and forth between Arthur and Ruby, waiting for answers.

“That we’re not so sure about, but judging by this,” Ruby indicated to Arthur who pulled the black book out of his inside pocket and handed it to Abberline. “For some time.”

Abberline began to scan the now loose pages for their content. His face couldn’t hide his feelings.

“It’s a list of people he can bribe Inspector, says it’s for his retirement,” Ruby informed him.

Abberline clenched his jaw and as he continued reading. His hands curled into fists and a flash of anger crossed his face before he managed to regain his composure. His brow furrowed with suspicion, "for heaven's sake Bernard, you are one corrupt bastard along it appears with most of the parliament," he hissed through clenched teeth. He paused for a moment, then met their eyes again. "What else?" he asked coolly.

Ruby unfolded the second piece of paper, her fingers trembling slightly as she passed it over to Inspector Abberline. He scanned it carefully and rubbed a hand across his brow as he read the words. “Rupert Constantine, Mrs Byford and Clifford Byford the MP and an address of a cemetery.” he murmured, looking up at them both, his dark eyes intently searching theirs for answers.

Arthur nodded in affirmation and then glanced sideways to Ruby who had gone pale in reaction to the names. “Yes, that’s right. She’s Royal’s sister-in-law,” Arthur said slowly.

“We paid her a visit this morning,” Ruby added hesitantly, “and she denied any involvement ... after her reaction, I must say I believe her. Plus, her husband, Clifford Byford is dead, so why his name is down there…”

As if on cue, Inspector Abberline stood up from his chair with the book still clasped in one hand. He looked between them both before settling his gaze on Arthur. “What does Royal have to say about her?” he asked.

“He mentioned her name - at least that’s what Billy told me. But we haven't spoken to him ourselves yet. He’s down in the cellar at the pub.”

The inspector gave a solemn nod before turning away from them and striding confidently towards the door. “We need to bring Royal in for questioning then,” he announced over his shoulder as he pulled open the door, “let's go.”

“He met with a bit of an accident,” Arthur offered, as he stood up a sly grin played on his face, “fell down and bruised his kisser badly,” he continued. “You know how these things happen Inspector, uneven ground and all that.” He glanced across and winked at Ruby, after checking that Abberline wasn’t looking.

Abberline held up his hand and then wearily scratched his forehead. “Mr Morris, let’s just get him to the station shall we.” He said as he made his way to the parlour door. “We’ll discuss his condition later, I’m sorry Emma, we’ve no time for the tea,” Abberline called. “I need to go back to the station, don’t wait up.” He stood in the hallway and shrugged his coat on.

The disembodied, muffled voice of Emma was heard from the kitchen as the three of them opened the front door and stepped into the night.

Chapter Thirty-Seven

The three of them trudged to the main street, feeling an impending sense of dread. Abberline had flagged down a Hansom and Ruby and Arthur climbed into it. The mood was heavy in the cab, as the reality of their situation had set in.

When they arrived at the hostelry, Arthur leapt out of the cab and declared he would meet them at the station in ten minutes. With that, he vanished inside the pub leaving Ruby and Abberline to continue on alone with their sombre thoughts.

Ruby broke the silence, “Inspector, how far do you think Royal’s corruption has gone?” Fear filled her eyes as they both pondered what further secrets lay waiting for them.

“I dread to think, Miss Myers.” he grumbled as he stared out the window of the cab, his face intermittently illuminated by the faint yellow glow of passing gas lamps.

Ruby eyed the Inspector, feeling a strange sense of admiration. Despite the discoveries that had been made, he still believed in justice and searched tirelessly for answers. With her gaze now fixed on the window, she said softly, "I'm sorry, Inspector Abberline, that your friend became what he is today."

His eyes flicked over to her, and he nodded solemnly.

Ten minutes later they pulled up outside the station. There was a low light burning from the police lantern up on the wall and Ruby noticed that the reception was well lit too.

Abberline helped her down from the cab and then she followed him as he strode purposefully into the building.

A tinkling of laughter could be heard from a room further down the hallway, which ran parallel to the front door.

The fire burned low in the hearth and paperwork was strewn all over the desk adjacent to it.

The place was empty, no one at the desks.

His forehead creased in confusion, Abberline marched towards the direction of the noise. This wasn't how the station usually was, it had once bustled with activity, it was now quiet and abandoned.

Ruby hesitated and chose to remain where she was until being invited through. She heard a door open. "Good god Constable," Royal suddenly shouted. The suddenness of the statement made Ruby flinch where she stood.

A woman screamed, and then giggled, followed by a man's voice calling for her to cover herself up.

"How dare you conduct such intimate business on these premises. Madam, make yourself decent and you constable go home to your wife, I will deal with you in the morning."

A few moments later a partially dressed woman, hastily adjusting her skirt, followed by the constable dragging up his trousers came into view. The woman was still grinning as the pair passed her, but the constable looked shaken and ashamed.

"Oops," Ruby couldn't help her sarcasm as she watched the pair disappear out of the building.

Abberline came back into the room, "Apologies Miss Myers, please follow me." He invited.

He showed her into a small, untidy office, different to the one she'd been in before. The fire in the hearth had long burnt out and the chill in the room made Ruby shudder. Abberline gestured at a chair near to the back wall and then hung his coat on the standby the door, as Ruby sat down.

"Could I take your coat for you Miss Myers?" Abberline asked politely.

"Don't worry, I feel a bit of a chill, so I'll keep it on thank you." She replied. "Arthur should be with us in a few moments," Ruby added trying to break the tension that had accumulated in the room.

"Yes, I'll have to wait for him out there," Abberline pointed over his shoulder, "the other constable that was on duty appears to have also vanished." He lit the oil lamp on the desk and turned up the wick, then pushed his hands into his pockets as he left the room.

Ruby glanced around the space which was a hotchpotch of files, dust, and office furniture. She couldn't help but wonder how many hours had been spent in the room with the occupant trying hard to catch the lawbreakers within the district. A plague on the desk said Det. Insp. Edmund J.J. Reid. This was his office then.

She looked up at a picture that hung lopsidedly on the wall near the desk. She stood up and moved closer to gain a better look. Two men stood with chests out, both were holding a glass in one hand and a cigar in the other.

The room behind them was decorated with dark wood panels, burnished leather chairs and sofas, and large portraits of important figures from the 1800s. The walls were lined with bookshelves filled with old tomes. A fireplace at one side of the room provided a warm glow to the atmosphere. Chandeliers hung from the ceiling, provided soft illumination. In the centre of the room, several tables were set up for card games and other activities. A dark wooden bar was at one end of the room, appeared to be stocked full of fine spirits. Both men had straight faces. The small plaque underneath displayed the names Clifford Byford MP and Inspector Edmund Reid. So, one of these men was Mrs Byford's late husband. Interesting.

As she pondered, she heard Arthur's voice along with Billy's. Moments later they entered the room dragging a limp Inspector Royal.

Abberline followed them in as they dropped Royal into a waiting chair. He slumped forward, so Billy grabbed his hair and held him back in the seat to keep him upright. Royal's face was badly bruised, dried blood caked his hair and parts of his features, one eye was swollen shut, the other kept rolling back into his head as he drifted in and out of consciousness.

"Don't think we'll get much out of him this evening," Abberline observed. "He can go down into one of the cells until morning. I'll call the doctor to take a look at him and then we'll question him further."

“That’s if he survives the night,” Billy added. “That was a pretty bad fall he suffered earlier, wasn’t it Arthur?”

“It certainly was.” Arthur agreed. “Shall we take him to the cell, Inspector?”

Abberline nodded, “This way, gentlemen.” He indicated for them to follow.

Arthur glanced across at Ruby and was just about to lift Royal from his seat when he happened to notice the picture on the wall behind her. “Wait a minute, who’s that bloke in the photo?”

“One of them is Mrs Byford’s husband, Arty but I don’t know which one,” Ruby told him as she turned her attention to the picture again.

“It’ll be the one on the left,” Abberline offered, “the other is the recently deceased Inspector Reid, died from a heart attack. Why’d you ask Mr Morris?”

“Well, that can’t be Byford’s late husband as that’s the bloke I saw hanging around outside my pub, remember Rubes?”

Ruby’s head snapped around at the picture again, “which one, him?” She asked as she stared at the man with his overly oiled hair, small moustache, and a mole on his cheek.

She watched as Abberline's eyes widened and he fumbled in his pocket and produced the small, ornate, silver snuff box. He held it up to inspect the picture on its lid and inhaled sharply. “Well, I’ll be damned,” he said, disbelief in his voice. “That’s not a church, it's an old picture of the bloody House of Commons, before it was renovated. Ruby leaned forward, her curiosity palpable. "And it appears," she added softly, "that Clifford Byford isn't actually dead."

Chapter Thirty-Eight

Ruby and Arthur reluctantly climbed into the cart, energized for the journey to Mrs Byford's. Billy snapped the reigns and guided the horses in the direction of their destination. Abberline had agreed to stay with Inspector Royal and meet them at Mrs Byford's house once he'd secured another constable on duty.

The once-bustling streets were now empty, as if the buildings themselves were holding their breath, save for the occasional scuttle of a rat or the hoot of a distant owl. A full moon shone down, illuminating the road in front of them with its silver-blue light. Wrought iron fences spun past them like intricate spiderwebs, their long shadows stretching out over the cobbles. The cart rushed over the bumpy terrain, jolting them back and forth, as they held on to dear life. Each bump sounded like an earthquake and reverberated through their bones.

Ruby stomach knotted and she felt restless as they made their way back to the Byford household. The journey seemed longer than before, as if her feet were dragging through treacle, and her breath quickened with each step closer she took. Arthur held her tightly, his arm like an iron band around her shoulders, reassuringly whispering words of comfort. "It'll be okay Rubes," he murmured against her head, "We'll track down Mr Byford; that shouldn't take too long once I get the usual lads involved." He kissed the top of her head before guiding her up the path towards the foreboding house.

A light was still burning brightly in the hallway window and Ruby shuddered involuntarily at its beacon-like call.

The three of them stared in disbelief as the maid opened the door, her face drained of colour and her eyes wide with fear. She barely opened the door enough to step outside before quickly slamming it shut.

"You have to go," she begged in a hushed whisper, terror radiating off her body as her gaze darted between the two of them and back over her shoulder. "I've been told not to let anyone in. Please," she begged again, her voice on the brink of hysteria. "It's not safe."

Arthur had endured enough of the conversation; with a sudden surge of energy, he shoved the maid aside and stormed into the hall. Ruby and Billy scrambled to keep up, barely managing to follow him in before he slammed the door shut.

Disembodied voices were coming from behind the door on the left. One was female and could be recognised as Mrs Byford's the other, was male.

"Billy keep an eye out in the hallway, we're expecting Abberline at some point." Arthur instructed. "Me and Ruby will be in there." He pointed in the direction where the conversation could be heard.

Ruby and Arthur stormed over and burst into the room. The swift action had the man out of his chair and Mrs Byford let out a blood-curdling shriek of terror as her whole body went rigid.

Byford had gone completely white, her eyes wide, her form trembling and rocking back and forth in an attempt to comfort herself. When she realised that it was Arthur and Ruby stood before her, she managed a weak, "Please help me, I think I'm going mad. Do you see a man sat in that chair?" She pointed across at the man opposite her.

Ruby rushed over and wrapped her arms around the woman, trying desperately to calm her down. "It's okay Mrs Byford, we're here to help, yes, we see him too." She said gently.

Arthur stepped forward and bellowed out, "Well if it isn't the late Mr Clifford Byford MP!" The words dripped with malice.

The man stepped confidently across the room and stopped directly in front of Arthur, meeting his eyes with an icy gaze. Arthur had seen that look before, and he knew what it meant, danger. The dark-haired man's heavily oiled hair was cut short around his ears, accentuating a strong jawline. A small mole perched on his left cheek, below a large black moustache, which twitched under his nose. His five foot eleven frame came dressed in a well-tailored blue suit. He looked around the room at each of them in turn.

"So, you've worked it out, how clever. You do realise of course that neither of you will be leaving here alive" Clifford said with an unearthly smirk, holding up a hand in warning. "It's Rupert Constantine now, but my name in my previous life is that of Clifford Byford." he said over his eyes never leaving Arthur's.

“I think it’s best if I take Mrs Byford back to her bedchamber, she looks quite ill.” Ruby suggested, helping Mrs Byford out of her seat, and firing a concerned look at Arthur.

Ruby caught sight of Clara with Billy in the hallway and helped Mrs Byford to the door, before calling the maid over. “Clara take her to her bedroom and stay with her until I arrive. Lock the door and don't open it for anyone but me," Ruby commanded harshly.

The maid didn’t argue, just nodded meekly, and led Mrs Byford upstairs.

Ruby strode back into the room, finding Arthur still standing in the same spot, arms folded tightly against his chest and rage written plainly on his face. She sat down in the chair vacated by Mrs Byford.

“Speak, now!” She shouted her voice so sharp it seemed to sting. Clifford was now sitting in the chair opposite Ruby. He leisurely pulled out a leather pouch and smoking papers. He meticulously rolled a cigarette, his fingers dexterous with practice, as if he had all the time in the world.

Rage coursed through Arthur's veins as he lunged at the man, grabbing him by the shoulders and lifting him off the seat, the pouch of tobacco and papers were scattered to the floor. His eyes were wild and vicious as he shook him. “You need to tell us how Mrs Byford is involved with the brothel and why you faked your own death.” He let him go and he dropped heavily back into the seat.

"Mr Morris, it appears your etiquette has not been refined." he sneered with a malicious glint in his eye.

"If you don't answer me, I'll yank out your tongue with a teaspoon," Arthur snarled.

Ruby glared at the man in front of her, "Answer his question," she demanded.

Constantine picked a loose grain of tobacco off his tongue. "I merely wanted to see what I was up against, to learn something about your lover, Miss Myers." His eyes traced all over her body as he spoke.

Ruby shivered under his gaze, stood up and walked towards Arthur. "You killed all those innocent girls, didn't you?" She asked.

Constantine sniggered, exhaling a stream of smoke from his cigarette. His cold, calculating gaze met Ruby's piercing stare. He barked out a laugh and took a drag on his cigarette. His face was illuminated by its flame, revealing the darkness in his heart. "Innocent girls, indeed," he sneered. "Like pigeons spreading their filth! They need to be eliminated like animals!"

Ruby's face contorted and her body tremored as she looked away. She pursed her lips, and her eyebrows furrowed in a display of pure revulsion. "No one deserves to die like that. What you did was wrong, immoral - they were all human beings, not some meaningless pawn in your twisted game!" She screamed, her voice echoing around them.

Arthur's eyes narrowed into razor sharp slits. Ruby trembled in his arms, and he instinctively drew her closer, his body like a shield between her and Constantine.

"Why?" Arthur boomed through gritted teeth. "What was the sense in killing them, they'd done you no harm."

Constantine's expression shifted from smugness to pure malice as he leaned in close. His eyes were cold and determined, and a sinister smirk formed on his lips. "As you won't be leaving this house alive," he whispered darkly, "so I'll tell you." Yes, the girls were my work –a cleansing ritual. I killed them because I was unsure which one originally gave me this damned disease. It was of course their fault, filthy, diseased animals." He raised a single finger into the air before adding slyly, "All except Jane and Martha; Jane got caught up in the wrong place at the wrong time when I couldn't get at you," he pointed at Ruby, "so I chose her instead. And Martha," he laughed a cruel, chilling laugh, "was just an added bonus." He waved a hand dismissively and uttered, "C'est la vie," as they say in France." He peered into their souls, his voice dripping with sadistic pleasure. "Oh, and I swiped those calling cards from that associate of yours, Mr Morris before he passed away," he said coldly. "Then for a bit of fun, I wrote a little poem, just for Ruby, did you like it my dear? Left at the theatre before your darling Elsie was tragically taken from you." He sneered at her and seemed to look right through her, deep into her soul.

Arthur's jaw clenched, and he held Ruby tighter to him.

"Then lastly, just for a bit of amusement, I ripped out the tongue of one of the women - I can't recall which - and posted it to Inspector Royal with a warning to stay quiet." A sneer crossed his face as he relished in his own deviousness. He leaned forward, his fists clenched tightly and fingers white-knuckled as they curled into the worn fabric of the chair's armrests. His gaze was piercing and unforgiving as he spat out his words.

Ruby's voice quivered with raw emotion, "Why Elsie? She didn't do anything to you, and you left the evidence of a potential pregnancy too!" Tears streamed down her face unchecked.

Ruby stared at him in disbelief, shock and terror contorting her face as his words sunk in.

His eyes burned into her like embers of a raging fire. "Ah, Elsie... I had to take something from you Miss Myers that meant as much to you as my stillborn child." He spat out the words with such force it almost felt like an attack, battering her senses. " I came backstage to invite her for dinner, only to be welcomed by the sight of you two locked in a passionate embrace as the door was ajar. I found an illegal abortionist willing to accept payment for the material that they removed, and I thought it would give you food for thought - I wanted you to understand that maybe Elsie was not just having a relationship with you, my dear." His cruel laugh echoed off the walls as he continued. "It's not nice when someone has control over something so precious, is it? All that and the fact that I was dead...the perfect way to put my plan into action, no one would suspect a dead man after all. As it is, I've only a few months left myself, and I see no reason why I can't be completely candid with you both. I won't be far behind you two actually, and because of this illness I certainly won't be swinging from a rope either." A sinister smirk spread across his face as he revelled in the power, he held over them.

"So why the coins?" Arthur spat through gritted teeth.

Constantine raised an eyebrow, and a sickeningly sweet smile spread across his face as he spoke. "Oh, that, my little calling card." He stood up from his chair and cast aside the stub of his cigarette into the fireplace in one swift motion. "Years ago, I met a beautiful woman," he began.

"Yes, yes your wife, Mildred." Arthur snapped back.

But Constantine continued undeterred. "No, actually it was her sister, Penelope. I fell head over heels in love with the girl. But sadly, she loved another man - your friend Inspector Royal."

Arthur growled low in his throat. "He's not our friend," he said darkly.

Constantine proceeded on, unperturbed by Arthur's ire. "Well anyhow, I thought the best way to stay close to her was to marry her sister - which in time I did." His face shifted into a wistful expression as he made his way over to one of the windows and pulled one of the drapes back. A watery ray of early morning light illuminated his sallow complexion and sunken features.

"If I'm honest," he said quietly, "the woman was a good and loyal wife, but we didn't connect in the bedroom, I've certain preferences, you see." With a terse laugh, he added, "So I took my preferences to a paying establishment instead as my wife was unwilling to partake in such… for want of a better word… activities." He turned slowly and looked at them, his eyes dark and piercing. Without a word, he strode back to the fireplace and placed his hands on the mantel, looming over them like a vulture eyeing its prey.

"Go on," Arthur prodded him, his voice solemn to match the mood that had taken over the room.

"So kind," Constantine spat out the words, his voice dripping with venom. "Eventually, the loyal wife became pregnant, we were both ecstatic at the prospect of having a family. Sadly, and this is where the story takes a tragic turn," He locked eyes with Ruby, his mouth contorted in a snarl. "Sadly, it wasn't meant to be. Although the pregnancy went to term, my wife delivered a stillborn. As if that weren't enough, the baby was horribly deformed. Now, after all these years, it's catching up with me." His gaze drifted to the floor as he spoke. "Our physician ran some tests on me not long before that day. But he didn't give me the results and when he did, they came far too late." He paused to wipe away a tear that had escaped from his eye. "I've got Cupid's disease, and not only did it deform my child, but it's also deformed me too." He touched his temple with his finger. "The doctor did say that it would happen when the illness takes hold and now, I do believe that is the case, I'm going quite mad."

The room fell silent as they absorbed everything he'd said, every detail sitting heavy in their minds.

"And the year this happened?" Ruby asked softly.

He met her gaze once more, his face etched with pain. "1855," he murmured.

Arthur narrowed his eyes and prodded again. "Royal has your name and also your wife's name in a book intended for bribery." he said with a demanding tone, "and that of a cemetery too, for what reason?"

It was six months after I faked my death," Constantine continued with a deep breath, "I was residing in Brighton, one evening I decided to take a stroll along the seafront. Unfortunately, I happened to bump into Sir William Thackeray Marriott the MP for the area. Of course, I denied being me, said I must be a very close lookalike and thought I'd convinced him, but Marriott decided to voice his suspicions to the police. Word trickled back to Royal, and he had great pleasure telling me that he had worked it all out. He decided to take a look at my grave, paid some thugs to dig it up and they found nothing but bricks in the in the casket. Then he tracked me down and took great pleasure in telling me I now owed him." Constantine said matter of factly.

“But that doesn’t explain why your wife’s name is in that book too,” Ruby mentioned.

“Royal thought she was involved, even though I’d told him differently.”

“So, Mrs Byford still doesn't know what happened,” Ruby said with a pang of guilt and relief. “But why did you have to fake your death?” She asked quietly.

“I’d gotten into some underhand activities within parliament, nothing too serious, but enough for it to end my career.” A look of wistfulness briefly crossed his face as he continued, “plus I’d begun a relationship with a former prostitute, the very girl I met at your establishment Miss Myers, my dear Scarlet, sadly she’s dead too, annoyed me one evening, saying she was leaving, so I had to put an end to that.” He stared thoughtfully into the air, then, “also it was common knowledge of my frequenting the local brothels in the area. No one in parliament knew of my diagnosis, it wasn’t something I wanted to be common knowledge.”

“Have you been involved in the trafficking of innocent people as well?” Ruby spat at Constantine, her patience worn to a razor-edged sliver.

Constantine shot her a look of mock indignation, “Of course not, my dear girl. Do you really think I would engage in something that wicked?” He sighed and dropped his gaze to his hands, nervously picking away at his nails. “My odious brother-in-law did ask me if I wanted to be involved when he started it several years ago, but I declined. He involved my wife's nephew – as he lives in Paris and has the contacts apparently. His art school never did very well, so…” He let the sentence hang in the air unfinished, the picking at his nail had become more intense, a sign of his boredom with the conversation topics.

Ruby clenched her fists and her jaw tightened, fiery heat building within her chest until it seemed like she would burst. Her face flushed with anger as the rage pulsed through her veins. She wanted to tear him apart with her bare hands, rip out his eyes for what he had done. “You’re a sick man, Byford, and it’ll be you that won’t be leaving this house alive.” Ruby snarled, her voice low and menacing, “You’ve no chance.”

Arthur moved to intervene, feeling Ruby's body tense at his touch. – But he was too late.

Ruby lunged forward, her fingers curled into claws that tore at the flesh of her target.

A furnace of hatred enveloped her body, and she felt an unholy strength surge through her veins, crackling like lightning. She lunged at Constantine with ferocious intensity, lashing out viciously with her clenched fists and razor-sharp nails.

Her heart raced as she watched the man hit the floor, then sat astride him as he writhed in agony beneath her. With each of his pained cries, she felt a flush of righteous vindication. He was a criminal who caused untold suffering to countless innocents, and now it was time for him to receive his due punishment. She had no room for pity or remorse; only a single-minded mission to bring justice for the wronged and their families. There was no escape for him; she would make sure that he felt every ounce of pain and terror that he had inflicted on others before finally releasing him from this life.

He made desperate grabs for her hands, but her fury was too powerful. Each punch felt like a white-hot bullet and each scratch bled like an animal cornered by its hunter. She was determined to be the one to take his life.

Ruby wept as she straddled the man who had caused such pain and suffering. She pulled her dagger from its hiding place. A ray of morning light struck the blade with an eerie, almost heavenly glow, giving it the unearthly beauty of the angel of death, as if she had come to deliver her vengeance. Her rage and grief fuelled her every movement as she plunged it into him again and again, each thrust representing all the innocent lives he had so cruelly taken.

She felt no forgiveness, only a burning fire within her chest that demanded vengeance until finally, he fell still beneath her.

Throwing the weapon aside, Ruby rushed towards Arthur, and they embraced tightly.

"It's done Rubes, it's finished," his voice quivered with emotion.

It was over, she'd done it, for all the people's lives he'd brutally taken, all the individuals who weren't given a choice. Ruby had done it for them all, she'd finally slain… the devil.

“Billy!” Arthur bellowed. “Help me move this dead man before Abberline arrives! We must get him into the cart and out of here now! And I’ll get some mops and salt water and clean up this blood and find something to cover the wet patch on the floor, that’s the best we can do before the Inspector arrives.” He quickly grabbed the corpse by its ankles and dragged it closer to the wooden cart, his breath coming in ragged gasps as sweat dripped from his brow.

He turned to Ruby, “Quickly go with Billy. Get back to the townhouse and clean up, change your clothes, make sure Rose washes them thoroughly.” His voice held a desperate edge as he hoisted the corpse higher onto the cart, covering it completely with old sacks.

“Here you go Rubes.” Arthur said as he helped Ruby into her seat. “Billy take the long way back, so you won't run into Abberline, I'll sort everything inside and talk to Mrs Byford and the maid. Now go!” With a sharp slap on the horse's behind, it jolted forward at breakneck speed.

“Hang on there, mate - let me get up front first!” Billy yelled hanging on for dear life. “No problem, I'll have Ruby back safe before you know it.”

With that, the cart took off over the cobbles and disappeared into the night.

Chapter Thirty-Nine

Three Weeks Later.

Ruby sat on the hard, wooden seat in the graveyard. It was late afternoon and soon the sun would begin to set over the horizon of a blue sky. The last of the mourners had now left safe in the knowledge that their family member could rest in peace. She watched a large, black crow picking out the worms from the freshly turned earth, Ruby pulled her coat around her shoulders. The only way to keep away the cold that slowly crept through the ground where she sat. Her thoughts played around in her head, trying desperately to sort out what she needed to do next. After everything that had happened, do they both stay in Whitechapel or move on?

She looked around and noticed Abberline approaching. He walked up respectfully before bowing slightly and sinking down onto his haunches, so he was sitting opposite her on a patch of dry grass that wavered slightly in the evening breeze.

"Miss Myers," he greeted as he removed his hat briefly. "May I?" He pointed at the space next to her.

"Yes, Inspector," she answered politely as she slid sideways so he could join her.

"Please give Mrs Byford my heartfelt condolences," he said with sincere concern in his voice.

"Of course," she replied calmly but flatly, acknowledging his sentiments while not really accepting them fully yet or perhaps ever. "I know you did your best but…"

"We got him though, found him floating in the Thames, been there awhile by all accounts, so lord knows what happened after he escaped from Mrs Byford's that evening, but it is justice for Mrs Byford," he pointed over at the grave – "for everyone today," he added as an afterthought.

A very brief, relieved smile crossed her lips as she realized Abberline was none the wiser about her role in disposing Mr Byford's body. She let out a big sigh, like the weight of the world had been lifted off her shoulders. "Ah yes," she said with a calming breath. "Would you kindly answer a question for me regarding Inspector Royal?"

"What about him?" Abberline replied, his voice tight with frustration as he clenched his jaw. His brow furrowed and Ruby could see the remnants of pain in his eyes. He shook his head and looked away, letting out a sigh before facing her again. "What was it that you wanted to ask me?" A slight breeze blew around his neck. He shuddered before he adjusted his coat collar, then his gaze met hers expectantly.

Ruby gave Abberline a penetrating stare that didn't waver. "Did he die in that cell that night or do you think someone helped him on his way?"

Abberline glanced away, unable to meet her inquiring gaze. He cleared his throat and shifted uncomfortably on the seat before responding. "Miss Myers, Doctor Sequeira came to check on him for me very late in the evening. When I saw him last, he seemed comfortable, despite his fall. Sadly, when the constable checked on him later in the night, he found Royal deceased in his cell. The injuries were not as simple as originally thought." He cleared his throat again. "That's the facts and a report has been filed of that nature." He concluded.

Ruby's expression grew solemn, her eyes fixed on the grave. "All that matters is that he's dead," she whispered, turning towards Inspector Abberline. "and he can't cause harm to anyone ever again. Mrs Byford has seen to it that he's a long way from the family plot too."

Abberline nodded in agreement, pushing his hat up ever so slightly. "Ah, yes. Mrs Royal - god rest her soul." He paused for a moment before continuing. "I can't help but feel total sorrow for her, the poor woman," he said, gesturing towards Ruby with an open hand.

Ruby looked down at her gloved hands. "If you will excuse me for one moment?" She stood up and made her way across to the freshly opened grave and to where a wreath hung from a post. She stayed there for a minute or two, picked up some dirt and threw it in on top of the coffin and then returned to sit beside him once more. "The misery she must've endured under his grasp, I'm just thankful for the letter she wrote me." She took a deep breath as she looked across the graveyard, her face slowly beginning to show signs of relief. "We may never have got to the bottom of all this if that hadn't pointed the finger in Royal's direction. It took a lot of courage for her to write it to me, even though she didn't live to see the outcome."

Ruby shuddered and stood up, then began walking down the cemetery path. Abberline followed closely behind. As they talked about how Mrs Byford was coping with recent events, a constable appeared in the distance, running towards them.

"I'm sorry," he called out between breaths, stopping right next to them. He straightened himself up and addressed Abberline. "Inspector, Miss," he said, "Sir, I've been sent with an urgent request to visit Doctor Sequeira's residence."

"The Doctor, why, what on earth has happened?" Abberline asked, taken aback by the news.

"I'm so sorry to tell you, Sir, that Sequeira and his wife have been found dead. The Doctor currently at the scene has said, that it appears to be joint suicide, Sir." The constable informed him.

Abberline's face paled and his eyes widened as he swiftly followed the officer down the path.

Ruby watched the retreating figures for a moment before she stepped away from the main pathway and weaved through the aged headstones and deep long grass. She stopped in front of four graves marked by fresh marble headstones. These were her family members. Clenching her fists, a wave of sorrow washed over her. The deep void she had felt in her life since their passing was still raw even after all these years. No matter how much warmth and support she received from her chosen family, it just wasn't the same.

"I thought I'd find you here," Arthur said his voice piercing through Ruby's reverie.

She turned towards him, "Don't the new headstones look lovely?" Ruby looked back at them.

“They were worth every penny, Rubes.” Arthur came up beside her holding four bunches of flowers, he stepped forward and placed each one down. Then stood back and took her hand in his. “Time to go home, my girl it’s getting dark, and this isn’t a place for a lady on her own at night.” He began to lead her back down to the path.

“So, you say, Arty, but I’ve recently learned it’s not the dead that can hurt you, it’s the living.” She said as she followed him in the direction of home.

A Note from the Author.

I do hope that you've enjoyed Ruby and Arthur's first adventure. The topics that were covered in this book are true of the era. Sadly, women and children were trafficked even in the nineteenth century and for the purposes that were written of in this story. There are some real people included such as Inspector Abberline, his wife Emma, Dr Sequeira and his beloved and also Dr Barnardo, but events have been fictionalised. The plot as you may have gathered is based loosely around Jack the Ripper, a case Abberline did investigate and Dr Sequeira did assist in, albeit briefly. Dr Barnardo was of course the man who opened up the first children's home back then.

The information and research allowed me to use some of the language of the era and has hopefully, given you, the reader, a taste of society back in the day. Traditionally, the discussion about trafficking has been linked with prostitution, particularly that of women and girls sold for the sex trade. In the nineteenth century, discourse about prostitution came from England and other Western countries, incl uding the United States.

British regulators considered prostitution a necessary evil and approved a national system of licensed brothels. Members of parliament and the public viewed prostitution as an epidemic which caused the spread disease.
One of the Antivirus Acts introduced by the British government sparked moral outrage from women such as Josephine Butler. She opposed forced feminization.

Butler and others, known as abolitionists, blamed prostitution on men who had immoral desires and believed that woman who engaged in the sex trade were embroiled in white slavery. This meant forcing a girl into prostitution against her will through violence, fraud, or drugs.

With the encouragement of refomerers in the chastity community working with activists, stories of white girls being forced into prostitution began circulating through the newspapers, gaining public support to punish anyone who encouraged women to commit a sexual act involving money.

A movement focused on morality, led by reformers in the purity community, soon replaced the abolitionist agenda. The British Criminal Amendment Act (1885) and the American Manning Act (1910) criminalized prostitution. (source: Mini Singh, Research Analyst, FSE, Raja El Habti, Research Assistant, FSE)

Sadly, as many know, the Jack the Ripper case has gone unsolved to this day, and although there are many theories as to who the killer was, he or she was never apprehended. Abberline had a deep regret about his failure to bring the murderer to justice. Once he retired from the police force, after 30 years of service, he would never speak of the case again.

He passed peacefully away at the age of 86 on 10 December 1929 at home in Bournemouth and was initially buried in an unmarked grave, not far from where he lived. A headstone to mark his grave was erected almost 80 years after his death following a campaign by retired Metropolitan Police officers. Although the case illuded him, he won the admiration of the community and to many he became the hero in East End London. Emma joined her beloved husband in 1930 when she died. The two now reside together and are remembered on the same headstone.

Although my book has been fictionalised, I would also like to draw attention to the women that were the true victims of Jack the Ripper. It is out of the greatest respect for them that I would like to acknowledge these women here. Mary Ann Nichols DOD: 31 August 1888, Annie Chapman DOD: 8 September 1888, Elizabeth Stride DOD: 30 September 1888, Catherine Eddowes DOD: 30 September 1888 and lastly Mary Kelly DOD: 9 November 1888. Your final moments were horrific and terrifying, and I hope that each one of you will now rest in peace.

Thank you for reading my first novel, another Ruby Myers adventure is on the way. Until then happy reading and if you would like to take a moment to leave some feedback on my Amazon or Facebook page, I'd be extremely grateful.

With thanks, Lillian Maddison.

ISBN:978-1-7395722-0-4
ISBN: 978-1-7395722-1-1
ISBN:978-1-7395722-2-8

Printed in Great Britain
by Amazon

32897247R00236

MARY LAY

EQUALLY WRONG

MARY LAY

First published in Great Britain in 2024
Mary Lay Stories

Equally Wrong is a work of fiction. All incidents, dialogue and characters are products of the author's imagination. Any resemblances to persons living or dead are entirely coincidental.

A CIP Catalogue of this book is available from the British Library

ISBN 978-1-7394517-0-7 (Paperback)
First e-book edition 2024
ISBN 978-1-7394517-1-4 (ebook)

Cover and layout design by Chandler Book Design
www.chandlerbookdesign.com

Published by Mary Lay Stories
www.marylaystories.com

Printed in Great Britain by
TJ Books, Padstow, Cornwall

ALSO BY MARY LAY

CATCHING UP

THE PRICE OF COAL

BIRDS OF THE STORM

SHORT STORY COLLECTIONS

THE PREVIOUS ADVENTURES OF ...

NOVELLA

A WOMAN LIKE THAT

For the risk-takers

CONTENTS

1

WHEELS IN MOTION

The six houses that comprised Westmorland Terrace, perched halfway up the hill overlooking the small coastal town of Watchet, were completed in March 1928. Originally intended to be a row of three, having sold those the builder then purchased an adjoining parcel of land and extended the terrace. Each house had large bay windows to the front, giving good views of the Bristol Channel. Numbers three and four in the middle of the terrace were double-fronted with four bedrooms, whereas the others had only three bedrooms. Noah Kingston collected the keys to number three at the end of the second week of March from the agent in Watchet after the completion of the sale and the transfer of the sale price from his bank in Williton. He had taken a rare day off work from his coastguard duties and hurried to the railway station to meet his fiancée, Caroline Munhead.

Caroline added a little more powder to her nose as she stood in front of her hallway mirror. Quantock Cottage was comfortably quiet, save for the ticking of the clock in the sitting room and the occasional shift of the coals in the kitchen range. She had lived there for nine months on a twelve-month lease. In that time, she had proved to herself that she was capable of running a home; she had learned about gardening and improved her cookery skills thanks to her neighbours Ron and Vi Saddington and had established a social presence in Doniford and nearby Williton and Watchet. Her father, George, had been concerned that she might be lonely, but Caroline had discovered she enjoyed spending time with others so much more when she had her own little home to return to by herself. And soon, all of that would change.

Caroline closed her compact and put it onto the narrow shelf underneath the mirror. She looked at her reflection for a moment longer. Her bobbed light brown hair with its slight natural wave needed a trim. She peered closer, was that… goodness, yes, a grey hair! Caroline plucked it from her head and dropped it to the floor as if it were an insect. I have only just turned twenty-four, she thought to herself as she gathered her gloves and pulled her plum-coloured cloche hat firmly onto her head; now is not the time for grey hairs!

Ron Saddington was in the back garden of Quantock Cottage digging compost into the vegetable patch. Caroline closed the kitchen door and called out to him.

"Do you really think we'll have any vegetables before I leave, Ron?"

"Oh yes. I've some early carrots and radish to go in, beetroot, and I thought we could give the lettuce another try. And of course, you'll have the rhubarb. I'll take the bell off the crown before I go and see how it's doing. If there's any stalks worth cutting, I'll leave them on the doorstep for you."

"Thank you, Ron. I do hope the new tenant appreciates all your hard work here as much as I do."

"You off to see the new house?"

"Yes, Noah was due to collect the keys this morning and then we are going on to Minehead to buy some furniture and have dinner with friends. Oh look, the robin is watching you!"

The bird had landed on the edge of Ron's wheelbarrow and was looking at them intently.

"He knows when there's grubs to be had. You enjoy your day."

At Doniford Halt, Evans the Station Master was reading a newspaper behind the ticket counter.

"Good morning, Mr Evans, could I have a single to Watchet please?"

He folded the paper and rested his pipe on the counter, "You can indeed Miss. Is it today you're visiting the new house?"

"It is. I noticed a man in a suit just now looking at the footbridge. Is everything in order here?"

"Oh no need to worry about him. I asked the board to send someone to have a look at it after the storms last year and they've only just got round to it."

"He didn't look like a workman."

"He's not. He's here to write a report. He'll send it to the board and then they'll decide if any work needs doing, part of their new Safety Movement. There's a couple of treads on the far side that need replacing. Might see a workman in another six months if we're lucky." He could see the concern on Caroline's face, "It's safe enough for now though, don't you worry! Here's your ticket, the next one'll be in shortly."

The journey was not a long one; Caroline had made it numerous times over the previous year. The carriages were typically occupied by tradesmen, young mothers and older housewives travelling between villages to do their shopping or visit friends or relations. Fifteen minutes later Caroline stepped onto the platform at Watchet and looked around for Noah. He emerged through the steam and smoke; his tall frame topped with a cap that covered his short sandy hair. He wore his usual navy-blue sweater and rough dark trousers, today with a dark woollen jacket.

They greeted each other with a kiss on the cheek and crossed the footbridge to the exit.

"Did you bring your notebook?"

Noah patted his pocket, "And a pencil, yes. Are you excited?"

"A little. I know you have lived in the boathouse for years, but I am becoming used to moving into new accommodation. This will be the third new home for me in just over a year."

"But this will be our first home together. I thought you might be a bit more keen."

"I am curious to see what it looks like from the inside, having seen it emerge from the hillside. Do you know if the other houses are taken?"

"We will be the third to move in. Well, I will be at least," he shot Caroline a glance.

"We've discussed this. My agreement for the cottage runs until the last day of June, and I'm still hopeful that Mary will bring Angelica to stay next month for a few days. But as soon as there is furniture, you should move in and not wait for me."

It was a well-finished house. Elevated from the road, six steps led up from the wooden front gate sandwiched between two banks of freshly laid turf. Noah opened the wide, black painted front door onto a hallway with black and white floor tiles leading to the rear of the property where the kitchen, scullery and bathroom were behind the staircase. To the right and left of the hall were doors to large bright reception rooms. Each had wooden parquet floors with a fresh coat of varnish. After exploring the ground floor, Caroline and Noah climbed the stairs. They found a linen cupboard on the landing and four good sized bedrooms. The rear bedrooms looked out over a square of garden that started level to the house and rose gently from about halfway to meet a large, long, squat building that ran along the far end of most of the terrace gardens.

"What is that?" Caroline asked as they looked out of the third bedroom window together.

"The rope shed. They make ropes and nets for the fishing boats, and nets for sheep pens."

"I've never noticed it before. Will it be noisy? I can see the chimney stack at the end there."

"I shouldn't think so. The chimney is only to power the small static engine that turns the twine. It used to be hidden by some trees but they were cleared so that the new fence could be put along the property boarders. I'll take you to look around one day if you would like?"

They spent the next hour, walking from room to room with Noah making notes of the furniture they would need. They could no longer avoid the conversation that they had been tiptoeing around: who would sleep where.

"Of course, when we get married, we'll move your art equipment and my desk into one of the bay bedrooms and sleep in the other." Noah was resting his notebook on the mantlepiece in the larger reception room and making some final additions to the list.

Caroline put on her gloves. "When?"

"Well, yes. Your ring was a declaration of intent remember; I do mean to make you my wife eventually."

Noah was smiling, and Caroline returned his smile but felt uneasy at the words he had used. To make her. There was something in her that recoiled, and she had no idea why. She was attracted to and very fond of Noah, though she still could not say if it were love. She wasn't opposed to marriage in principle; it seemed to work for other people, even for her dear friends Helen and Tommy who despite being attracted to others of their respective sexes had married for convenience and were on the whole prospering. But something kept snagging at her each time the subject was broached between her and Noah, like a nail on a doorframe. The ring in question hung on a chain around her neck and in that moment felt heavy and cold against her skin.

They caught the next train to Minehead. The afternoon had brightened with the sun flashing through gaps in the dishwater clouds. Passing Blue Anchor Bay, Caroline gazed at the sea from the carriage. She wondered if it would be warm enough for her to swim before Easter. She loved sea swimming, much to the consternation of Vi who regularly declared Caroline would "catch her death" from doing so. Her bathing costume would need an inspection to make sure the moths had not made any holes before she swam again, and she made a mental note to check it.

The showroom floor of McIlroy's department store held a wide range of furniture from manufacturers and workshops across Europe. Though Noah had savings that had not been completely swallowed by the house purchase, they had agreed that they would only buy a few items new and make do with second- or third-hand for the rest. The style of much of the European furniture was becoming more angular, less organic and fluid and in some ways less decorative. Local pieces were of a traditional style and with less adornment.

Noah had set himself a budget of fifty pounds to cover two beds, two fireside chairs, a gramophone, dining table and chairs and several rugs and pairs of curtains. Caroline decided to spend some of her own money from her savings on a dinner service, a range of Czech crystal glasses, a canteen of cutlery and some enamel cookware. After an advance from her father of fifty pounds in the year she turned twenty-one, her income now derived from shares in National Benzol and one or two other companies, along with irregular profits from paintings that her friend Elsa House sold on Caroline's behalf in London. The ones that sold fastest and for the most money were of a subject matter that Caroline knew she could never display at Westmorland Terrace.

She felt lightheaded as they left the store and walked along the busy streets towards Blenheim Gardens.

"Are you alright, Caroline? You seem a little quiet."

"I have never spent as much money as that on anything before."

"Do we really need the glasses? We can always cancel some of it if you've changed your mind."

"There is little point in having a new dinner service but no glassware. No, it's alright, I'm just not used to it. We shall need to be less extravagant with the rest though. I saw a notice for a house clearance sale in Williton, I thought I might go along. I was going to ask Daisy if she would come with me."

"Not Helen?"

"Helen is so busy now with her duties as Councillor. I'm looking forward to tonight with them, I haven't seen them since my birthday."

Helen and Tommy Gersen-Fisch rented a large house that looked out over the recently laid Blenheim Gardens and the sea beyond. Caroline had been at school with Helen, and their friend Midge who was newly married and recently returned to Africa to complete her missionary appointment with her husband Oliver. Helen and Tommy had become friends in London, both of them revelling in the sexual freedoms the city afforded. Helen had a tendency to display provocative behaviour after having a few drinks, the result of spending much of her childhood overlooked by her parents as their middle child of five. Her eldest sister had become surrogate mother to Helen's two younger brothers, while their mother travelled Europe with Helen's closer sister Sophia. Sophia was in need of a cure for tuberculosis which ultimately proved elusive, and she died just a few months after her marriage. Despite her lesbian relationships and outrageous behaviour in London, Helen had inherited her mother's political ambitions and had secured a position as local councillor the previous year.

It had been hard fought, and Tommy's own relationship with a chemistry teacher, Christopher, had come close to toppling Helen's carefully crafted professional persona. Tommy and Christopher had become involved in a brawl in an Exeter club known to be popular with gay men. After a night in the police cells, Tommy was charged with drunken disorder, fined and sent on his way. He had not seen Christopher since. It had been a watershed moment for Tommy; he had spent some time in Malvern considering his life options and returned to apologise to Helen with details of a new opportunity his cousin's husband had set up for him. He had needed something to channel his nervous energy and compulsive, addictive passions into. He had found it with a group of ex-air force pilots at a small airfield between Taunton and Bridgwater. The Sunray Air Company had saved Tommy's skin.

1928 had so far proved to be a more positive year for Helen and Tommy. The chatter in the town about Tommy's arrest had died down to an occasional sideways glance, and everyone seemed to have accepted them as a conventional young married couple, which was exactly Helen and Tommy's plan when they had married in Blackpool a couple of years earlier. Naturally, no eyebrows were raised when Daisy Clare, bookseller and printer from the village of Dunster, stayed the night at the Gersen-Fisch home, and Helen never stayed the night in Dunster. Yet their relationship had also found a comfortable level that was neither claustrophobic nor extravagant but had appeared to Caroline to be waning since its first flush of intensity. It suited both women and gave them what they needed.

Daisy would be joining them for dinner that evening. Helen was a considerate host: an odd number of guests was only usually permitted when a large party was being thrown, and those had become less frequent now that her place on the council was secure. However, all five knew each other well and the odd number was overlooked. Caroline and Noah were admitted by the housekeeper Mrs Rich and shown through to the garden room at the rear of the house where Helen was reading a magazine.

"Caro! Noah! Goodness is it that time already? Mrs Rich, some tea if you please and a plate of those delicious biscuits of yours."

"You look well, Helen. Is Tommy out painting?" Caroline sat next to her friend on the double cane seat and Noah took a single chair.

"No, I am reliably informed that the car is 'running hot' and requires some attention. He has taken it over to the garage and is no doubt up to his elbows in oil and grease trying to help fix the infernal thing."

Tommy arrived a little after six and announced that the car had been stubborn but that he and the mechanic had beaten her into submission. Tommy and Noah discussed the engine over dinner while Helen and Caroline ate in relative quiet. Caroline was pleased that Noah was at least able to hold a conversation with Tommy, despite disapproving of his homosexuality. It would have made things terribly awkward if Noah had been against Tommy on principle, Caroline decided.

Later, as they were getting ready to leave and catch the last train home, Caroline and Helen found themselves alone for a moment in the hallway.

"Is everything quite alright Caro? You've been rather quiet this evening."

"Yes. At least, oh I don't know I'm probably being silly."

"What? Come along, a problem shared and all that."

"Noah keeps mentioning marriage. And every time he does, I feel this need to run away. There, it's quite ridiculous, isn't it?" She put on her hat and tied the belt of her coat.

Helen did not reply; Noah and Tommy came into the hall at that moment and the goodbyes began in earnest.

Sitting in the bouncing, swaying carriage, passing Dunster station, Noah said, "I think it's time I introduced you to my parents."

"That's fair, considering you have met my father already." Caroline recalled the Boxing Day afternoon she had spent at Quantock Cottage with Noah and her father three months before. It had been when the two men had conspired to surprise her with news that Noah had bought the house and wanted Caroline to marry him and live there with him.

"Mother keeps asking when I'll take you over there. I thought perhaps Easter weekend, on the Saturday if I can find a boat heading that way."

"It's a nuisance that the train doesn't run through Porlock." Caroline yawned behind her gloved hand, "But I have never been on a boat, so that would be exciting."

"Leave it with me then, if there's no passing boat, I can always ask Chancy to take us on the *Merry Jen*. He has family just inland from Porlock too."

"As long as I am home again by that evening. Mary and Angelica are due to arrive on the following Tuesday and I shall need to get everything ready for them on holiday Monday."

"Oh of course, yes, I had forgotten. I will ask Chancy then, and he might let me take the *Jen* myself."

"Have you sailed it before?"

"I've sailed others of a similar size and worked with Chancy a few times on the *Jen*. She handles well, and we'll only be going along the coast, not out to sea. We can be there and back again in a day with no trouble at all."

"I should like that."

They were approaching Watchet. Noah put on his cap and stood up as the brakes were applied to the wheels.

"I wish you would let me see you home."

"There's really no need, Mr Evans looks out for me, and you'd only have to walk all the way back to Watchet again."

Noah bent and kissed her cheek. "Not long now and we'll be getting off at the same stop anyway." He smiled and left the carriage.

Caroline sat back in her seat for the final twelve minutes of her journey. She was excited to take a trip on a boat with Noah, but the reason for the journey felt like a weight pressing down on her head. She knew it would be another step towards marriage, another official act in the scripted performance she found herself in. She didn't understand why she felt the way she did. She was very fond of Noah, she enjoyed his company and found him attractive. He had a good, steady job and though his health was not robust due to injuries he sustained in the war, he was capable, practical and had the respect of almost everyone in Watchet. And yet, she felt as if she were being dragged towards an inevitable fate, instead of happily skipping along.

The house clearance sale had drawn quite a crowd. Caroline joined Daisy Clare on the train rather than riding her bicycle to Williton as she usually did, and the two women squeezed themselves into the hallway of the already bustling large house on the southern edge of the village some twenty minutes before the auction was to begin. Daisy wore her long raincoat despite the sun shining brightly outside, and her wellington boots met the hem of her woollen skirt showing just a narrow glimpse of black stocking. Her wide-brimmed felt hat sat at an angle on her head, her dark hair escaping in all directions underneath and around it. Caroline had liked Daisy from the moment they had met at the bookshop Daisy had inherited from her aunt and uncle. Though ten years older than Caroline and Helen, Daisy was the sort of woman who was comfortable with people of any age, any class and any origin. However, spending a large amount of time in her own company meant that Daisy often chattered away nervously when around other people. Her house companion, Gladstone, an old tabby tom cat, was not an avid conversationist.

The crowd milling and jostling throughout the house was two thirds' men to one third women. Caroline wondered if it had been the same when the contents of her childhood home had been sold, and then the house itself auctioned. She had been staying with Helen and Tommy that weekend and had missed the excitement. Her father George had sold up only a few months after his wife Elizabeth died, and bought a modern, newly-built apartment near the Park in Cheltenham. The thought of rattling around their family home with the ghosts of Elizabeth and their son Freddie was too much for George to bear. Freddie had been killed just a few days before the Armistice, at the bottom of a canal that his company had been attempting to advance across. There had been no victorious return to celebrate; Elizabeth had rapidly descended into a laudanum-supported torpor and then a long period of delicate health that Caroline had spent her teenage years attending to. It had been the reason Caroline had missed out on the usual activities to which young women of her age were usually exposed.

Daisy spotted a bookcase crammed with a disarray of large and small hard-backed books. She pulled one out and blew off the dust before opening it somewhere close the the middle.

"Found something of interest?" Caroline asked, arriving at her elbow.

"Possibly, yes. A second edition of this sold for several guineas last year, and look, this is a third edition from 1877. I wonder, do you think we have to bid for the whole case of books?"

Caroline turned the pages of the catalogue until she found the entry for the bookcase, "It says bookcase and contents. That sounds as if you would need to bid for the whole thing. The guide price is ten shillings."

Daisy closed the book carefully and replaced it on the shelf, "Let's not draw attention to it. Shall we go and look in the kitchen?"

Three hours later, Caroline and Daisy emerged from the house clutching various receipts. The auction was still in progress but both women had spent their allowances and were in need of refreshment. They headed to the tearoom on the high street and ordered tea and sandwiches. Daisy could hardly sit still; she was feeling extremely pleased with herself.

"Twelve shillings! I still can't quite believe it. All of the books and the bookcase itself, though goodness knows where I shall put that. But twelve shillings, and not only that third edition but a signed copy of Hardwicke's *A Pair of Blue Stockings* as well! The auctioneer was clearly unaware of its existence, not to mention its value. I'm sure I can resell the third edition for at least five guineas, and the rest of the books will sell eventually. But I think I shall keep the Hardwicke for myself, it's been years since I read it."

"What is it about? I saw you tuck it away behind another book, but I didn't realise it held any particular value."

"Oh, it doesn't really, not in polite society anyway. It's rather a … difficult novel. The translations were more popular, French and Dutch."

"Difficult in what way? Don't be so cryptic Daisy!"

"Well, the subject is a young girl who," Daisy looked around and dropped her voice to a whisper, "is seduced by a lord and then in turn seduces the lord's wife."

Caroline looked at Daisy with wide eyes. She generally took these things in her stride and was rarely shocked by the behaviour of others. Rather, Caroline found it all curiously interesting and was an avid spectator of other people's activities. She knew though that she was often a little slow to understand when people explained scandalous gossip or stories.

"Are you pulling my leg?"

"Absolutely not! I read it years ago in the French translation, but this copy is in English, so you can borrow it if you like once it arrives at the shop. Even if I were happy to sell it, I think it would be too difficult to publicise. These days the subject matter would be called indecent."

"But you don't want to sell it?"

"Oh no. Why?"

"Well, I just thought, you know the gallery that I send my paintings to in London? I think the owners might be interested in a novel of that kind. Or know someone who might be, at least."

The waitress brought the tea and caused the women to pause their conversation. When she had left them, Daisy smiled and shook her head.

"I won't be selling it. The first time I read it, I remember feeling a connection to the heroine, Julienne. I had only borrowed the copy I read, and I've not seen another in all these years. I shan't be letting this one go. Are you happy with your purchases?"

"I was disappointed not to get the mirror I bid on. That woman in the green coat was obviously determined to have it and I couldn't have spent the amount she did in the end. The occasional table and the mantle clock were a little more than I had hoped to spend but the lamp is gorgeous."

"And a bargain at six shillings."

"Yes. I noticed that there were some more recent novels in the collection you bought. Would you mind if I gave you sixpence for the Victoria Woolf? I've been meaning to read some of her work."

"Have it, no need to pay. She has a curious style, I'm not sure I always fully understand what she is trying to say in her novels, but they are certainly thought-provoking."

"Thank you."

Caroline stirred the sugar into her tea and gazed out of the window into the sunlit street. The post office opposite stood with its door open and the board advertising the latest newspaper headline read 'Nora Bayes, Singer, Dies!' She wondered whether James had finished making his film about Welsh miners and what project he would be taking on next. James Baker had been the one to introduce Caroline to film acting and had told her so often that he was not husband material that when he proposed, she had declined. Not for the first, or last, time she wondered if she had made the right decision.

"… Caroline?"

"Sorry Daisy, I was miles away there for a moment."

"I asked if you and Noah had set a date for your wedding yet. I know you were going to wait, but a date helps focus the mind and if you'll be living together then a long engagement isn't really necessary, is it?"

"No. No date. Those sandwiches look delicious, egg and cress together look so jolly, don't you think?" Caroline smiled without looking at Daisy.

The second post brought Caroline final confirmation that her friend Mary Rose would be bringing her daughter, Caroline's Goddaughter, Angelica to stay at Quantock Cottage on the Tuesday after Easter. Caroline's neighbour Vi had called in for a chat about Easter bonnets for the Church Women's Guild when the letter arrived.

"And they'll be staying the week then?" Vi asked.

"Only until Saturday. Mary's husband is the vicar of St Mark's, and she likes to be there for the Sunday service. I am so excited to have Angelica here, it will be wonderful for her to see the sea. I do hope the weather will be warm enough for us to swim."

"Ron says he thinks this sun will hold a while yet, so maybe it will. And you say your friend is from Bristol?"

"Yes, well Trinidad originally, but she grew up in Bristol."

"Trinidad? Where's that then? Somewhere in Wales?"

"No, it's in the Caribbean. Close to South America. Mary's father is in the British Army, he is serving in India at the moment I believe."

Vi considered this information for a moment, "Do you mean she's a darkie?" She finally asked.

"She has brown skin, yes. Angelica of course is much fairer. There are a lot of people like that in Bristol."

"I'm sure there are," Vi crossed her arms over her chest, "not so many here though. Still, I'm sure you have enough plain English cooking under your belt now, you won't be needing me while they are here."

"You're welcome to come and meet them, Vi. I'm sure you'd like Mary and Angelica is such a bright little girl."

"We'll see. I'd better get back; potatoes don't peel themselves."

2

MESSAGES LOUD AND CLEAR

Chancy Pritchard was waiting for Noah and Caroline on the quayside where the *Merry Jen* was tied up. He had landed his catch the evening before and was happy to have a couple of day's rest and let Noah take the boat out along the coast. They had known each other all of their lives, Chancy (or Charles, to give him his proper name) being five years older than Noah.

"You sure you don't want young Ben to tag along with you and crew?" he asked as he shook Noah's hand.

"No need. He deserves a day off as much as you do. Is she ready to go?"

"She is. Chance of rain later though, so the waterproofs are in the wheelhouse. Help you on, miss?"

Caroline was nervous and excited to be taking her first real boat trip. She took Chancy's offered hand and stepped up onto the crate he had set on the harbour edge so that she could more easily climb onto the deck. Noah having jumped on board first, took her other hand as she stepped up from the crate. The boat moved gently under her feet, not unlike a train she thought.

Chancy untied the ropes and threw them to Noah, then waved them off. With the engine throbbing and the smell of oil and fish in the air, Noah steered the boat expertly out of the harbour and turned west. Caroline sat on the deck, safely buckled into her life jacket, trying not to clutch too tightly onto the side of the boat as the sea swell rocked it more determinedly. Noah had insisted that she wear a life jacket, despite not wearing one himself, and had explained the radio system and emergency flare to her while they had waited on the quayside for Chancy to arrive.

Caroline held her hand up to shield her eyes from the sun and looked back towards the east and the white churn of the water they were leaving behind them. Watchet looked very different from the sea. The jumble of whitewashed and brick houses scattered up the hillside reminded her of St Ives in Cornwall. She had visited there almost two years before, staying a week at an artist's retreat. She had met Max there.

She couldn't prevent the flush of colour as it rose from her throat, but had Noah noticed she would have blamed it on the sun and the keen sea breeze. Caroline was on her way to meet her prospective parents in law, and she had to find a way to stop these thoughts of Max and their night together coming to her like this. It was impossible; she would never see Max again, they had known, agreed. He was married, he lived in Bath, their paths were as likely to cross again as Caroline was to meet an Indian princess or a South African diamond smuggler. And yet she had met Galina Bassett, daughter of a Russian diamond cutter and widow of an international jewel trader who had died (or been killed, if Galina was to be believed) because of a deal gone bad. Galina had moved into the same block of apartments as her father, and Caroline had later discovered that her father had been the person who had helped Galina purchase her apartment.

No one would have believed that, Caroline thought as the *Merry Jen* bounced over a larger wave, if they read it in a novel and yet it was all true.

No, she had to live in reality. Noah need never know about Max. Helen had assured her that men couldn't really tell if a girl had lost her virginity as long as she made all the right sounds and played just a little shy and frightened on her wedding night. A lone gull flapped determinedly alongside the boat as Caroline looked back towards the wheelhouse. Their eyes met for a moment before the bird turned away, disinterested now that it knew no fish were to be stolen.

The cottage where Mr and Mrs Kingston lived was set along a narrow lane that led inland from the harbour at Porlock. It was not as picturesque as some of the cottages huddled around the harbour in Watchet, or on the High Street of Dunster. It was a small low-ceilinged home with a door that led directly from the street into a small sitting room with a larger kitchen and scullery beyond. Stairs led from the kitchen up to two small bedrooms with fires that smoked from chimneys that wanted sweeping.

Mr Kingston had been a fisherman but had lost his arm in an accident with some rope. The family had relied mostly on Mrs Kingston's wages from her job as the local school cleaner and cook for a while before Noah's brother Peter became Coastguard at Watchet. He lived much as Noah had been, sleeping in the rooms above the boathouse and sending money back to his parents each week. Then the War came, and Peter was killed in action, leaving Mr and Mrs Kingston again reliant on her wages. They had been fortunate that an elderly relative on Mrs Kingston's side of the family had died and left Mrs Kingston the cottage they now occupied. It was a weight off their minds as they had often struggled to pay the rent on their previous home.

Mrs Kingston still cooked and cleaned at the little village school, though the roll was diminishing with every new school year. Over lunch, served at the kitchen table, Caroline learned that the coming July would see the middle class' teacher retire, and the county education office had decided that the two remaining teachers would have to take slightly larger classes: one for infants and one for juniors. Caroline had never given much thought to how children were educated, and whether her experience as a pupil at Mrs Pendersen's school for girls in Pittville was typical of children in 1928. Mrs Kingston was happy to enlighten her over roast duck with roast potatoes, boiled cabbage and swede, and a rather thick gravy.

Noah and his father ate mostly in silence. Noah was pleased that his mother and Caroline seemed to be getting along well. Once or twice he glanced at his father across the table, and the older man nodded slightly to give his approval at whatever Caroline had just said. Mr Kingston listened to the young woman and wondered if she would make a good wife for his son. She would obviously make someone a good wife one day, but for Noah? Would she be prepared to wait at home while storms raged, and her husband took charge of rescue attempts for vessels in distress? He watched her surreptitiously during the meal and decided that she might grow tired of life in a sleepy fishing village. She was, however, the first girl Noah had brought to meet them in three years, so he would not do or say anything to sour the union.

Caroline insisted on helping Mrs Kingston wash up the lunch things while the men retired to the sitting room. Afterwards the teapot was refilled, and the conversation found its way to the losses of the Great War as all four gathered around the fireplace on upholstered chairs. Mr Kingston handed Caroline a framed portrait photograph of a young man who looked as if he could have been Noah's twin. Peter had been dressed in his army uniform; the photograph taken in Portsmouth just before Noah had been called up. Mrs Kingston wiped a tear away with her handkerchief as she said how she wished her sons had had their photograph taken together, she would have liked that on her mantlepiece.

"Your brother died as well? In France?" Mr Kingston asked Caroline while his wife poured more tea into their best china cups.

"Yes, Freddie. Just before the Armistice."

"How dreadful for your family," Mrs Kingston said quietly.

"Mother took it very badly. I had to look after her. You are very lucky to have a photograph of Peter, we don't have any of Freddie. I suppose we were all so sure then that he would be coming home again."

The silence sat heavily upon them for a few moments as the mantle clock ticked on.

"It's the next generation we need to be looking to now," Mrs Kingston said trying to lift the conversation again, "Children bring such joy to a couple, don't you think, Caroline?"

Caroline dropped her eyes to her teacup. This was not a topic she particularly wanted to discuss on her first meeting with Noah's parents. She had assumed that marriage would be mentioned at some point but children and to have them or not was a minefield.

As she was thinking, Noah shifted uncomfortably in his chair, "We're not even married yet mother."

"But you will be soon and then children follow just as night follows day. Carrying on the family name. There have been Kingstons here for generations you know."

As Noah moved the conversation on to other relations and their well-being, Caroline looked up from her tea to find Mr Kingston studying her as he sucked on his pipe. He had a kind face; Caroline had felt a warm welcome from both of Noah's parents but his father's quiet consideration of everything she had said since she arrived now showed in his expression. In that moment, Caroline knew that Mr Kingston had seen her reservations about her relationship with Noah.

Noah's parents accompanied Noah and Caroline back to the *Merry Jen* when the tide was high enough for her to sail again. Caroline carried a small basket containing a fruit cake and a dozen eggs. After some last-minute chatter on the quayside, Caroline stepped aboard the boat and watched with curiosity and respect as Mr Kingston used his remaining hand to untie the ropes holding the *Merry Jen* close to the quay wall and threw them onto the boat's deck for Noah to coil and stow. As Noah put the engine into gear, Caroline waved farewell to the two figures on land.

On Easter Sunday Caroline rode her bicycle to Williton to attend the service at St Peter's church. Since meeting Noah's parents, her feeling of unease about her relationship with Noah had been gnawing at her and she had woken from a fitful sleep that morning in need of clarity. Though she was not an avid church-goer since leaving Cheltenham, she had grown to like the wide grey church of St Peter and the congregation that appeared to be mostly women. The vicar was a middle-aged man with a shock of red hair that he continually pushed away from his face to one side. Caroline had frequently wondered why he did not grease it back as many other men did.

Easter, like Christmas, was a time when even the most reluctant members of a parish would make the effort to sit through a two-hour service. As Caroline entered the cool church interior, she realised she would have to squeeze into one of the pews near the entrance as the church was already almost full. She found a spot next to an elderly woman in a grey woollen jacket and matching skirt who smiled warmly at Caroline and complemented her on her "healthy complexion". Caroline thanked her and did not explain that it was the result of riding the two miles from Doniford on her bicycle into a fresh easterly wind.

The service was a traditional one, with references to the resurrection and how the believers were not themselves believed yet maintained their faith. Caroline sat with her hands in her lap and waited for some divine inspiration. She wanted to hear a phrase or sentence that would identify the unease she had been feeling and show her a way to resolve it. She found her gaze resting on a board that hung on the church wall listing the names of the 23 men of the parish who had been killed in the Great War. There was a Frederick among them, Private Frederick Emmerson. Had he been one of the first to fall, Caroline wondered, or had he, like Freddie, been carried almost all of the way through the conflict only to die in the final moments. Had this Frederick been a dashing young hero, or a scared boy cowering in a shell crater with the remains of his battalion scattered around him like feathers from a burst cushion? Had he left a wife and perhaps children behind? Were they, at this moment, sitting only a few feet away on another pew? Or had he left a childhood sweetheart with the promise of marriage upon his return unfulfilled?

It had been a sermon delivered by the Reverend Canon at Christ Church in Cheltenham that had prompted Caroline's decision to begin her efforts to catch up on the years she had missed by attending to her mother after Freddie's death. It had been an image of Freddie, half seen through bright sunlight, that she had interpreted as a direction to investigate a strange light on Cleeve Hill. That light had turned out to be the glint of sunlight on Noah's binoculars. She missed her brother with a sudden burning hole in her chest that brought tears to her eyes. The lady in grey next to her offered a crisp white handkerchief and muttered how particularly moving the sermon was.

This brought Caroline's attention back to the words the Vicar was saying.

"... but what is the point of resurrection if life is not then lived to the glory of God? How do we honour this second chance if all we do is look back and not forward? Friends, the gift of eternal life is here, right here, with us now. While there is comfort in the old ways, the traditions that we all hold dear, we must also use this second chance to look to the new! Renew our faith while at the same time renewing our engagement with life! Forge new friendships, find comfort in communion not only with those we know and love, but with strangers, that we might convert them to friends also..."

Forty-five minutes later Caroline stepped out into the sunshine hungry but no less perturbed. The direction she had hoped for had eluded her. It had been pleasant to be in the company of others for a while, but now all she wanted was to ride home to the solitude of her little cottage by the sea and her paints and the lunch she hoped would not be burnt and filling the kitchen with smoke. She walked around the side of the church to where she and others had left their bicycles. A woman was crouched down her fingers black with grease.

"I say, can I help?" Caroline asked as she approached.

"No, thanks awfully, but the blasted thing is back on now. I swear that chain knows what day of the week it is, it only ever slips off on a Sunday!" The woman stood up and faced Caroline.

"Here, take this for your hands," Caroline offered her own handkerchief, rather than the one from the lady in grey which she intended to wash and return.

"Oh, you're too kind. I couldn't possibly spoil it. I have my own here," she deftly pulled a handkerchief from her handbag with the tips of her blackened fingers. "Forgive me, but I don't know your name though I recognise your face."

"Caroline Munhead, pleased to meet you, Miss...?"

"June Emmerson. Pleased to meet you, I won't shake hands."

The two women chuckled and took hold of their bicycles. They began to push them along the gravel path towards the churchyard gate.

June sneezed into her handkerchief suddenly, and when she had wiped her nose she said, "I know where I recognised you from now, it was the auction the other day. You were bidding on a lamp that I had my eye on."

"Yes, that's right. I'm sorry that I prevented you from having it. Oh, you have a grease smut on your nose now from your handkerchief!"

"Oh Lord, where? Could you?" she handed Caroline the piece of cloth and Caroline gently rubbed the grease away.

"That's better."

"Just like mother. She was always rubbing at mine and Fred's faces with her handkerchief. I don't know how she stood it really, the very last thing I want is to be wiping dirt from children for the rest of my life!"

Caroline said nothing. They reached the gate, passed through in single file and turned to their opposite homeward directions.

"June, may I ask you a question before you go?"

"Of course, go on."

"Do you think it wise to settle for something you like but don't love, or would you wait until you found something you feel you can't live without?"

June studied Caroline for a moment. "You're not talking about that lamp are you."

"No, no I'm not." Caroline admitted.

"Then I would say that impulse purchases are often regretted later, but if you really truly want something, nothing else is ever going to give you satisfaction. You'll forever be wondering what if."

Caroline nodded. "Thank you. I'd better go and rescue lunch – good afternoon!"

The small joint of beef was not burnt. As she sat at the kitchen table and ate her lunch, Caroline considered June's advice. She felt it was no coincidence that the sister of another Frederick, the very same one she had been musing on during the sermon, should be the messenger on that particular day and subject. God indeed moved in mysterious ways.

Mary and Angelica Rose arrived in a swirl of steam on Doniford Halt platform. Caroline had told Evans the Station Master that she was expecting her friend and her little girl, and that they would require some assistance with their luggage. There was a momentary pause as Evans saw Mary, who had dressed soberly for the journey in her navy-blue coat with a wide collar edged with cream piping and a hat to match. Their eyes met as Mary handed him a small suitcase; she recognised the look. Then Angelica pushed around her mother's skirt and shrieked "hat!" while pointing to Evans' head.

Evans melted. Angelica's big brown eyes, her excited giggling and determination to get off the train and explore demolished any hesitancy he might have had. Evans picked up the little girl and carried her across the platform to where

Caroline was waiting. More shrieks of delight followed from Angelica while Mary brought the remaining case to join them. At the very last minute she had decided against bringing the large pram that she still used for Angelica around Cheltenham, thinking it would do the little girl good to walk more now that she could.

The women hugged each other as best they could with Angelica clinging to Caroline's neck. Evans shepherded the trio out through the ticket office to the waiting taxi and waved them onward the short distance up the lane to Quantock Cottage.

As the taxi stopped at the crab apple tree by Caroline's gate, Mary said in her lilting Trinidadian-via Bristol voice, "Is this it so soon? Miss Caroline, you should not have taken the trouble to get a motor car, we could have walked it just as easily!"

Caroline smiled at Mary's usual formal way of addressing her; she had missed it. "I thought you might have the pram with you, or that you would be tired after your journey. It's really no trouble to arrange."

There was nothing on which Angelica could hurt herself in the garden, so after showing Mary their sleeping arrangements, they took tea on the back lawn while Angelica ran up and down the pathway between the vegetable plots, making piles of stones, twigs and snail shells at either end.

"She has grown so much since Christmas!" Caroline observed.

"Yes, and she has a few words now too. Not always complete, but we understand her."

"And you, are you and Philip well?"

Mary gave a small, tight-lipped smile, so unlike the wide generous grin she shared with her own mother, Celestine Vincent.

"Philip and I are very well. And I will tell you, I am due another child in September."

"Really? Oh, Mary how wonderful for you! I'm sure Philip is delighted too."

"He is. After… after Mark, I had not wanted another. But my other piece of news has made me feel that this one will be alright," Mary and Philip's baby son Mark, named after the parish, had died from whooping cough the previous autumn.

"What news is this?"

"There is a possibility that we, or rather Philip, could be granted a new parish. Away from Cheltenham."

"Oh, but I thought you were both happy at St Mark's."

"Yes, Philip is, but I am not happy to have more of a family there. Not now. It was a blessing that news of this new parish came at the same time I realised there would be another child. Philip will go and see the place while I am here, and I shall know when we return home."

"Well, that's rather exciting. I'm sure the congregation at St Mark's will be sorry to see you go, but perhaps if you feel more comfortable in the new one, it will be a good move. Where is it?"

"A few miles from Bath, a place called Bradford-on-Avon. Do you know it?"

"No, I don't think I have ever heard of it. We should look on the map when we've finished our tea."

Angelica brought a twig for Caroline to look at. "'Ani Car, this!" she said, proudly.

"Yes, it's a twig, or a stick. Can you say stick?"

"This!"

"Not quite, but it's a lovely stick. Can you find another?" The little girl ambled off.

The following day Caroline had arranged to meet Helen in Minehead and show Mary the town. They would have a picnic in Blenheim Gardens as the weather was dry, with Mrs Rich providing a basket full of food and drink for them all. This time they walked down to the train station with Angelica in between them holding both Mary's and Caroline's hands. She was dressed in a short lemon frock with a cream knitted jacket and a yellow ribbon to keep her hair out of her eyes. At two and a half years old, she was now her own distinct little person and Caroline was fascinated by everything she did.

Evans sold them their tickets and handed Mary a small paper bag containing Fruit Salad and Black Jack chews, "For the little one."

"Thank you, very kind." Mary tucked the bag into her handbag quickly before Angelica noticed them. Once they were on the train, she told Caroline, "But Angelica is too young for those kinds of sweets. We shall have to eat them for her."

"Mr Evans is quite taken with her isn't he," Caroline said as she held Angelica on her knees so that the girl could see out of the carriage window.

"He seems a nice man."

"He is. When I come home late from Watchet, he always comes out of the station to watch as I walk home, even though it's just a short way."

"And why would you be coming home late?"

"Ahh, well, if Noah and I go to see a film, or if we have been to Minehead, I often catch the last train home at night. It makes no sense for Noah to come to Doniford and then have to walk all the way back to Watchet again. He used to insist, but I have convinced him now that I am perfectly safe under Mr Evan's watchful eye."

"Will I be meeting this Noah while I am here?"

"I do hope so. The trouble is, he works often such long hours. He said he would come over to Helwell Bay tomorrow and I thought we might take Angelica to the beach, especially if the weather is as nice as today."

Mary was still wary of allowing Angelica into the sea as she had no inclination to swim herself. But she trusted her friend and nodded her agreement to the proposition.

The railway station at Minehead was the end of the line and all of the passengers had to leave the train. The engines were then guided onto a large turntable which spun them slowly around to face the way they had previously come. From the turntable, the engines proceeded along a short length of track to just beyond the end carriage, then reversed until they could be hitched to the carriage again for the return journey. Caroline, Mary and Angelica stood at the end of the platform and watched the manoeuvres, Angelica pushing her face between the railings to get the best view. She did not want to leave once the engine was reattached and passengers were being allowed to board, and cried briefly as Mary carried her out of the station. Heads turned and women muttered under their breath.

Caroline noticed, though she could not hear what was being said. Mary kept her eyes looking straight ahead, talking softly to Angelica the whole time until they reached the main shopping street of the town. Then Mary put the little girl down and instructed Angelica to hold her hand, which the girl duly did. They walked slowly because of Angelica. The sun was warm and many of the town's inhabitants were out making purchases or meeting friends. As they passed a small white terrier that had been tied by its lead to a lamp post, Angelica stopped and crouched down to talk to the dog. The dog was elderly and not at all inconvenienced by

Angelica's interest; he sat with his short tail wagging on the dusty pavement, his head tilting comically from side to side as if listening to Angelica's babbling conversation.

Caroline was about to crouch down alongside her God-daughter when a woman came hurrying out of a nearby shop.

"No! Get away! Get that child away from my dog!" She shouted dramatically.

Caroline turned to the woman who was now untying the lead, "It's quite all right, Angelica was only saying hello to him."

The woman ignored Caroline and rounded on Mary, "You people should keep better control of your children! If my back had been turned for a minute longer no doubt you would have stolen Parson! This is a respectable town, and we don't want your kind here!"

"How dare you speak to my friend like that! She has every right…"

"Miss Caroline, please…"

"How dare I? Madam, I live in this town, I pay rates in this town and my husband pays his taxes, I have every right…"

"There is no reason at all to be rude…"

"Caroline, we should go…"

Angelica was still crouched by the dog, who still sat wagging his tail while his mistress' voice grew louder.

People stared as they walked by. Some stopped to watch the scene. Mary desperately wanted to leave, but Caroline stood her ground and was arguing with the older woman. A policeman arrived, pushing his way towards the women through the onlookers, some of whom melted away at the sight of him.

"Now ladies, what seems to be the matter here?"

"Constable, this child was antagonising my Parson, and then this young woman has been quite rude to me…"

"Utter nonsense! Angelica was simply interested in the dog, and if anyone has been rude, then I should say it is you, accusing my friend of being unwelcome here and trying to steal the animal."

The woman took a breath as if to start a fresh accusation when the constable held up his hand to silence her. He looked at Mary.

"Is this your little girl, madam?"

"Yes, officer."

The dog had offered Angelica his paw and as she tried to take it in her hand, Angelica wobbled and sat on the pavement with a bump. The dog, old as he was, thought it was a new game and tried to jump onto the little girl, which shocked her and she burst into tears.

The policeman bent down and picked Angelica up out of the way of the dog's attempt to lick her face. He turned her around so that they were nose to nose and she immediately stopped crying, her eyes wide and her lashes wet with tears.

"Well now," he said looking directly at Angelica but speaking loud enough for everyone to hear, "What a pretty young miss. How nice it is to see visitors to our town. Now you go back to your mother and I'm sure Mrs Cottismore will take Parson home and give him a nice juicy bone because nothing has happened here. Isn't that right Mrs Cottismore?" He handed the girl to Mary and untied the dog's lead from the lamp post as he waited for a response from the red-faced older woman.

"Constable I really think..."

"Yes, Mrs Cottismore?"

"Well. Of course, it is almost lunch time. We shall be getting along. Come, Parson!" She turned on her heel and walked off, head held high and dragging Parson behind her, through the now dispersing crowd.

"Are you alright madam?"The officer asked Mary as she wiped Angelica's face with her handkerchief.

"Yes, thank you."

"What a horrible woman! The things she said…" Caroline stared after Mrs Cottismore.

"Yes, madam, well some people are set in their ways. No harm done though I hope."

Mary shook her head, "No, Miss Caroline shall we carry on?"

"Yes, yes let's. Thank you, officer, I shall mention you to my friend, she is a Counsellor here, Mrs Gersen-Fisch."

"No need madam, just doing my job. Have a pleasant day," He winked at Angelica who was now sucking her thumb with her head against Mary's neck.

She smiled at the policeman without taking her thumb from her mouth and said quietly, "Hat".

They had walked to the end of the main street in silence. Caroline was furious with Mrs Cottismore, the more she absorbed what the woman had said the hotter her rage burned. Mary meanwhile was trying to stop the trembling that had overcome her as the crowd had begun to gather. The relief at finding a sympathetic policeman only partly made up for her embarrassment at being a spectacle for the locals to stare at.

They crossed the road and Angelica was allowed to walk again.

"What an awful woman," Caroline gasped, shaking her head, "I'm so sorry about all of that Mary."

"Miss Caroline, there is nothing for you to apologise for. It happens. People, older people, they often think I want to steal things. Or harm them. Or curse their babies or poison their food or sour their milk or put weevils in their flour. They think I am dirty, that I don't wash, that Angelica has lice or fleas or that Philip has lost his senses for taking me as his wife. Do you know, someone asked him the other day if he was going to marry a white woman as well? With me standing right there next to him!" Mary's voice became more noticeably Caribbean as her emotions flowed.

"Oh Mary, how awful for you. Some people are simply too rude for words."

"One day I will go back to Trinidad. I will take Angelica to meet her relations there. I want her to see that people can be good and not always thinking the worst of us."

"Would Philip go with you?"

"Yes. We have talked about it many times. He wants to have our children in England so that they will always be able to stay here, but when they are older, we will both go. He says the church will help us."

"Do you remember anything of Trinidad?"

"I remember the sun. Celestine tells me of the people and places, and I try to remember, but I was only Angelica's age when we came to Bristol."

Helen greeted them with her usual generous and warm hospitality, offering them cool drinks or tea, and suggesting that Mary might like to take Angelica up to one of the bedrooms for a nap. Mrs Rich led them upstairs and Caroline and Helen went into the sitting room. Caroline repeated the episode with Parson the dog and Helen agreed that the constable was a good sort and that she thought she knew who the woman was.

"But Caro, you know many people feel the same way as her."

"Yes, I do, but it is always a shock when one experiences it raw, as it were."

"One can only imagine how much more shocking it must be for Mary. Unless one gets used to it."

"I don't think I would ever truly get used to it. She looked so embarrassed, and then so grateful when the policeman was kind to Angelica. It was not how I'd imagined our visit here would be."

"Indeed. But what of your visit to Mr and Mrs Kingston, did that play out how you imagined?"

Caroline gave a review of her meeting with Noah's parents. Mrs Rich brought in tea while she talked, and Helen listened carefully without interrupting. When Caroline had finished, she sat back in her seat and closed her eyes.

Helen lit a cigarette.

"Forgive my bluntness, but you don't seem as enthusiastic as you were even a few weeks ago when you two came to dinner. Has something happened between you?"

Caroline opened her eyes and sighed, "No, nothing has happened. Helen, I keep thinking everything is alright and then something will irritate me or make me wonder if I really know Noah well enough to be living with him. And he mentions marriage a lot more now, as if he didn't really want to have a long engagement in the first place."

"Perhaps he thought it would be the only thing you would agree to. Or your father would agree to."

3

SEEKING COUNSEL

Their picnic had been a success. Mary had slept for a short while next to Angelica on the bed and felt better afterwards. They had carried the picnic basket and rugs down to Blenheim Gardens and Angelica had played on the grass with another little girl whose mother Helen knew.

The return journey to Doniford was uneventful and Mary put Angelica to bed early. The women spent the evening knitting on either side of the fire in the sitting room, with a small glass of sherry each and the radio playing a concert by the Royal Philharmonic Orchestra. It was peaceful and Mary wondered how Caroline could bear to leave the cottage at the end of June as she was planning to do. She also wondered about Noah and his and Caroline's relationship. Mary had not been surprised to hear about the engagement, she knew Caroline was not always one to follow convention. But there was something not quite right when Caroline talked about the new house and her future with Noah, and Mary did not ask more questions than she thought polite.

The next day was warmer still. After breakfast, Caroline gathered towels and her bathing costume, and the three of them set off down the lane to the beach. Mary was still unconvinced of the water's benefits but allowed Angelica to be undressed and play naked on the sand. They built sandcastles and inspected the rockpools. Angelica shrieked with delight at a crab they found, and when Caroline placed it on the sand, the little girl crawled on her hands and knees alongside it for several yards as the creature attempted to find another shallow pool to hide in.

As the sun reached its height, Caroline changed into her bathing costume and led Angelica down to the water. At first, they simply stood at the edge of the water as the gentle waves lapped at their toes. Angelica was keen to go further in, so after a few minutes Caroline picked her up and they walked forward until the sea was at Caroline's waist. Then she carefully lowered the girl into the water a few times to let her get used to the cold. Next Caroline turned Angelica so that she could support the girl's head and shoulders but leave her body and legs free to float on her back in the water. Angelica instinctively kicked her legs and chuckled as Caroline laughed at the splashing.

The tide was on its way in, so Caroline moved them a little closer to the shore before turning Angelica to face her in the water. She held the girl at arm's length and after the first few splutters and mouthfuls of seawater that Angelica swallowed, Caroline slowly walked backwards as Angelica half floated and half kicked her way through the water. After a while, Mary got up and went to the tide line holding a towel, and Caroline guided Angelica back to shallow water before letting the girl run through the surf and into the waiting arms of her mother. Mary carried her daughter back to their belongings while Caroline stretched herself out and swam in the deeper water. On her third 'length', she spotted Noah walking down the cliff path towards them and made for the shore to meet him.

By the time Noah reached them, Caroline had changed back into her dress and was rubbing the ends of her hair dry with the towel.

"Good morning! How was the water?" Noah asked as he sat down on the nearest rock.

"Cold still, but invigorating. Noah this is my good friend Mary and her daughter Angelica."

"Pleased to meet you Mary," Noah did not offer his hand.

Mary noted the lack of handshake, "Good morning. Miss Caroline has told me so much about you."

Caroline did not see Mary's thin smile but heard the slight edge to her voice. They talked for a while, as Angelica ate slices of apple from a bowl. Noah asked about their day in Minehead but neither of the women mentioned the unpleasant Mrs Cottismore.

"Will you come back with us for lunch?" Caroline asked.

"Not today I'm afraid. I need to get back. In fact, I should get going. Oh, the dinner service and glassware arrived yesterday. I left them in the crates in the kitchen as we have nowhere to put them until we can find a dresser. You'll come over on Saturday for the *matinée*?"

"Yes, I'll come and find you at the harbour."

When Noah had gone, they sat in silence for a while, watching the gulls bobbing on the water and Angelica burying her toes in the dark sand.

"Mary," Caroline said at last, "When Philip asked you to marry him, did you say yes straight away?"

"I did not. He asked his Vicar at the time and his own parents before he asked me. I told him how hard it would be for him. I did not want his work to be affected if we married."

"But it hasn't been, has it?"

"The Bishop has been good to us. But sometimes… no, it doesn't matter."

"Go on."

Mary sighed, "Sometimes I think the Bishop uses Philip and I as if we were trophies. Something to show off to people."

Caroline considered this for a moment. "Do you mean, if he sends you somewhere, it is because he thinks you will prove people wrong who are against coloured people being here?"

"Something like that, yes. Not just for them to look at me and say, 'the black woman is a lady like you all' but also for them to look at Philip and say, 'if a man of the cloth can take one as his wife, they cannot be so far from God'. I have seen it before, and I did not want it for Philip, but it has come to us anyway." She sounded sad and resigned to their fate.

"So even though you loved Philip and wanted to marry him, you said no because you cared for him?"

"Yes."

"But he convinced you eventually."

"He did. Celestine was impressed by him. She told me to marry him, so I did."

"I think my father would want me to marry Noah."

"You say he helped Noah buy the house? Then he must think something of him. But you are his daughter. He would want you to be happy," Mary looked at Caroline, "Will Noah make you happy?"

"Oh Mary, I don't think he will. And I feel awful about it because he has bought the house and we have bought furniture and other things for it, but I don't think I can marry him and the more he talks about it the less I want to go through with it. And I don't know how to tell him!"

"You must find a way."

Once Mary and Angelica had returned to Cheltenham, Caroline fell back into her usual routine of painting, walking and swimming. She sorted through the sketches of Tommy that she had made the previous year and worked up two fresh canvases featuring his reclining naked body to send to Elsa for Bobby's gallery in London. Caroline enjoyed the flow of the charcoal as she made her fluid marks across the canvas; it was a liberating medium that matched the subject matter well. As she packed them carefully, she wondered if Tommy would ever walk into a room and see himself as her artwork on a wall. She did not think he would be embarrassed if he did.

When the paintings had been sent off to London, Caroline felt restless again. She visited Daisy Clare one Thursday when the Yarn Market was in full swing in Dunster. It was named because of the ancient reliance on sheep fleeces in the area, but now was a thriving collection of livestock and farm kitchen wares. Caroline had finished reading Virginia Woolf's *Day and Night* and had felt a strong connection with the characters in the story, particularly Mary Datchet. She hoped that Daisy might have another of Woolf's novels in her shop and was pleased to find a battered and slightly water-stained copy of *The Voyage Out* which Daisy again let her have for free.

With cheese, goose eggs and a shoulder of pork in her basket, Caroline walked with Daisy along the High Street to the café for lunch. Over pressed tongue and mustard sandwiches, Caroline tried to explain how she felt about Noah. He had not been in favour of Tommy sitting for more sketches when Caroline had mentioned it to him. He had tried to persuade her to paint more dainty watercolours instead.

"I think we are just growing apart, wanting different things," Caroline finished and took another bite of her sandwich.

"That doesn't sound like a good foundation for a happy marriage. You must speak to him about it. I have been feeling a similar way myself recently. Now that Helen is so involved in her work on the council, I feel rather surplus to requirements. I suppose it is just the way these things go."

The two women stirred their cups of tea thoughtfully, ignored by the other patrons of the café.

At the same time Daisy and Caroline were drinking their tea in Dunster, Noah and the harbour master at Watchet were enjoying a lunchtime pint of beer at the Anchor Inn just behind the boathouse on the quay. David Escott had been instrumental in initially convincing Noah that marriage could wait, if it happened at all.

"Albert'll bring the lorry around at five, we can go and collect that bed from Blue Anchor." Escott took a box of matches from his waistcoat pocket and lit his pipe.

"I think I might need two before June." Noah stared into his pint.

"Not going well with Caroline?"

"I don't know. We carry on as we have been, we've not argued or anything like that. Yet, I get the impression she is having second thoughts. And there are some things that now I know more, I'm not sure I agree with."

"Best to get it sorted out sooner rather than later, boy."

"I think if I try, I could make it worse. Caroline is … she is like a fish I'm trying to land and every time I think I've got her, she flips and slips away from me."

Escott drew on his pipe and breathed out the smoke away from Noah, "Then you either need to get a net and have her secure on board, or you cut the line. Depends how much you want to land her."

Caroline decided she must talk things over with her father before tackling Noah. As Quantock Cottage had no telephone, she wrote to him to say she would catch the train and be in Cheltenham on Friday 4 May and stay until the following Tuesday so that they could spend the bank holiday weekend together. She had not seen George since Christmas and was keen to satisfy herself that his health had not deteriorated since his diagnosis of diabetes. She had always been close to her father, and now they were the only two left of the Munhead line she often wished he would retire and move closer to her. Except now, Caroline thought as the train pulled into Cheltenham Spa station with a squeal of brakes and bellows of steam, she might well end up asking if she could move back to the apartment with him again.

She hailed a taxi from the station and arrived at Norwood Court apartments just as Sara Johnson, her father's daily housekeeper, was leaving through the glass doors with their curved brass handles.

"Good afternoon, Sara! Are you well?"

"Yes, thank you ma'am. I wasn't sure what time you'd get here, but there is cold chicken and vegetable pie for yours and Mr Munhead's dinner."

"Excellent. And how is Miss Kettle?" Sara's services were shared between Caroline's father and Agatha Kettle, a retired schoolteacher who lived on the ground floor.

"She's away for a few days, ma'am. That's why I'm off a bit early today. Mother's not so good at the moment so I shall be able to see to her before Father gets home."

"Give her my regards and I hope she is feeling better again soon."

Sara's mother had suffered from arthritis for many years and was virtually housebound. Sara was the youngest of the four Johnson daughters and had an interest in becoming a nurse when the current overabundance of nurses (or women who felt they could nurse just as well as trained professionals since the war had required them to) declined. Sara's oldest sister Annie had been the Munhead's maid throughout Caroline's teenage years and had only left the family to have a child of her own with her husband Jacob Jenks. Their son Victor was almost a year old, and George Munhead was one of his Godfathers.

Caroline carried her case into the apartment block, and was met by the doorman, Ferris. After exchanging warm greetings, he carried her case up the central stairs to the top floor when her father's apartment was situated. On that short climb Caroline learned that Miss Kettle was staying with a great niece in Brighton for a week, and that Captain McTimony on the second floor had taken a turn for the worse and things were looking bleak. There was still no occupant of the other second floor apartment. It had been empty since the hasty departure of optician Vaughan Rickard with his still-married elopee, Florence Curzon. Caroline was relieved to close the apartment door behind her.

The apartment had not changed in her absence. She could smell the pie Sara had left for their dinner, mixed with the aroma of lavender and polish. The narrow hallway contained the prized telephone standing on a slim table, and doors leading to the sitting room, bathroom and two bedrooms. Caroline took her case into her old bedroom and unpacked her clothes. Her old wardrobe with its brass key and mirror on the inside of the door was a familiar comforting sight. She looked at her watch, saw it was just after five o'clock, and wondered where her father was. He would normally have left the office of the Cheltenham and Gloucester Benefits Building Society at four o'clock on a Friday and walked the twenty-minute route to Norwood Court apartments. Caroline decided to run a bath and had just stepped into the hot water when she heard her father open the apartment door. She called out a greeting and said she would be decent in half an hour if George could turn the pan of potatoes on to cook. George smiled to himself at the word decent but did as he was asked and then took the evening newspaper into the sitting room to read while he waited.

Over dinner George explained why he had been late home.

"I called in to the Everyman and bought tickets to the *Pirate of Penzance* for us for tomorrow. I thought it might make a pleasant change from the picture house for you. And for me as well."

"Oh, how lovely! What time does it begin?"

"Eight. We will have plenty of time to eat before the performance. Would you like to go out for dinner?"

"You are being uncharacteristically extravagant, Father. Is everything alright?"

George chuckled. "Yes, everything is perfectly alright. I simply thought it would be an enjoyable way for us to spend the evening, and as I have been on the diet that Dr Riley insisted on since before Christmas, I feel I deserve a little extravagance while you are here."

After dinner they moved to the sitting room and over glasses of port Caroline explained her growing feelings of reluctance to moving in with and marrying Noah. George listened carefully. He knew Caroline needed to talk out the whole situation without interruption and would then wait for his considered opinion. As he learned more, he nodded and took on some of the sadness his daughter was expressing.

George had liked Noah from the start when Noah had written to him at the Building Society and asked not only for Caroline's hand in marriage but also advice and assistance in obtaining a mortgage on the house in Westmoreland Terrace. They had subsequently talked several times on the telephone and by the time they met at Quantock Cottage at Christmas, George felt completely comfortable that Noah would make a good husband for Caroline. However, he was also conscious that he and Noah had assumed a certain patriarchal authority in arranging things without consulting Caroline and it had been his one reservation about the whole endeavour. Now it seemed he had been right to be concerned on that front.

"You still wear the ring?" He asked when Caroline appeared to come to a stop.

"Yes, but I shall give it back."

"That sounds as if you have made a decision."

"I don't see now how I can go through with it all. I feel utterly wretched about it. He is a good man, I just don't think he is … the right man."

"Caroline, you will always have a home here with me. Perhaps it would do some good to put a distance between yourself and Noah for a while?"

"I just don't know." She said quietly.

"Well, I am not going to give any further advice this evening. It is late and you have had a tiring day. Do you have plans for tomorrow?"

"I thought I might visit Lottie and the twins. I shall be back in plenty of time for dinner."

"Then let's say no more this evening. I will think over all that you have told me, and we can talk of it further over the weekend."

Lottie Price, nee Lewis, had befriended Caroline when they worked together for a few months at Sunningend Engineering in Cheltenham. They had been employed in the sewing room, stitching heavy canvas sheets onto wooden frames that were then coated in a resinous mixture and allowed to dry, before being assembled into aeroplanes. Lottie's husband Eric had volunteered during the General Strike two years before to assist the police in distributing supplies. It was the incentive to apply to become a police constable and he had completed his training while he and Lottie married and lived with her parents near the gas works in Cheltenham. Once enrolled as a constable, he was posted to Stroud and the couple wasted no time in starting a family to fill the police house they were allocated. Alice and Edith Price had been born and christened in January 1928. Eric enjoyed his work immensely and Lottie managed the twins with the help of regular visits from her mother.

Caroline decided to walk from Stroud station up to the pair of police houses at the top of the town as the weather was dry with streamers of white clouds blown across the azure sky. She knew she would have to recount much of what she had told her father when she saw Lottie, but it was proving to be cathartic and helped her to organise her thoughts on the matter. She had not warned Lottie of her visit and she hoped she would find her friend at home. Thankfully Lottie had been standing over a copper drum with a pair of wooden tongs, boiling the girls' nappies; she opened the door with a squeal of delight to see Caroline.

The twins were napping, which gave Lottie a chance to boil the kettle and make a pot of tea while keeping an eye on her laundry. The peace was broken after an hour by the children waking to be fed and changed. Caroline assisted as best she could and was not surprised to be given a bottle of evaporated milk mixed with water to feed Alice while Lottie made up another to feed Edith.

"The District Nurse suggested it after three months. The girls were forever hungry no matter what I did, and we were getting next to no sleep. Worked a treat."

"They say it's as good as the mother's milk," said Caroline, remembering a public health talk she had heard recently on the radio.

"Oh yes, and on Eric's wages we can afford it. They'll be starting on solids soon anyway."

While burping the babies, Lottie asked Caroline about Noah and the house on Westmorland Terrace, and Caroline's retelling began. Though she said less to Lottie than she had to her father, it took as long because Lottie regularly interrupted with questions. By the time Caroline had finished, the girls had drifted off to sleep again and the copper had been switched off. Lottie took the babies back upstairs to their cots and when she returned, she used the tongs to put the nappies into an enamel bucket and invited Caroline out into the back garden while she ran them through the mangle.

Caroline turned the mangle handle while Lottie fed the squares of terry towelling through the rollers and into a second waiting bucket.

"You know Bob is still not married," Lottie's older brother had long held a candle for Caroline, but though he was securely employed at the gas works and had his own home in Prestbury village on the edge of Cheltenham, Caroline had always felt she could not happily live the domestic life he offered her.

"Lottie, I can no more marry Bob than I can Noah. They want the same kind of wife, and I am not she."

"So, what *do* you want? To end up an old maid?"

"I don't know what I want. I only know I don't want to get married or live with Noah as if we were."

"Perhaps you should join a nunnery."

"I'm not a Catholic. In any case, I'd like to travel and see a bit of the world. My friend Helen's husband Tommy has got in with a group of pilots who are running flights to London and Scotland. They say it's going to be the next big thing."

"I thought the motor car was going to be the next big thing! Well, perhaps you need to marry a rich pilot."

"Why do I have to marry someone just to be able to do what I please? Why can't I do it by myself?"

Lottie shook her head and picked up the second bucket to peg the wrung-out nappies on the washing line, "Because you'll need a man's wages to do it all."

Caroline enjoyed her dinner and trip to the theatre with her father. They did not discuss Noah further that evening, nor on their way to or from Christ Church the following morning. George had continued to belong to the congregation despite moving out of the parish. On their return to Norwood Court, they heard the sound of Galina Bassett's phonogram playing her beloved Russian composers. After lunch Caroline knocked on Galina's door.

"Caroline, what a lovely surprise! Come in. You heard Borodin, yes?" Years of English education and international travel had removed almost every trace of Galina's Russian accent, but not her love of her musical countrymen.

"I thought it was Borodin, but I wasn't sure. How are you?"

They went into Galina's sitting room and she poured Caroline a measure of vodka before lighting a cigarette.

"You still don't smoke? Well, I am very well if a little bored."

"Cheltenham isn't the most exciting town," Caroline sat on the sofa with her drink.

"It is not Cheltenham. I can remove myself to wherever I choose. No, I am bored with being a single woman."

Caroline was no longer shocked at Galina's candid honesty. It was one of the reasons Caroline had hoped to talk with her while visiting. A woman of the world and greatly travelled, Galina was often even more frank than Helen.

"Your affair has ended?"

"Yes. Rather like a puppy that grows up to be a bloodhound, he became unmanageable. He will never leave his wife, and yet all the talk of futures and plans. It became tiresome."

They did not need to speak his name. Caroline knew that Galina had been spending nights with Matthew Monk from the other ground floor apartment at Norwood Court in an Oxford hotel. A serial adulterer, he had moved with his wife Rebecca to Cheltenham after an affair with a young typist at the airbase he worked at training reconnaissance pilots. Rebecca Monk had devoted herself to nursing Captain McTimony after he suffered a stroke the previous year.

Galina also knew about Max. Caroline had eventually needed to confide in someone with relevant experience after she returned from Cornwall, and Galina was the obvious choice.

"I rather have the opposite problem," Caroline sipped her vodka.

After explaining briefly while Galina smoked her cigarette, Caroline waited for her host to pronounce her verdict on the situation.

"Yet another man who wants to marry you. In polite circles you might be considered a tease you know."

Caroline frowned, "That's hardly fair, Galina. I don't intentionally lead anyone on."

"And yet, here you are. How many proposals have you have so far?"

Caroline used her fingers to count, "Bob, Luke probably would have, James, Vaughan, and now Noah. Five. Is that so very many?"

"For a princess or an heiress, perhaps not. You are neither of those things. These offers will not continue forever."

"I really don't think I want them to. I like meeting new people; I just wish I could do it without the men I meet falling in love with me!"

Galina poured more vodka.

"Your agreement on your cottage ends next month, yes? What do you plan to do then?"

"At the end of June, yes. Come back to Cheltenham I suppose."

"And you will not be happy. You will find yourself with yet more proposals from men you have no real interest in, and eventually one will wear you down and you will become a wife who resents her husband for his freedoms and his money. Have you forgotten what I told you about finding a man who shares your passions?"

"The only man who shares my love of art is married to Helen and prefers men. It is hopeless Galina. I feel I am missing something, and I don't know what it is or how to find it!"

"Caroline, you are floating. You are allowing yourself to drift like a feather in a breeze. You must focus, take control, make a decision and take action. Do not waste time on anything that does not excite you. Seek out that excitement. Heaven knows there will be time enough for knitting by the fireside and tea with the vicar when you are an old woman!"

On the bank holiday Monday, Caroline and her father took a stroll around The Park opposite Norwood Court apartments. Cheltenham had several large public parks, but this one had always been known simply by that name. They sat on a bench near to the ornamental lake and threw pieces of stale bread to the ducks and pigeons that gathered around them. When the bread had been exhausted, and the birds dispersed, George turned to face his daughter. He had enjoyed having her in the apartment again but understood that she would be leaving the next day and even if she returned at the end of June, it would only be on a temporary basis. He had prepared his advice and it was time to give it.

"Caroline, you must tell Noah as soon as possible of your decision. It will do him no harm to have purchased the house, but you will need to arrange to have your belongings sent here or stored somewhere. You are sure that you do not want to renew the lease on the cottage?"

"No, I love it, and I love being so close to the sea, but I do not love the thought that it could flood in bad weather."

"Then I shall inform the owner's solicitor. You will need to cancel all of your regular services in good time. You have a little over sixty pounds in your bank account, how much do you have in your Post Office account?"

"Around twelve pounds, I spent rather a lot on things for the house. I should ask Noah if he wants the dinner service for himself, and the glassware. Oh, but I bought the most beautiful lamp at an auction, I should like to keep that."

"You will need to make arrangements with Noah yourself. This is your decision and all part of being a responsible adult. Twelve pounds should last you a few weeks, but you will need to consider obtaining employment if you are not going to move back here, and you should consider it anyway for your own benefit even if you do."

"Yes. I could do all that Sara does of course, and save you the expense of having her, but that would mean she would be out of a job, and I don't want that for her. If she had to work elsewhere, then Miss Kettle would also lose Sara. I don't know what type of work I could do though," Caroline sighed dejectedly, "I feel I have come full circle and the past two years have been wasted. Except now it will be Sara I am reading out the situations vacant column to instead of Annie. I will have to register with the Agency in the Promenade as well this time."

"It would be sensible. Naturally I shall ask about suitable vacancies through my acquaintances. You still have your reference from Sunningend?"

"I do somewhere, yes. I suppose I could ask there for my old job back, though Lottie says the night shift was withdrawn recently so I expect some of the girls will have taken up any vacancies during the day in the sewing room."

"I shall tell Sara and Ferris to expect delivery of your larger belongings at the end of next month, the wireless set and anything else of that kind. I will cover the packing and transportation costs for you, so let me have the details when you have made the arrangements."

"I'm sorry that I am being such an inconvenience. I wish I didn't feel this way."

"If you are not happy, my dear, then it is not an inconvenience. And I should apologise for taking too much for granted when Noah and I came to our arrangement. It seems we were equally wrong there."

It was the beginning of June before Caroline finally told Noah that she could not move into Westmoreland Terrace with him when her tenancy of Quantock Cottage came to an end that month. They were sitting in the garden at the cottage, drinking beer after dinner one Friday evening. The sun was about to dip below the trees that edged the Saddington's garden, and the eight-forty train had just left Doniford Halt for Williton.

Noah inhaled cigarette smoke and put his glass down on the path beside his chair. "I guessed as much. Good thing we haven't sent out any invitations."

"I'm sorry. I have been trying to tell you for weeks but there has never been a good time. I'm very fond of you Noah, but…"

"Don't, please Caroline. Don't try and soften the blow now that you've told me. I had convinced myself that it was just nerves on your part."

"It's not nerves. You asked me not long after we met if I was scared of commitment, do you remember?"

"Yes, and you said you weren't. What's changed?"

"Nothing has changed. I'm not scared of it. But marriage is a commitment, and I'm just not ready to take that step. I may never be."

"I've always said that we need not get married straight away."

"Yes, but almost every conversation we have now, it crops up at some point between us. I like your mother, but when we visited them last weekend and you went to the pub with your father, it was all she talked about. Had I chosen a date, what flowers had I picked out, what style of dress. It was all very awkward, and I don't think it would stop once we were living together. If anything, I expect it would become more so."

Noah finished his cigarette and stubbed it out with his toe in the grass, "So, what will you do? Stay here for another year?"

"No. I shall miss this cottage very much, but it came so close to flooding last year I am in no hurry to wait and see if the sea does reach this far. Helen has said I can stay with them for a while so I will send some of my belongings back to Cheltenham and take the rest to Minehead."

"And is this the end?" He leaned forward with his elbows on his knees, "The end for us, I mean."

Caroline reached out and touched his hand, "I think it must be. I feel wretched, about us and about the house, and I would always want to be your friend Noah, but I cannot ask you to wait while I live my life on the chance that one day, I might change my mind. You do see that, don't you?"

Noah took her hand in his. He had felt on their journey home from his parents the previous weekend that something had crystalised in Caroline, that she had reached a decision about something, and he had feared this moment. They had not seen each other all week, and he had been nervous about going to dinner that evening with her. But now the words had been spoken, he found he was a little relived too. They had been dancing around the subject for too long.

"I'm sorry that I can't give you what you want Caroline."

"I'm not even sure what that is. I just know it's not marriage, not now, and the pressure to do that would be enormous if I moved into the house with you." She withdrew her hand gently, "You must have this back too."

Caroline undid the chain around her neck and slid the ring off into the palm of her hand. She held it out to Noah, who took it and put it into his pocket without a word.

4

EVERYTHING IS BETTER IN THE SUNSHINE

"Do you have sixpence for the meter?"

Caroline had been in Minehead for just over a week and was helping Helen in her office at the parade of new shops in her Alcombe South constituency.

"There are some in the biscuit tin on that shelf. Feed it two or three would you, so that it lasts the rest of the week."

Helen was preparing for her weekly surgery where anyone could visit the office and talk about, ask, or as was often the case, demand her attention to some issue. She had chosen Tuesday afternoons for the surgery as all of the shops were open and the local residents would naturally be in the area. Wednesdays were half-day closing in Minehead. Her constituents were welcome to visit by appointment on any other weekday, so that she could fit them around her committee meetings and visits.

Caroline's arrival had been synchronous with the request for a leave of absence by Helen's regular assistant, Monica. A sickly aunt required Monica's attention, and Helen was able to appear benevolent in both directions while solving her own problem at the same time. Monica had telephoned that morning to explain that she would need another week, on the orders of her aunt's doctor, but that she hoped to return after that if Helen could hold her position open. Helen was relaxed and sympathetic, not wanting a good secretary to slip through her fingers. Of course Monica could take another week, of course her position was secure, best wishes to the aunt for a speedy recovery.

Caroline emerged from the meter cupboard and went to the hand basin in the corner of the office to wash the grime from her fingers. The office was laid out as two rooms with a lavatory in a partitioned space off the rear room where they both currently stood. The front room contained a desk and some utility wooden chairs. The women had partially covered the inside of the large front windows with posters and notices to afford the visitors a little privacy without cutting out all of the light. It was sandwiched between a butcher on the left and a tobacconist on the right, with a post office, hair salon and a chemist occupying the other units. The proprietors of the shops all lived in the storey above in purpose-built apartments. The apartment above Helen's constituency office was rented by one of the teachers at Saint Theresa's convent school in the town.

"Do you think Tommy's pals will agree to him taking a month off?" Caroline asked, drying her hands on a small towel.

"I should think so. In any case, he's not actually employed by them, he is a small shareholder and donates his time to their cause. He can come and go as he pleases."

"It was very good of your father to offer the house for a whole month. I think it will do me some good to be out on the moor again. Not that it's not wonderful to be staying here in Minehead with you of course." Caroline added quickly, not wanting to offend.

"I quite understand. I wish I could stay longer with you both, but my work here simply could not withstand an absence of that duration, even with Monica to keep the ship sailing. There is so much to do to make sure all the women of Minehead understand they have a vote now, since the Act passed. So many of the menfolk are against it all, and really, you'd be shocked Caro to hear some of the women's opinions against it as well. A week will be plenty long enough for me to get my golf swing back up to standard. We are lucky that Mother and Father are staying in Harrogate for the summer with some army friend of his, and that William is in Aden although whether that is lucky for everyone else in Aden remains to be seen."

"Did you say he was working for the British Consulate?"

"Yes, some clerical role. One can't help but wonder if these punishments Father contrives are actually rewards to William. He certainly sees a lot of the world at the government's expense."

"I hadn't thought of it like that, but Aden is rather dangerous at the moment, isn't it?"

"Everywhere in the middle east is dangerous if you are with the wrong tribe, Caro. It will give Jolyon a break from having to plead our brother's case before the magistrates at least."

"Is Jolyon very much like William?"

"Couldn't be more different! Jolyon is very much like our sister Roberta, possibly because she spent such a lot of time with him when he was a baby. William was older, and naturally had developed his own personality already when Roberta was put in charge of them both. I wouldn't be at all surprised if Roberta and Jolyon end up living together at the villa when Mother and Father have gone. Roberta is far too old to marry now in any case."

"Oh Helen, surely not! Roberta is what now, forty? That's not too old. She might find a widower and fall in love."

"Thirty-eight. Had the war not cut a swathe through the male population, she could well have snapped up a widower by now, but sadly I think she will end her days doing her good works around Plymouth as a spinster."

"So might I." said Caroline quietly.

It had rained heavily in the night. As Tommy drove Helen and Caroline west into Devon the next morning, there were large puddles across the road which he tried to avoid in case they were hiding deep holes that would damage the car's tyres or suspension. He was in good spirits. The airfield had taken up plenty of his time (as he had hoped it would) and he had spent far less time painting than he would otherwise have done. A month on the edge of Dartmoor was the perfect balance to his recent industry and he was happy to have Caroline as his companion. He looked on her as if she were his sister; Tommy had no other living siblings. His only family were his father and two distant uncles (who were really second cousins or great uncles once removed), and Lina who lived in Great Malvern and was an even more distant cousin on his late mother's side.

The Sunray Air Company was now his passion. Having invested a thousand pounds initially, he had written to his father and was now hoping for an advance of another five hundred. The ground crew, four young men who had been pilots and engineers at the end of the war, had accepted him as one of their own and he felt sure it was not just because of the money he had contributed. The two small aeroplanes they had acquired and overhauled were now in operation running three trips a week to Glasgow, and daily to Ashford in Kent. Almost turning a profit, they had recently been discussing a number of different ways to expand their operations. It had given Tommy and idea about how to help Caroline resolve her current transient situation but for now he was keeping that to himself.

Caroline sat in the back seat of the motorcar and watched the the landscape change subtly from coast to moor to open farmland. There were sheep looking rough and unclipped, and stocky chocolate brown ponies with tousled dark manes and extravagant eyelashes. Glossy black crows patrolled the fields in search of edible treasure. Caroline was very much looking forward to a month in Tavistock. Though her previous visit had not started on the best note, having been assaulted by one of the young men in the house party she, Helen and Tommy had attended, the little moorland town had enchanted her. The view from her bedroom window out across the purple moor was one she could stand looking at for hours. The way the clouds bubbled up and chased each other across the sky was as entertaining as any moving picture.

Helen's father had bought the house new from the builder three years before, as a place to entertain his golf-loving friends. Colonel William Postgate spent much of his time at his club in Plymouth, while Helen's mother Lady Rosalind whose noble Romanian heritage showed in her small stature and dark hair, devoted herself to the advancement of women's suffrage and health care. She moved in the same circles as the Astors, and the Postgate's villa in Lipson was often filled with well-dressed and serious women discussing the provision of maternity or children's services in the city. Plymouth was rich with merchants, and poor with mile after mile of squalid shared housing radiating from the Dockyard. The Victorians had done their best to provide better homes for the railway workers and their families, but there were still acres of slums where the stench kept all but the hardiest philanthropists away.

Helen had spent very little time in Plymouth once she was old enough to go away to school. She was boarded at Mrs Pendersen's School in Cheltenham while Rosalind travelled Europe with Helen's consumptive sister Sophia. Helen hadn't minded; at school she could be the centre of attention if she chose to be instead of the disappointing third daughter quickly overshadowed by her younger brothers. She had revelled in the female community, growing to understand her own attraction to other women while absorbing the information and culture brought by the other girls from around the world. Around the world, and in Caroline's case, across town. They made an unlikely trio along with Midge Frampton, or Midge Gregson as she now was.

Thinking of Midge, Helen turned in the front seat to say to Caroline, "Did you remember to write to Midge and let her know you would be staying with us?"

Caroline blinked as she dragged her eyes from the bright countryside to the darkness of the motor car. "I did, yes. Though if she has written recently, Mr Bright at the post office has your address to forward any letters to. He is such a dear man, I shall miss him, and Mr Evans at the station."

"Do you girls fancy stopping at Okehampton for some lunch, or shall we keep going to Tavistock?" Tommy asked over the noise of the engine.

They agreed to stop and as well as having lunch at the White Hart Hotel, they purchased some supplies for dinner and breakfast in case Mrs Danks, the retained housekeeper, had not been made aware of their arrival. Helen did not trust her father's secretary to have delivered the message. They bought sausages and bacon, a pound of cheese and a dozen eggs, two loaves of coarse bread, a pat of butter and two pints of milk. Caroline piled their provisions up on the back seat of the car next to her, their luggage having taken all of the other space.

That evening, tired but happy, Caroline lay in the narrow bed in the little yellow bedroom in complete darkness. She could hear the radio playing the end of the evening concert in the sitting room where Tommy finished his glass of whiskey. Helen had gone to bed early after taking a bath. If only they could all just stay there forever together, she thought. They had laughed and joked together over their simple dinner and found a pack of playing cards in the sideboard to play a few hands of Rummy before Helen had declared her need to wash the dust of the roads off her person. Tommy seemed relaxed too, Caroline mused. He was so often a bundle of nervous energy, she hoped he had truly put his disastrous affair with Christopher behind him. They had decided to play golf the next day if the weather held and reacquaint themselves with the other club members. The High Moorland golf club lay at the end of Down Road and was the reason the houses along the road had been constructed. She would enjoy the exercise after being sat in the motor car for much of that day.

Helen stayed the week as she had promised. The following Friday she packed her case and kissed Caroline farewell before Tommy drove her down to the little railway station in the town. She did not want to leave; she had been invigorated by the fresh air on the golf course despite her view of Tavistock as a depressing little town dressed in grey moorland granite. Yet, she was also keen to return to Minehead, to her work, and to Daisy whom she hoped would meet her at the railway station and stay the weekend. Her life felt removed from her Devon roots now. Helen had found an understanding in Daisy that she had never felt with previous lovers; Daisy too had her own life and interests, but on the occasions that they came together intimately they found each other to be equals. That was what Helen needed, she decided as she boarded the first of three trains she would take that Friday.

Left alone in the house, Caroline made herself a pot of tea and took it into the rear garden. The boundary hedge of clipped beech had been kept deliberately low so as not to obscure the view of the moor beyond. A young rowan tree had been planted on one corner of the garden and would never provide any shade to the owners being in the wrong position. It looked somewhat sickly to Caroline as she inspected it more closely, its shivering leaves a mottled yellow-green in the sunlight.

"Is to keep witches away, so they do say."

Caroline gasped at the voice behind her. "Oh Mrs Danks, I didn't hear you cross the grass, you made me jump!"

"Sorry for 'um. Is there three for dinner this eve' or no?"

Caroline had grown used to Mrs Danks' soft broad accent and had no difficulty understanding most of what she said now.

"Just Tommy and I from now on. Could you bring out some more hot water for the teapot please?"

Mrs Danks nodded and turned to go. Caroline remembered something she had been meaning to ask. "Mrs Danks, do you know if there are stables nearby where we could hire horses for a day?"

Mrs Danks looked blankly at her. "To ride?"

"Well, yes. Across the moor, perhaps as far as Princetown."

"End of the road, then left a way. Stables might lend you horses and saddles and such. Don't be fooled by the sun mind; the bogs still suck people in even in the summer." She turned and went into the house.

Caroline smiled despite Mrs Danks' stern warning. She had never ridden for pleasure and had been a little scared of the hunters and polo ponies she had met in Dunster under the care of Jack Herridge. It was not the season for hunting with hounds, and Caroline would not have wanted to join a hunt in any case, but the thought of slowly and quietly crossing the moor on horseback appealed to her. A conversation overheard at the golf club had placed the idea in her mind, and she felt sure that Tommy would also enjoy an excursion.

She told him of her plan over their dinner of cold chicken and salad that evening.

"Have you ridden before? I'd never have put you down as a horse lover." Tommy inspected a lettuce leaf before taking a bite.

"Not ridden in the way I think you mean, no. I have sat on a horse, and also on a donkey one year at a summer fayre. I thought perhaps that it would give a different perspective of the scenery, being higher up."

"Yes, there is that. Tricky to sketch while on a horse though. And we'd have to travel light, just a sketch book and some pencils. Did you bring that old backpack of yours?"

Caroline had acquired the backpack while staying in Dunster the year before. It had been left at the boarding house by a previous traveller and her host had offered it to Caroline.

"I did. It's been such a useful thing, though I would never have thought to buy one for myself."

"Well let's go and see the stables tomorrow and arrange a day for it. I say!" he held up a lettuce leaf with his fork and a small green caterpillar raised its head in greeting.

Tommy, to Caroline's surprise, was an experienced horseman. Although it had been some years since he had ridden, he was confident around the animals and spoke knowledgeably enough to the stable owner that she willingly agreed to loan two of her mares for the day. They arranged to take them the following Monday, as Sundays were universally observed as a day of rest in the district. The golf club remained closed, and there were regular petitions to suspend the railway operations through the town on Sundays, to no avail. Caroline and Tommy were content to sit in the rear garden and listen to the various church bells calling the faithful to prayer, breakfast on a Sunday being a self-service affair without Mrs Danks' assistance.

"I hadn't realised that Tavistock was quite so puritan." Caroline said as the last bell ceased.

"Mostly Methodist here." Tommy replied from under his straw boater hat which was shielding his face from the sun. "There's a catholic church in town I believe and several non-conformists too. But I'm told that the further you venture onto the moor, the people become more pagan."

"What does that mean exactly?"

Tommy removed his hat. "The ways of the countryside, no doctrine, no scripture. Though I do know that in some instances remote rural communities become extreme zealots in their religion. All Old Testament and brimstone and fire."

"Yes, but what does 'ways of the countryside' mean?"

"Planting by the phases of the moon, if you believe in that kind of thing. Knowing which wild plants to use for treating illnesses, keeping a black cat and a beesom in their gingerbread cottage in the woods." He smiled, waiting for Caroline to catch his joke.

"Oh Tommy, don't tease!"

"I'm sorry Caro, it was too easy. But these fairy tales must come from somewhere, and there was an old woman who lived in a run-down hovel near where I went to school. Everyone thought she was a witch; she had the obligatory black cat. As far as I know she often carried out midwifery to the locals, though we never saw her in church."

"Didn't you go to school here in Devon?"

"Near Totnes. Father pulled a few strings to get me in, on account of our family not being Christians. The Brothers were rather strict in some areas and incredibly indulgent in others."

"Is that where you learned to ride?"

"Yes, we had several horses there. The school had a lot of land and we had to help cultivate it otherwise we would have starved during the winter. We would have formal lessons in the mornings and then after lunch we'd all be outside whatever the weather until supper. I soon worked out the stables were the driest place to be. What about you? Helen never talks much about your school days together. What kind of place was it?"

"Mrs Pendersen's was a very large house close to Pittville Park, that's the largest park in Cheltenham. There weren't many girls there when I started, but by the time we all finished there were girls staying in other houses around the edge of the park who would come to the main house for lessons. I stayed during the week but went home on Friday afternoon and returned on Monday morning. We spent a lot of time outside too, but mostly doing exercises. There was something of a mania for co-ordinated exercise routines at the time, every school would put on a display for fêtes and summer shows and the like. And of course, we were taken swimming twice weekly at the baths at Montpelier."

"Ahh yes, the spa waters. That certainly explains your love of swimming now."

"It's a pity that there is no pool here. I miss being able to walk to the beach every morning for a dip."

"Look here, we don't have to stay in Tavistock for the whole month you know. The south coast has some perfect spots for swimming, why don't we take a drive there later in the week?"

"Could we? I brought my bathing costume just in case."

"Yes, let's. I'll fetch a map and we can look for likely beaches."

Monday dawned under a disappointing cover of low cloud. The air felt damp and although it was still warm, Caroline and Tommy were glad of their jackets. Caroline put on the pair of Freddie's old trousers that she had been wearing more often since moving to Somerset. On days when she was not expecting visitors and had no plans to go any further afield than Helwell Bay, she had found them far more practical for pottering around the garden in. It also meant she did not have to bother with stockings; the socks that Midge had given her had been joined by several pairs Caroline had knitted for herself over the winter.

The stable owner approved of Caroline's outfit.

"I had wondered if you'd want a side saddle." She said as she handed Caroline the reins of the second mare.

"Oh no, this will be perfectly alright, thank you."

"Well, this is Brimstone. She's as docile as they come. Just don't pull on the bit too much and she'll walk all day."

Caroline glanced at Tommy, who was trying not to laugh from his seat on Firefly. "Brimstone, what an unusual name."

"After the butterfly. She was much lighter in colour when she was a foal and was born in the spring when the Brimstones are first about. Leg up?"

Once Caroline was in the saddle, they left the stable yard and headed down into Tavistock and then out on the Mount Tavy road. As they left the town behind and climbed steadily up onto the moorland towards Pew Tor, the breeze replaced the sounds of industry in their ears. The sun had begun to burn away the cloud. Skylarks leaped high and sang as they descended again to the scrubby grass. They saw wild ponies in the distance, and a herd of deer shepherded by a large stag who watched them carefully as they rode past at a safe distance. True to her owner's word, Brimstone plodded along at a steady pace and Caroline needed to do very little to encourage her to follow Tommy astride Firefly.

It was a brutal landscape. The lack of trees and human occupation was disorienting. The only sign of a human hand at work besides the roads were the miles of low stone walls, some well-tended, some in complete disrepair, which marked the boundaries of hardy farmsteads. Caroline tried to imagine the scene in various weathers: driving horizontal rain, dense fog, deep snow, baking blistering sunshine. It was no wonder that so few people had decided to make their homes on Dartmoor, preferring instead to colonise the fringes of the moor where trees would grow and provide shelter and fuel.

What then of the inhabitants of Princetown, she wondered. She knew as much of the prison there as anyone did. A notoriously harsh environment, first built by prisoners of the Napoleonic wars and now housing some of the most dangerous criminals in the country. What would persuade a man to bring his family to such a remote and potentially dangerous place? She could see the reasoning to build a prison there, but for anyone to actively want to live alongside it, she could not comprehend their state of mind.

They heeded the warnings about boggy areas and kept a lookout for the tall straight reeds that grew in the pools. By the time they had skirted Pew Tor and could see Princetown and the stern face of the prison in the distance, the sun was warm on their heads although the breeze was still keen. Tommy suggested they stop at the edge of the settlement and sketch for a few minutes before taking refreshment in whatever business they could find open in Princetown.

Caroline was nervous about leaving the horses in case they should wander off, but a little further along the road they came to a rather strange gateway without a wall on either side. The remnant of some long-abandoned cottage was just visible a few yards from the road, now overgrown with gorse and moss. They tied the horses to the gatepost and made use of the tumbled cottage walls as a place to sit and sketch the vista before them.

"Isn't it strange how a landscape so baren and rough can be so beautiful?" Caroline was looking at the purple tors in the distance.

"Didn't they teach you at school about the picturesque style?"

"Not that I remember. Our art classes were mostly apples and flowers in vases."

"Well, it sits in the middle between the beautiful and the sublime. What the Renaissance painters considered beautiful were scenes that were calm, tranquil, well proportioned, nothing jarring on the eye. They considered the sublime to be the opposite, so scenes of death and destruction. In between those emerged the picturesque where the composition is much more natural, there is less symmetry, less harmony, and often the works appear more like sketches than the finished article."

Caroline absorbed this new information, a little disappointed that she had not been the first person ever to see the wonder in a harsh landscape but accepting that her emotional response was at least validated. "You know so much, Tommy. I wonder how you remember it all."

"When I first went up to London, I spent a lot of time in the galleries and museums. I read a lot of books and talked to people about the art as a way of making friends. I'm not that clever Caro, I simply pounce on a subject now and then and devour everything I can find about it. Rather like the aeroplanes. My mind holds certain facts that are quite useless until the opportunity presents itself in a conversation where I can pull them out and astound the listener."

"I was often a daydreamer at school. I don't think I've really studied anything in the way you have. Perhaps that's why I seem unable to find something to settle down with? I still have so much to learn."

"You have a natural ability in art. I rather like that you're not weighed down by convention, the way you mix the charcoal and the watercolours in your work is marvellous. Some of us are born to drift, dear heart. We can't all be as dedicated as Helen or Midge to a cause."

Caroline closed her sketch book and put her pencil back into her rucksack. "What I would really like to do is some more acting, but I don't think I have the dedication to that kind of lifestyle. I don't mean to be rude, but I'm feeling a little unsettled being a guest of yours and Helen's at the moment. I know it must come to an end, but I don't feel that returning to Cheltenham will be satisfactory either. And before you suggest it, I am not going to marry someone just so that I can secure a home!"

Tommy looked dramatically wounded. "I would never suggest such a thing! If that had been your master plan, no doubt you would be settled with the good Mr Kingston by now and we would not be here having this conversation."

He too put his sketching equipment away, "But I do sympathise with your situation. If you don't feel a strong enough call to the stage, what does call to you?"

Caroline considered for a moment, "I like meeting people. I like talking to different people and visiting new places. I seem to be reasonably good at that, though I don't see how it could provide me with any form of income."

Tommy grinned, "I have an idea that might interest you. Come on, let's go and find some lunch and I can explain."

Caroline was glad of the trousers she wore as she remounted Brimstone in the most unladylike fashion imaginable. The horse was unperturbed and stood still while Caroline made herself as comfortable as possible. Firefly was more reluctant to stand for Tommy once her reins had been untied from the post. She led Tommy in a comical dance as he hopped on one foot with the other in the stirrup, the horse turning in circles. Finally, his bounce coincided with Firefly's movements, and he was in the saddle once more.

They entered the village passing the prison on their left and could see the steam from the trains on the railway that joined the Tavistock line some way in front of them. The church stood on their right, with the only trees in sight lining the graveyard around it. There was no one about in the main street. All was quiet and a cloud moved in front of the sun as they reached a gentle bend in the road that made Caroline shiver. Everything was so grey! There were no flowers in front of the houses, or flowerbeds in the grassy mounds between them. No window boxes, and the woodwork on the houses was a uniform dark grey as if a job lot had been purchased on behalf of the whole village. On her first visit to Dartmoor, Helen's brother William had driven them out to Princetown, but they had only stayed a few minutes before moving on to Postbridge.

The horses continued at a slow walk until they came closer to the railway station where they found a pub and the Clearview Tearooms. They chose the tearooms and tied the horses again to a lamp post to one side of the entrance. Conversation stopped for a moment as they entered, and all eyes appraised them. A table in the window was vacant and they quickly took their seats as the murmur of voices began again.

"What would you like, old thing? My treat," asked Tommy.

"That's very good of you." Caroline picked up the menu.

The waitress arrived, a very young girl of no more than twelve Caroline thought. She stood with her hands clasped in front of her, and her squinting eyes looking at Tommy and at the door at the same time. Her uniform was at least two sizes too big and had visible signs of mending along the front button placket.

"I say, do you have any of those pasties?" Tommy asked, a little louder and slower than his normal speaking voice.

The girl blinked and nodded her head without speaking.

Caroline touched his hand, "I don't think she is deaf." She looked up at the girl, "Could you bring us two pasties and a pot of tea please?"

The girl again nodded and turned away.

"What an odd little thing!" Tommy said, running his hand through his mop of black hair, "I wonder that she's not in school."

"I suppose they must have finished for the summer. And really, how lucky for her that she has some employment. There can't be many opportunities for young girls in a place like this."

The girl returned with a teapot and a small jug of milk, then silently left again.

"Tell me this idea you said you had," Caroline was curious and hoped it might be an opportunity to repay her friend's generosity in some way.

Over their lunch Tommy explained that the Sunray Air Company was operating well, but that the ground crew were finding it difficult to keep on top of all the paperwork that went with the venture.

"Invoices, permits, inspections, safety requirements, honestly Caro you wouldn't believe the number of forms required, most of them in triplicate and to be sent to various ministry offices. David is doing his best, Rupert simply wasn't made to sit at a desk and the rest of us have no idea what the other has done or signed off most of the time. We all agree that we need a secretary, but it would have to be just the right kind of girl. Someone who could greet passengers, manage the office, order parts and fuel, and put up with us menfolk!"

"And you think I might be that kind of girl?"

"Well, why not? You said before, you like meeting people and there would be a lot of that. You're organised, you couldn't have managed the cottage by yourself otherwise. I'm sure the crew would have you on board in an instant."

"But the airfield is in the middle of nowhere you said. How on earth would I get there? Where would I live? I know I don't mind my own company, but it seems rather cut off from everything else," Caroline wasn't convinced.

"That was my other plan for our stay here on Dartmoor. If you could drive a motor car, then you'd be able to get about wherever you wanted to go. I think we should resume our lessons."

"Tommy, you have such fantastic dreams! Even if I could drive, I have no money to buy a motor car. I only have around forty pounds a year plus whatever I get from the paintings and there is no certainty that they will keep selling or that I will keep painting them."

Tommy was almost bouncing on his chair with excitement, "You haven't heard it all yet. There is a car that you could have at a very reasonable price. It's a baby Austin, needs a bit of work and some new front tyres as she's been in a field for a while, but we brought her back to the airfield a couple of weeks ago and I've been tinkering with her. Her engine is sound, just some cosmetic dents to put right. A thorough clean and she'll be as good as new."

Caroline shook her head, "Tommy, you're not listening. It would have to be less than, I don't know, say twenty pounds, for me to be able to buy it. I do appreciate you thinking of me and trying to help, but it's simply not possible." She finished her pasty and put her knife and fork together on the plate.

Tommy sipped his tea and thought for a moment, "What if, and of course I'd need to clear this with the crew, but what if the cost of the motor car was deducted from your salary, over a year. Rodney suggested fifty pounds as a sale price, so could you manage a pound a week for a year?"

"That would very much depend on what the salary was in the first place. I don't even know what a secretary would earn. How much does Helen pay Monica?"

"I believe Monica is paid from the party funds, but it will be somewhere around two pounds a week. Will you at least consider it? You don't need to make a decision this very minute."

Caroline agreed she would.

Tommy was careful not to press Caroline for a decision. Over the following few days, he did not mention the airfield at all unless Caroline did. He tried to give her some time to herself to think things over, playing more golf than he normally would have with a young man called Sidney he had met at the club, and as the weather turned wet, they postponed their trip to the south coast until the sun returned. Caroline finished reading the copy of *The Voyage Out* that Daisy had given her, and again found an emotional response to the character of Rachel. She understood the excitement of a journey into the unknown and was fascinated by the different characters on the ship. Caroline daydreamed of sailing away to new lands, or perhaps flying if the job Tommy had described to her could be secured.

They were at the start of their third week in Tavistock when the morning sun streamed through their bedroom windows, and both agreed at breakfast that they should go to the sea that day. Mrs Danks made up a picnic basket for them, and armed with towels and bathing costumes, they set off towards Yelverton and then down to Plymstock before turning towards the coast. Their first stop was Bovisand, which Caroline had suggested must have a beach of some sort because of its name. What they found was a stone fort built into the side of the headland and a long slipway that led down to a rocky shore. It was impressive, and they spent a little while sketching the fort as it was so unusual to them, before returning to the car. They consulted the map Tommy had brought and could see that the river Yealm cut through the headland to the east. They would need to travel inland again to find a crossing. Caroline pointed to Noss Mayo on the other side of the river and asked Tommy if he'd been there.

"Not to my knowledge, which is a good reason to explore it today, don't you think?" He said, folding the map and handing it to Caroline.

The roads of the South Hams were deep set with more of the now familiar stone walls and hedges. They had numerous bends, some of them very sharp, and the going was slow. Tommy and Caroline didn't mind, they were not in any hurry and made frequent stops to admire the view as suddenly the road rose and revealed a deep valley or an expanse of glittering blue sea. Even when they found themselves behind a slow-moving herd of russet-coloured thick-coated cows returning from their milking parlour, they simply pulled over and waited until the beasts were safely back in their field before moving on.

It was almost midday when they followed a narrow lane from the road that led to Newton Ferrers, crossed the river

Yealm once more and descended towards Noss Mayo. At a bend in the road, Tommy pulled the car over into the driveway of a property not visible from the highway. He reached behind onto the rear seat and brought out his A.A route card. It had details of the route between Yealmpton and Newton Ferres, including a mention of Noss Mayo, and on the reverse some points of interest.

"I think this must be the entrance to Thornley House," he said, putting the card back on the rear seat. "Shall we see if anyone is at home?"

"Can we?"

"Of course! These big old houses practically expect visitors to drop in on days like this."

He reversed a short way and then turned into the drive. The front courtyard of the house was open to one side and the river could be seen at the bottom of the valley beyond. Caroline stayed in the car while Tommy bounded up the front steps and rang the doorbell. After a short conversation with someone in the shadow of the entrance hall the door closed, and Tommy returned.

"The family are away, but the housekeeper says we can have a wander round the gardens as long as we stick to the paths."

Caroline got out of the car and decided to keep her hat on to help shade her eyes from the sun.

"Who are the family?" She asked.

"According to the A.A., this place is owned by the Hebblethwaits, you know, from the cotton mills. New money, rather like my family."

Caroline could hear no trace of pride or depreciation in Tommy's voice. She remembered her father once saying that "new money was still money" and spending money was what kept the economy flourishing. As they rounded the side of the house covered in wisteria, it was clear that the Hebblethwait family were spending their money on their garden. There were numerous young trees and newly dug borders with plants not yet filling the spaces between. She could see from the foliage and what flowers were blooming that in a few years' time it would be a tapestry of rich colour. The lawns were manicured and separated from a formal rose garden by a low stone balustrade. In the midday sun, the scent of the roses was heavy and sweet.

They decided not to go too far along the Long Walk, conscious that it would be an uphill return and that they had still to find a beach and go swimming. They were also starting to feel hungry, so they retraced their steps to the car.

"Wasn't that beautiful? I'm so glad we stopped now," Caroline sighed as they pulled away up the drive. "Imagine living in a place like this. How wonderful."

"If I remember correctly, the family still have a much larger house in Yorkshire and property in London of course. They spend most of their time in the north."

"And yet they are clearly investing in the garden here."

"I imagine the climate in Yorkshire doesn't allow for such a range of plants. Did you feel the change in the air temperature as we walked down the slope? You have to be seriously rich to manage their portfolio of properties. The death duties would cripple one, and that's something I am very much hoping father manages to put off for as long as possible."

"Will it be a large amount for you to find?"

"Not so much for me to find; it will be taken from the estate. Around six or seven percent the last I heard, which is not an inconsiderable sum. Still, he's in rude health and I doubt very much I shall have to do the calculations."

"And you don't want to return to your family home when the time comes?"

"Absolutely not! Sell the whole bally lot of it I say, and then I can find something worth while to invest in like the airfield." It was the first time in days he had mentioned it.

They continued their drive through the very narrow lanes of Noss Mayo, a small hamlet with its larger neighbour Newton Ferres visible across the river. Caroline spotted a sign that announced, 'Stoke Beach' and Tommy continued until the lane became too rutted and uneven to risk grounding the car. He pulled into a gateway, and they carried their lunch and bathing things the last half mile down a steep footpath to the sandy bay below. There was no one else around.

"We really shouldn't swim on a full stomach," cautioned Caroline, "so I'm going to bathe first."

Tommy agreed and soon they were both in the water. Caroline swam strongly for a while and then relaxed on her back with her eyes closed, the sun warm on her face. Tommy was a less strong swimmer and was back on the sand after ten minutes of exercise. He was investigating the contents of their basket lunch when Caroline emerged from the azure water and walked up the beach to where they had left their clothes.

"This is glorious!" She said dropping down onto a towel. Her skin was already drying in the sun as she removed her bathing cap.

They ate the sandwiches, fruit and cake that Mrs Danks had provided, and drank cool ginger beer from two stone bottles. It wasn't Caroline's favourite drink, but she was thirsty, and Tommy agreed to stop at the next opportunity to have some tea. After lunch, Tommy walked along the high tide line looking for interesting pebbles and shells and Caroline changed back into her clothes and sat watching a seal out in the bay. Its head resembled a dog's and at first she had thought it was one. It would rise out of the water for a moment looking around and then dive again, only to appear moments later a little further along the bay.

She felt that this beach, and that day, was one of the most perfect she had ever known. The pale sand was warm around her toes. The only sounds were those of the gentle waves and an occasional gull overhead. If I could stay here forever, I would be content, she thought. She knew it was an impossible dream; her practical conscience chipped in unwanted and reminded her that the sea was not always a tranquil pool of blue. But surely, she reasoned with herself there must be a way to live close enough to the sea to visit regularly, yet near enough to an urban location where one could find employment.

Caroline looked towards Tommy, returning along the shore. She couldn't stay with her friends forever, no matter how much she loved them and they her.

Tommy reached their picnic spot. "Are you ready to go home or would you like to explore somewhere else?"

"We could go back, but Tommy sit down for a moment, would you."

He did as she asked. "What's up?"

"The secretary position you told me about when we went to Princetown. If I were to learn to drive properly with you, and if I were to have the motor car you mentioned, do you think I would really have enough left to live on?"

Tommy couldn't help but smile, "With your income, and the sale of your paintings if you chose to continue with them, I do believe so yes. Of course, there would have to be an end to the wild parties, and you'd need to find somewhere modest to live, but I'm sure it could be done."

She chuckled, "Be serious, can't you? Could we do some more sketches, of you I mean, perhaps out on the moor? I'd like a few more poses that I can work from if you don't mind."

"Of course I don't mind. The chances of us being seen are so remote, we could go tomorrow as long as I get some petrol on our way back this afternoon. I've never liked to ask, but how much do they sell for?"

"The last ones I sent up to Elsa made four guineas each. Elsa and Bobby take a portion to cover the framing and their fee, and I received around three pounds for each one sold. Elsa says if I can find larger canvases they would naturally sell for more, but they would require much more packing so as not to get damaged on their way to London."

"Still, three pounds a time is not to be sniffed at. Even selling one a month would be more than enough to cover the cost of a motor car." His grin was infectious, and Caroline felt a tingle of excitement.

"Do you really think I could do it all?"

"There's only one way to find out."

5

OPPORTUNITY KNOCKS

The month at the house in Tavistock had come to an end. Caroline and Tommy bought a box of chocolates for Mrs Danks to thank her for her service and left them on the kitchen table with a note. They closed all of the windows, took one last look around to make sure they had left nothing behind, and pulled the front door shut behind them. Tommy had spoken to Helen on the telephone twice since she had left them. Monica had returned and Caroline would not be needed to help out in the constituency office when they got back to Minehead. There were several letters waiting for Caroline.

Tommy decided to drive a different route home than the one they had taken from Minehead a month before. They went for one last time across the moor to Moretonhampstead, around the northern edge of Exeter and then northwards through Tiverton and beyond. Caroline sat quietly in the passenger seat holding the map should it be needed. They stopped briefly in Tiverton, where Tommy asked her if everything was alright.

"Oh yes, I'm just sad to be leaving Devon. I've had such a lovely time there."

"I think once we get to Dulverton you should take over the driving."

"Oh, I don't know..."

"You are perfectly capable, and the roads will be very quiet over Exmoor."

"Alright. I must keep practicing, mustn't I. I was so much better yesterday."

"You can drive. Just keep reminding yourself of that."

And she did. They might not have gone as fast as if Tommy were at the wheel, but they made their way steadily and safely across Exmoor and Caroline found herself smiling as she navigated the lanes. Tommy fell asleep beside her, which made her nerves return when she noticed but she slowed the motor car a little for a while until she felt more confident again. There was a difficult moment when she met another motor car as they crossed a stone bridge. Tommy woke with a start at Caroline's sudden braking, then talked her through reversing to allow the other car to pass. Thankfully Caroline noted, the other driver was also a woman who did not seem to be too inconvenienced by Caroline's slow manoeuvres.

It was agreed that Tommy would speak to the rest of the ground crew about appointing Caroline as company secretary the next time he went to the airfield. In the meantime, Caroline wanted to speak to her father about it all. She telephoned when she thought Sara might be in the apartment to take a message, and then called back that evening after her father would have eaten his dinner. They spoke for almost twenty minutes, Caroline very conscious that a long-distance call would be expensive for Helen and Tommy.

George had some reservations, as Caroline expected him to. How, he asked, would she manage if she could find no accommodation? Would she require the small pieces of furniture currently stored in her old bedroom at the apartment to be sent down? Did she feel confident enough to manage a motor car by herself? In all weathers? What if it broke down? Caroline could not answer all of his questions, but they were designed more to ensure she was considering the proposal fully.

Finally, George asked, "Will you require any further funds to establish yourself?"

"I really don't know, Father. As I say, if the men at the airfield agree with Tommy, then I shall go down and meet them all next week and have a trial run. I can stay at the inn that Tommy uses for that, in my own room," she added quickly, "and if that works out alright then I shall probably take rooms in Taunton to begin with. You remember we saw quite a few notices when we visited last year."

George remembered the rows of terraced houses behind the wide Parade in the centre of the town and hoped that Caroline could find more than one or two rooms in a shared house.

"Write to me as soon as you know what you will be doing. It may take a few days to arrange any agreement for your lodgings, but Caroline," his voice was stern, "it must be agreed with a legal contract. I do not want you to verbally agree weekly terms with anyone and then find they put the rental amount up substantially at the first provocation."

"Yes, Father. I shall make sure everything is quite so."

"Very well," he sighed, "I shall wait to hear from you. Goodbye my dear."

Caroline returned the receiver to its cradle and stood in the hall for a moment. She felt overwhelmed. Why couldn't she have just married Noah and settled down in that lovely new house? She knew instantly that she would not have been happy there, once the early wedding euphoria had worn off. She had to take control of her own affairs.

Helen emerged from the sitting room, cigarette in hand, and leaned on the door frame.

"Everything alright, darling?"

"He sounded concerned."

"One would be surprised if he had not. I'm sure the thought of you working with a handful of hot-blooded pilots would be enough to concern the most liberal of parents."

"It was only when I said it out loud to him that I realised how it might sound."

"The thing is done now. I see no reason why Tommy's chums would decide not to at least meet you next week. They all seem very decent and dedicated to their enterprise."

There was a pause, where both women mentally said the words "eligible bachelors".

"No." Caroline spoke as if they had said the words out loud.

"No." agreed Helen. "Anything of interest in your letters?"

"Oh yes! Mary and Philip will be moving to Bradford on Avon on August 1st. She sounds so relieved in her letter. I really think she was dreading having another baby at St Mark's. Midge sends her love and says she and Oliver will be staying another six months in Africa. He seems a good sort, don't you think?"

"A very good sort and just the man for Midge. I wonder if there will be children there before too long."

"Well, the third letter was from Annie and there will be more children there at the end of this year. Victor will have a little brother or sister. If ever there was a woman content with being a mother, I should say it was Annie."

"Some women are born for it, dear heart, and others find themselves completely incapable of it. Better that we leave it to those who relish the idea." Helen looked keenly at Caroline as she spoke.

"No chance of anything of that kind here, not for a long time!"

"Good, well, let's take a look at the train timetable and see when we can get to Taunton on Saturday shall we?"

Tommy returned on Thursday evening with news that the ground crew were very interested in meeting Caroline the following week. He offered to drive the women to Taunton, but they declined saying they would enjoy the journey by train. Tommy even offered to lend them the car, but Helen told him to save the fuel.

"Just because Caro has shares in National Benzol, there is no need to spend where it is not necessary."

Although it was late July, the sky was grey, and a light drizzle fell as the two women walked out of the railway station at Taunton. They opened their umbrellas and turned towards the Parade where they planned to begin their search. There were several estate agents in the town, and all had a number of properties that they were more than willing to show the ladies. Caroline and Helen also looked in various newsagent and tobacconist windows and on noticeboards jotting down telephone numbers and names in the pocketbook they had brought for just that purpose.

Over lunch in a small restaurant, they went through the papers the agents had given them. It had been the same at every agent office, the explanation that Caroline's father would be handling the finances and the tenancy agreement, yes she would be living alone, yes she had employment. By the third inquisition Helen was becoming impatient with the questions and elevated George Munhead to 'bank manager' status and introduced herself as Councillor Gersen-Fisch, with the desired effect. The friends had agreed that if anything stood out as close to perfect, they would try and arrange a viewing that afternoon. Others less suitable would not be discarded completely but taken back to Minehead and studied further once Caroline had visited the airfield. Helen held out one paper for Caroline to read.

"This looks like a possible."

"Clarence Street, isn't that one of those the agent said was near the river?"

"Oh, quite possibly. This one is Belvedere Road; I believe we walked past there from the station. Mark that one to view."

Caroline put a cross at the top of the paper with her pencil. Many of the properties sounded the same in their descriptions; two and three bedroomed terraced houses built for the Victorian railwaymen. Helen handed her another paper for a house in Leslie Avenue to the north of the railway, and one more for apartment rooms in a larger house on Alma Street. The street names meant very little to Caroline or Helen, they were simply looking for a reasonable rent. Caroline was very aware that she did not have enough money to rent a property on the scale of Helen and Tommy's house in Minehead with its five bedrooms and three reception rooms. She was glad of Helen's help but hoped her friend wouldn't stretch Caroline's budget too far.

After they had eaten, they had three properties that looked the most promising and went back to the two estate agents to ask to view them. It would be quite a distance for them to walk, although they hoped to be able to catch a bus back to the town centre from each property and then to the railway station when they had seen them all. The first agent was a very short man who barely reached Caroline's shoulder. He reminded her of the agent who had shown her and her father around the apartment block at Norwood Court before George had made the purchase. She wondered if all estate agents were by default short men.

Belvedere Road was the first on their list. As soon as the agent opened the front door the women could smell the damp. They gave it a perfunctory look round, but the peeling wallpaper and the lack of an indoor toilet allowed them to quickly cross it from their list. The second agent had both Leslie Avenue and a house on Holway Road on their books. This time instead of a male agent to accompany them, a woman of similar age to Helen and Caroline stepped forward to shake their hands. She introduced herself as Miss Edna O'Neil, the daughter of the senior partner in the estate agent business. With Miss O'Neil's assistance, they caught a bus most of the way to Leslie Avenue. It was a wide, straight street with terraced houses on both sides. All had wide doors and windows and were made mostly of a honey-coloured brick with white brick details. There were a few motor cars parked in the street and two young boys were playing marbles outside one of the nearby houses.

Number forty-two was at least not damp. The front windows gave a good amount of light into the sitting room (off the entrance hall) and the bedrooms upstairs. A second reception room led to the kitchen with a toilet attached. It had three bedrooms on the first floor, two of which had open fireplaces. It was in truth similar to thousands of workers houses that had been built at the end of the previous century across the country. Caroline thought it much like Lottie and Bob's parent's house near the Cheltenham gas works, although this had an indoor water supply and a larger enclosed rear yard. The rental, Miss O'Neil confirmed, was twelve shillings a week in advance.

There was no direct bus service from Leslie Avenue to Holway Road. The three women walked briskly and caught a bus from the end of the Avenue into the town centre, and then caught a second along South Street and got off before it turned towards King's College. The house for rent was on the corner of Holway Road and Eastleigh Road and stood opposite a small greengrocer's shop. It was listed as partially furnished, which Helen pointed out could mean anything from a few chairs and a bed to a store for the landlord's unwanted furniture from other properties. The stone above the newly painted black front door read 'Elmsworth' and the hedge to the front and along the Eastleigh Road perimeter was neatly clipped. Caroline stood for a moment looking at the quiet street that curved gently while Miss O'Neil sorted through her ring of keys to find the correct one.

Once inside, Miss O'Neil informed them that Elmsworth had received considerable interest already. Helen asked how long it had been empty, while running her gloved finger along the mantlepiece in the front sitting room.

"Getting on for ten months now."

"Really, for such a pretty house?" Caroline said as she inspected an under-stair cupboard. Helen frowned at her, but Caroline wasn't looking her way.

"Yes. Well, I should be honest with you since you would hear it from the neighbours if you asked. The old woman who lived here before died."

This was by no means unusual, people of all ages died at home even with the new hospitals being built. There was something in the way Miss O'Neil said the words, and the way she avoided Helen's eye when she said them.

"Died how exactly?" Helen asked.

Caroline had gone along the hall and into a second reception room that looked out onto the narrow strip of garden on the Eastleigh Road side of the house.

"She had a lodger. Did you not read about it in the newspaper? Oh but of course, you are not from the town are you," Miss O'Neil lowered her voice, "She was found on the kitchen floor with her head bashed in, and the lodger was arrested in Southampton trying to escape to Canada. He must be coming to trial soon I should think."

Caroline came back into the front sitting room at that point, "There's a strange brown mark on the kitchen floor, could that be cleaned if I were to take the property?"

Helen gently shook her head as she and Miss O'Neil looked at each other.

"We would certainly make every effort to clean the house thoroughly," Miss O'Neil replied, "Would you care to see the bedrooms?"

As Helen and Caroline travelled back to Minehead later that afternoon, in a carriage that smelled strongly of cigar smoke, it was clear that Caroline had fallen for the Holway Road house. She chattered on about the unusual layout, the usefulness of the furniture provided, and how strange it was that it should only be offered for eight shillings a week. Helen could withhold the information no longer.

"The house has a history that appears to have made it rather difficult for the agent to let."

"Oh? I couldn't smell any damp in there, not like the first one, that was awful!"

"No, but you spotted the stain on the kitchen floor. Caro, I don't know how you will feel about this, but Miss O'Neil told me the previous owner had been murdered there a year ago."

Caroline was stunned, "Murdered? Good gracious, who by?"

"Apparently the old woman had a lodger. One hears about it regularly, but one never expects to come so close to that kind of situation of course."

"And has he been caught, this lodger?"

"Miss O'Neil said he will come to trial shortly. Caroline, it explains the lower rental. Don't feel that you must take it simply because it is so cheap."

They sat in silence for a while. Caroline had often read about murders and dangerous criminals from the lower classes on the run in the newspapers. She also enjoyed Mrs Christie's novels, and in those the culprit was often a middle- or upper-class scoundrel. It was not unusual for women on their own to be duped out of their life savings or have their jewellery stollen, but real murders in their own class were thankfully much rarer. Caroline wondered about the older woman whose home it had previously been. Why had she taken in a lodger? Could she have been a kindly sort who wanted to help a young man in need? Someone to share her pretty home with and not spend her days quite so alone. Surely a woman like that would not want her spirit to linger and upset a young woman such as Caroline who was trying to make her own way in the world. Daisy would no doubt suggest they held a séance to try and pacify any discontented soul still lingering, and yet Caroline had felt no presence. All she had felt was joy as she had explored the house.

Helen broke into her thoughts. "You're not seriously considering it, are you?"

"The Holway Road house? Yes I am. Why not?"

"You don't feel the slightest unease, knowing a poor old woman was battered to death in her kitchen there?" Helen raised an eyebrow with concern.

"I didn't feel uneasy when we were there. If there had been a bad presence, surely one of us would have felt it? And you didn't, did you? Tell me truthfully."

Helen sighed. "No, I did not. And I suppose lightning is unlikely to strike twice as they say. If the murderer is convicted, you wouldn't have to worry about his returning to the scene of the crime as they do in novels."

"If he is convicted, he'll hang. There's no coming back from that."

"There was nothing particularly wrong with the other one, Lyndsey Avenue."

"Leslie Avenue. No, it was perfectly alright, but the area around Holway Road seemed much nicer, and the little grocer's shop on the corner would be so convenient."

"No garage."

"None of them had a garage."

Helen felt she would not be able to dissuade her friend, however uncomfortable the idea of living in the house was to her. "It might have been let by the time you've been to the airfield," she said, hopefully.

Caroline's introduction to the ground crew of the Sunray Air Company was a whirl of information and endless coffee and tea. She was incredibly nervous as she sat next to Tommy in the car driving through Somerset, and Tommy was happy to remain silent on the journey. They first called at the Inn where Tommy stayed two, and occasionally three, nights each week while he was at the airfield. The landlord greeted him warmly and showed Caroline up to a very small room at the rear of the Inn. She would share a bathroom with four other rooms, but they were not always occupied he assured her. Caroline unpacked her clothes quickly and hung them in the slender wardrobe.

She had brought Freddie's old trousers, feeling they could be useful.

When Tommy pulled into the parking area at the airfield, David was sat on the bench they had added outside the office, smoking. He shook Caroline's hand and took her inside while Tommy went in search of the others. Over the next three days Caroline was shown how to use the telephone and how to dial through to the extension they had installed in the workshop. She learned about the flight routes for both freight and passengers, and the paperwork that was required for each. Rupert explained the list of companies they regularly ordered supplies from, and how much they had on account with each.

For her part, Caroline took control of the haphazard filing system the men had devised between them, gave the office a thorough clean to remove all traces of oily fingerprints, and made a list of things she felt would improve the wait that the customers had when they arrived for their flights.

"Houseplants?" Rodney asked when he saw the list.

"Yes, one or two. And perhaps some posters to advertise the locations you fly to, like those that the railway companies use."

David came into the office clutching a receipt for some cleaning products, "Be a good girl and file this for me, Caro. It's Dowlings, so under D, I assume."

"Yes, under D-unpaid, here I'll show you."

"No need, now you're here," he smiled and went out again.

"I think that means you've got the job," Rodney handed back the list.

"Truly? Oh thank you, how wonderful! And the motor car?"

"Tommy is just giving it a wipe over for you. We could go to Bridgwater and get a few of the things on your list if you like?"

The Austin Seven had royal blue bodywork and a canvas roof that could fold back in good weather. Caroline got into the driver's seat and adjusted the mirrors. She was taller than David, but shorter than the rest of the crew. Cautiously she pulled out of the airfield and onto the road and was soon rumbling along in third gear towards Bridgwater. It was a smaller town than Taunton and favoured by the men. Rodney directed her to where she could park, and they spent an hour purchasing stationary supplies and other small items that Caroline felt would be needed.

"Will I need any overalls?" Caroline asked as they returned to the car.

"I suppose you might want a housecoat or an apron for when supplies are delivered. It can be a dirty job to carry the crates."

"Rodney, do you think anyone would object to me wearing more manly clothes? A shirt and trousers, perhaps? I could wear a dress on the passenger days, if you'd all prefer. I just think a dress might not be very practical."

"I certainly have no objections, but let's see what the chaps say when we get back shall we?"

Peter was on the Scotland flight that week, but none of the men thought he would object to Caroline's suggestion. They all agreed that on the days when passengers were expected, Caroline should wear a dress and take on hostess duties while their customers waited to board. Work had still not been completed on the customer lounge area and passengers often remained in their cars until the aeroplane was ready to receive them. Caroline would be expected to work from nine each weekday morning until four in the afternoon, with the exception of days when their flights might be delayed and return to the airfield late.

Caroline explained that she hoped to take a house in Taunton, but that she might not be able to move until the start of September, given that August would begin in just a few days. A compromise was reached, with Caroline agreeing to accompany Tommy for the days he spent at the airfield during August, with the expectation that she would increase her hours from September. Everyone was keen to have her join the Company, and she was excited to be given what she considered a position of some responsibility.

Looking back, Caroline would say she had never had such an exhausting or exhilarating month as that August turned out to be. George was sent the details of the estate agent who also owned the house on Holway Road, and he took control of arranging for some furniture to be transported from Cheltenham to Taunton on Caroline's behalf at the end of the month. Caroline spent Mondays and Fridays scouring the *Western Mercury* advertisement columns for furniture for sale, and after two weeks travelling with Tommy to and from the airfield, she decided to take the Austin into Taunton and stay the night at a hotel in order to better acquaint herself with the town. As the property was vacant and the estate agent had received the first month's rent in advance already from George, Miss O'Neil agreed that Caroline could have the keys for the Friday afternoon so that she might leave some small items in the house such as linen and a rug that David had donated to her cause.

Caroline parked the Austin outside Elmsworth and switched off the engine. She sat for a moment looking down the street. An elderly man was walking slowly with an equally elderly terrier at his heel. It had been a showery day and a few spots of rain fell on the windscreen and obscured her view. Caroline suddenly felt a strong sense of trepidation. Was she really doing the right thing? She knew no one in Taunton besides Miss O'Neil, and it suddenly felt a very long way from Cheltenham and Minehead. She was lost in thought when there was a knock on the passenger window that made her jump. A woman's face appeared, staring at Caroline through the glass. Caroline got out of the car.

"Can I help you?" She asked.

"I noticed you parked here, I thought you might be lost," the woman had no hat and appeared to have come from the house next door. It had a similar stone over the door engraved with the word 'Ivydene'.

"Oh no, I shall be moving in here at the end of this month. I just came to drop off a few things and take some measurements."

"Moving in? Into Betty's?" The woman face showed concern that Caroline recognised. She decided to get the inevitable conversation over with there and then.

"Yes. I'm sure it must have been a terrible shock to everyone in the street to hear about her … death, but it is such a nice house and I'm not the least bit squeamish."

The woman folded her arms, "It will be nice to know someone is in there again I suppose, Mrs?"

"Miss actually, Caroline Munhead," Caroline went around the front of the car and offered her hand.

"Pleased to meet you, I'm sure. Winnifred Collier, my husband Johnny is a builder. Carpenter by trade but he can turn his hand to anything in the building line. He works for Carter's."

"I'm sorry, I'm not familiar with them. I'm quite a stranger to Taunton actually."

The rain was starting to fall more heavily.Winnifred nodded to the elderly gentleman as he drew level with the women.

"Well, I can't stand out here all day. I'm sure I'll be seeing you again Miss Munhead."Winnifred scurried back into her own home and shut the door firmly.

Caroline was amused at the woman's manner. Certainly, this neighbour would not be anything like Vi and Ron Saddington back in Doniford.Thinking of the older couple she had left behind lowered Caroline's mood as she pushed the key into the door of Elmsworth and let herself in. For a moment she stood in the doorway and listened.The house was perfectly silent as one would expect it to be.

"Would you mind if I stay for a while, Betty?" Caroline asked into the empty hallway.

Later that evening, while Caroline lay on her hotel bed and made yet another list of things she would need for her new home, Winnifred was serving dinner to her husband and their twelve-year-old son Jonathan.

"I met the new neighbour today.A Miss Munhead. Not married."

Johnny helped himself to gravy, "Moving into Betty's?"

"Yes. Seems unnatural if you ask me. A woman on her own too."

"Well, someone had to take it eventually, Win. We can't choose our neighbours. And there are more young women these days working and living by themselves."

"She has a motor car as well. I hope she won't be having parties every night like those flappers!"

"A motor car?"Jonathan looked up from his minced beef and onion, potatoes and carrots with wide eyes.

"Don't interrupt, Jonathan. And don't think you'll be hanging around outside, getting in the way." Winnifred surveyed the table and then sat down to her own plate of food.

"Don't be so hard on the lad. He might put his interest in motor cars to good use one day, eh son?"

"I'd like to, Dad. Mr Mitchum says next term we might be able to take an engine apart and then put it back together again!"

"What good will that be, taking something apart indeed. They should be teaching you important things like maths and science. I don't know what we pay the extra for, I really don't." Winnifred had said the same many times before, in response to a number of practical exercises her son's teachers offered their pupils. In truth, she was proud and protective of Jonathan's place at Renton House school; Johnny had been a pupil there as had his father and uncle, and as such his son received a substantial reduction in fees. Winnifred wanted more for her son than a career in carpentry, preferably in an occupation that came with a uniform and not overalls.

"It'll be good to have someone next door again in any case, it'll stop the place getting damp. And you'll have someone to talk to, Win. Did the lady say what work she did?"

"I didn't ask. I doubt it will be anything respectable, she didn't look like a teacher or a nurse."

6

SETTLING IN

Caroline woke on the morning of Saturday 1 September 1928 to the sound of birds chirruping, distant church bells ringing and someone whistling in the street outside. She rolled onto her back and stretched. The letter box in the front door flapped and the sound of post falling onto the hall floor made her open her eyes to the sunlight that was flooding the larger of the two bedrooms at Elmsworth. The whistling must have come from the postman, she thought. Caroline had chosen the rear bedroom as her own; it faced south and would have the sun all day, unlike the front of the house that would always be in shade. Miss O'Neil had told Caroline that the house would be cleaned and a few small repairs would be undertaken before she moved in, but then it was Caroline's to decorate as she wished. Caroline turned her head on the pillow and looked at the rolls of wallpaper standing on end in the corner of the room. They had a pattern of yellow flowers and greenery that had reminded Caroline of the bedroom at Laurel View in Tavistock that had been her home recently. She had bought them the weekend before at a bargain price as they were the last of that particular stock. She had no real idea how one attached them to a wall but was sure she would find someone to ask soon enough.

Her eyes moved to the small bedside clock and to her surprise she saw it was almost half past nine. She had slept like a log, falling into bed around midnight after unpacking the last of the crates her father had sent down. She had not stopped the day before, picking up the house keys at nine in the morning, then supervising the delivery of her possessions. At lunchtime she had slipped out to the grocer's shop on the opposite corner of the street and introduced herself to the owners, Mr and Mrs Farthing. Ted and Irene had run the shop for ten years and lived in the flat above it. The garden had been concreted and a small delivery van was now parked there painted in the same burgundy and cream livery that the front of the shop sported, the name Farthing's emblazoned on the sides. Ted was immensely proud to have been able to afford the van and was steadily increasing the reach of his delivery rounds each afternoon. Women, he had discovered, would spend more on provisions if they did not have to carry them home themselves.

Irene had been keen to tell Caroline the personal histories of every other resident of Holway Road. To divert her, Caroline had asked about the nearest church. Irene then reeled off the names of the two catholic churches, the Baptist, the Methodist and the Unitarian chapels before explaining that for Anglican worship Caroline would need to make her way into the town centre and seek out St James' or Taunton Minster, the church of St Mary Magdalene.

"There's a pretty little church in Blagden, I think it's St George's, if you want to go a bit further," Irene was gazing into the distance as if trying to see the towers and spires through the shop wall, "or St Andrew's over the other side of the railway. Yes, we're very well served spiritually here. And of course, you have your motor car, so you could go further still."

"I was rather hoping for somewhere within walking distance."

"Well, we are right on the edge of the town. And have you found the garage? You'll be needing petrol no doubt," Irene asked.

"I did see one on my way here, but I can't remember the name."

"Ted gets his van seen to at the Country Garage on Priory Road. I'm sure he would take you over there and introduce you."

"That would be very helpful, thank you Irene, though it really would just be petrol I would need. I have engineers on hand at the airfield if anything goes wrong with the motor car."

"The airfield?"

"Yes, I am a sort of secretary and general assistant at the Thurloxton airfield, it's not far from here towards Bridgwater. I haven't been there long, but it is very interesting, and I meet new people all the time." Caroline found herself smiling broadly. She really did enjoy working in the little office and showing the passengers where to wait for their flights.

Caroline assumed that Irene would be telling the rest of her customers all about her, and that soon people would be saying hello to her in the street and asking about the aeroplanes. It was such a novel occupation, and air travel was such a luxury, Caroline had found there was a general fascination about anything and anyone connected with it. She had been asked if she had met any famous people, particularly film stars, if she felt scared being so close to the aeroplanes, and if she had the opportunity to fly one herself. To all of those she had answered no, but one day, she said to herself as she crossed the kitchen and went into the tiny bathroom built on to the back of the house only five years before, one day I might meet a film star or even fly in an aeroplane.

More immediate occupations for the weekend before she had to return to work and begin her first full week at the airfield, were to stock up her larder with dried goods (she had only bought the barest essentials at Farthing's the day before), get to grips with the range in the kitchen and attempt to bake some cakes or biscuits to see her through the week, and explore the rather over-grown back garden. Caroline washed and dried her face in the bathroom, then put two white eggs into a pan of water on the top of the range next to the kettle to boil and went to retrieve the post.

Caroline had written to Midge, James, Lottie and Annie with her new address from Minehead over the previous weekend. She intended to write to Elsa in London and to Tommy's cousin Lina in Malvern who Caroline had got along very well with the first time she stayed in Devon with Helen and who's wedding to Albert Caroline had attended almost two years ago. Caroline would have liked to stay in touch with Lady Victoria Elmhurst, her host in London, but now that she and Helen were no longer an item, Caroline felt she should show some loyalty to her old school friend and had not made any attempt to contact Lady Vic in Egypt. While the eggs started to tap dance on the bottom of the pan, Caroline opened the letter that had arrived.

28 August 1928
Bradford-on-Avon

Dear Caroline,

Mary and I wanted to write to welcome you into your new home. As you know, we have been here now a little over a month, and although I was very sorry to leave St Mark's we have been welcomed by our new parishioners here at Holy Trinity. It is a most interesting church, Anglo Saxon in origin and I am sure you would find many of the carvings and adornments worthy of your artistic abilities. There is also a much smaller church just to one side of Holy Trinity, called St Lawrence's, which is undergoing some restoration work at present.

Mary is coming along well, and we are expecting our addition to the family at the beginning of October. Celestine will be joining us for Mary's confinement. The vicarage here is of similar proportions to St Mark's and we have plenty of room for everyone. Indeed, we would very much like for you to visit whenever you have the opportunity. I appreciate that may be difficult now that you have found full-time employment again, and our cosy Wednesday evening dinners won't be re-established, which is a great pity. Any time you would like to come and stay for a few days, please do let us know. We shall be having a telephone installed – the Bishop took some convincing – and when we do I shall send you our telephone number.

Please do tell us all about your new home. Mary is so looking forward to hearing from you.

In God's peace
Philip, Mary and Angelica

Caroline retrieved her eggs and poured water into the teapot. Not for the first time, she wondered if Mary could write, given that the letters Caroline received from them were always written by Philip. She knew Mary could read, and do simple mathematics, so perhaps her handwriting was poor. Caroline would not ask, and if the Roses were having a telephone installed, she would be able to speak to Mary and not rely on letters in any case. She would have to investigate the expense of having a telephone line put in at Elmsworth, as it was certainly becoming an important communication device. It would also help her to stay in contact with her father and Helen and Tommy now that she was some miles from them all. Caroline felt another little flutter of trepidation; had she bitten off more than she could chew? Could she really afford to live by herself, and run the Austin, and find some entertainment in her new surroundings?

After breakfast, and a visit to Farthings, Caroline decided to take advantage of the warm late summer weather and walked into the town centre. She and Helen had been so intent on finding estate agents that she had not taken in many of the other buildings and shops there. Now she retraced her steps from previous visits with Mrs Harding with whom Caroline had stayed on her first adventure to Dunster, and later with her father after she had moved into Quantock Cottage. She wandered around the usual grocers, chemists, stationers, fishmongers, bakers and ironmongers collected around the central war memorial. She found an outfitter's shop in Corporation Street and bought a cotton blouse to add to her work wardrobe.

"Would Madam like to see anything else?" the female assistant asked as she folded the blouse between two sheets of tissue paper.

"I did wonder," Caroline said furtively, "if you had any trousers that might fit me?"

"Trousers, for Madam?" She tried not to raise an eyebrow.

"Yes, you see I work at Thurloxton airfield and trousers are so much more practical to wear, only the pair I have are getting rather thin now and I could do with some more." Caroline had no intention of throwing Freddie's old trousers away; she would hang on to them to their last thread.

The assistant came around the counter and took her tape measure from around her neck. She asked Caroline to stand up straight while she measured her waist and as close to her inside leg as the assistant dared get. She disappeared into the back of the shop and returned a moment later with two pairs of woollen trousers, one in navy blue and one in a dark green.

"Would Madam care to try them on?"

Caroline agreed and was this time taken to the back of the shop where a small section of the workroom was curtained off. Caroline congratulated herself on dressing in a skirt and blouse that morning and stepped out from behind the curtain a few minutes later wearing the blue trousers with the bottoms turned up by an inch. She looked at herself in the long thin mirror to the side of the changing space. Curious, she thought, that I do not look like Elsa and yet I also do not look like a man. I look more like Midge, which is no bad thing. She told the assistant that she would take both pairs if they could be turned up at the hems and be ready for her the following Saturday.

Before returning home, Caroline checked the times of the Sunday service at the Minster and bought some pilchards for her dinner. She was coming out of the fishmonger's when she bumped into Edna O'Neil. After the expected pleasantries and enquiries about settling in, Caroline asked what entertainment there was to be had in the town in the evenings.

"Particularly at the weekends, as I shall be too tired to go out much after work." She explained.

"We have two picture houses, a small theatre, and there are sometimes talks and dances at the Guildhall. Or you could join a club or society, there are several that have posters in the library entrance. I was going to the Gaumont this evening, there is a new film with Betty Balfour, it's a comedy. Would you like to come with me?"

"Oh, if it wouldn't be any trouble, I should like to, very much!"

"Then let's meet outside at seven. Now I'd better get back to work. See you this evening!"

Caroline enjoyed the film. There were certain points where she saw a connection to her own life; Betty Balfour played a young woman forced to get a job after her father tells her he has lost all of his money. Yet the twist was that the father had only told Betty there was no money as a punishment for her wild ways. Betty also argued a lot with her on-off boyfriend, and Caroline felt uncomfortably reminded of Noah. Though they had not argued, Caroline was still unhappy that after saying he would be satisfied with a long engagement, Noah had become increasingly focused on marriage. As they left the cinema, Caroline asked Edna if she had a boyfriend.

"No one serious, not now. There was a man, but he had to go away."

"Didn't you want to go with him?"

"I couldn't."

There was a silence between the two women. Caroline felt that Edna wanted to say something more and was deciding how best to do so. When the couple in front of them crossed the road, Edna took a deep breath.

"I couldn't go with him because he went to prison."

"Oh," Caroline didn't know what to say. Then she had a thought, "Edna it wasn't the man who killed Betty was it?"

"No, no of course not. No, he wrote some cheques when he had no money to cover them." She frowned, "it's not something I tell everyone, you understand."

"Oh yes, of course. Well, I don't know anyone here in Taunton to tell, but I wouldn't anyway. I'm not a gossip. But goodness, Edna, how awful for you."

"Thank you. Yes, it has been rather difficult. Hugh was sentenced to five years. He has two more to do."

The women walked through the now dark streets between the pools of yellow cast by the streetlights, in the general direction of Holway Road.

"And are you ... waiting for him?" Caroline asked.

"My father would be apoplectic if he knew. I write to Hugh every few days. He writes to me but sends the letters to a friend. He is so very sorry for what he did. He swears he will never do anything like that again. I believe him." Edna lifted her head with her final sentence and looked directly at Caroline.

Caroline almost asked how Edna could trust a man who had been convicted of deception but caught herself just in time. She liked Edna and it wouldn't do to upset a new friendship with insensitivity. Instead, she asked, "How did you come to work at an estate agent?"

"It belongs to my father. He took me on as a typist, but I convinced him to let me become more involved in the letting side of the business. I'm saving up so that when Hugh is released, we can move away and start a fresh somewhere new." Now it was Edna's time to consider a question before she asked it. "Is that what you're doing, starting a fresh here?"

They had stopped walking as they reached a crossroads.

"I had been involved with a man, he wanted us to get married, but I didn't want to. I have been very lucky that my friends have helped me find a job. They helped me get the motor car as well. I don't think my father is entirely thrilled about me moving here but it is close enough to the airfield. So yes, I suppose it is a fresh start. It was either here or go home to Father."

"You won't tell anyone about Hugh, will you?"

"I promise I won't."

"Well, it's been nice to see you. I live just down there. Will you be alright getting home?"

"I'm sure I will. Do come and visit if you are at a loose end. You know where I live."

The girls chuckled and then said their goodbyes. Caroline considered Edna as she walked home along South Street and into Holway Road. Was Taunton a hotbed of lawlessness? Would she be safe there? But Edna seemed to be a nice young woman, certainly not someone Caroline would have picked out as a criminal sort. She clearly loved Hugh. Caroline hoped Edna was not placing her faith in someone who would eventually leave her penniless.

Caroline arrived home on Thursday 20 September to another letter from Philip Rose. Mary had been delivered of a baby girl whom they had named Grace Celeste. Mother and daughter were well, Celestine would be with the family until the weekend, and then would Caroline like to visit for a few days? Caroline had read the letter in the hallway as soon as she had closed the front door. Now she set the letter and envelope down on the stairs and took off her shoes.

It had rained for most of the day and her eyes were tired from concentrating on the road on her drive home. It had been a difficult day. Deliveries had been late. Passengers had been rude and unwilling to follow instructions with one woman marching out to the waiting aeroplane without checking in at Caroline's office and caused the flight to delay take off because no one realised she was already on board. Caroline was also becoming disenchanted with Rupert, who had taken to hanging around her office, sitting on the edge of her desk smoking and asking her ever more personal questions.

A trip to see her friends, and in particular the two little girls, was just what Caroline needed. She went into the kitchen and moved onto the range the pan of potatoes and carrots that she had peeled at breakfast and left in water all day. Then she carried a small enamel dish into the larder and unwrapped a pork chop that was on the cold shelf. She sniffed it to check its freshness and then placed it in the dish and returned to the range where she opened the small oven door and pushed the dish inside. The kettle still had water from the morning, and she moved it onto the hotplate to boil for tea.

As she moved around the compact kitchen, her routine tasks carried out without needing to concentrate, her mind returned to Rupert. It wasn't that she didn't like him, she liked all of the ground crew, but his comments and questions about what she was wearing, what she did in the evenings, and who she might be doing it with had begun to feel invasive. He had stood so close to her at the filing cabinets that afternoon she had felt his breath on her cheek. The kettle boiled and she made the tea in her china pot, a parting gift from Vi and Ron.

She would have to talk to Tommy about Rupert. There would be no good in her speaking to him herself; he was in many ways the leader of the ground crew and she knew that though that day had been difficult, most days were enjoyable and she did not want to be asked to leave. Unexpectedly, an image of Harry Gregory flashed through her mind, and his words, "no one will believe you," rang in her ears. But Helen had believed her. Caroline sighed. She must see about having the telephone installed. There would be more nights like this when she wanted to talk to Helen. She would ask Tommy if she could have some time off to visit Mary and Phillip too.

Tommy was sympathetic when Caroline took him a mug of coffee the next day at their mid-morning break.

"I'm sorry old thing. We've all noticed him doing it, but truth be told no one wanted to say anything in case you were welcoming the attention."

"Well, now you know I am not, and I would prefer Rupert to stay out of the office unless he has paperwork to see to."

"I'll have a word. I'll speak to David as well, those two are thick as thieves and Rupert will listen to David if he doesn't listen to me. You said there were two things you wanted to say to me?"

"Yes, I know I haven't been here very long, but I was wondering if I might have next Friday and the following Monday as a holiday. I'd like to visit my friend Mary and meet her new baby. It will be a long drive and I'm thinking of taking the train instead."

Tommy chuckled, "Still tied to the old iron horse, eh?"

"Yes, but I can relax if I'm not driving all that way and be refreshed when I come back to work." She smiled as sweetly as she could.

"You don't have to convince me you know. I'll let the others know. Perhaps it will help Rupert to cool off a bit too."

Caroline was met on the platform at Bradford-on-Avon railway station by the whole Rose family. Angelica had been excitedly skipping around the pram containing her little sister and Philip had grasped her at the last minute as she made to run towards the train. Mary was very happy to see Caroline again, and with Caroline's case stowed in the parcel space under the pram they walked slowly together pushing the pram behind Philip and Angelica towards the vicarage.

The town ran along the railway line and canal, and up the hillsides. Many of the buildings were constructed of a mixture of brick and the local pale coloured stone, and the houses with front gardens were neat and tidy with well-clipped hedges. The smell of industry and bonfires mixed with domestic coal fires crept along the lanes in the still air. There was another smell that Caroline recognised as chemical in nature from her time at the engineering works with Lottie. She mentioned it to Philip who explained it was from the old mill where rubber goods were now produced. Originally the factory made rubber capes used by soldiers in the Crimean War, but lately they had turned their processes towards producing tyres for bicycles and motor cars. It employed many people from the surrounding area, who made good use of the train service through the village. Unfortunately it also polluted the river, and Caroline could see how cloudy the water was as they crossed the stone bridge from one side of the village to the other.

It was lunchtime and children were out in the primary school playground as the Roses and Caroline passed by. Angelica was being carried by Philip and squirmed in his arms to better see the children, her fingers in her mouth and her eyes wide and inquisitive.

Mary noted her daughter's curiosity, "Angelica loves to be with other children."

"She has grown so much in just the past few months. Her speech is coming along too."

"There is a little girl next door to the vicarage. Angelica likes to play with her in the garden. I watch both girls while Julia's mother attends the Women's Institute."

"You don't go yourself?"

"No Miss Caroline, I have the Mother's Union meetings, and Julia's mother watches Angelica then."

"What a practical system! And so good for Angelica to have a little friend." Caroline was reminded of her childhood before she went to school at Mrs Pendersen's, playing with Florence and Timothy the twins who lived next door. She wondered how Florence was now, after her disastrous abortion and elopement with Vaughan Rickard to his parent's home in Cromer on the Norfolk coast. They had lost touch, and Caroline wondered if there might be a way to find their current address. She would ask Philip later.

The vicarage was a grey stone building set on the hill above the Holy Trinity and St Lawrence churches with various climbing plants covering the lower walls. Philip explained that it had four bedrooms, and a small vegetable plot in the garden that he was looking forward to bringing back to life next year.

With an increase in his stipend, Philip had been able to engage a maid. She was not a local girl. Philip and Mary had discussed at length who they might want to employ, with Mary being reluctant to be in such a position of authority until Philip suggested they take a girl from an orphanage or reform school.

On making enquiries, Philip visited the Muller Orphan House at Ashley Down on the edge of Bristol. He was introduced to a small group of thirteen-year-old girls in Number 2 House who were approaching the end of their legal schooling requirement and in need of employment. On seeing Audrey, Philip knew that Mary would agree to take her in. Audrey Jeffries had been at the Orphan house since the spring of 1919 after her father Ellis (originally from Barbados) and mother, Vera (a Bristolian), had both died from the Spanish flu. She was not the only mixed-race child at the orphanage but was the only girl of the appropriate age. She stood head and shoulders above the six other girls in the group, dressed in the blue cotton dress, white pinafore and white bonnet that was their uniform. Audrey kept her eyes down the whole time, whereas some of the other girls stared at the visitors and tried to make themselves as appealing as they could.

Caroline met Audrey in the hallway of the vicarage. The girl stood at the foot of the stairs waiting for instructions.

"Audrey, this is our good friend Miss Munhead, Angelica's Godmother. Could you please take her suitcase up to the spare room and then bring us some tea in the sitting room." Philip said.

The girl gave a silent nod and reached out to take Caroline's case.

"Thank you, Audrey." Caroline smiled at the girl but received just a glance in return.

When they had made their way into the sitting room and Angelica was engaged in a simple jigsaw on the rug in front of the fireplace, Mary explained, "Audrey is very quiet, Miss Caroline, she does not like to speak. She has an impediment, a lisp, but she is a good girl."

"Is she the only help you have here?" Caroline asked.

"Yes. I can still cook and sew, but Audrey does more of the cleaning and laundry. They are well treated at the orphanage. Audrey came with three pairs of shoes! They have swimming baths for the children to use, and picnics in the summer."

"Talking of Bath," said Philip, picking Grace up out of the pram now that she was awake, "I have to go up tomorrow. Would you like to come with me Caroline? I shall only be three hours at the most, and you might find the Roman baths interesting."

"I should like that very much, thank you. Can one swim there? I always pack my bathing suit just in case these days."

"I believe so. The water smells rather like rotten eggs though!"

Caroline and Philip took the train to Bath the next morning. It was overcast and misty, and Caroline was glad of her coat and hat. Philip walked with her to the Roman baths, and they agreed to meet in the station tea rooms at one o'clock before returning to Bradford-on-Avon. This would give Caroline time to bathe and explore some of the city by herself while Philip was at his meeting.

The baths stood near to the abbey in a precinct surrounded by shops and businesses. Caroline marvelled that the structure had survived the centuries largely intact. There were excavations taking place to one side of the buildings, but the main bath and changing rooms were open and for twopence Caroline was admitted and shown to the lower level. Under instruction not to drink the water in the pool, Caroline changed quickly and made her way to the green water. Philip was correct that the sulphur caused a smell of rotten eggs, but the heat from the water was enticing on such a grey day and Caroline was keen to get in.

There were two older women also swimming sedately around the pool. Caroline exchanged good mornings with them as she joined their circular route. She was used to cold water swimming but found the warm water if anything harder work. Like swimming in soup, she thought to herself on the second circuit of the pool. She copied the other women and swam slowly, and after three circuits, she climbed out using the stone steps at one end. Her whole body felt heavy from the exercise. She draped her borrowed towel around her shoulders and sat on the edge of the pool for a few moments with her feet in the water. One of the older women got out, her exercise completed for the day. Caroline waited for the remaining woman to reach the far end of the pool before shrugging off the towel and slipping back in, intent on completing another three circuits.

When Caroline left the baths, a fine drizzle was falling. To avoid it, she browsed in shops, bought a magazine and a copy of *Mrs Dalloway*, and explored the inside of the abbey. She sat for a while in the Lady Chapel until the warmth of the bath waters finally left her and she felt chilly. Looking at her watch, she still had an hour before meeting Philip. She decided to walk back to the station and have a cup of tea and look through her magazine.

The station tea rooms were busy. Caroline took a table against the wall furthest from the door just as a couple were leaving it to catch their train. She ordered a pot of tea and had been reading an article on kitchen refrigeration units when a voice caught her attention. Two tables away, a man was giving his order to the waitress; the woman's back was to Caroline, obscuring the man from her line of sight, but her heart was beating faster at the sound of his soft accent. As the waitress moved away, Caroline's curiosity was confirmed. She found herself staring into the face of a man she had believed she would never see again.

7

VISITORS FROM THE PAST

Max Bird had left his home early that morning and taken the train to Bristol for his appointment at the Eye Hospital. It was a routine visit, one of many that peppered his calendar and took him to various doctors, surgeons and psychiatrists across Avon and Wiltshire. He was growing tired of the experience; there seemed to be little more reconstruction anyone could offer him, and no more feeling had returned to his left hand, though the exercises had strengthened his leg so that he no longer needed a stick to help him walk. They had confirmed that morning that no further deterioration in his sight was detected, to which Max had replied with stoic humour that without his left ear he wouldn't have been able to wear spectacles in any case. The nurse had not shared his laughter. The doctor had simply nodded and continued writing up his notes.

Returning to Bath, Max gazed out of the window of the train carriage without seeing the fields roll by. He felt restless. Redundant. His war pension was just enough for him and Diana to live on when he could find no work but made him feel even more wretched for relying on it and on her family for support. With his useless hand, he could no longer continue as the draughtsman he had trained to be. He had taken two or three temporary positions as an office clerk since being confirmed as fit to work, but his frequent medical appointments eventually conflicted with his employer's schedules, and he had been asked to leave albeit with a good reference each time. It had been four weeks since his last pay packet.

Diana's family would not let them starve. Her father was a partner in a solicitor's firm and had been dubious about her marriage to Max from the start. Max had seen the glee in his father-in-law's face when Max announced he would be enlisting. Diana had begged him not to go. She had not forgiven him, not even when he returned with the first of his injuries, and certainly not when he declined a medical discharge and returned to the front for a second time. Now they hardly spoke. Max knew that his appearance disgusted Diana, though he thought she would never come right out and say so. She had always been a woman of reserve, their lovemaking after the first few encounters became a passive exercise for Diana and Max had gradually lowered his expectations to match her lack of enthusiasm. She had never refused him, but now they slept in separate rooms. It had been two years since he had made any overtures of that kind towards her.

It had been his return from the painting retreat in Cornwall that had been the last time. There he had spent a week with a small group of strangers, painting and sketching in the mornings and exploring various handcrafts in the afternoons under a clear blue sky with the pale sandy beach and turquoise sea as their inspiration. He had gone at the suggestion of his psychiatrist. He had returned to Bath at the end of the week having met a young woman who had treated him as a real man for the first time since the war. She had been kind without being patronising, pretty but not beautiful, and somewhat naïve which gave her a charm that he had fallen for. She had gone willingly to his bed on the last night of his stay and had agreed that they would never see each other again.

So why was he thinking of her now as the train approached Bath station? She lived, as far as she had said, up country and was probably married by now and raising a family. Max's stomach growled and brought him out of his reflections. He would never meet anyone like Caroline again. He simply had to carry on with Diana and try to find another job.

He waited until the train came to a halt before standing and leaving the carriage. It was twenty minutes past twelve. He could save money and return home for a muted lunch with Diana, or he could get something to eat in the tearoom and postpone the silence a little longer. The smell of fried bacon tempted him inside, and he picked up a newspaper by the door to read while he ate. Perhaps there would be some vacancy he could apply for that afternoon.

Passengers and those waiting for travellers to arrive were in a constant ebb and flow in the tearoom. He spotted an empty table in the centre of the room and concentrated on lowering himself into the chair without knocking it over or missing the seat and landing on the floor. It would not have been the first time if he had, but once again he gave thanks that at least his leg had improved some more over the past year. The waitress came with her notepad. Max ordered a mug of coffee (easier to manage with one good hand than a pot of tea) and a bacon sandwich. As the waitress moved away, Max looked around and straight into the grey eyes and surprised face of Caroline.

There was a moment, mentioned in romance novels to please the reader, where time seemed to stop. The sound of rattling cutlery, chatter, rustling newspapers, squealing train wheels and spurts of steam were all silenced. No movement interrupted their line of sight. Caroline realised she was holding her breath and gasped for air. Max made to stand up, but Caroline found her voice first.

"No, stay there, I'll come to you," she said, picking up her hat and magazine from her table.

The waitress arrived with Max's coffee, and helped Caroline move her tea things to his table. When she had gone, Caroline and Max sat for a moment simply looking at each other. They did not smile. They studied each other's faces as if they wanted to be sure they were not mistaken before committing to conversation. The waitress returned with Max's sandwich and asked if Caroline wanted anything to eat.

"Oh, no, not yet thank you. My friend will be here shortly."

Left alone, Max took a sip of his coffee. "It really is you. But you're meeting a friend?"

"He'll be here at one. Oh, but it's not what you think, he is my friend's husband. Mary has stayed with the children in Bradford-on-Avon and I came with Philip today so that I could swim. Philip is the vicar there."

"I never thought … you look well. Are you well?" His brow creased with concern.

"I am very well, thank you. Gosh so much has happened since … Cornwall. I live in Taunton now; I've only recently moved there. And I work at an airfield in the office. Oh, and I can drive too, and I have an Austin motorcar! But what about you, how are you? I see the stick is gone."

"My leg is a little better but everything else is much the same …" He didn't want to speak of Diana, but she loomed like a phantom in between them, a shadow that Caroline saw just as clearly.

"Please don't let your sandwich get cold, Max," Caroline said. His name felt like sunshine in her mouth. She could not stop looking at his face, just as she had found herself doing on the terrace of the Bohenna's house in St Ives. And just as then, she had a strong desire to touch him, his face, his hand, any part of him. She waited for him to finish chewing and swallow before she asked her next question.

"Do you still paint at all?"

"I sketch sometimes. I keep a set of pencils and a small sketchbook. I'm not always able to get canvases or have the time to paint." He took another bite. Diana had given his paintings a cursory glance when he had returned from Cornwall, and they stood now where he had left them in a corner of the bedroom that had become his. He had deliberately left the drawings he had made of Caroline behind in St Ives. The set of tiles he had made there were wrapped in sacking on the floor next to the canvases.

Caroline glanced at the large wall clock. It was ten minutes to one and Philip could arrive at any moment. She reached into her bag for the notebook and pencil she and Helen had used when they were looking for places to rent. She tore off a page and began to write.

"Max, please will you take this, it's my address. I want you to have it. Blast it, I wish I'd had a telephone put in sooner so I could give you the number, but the engineer won't be doing that for another three weeks yet. Anyway," she folded the paper in half and pushed it across the table towards him, "please take it. I feel as if it's important. I know we said we would never meet again, but now that we have, please just take it."

Max put his hand over hers, "Will you give me the notebook?"

She did so, along with the pencil, and after putting the scrap of paper into his waistcoat pocket, he quickly wrote a few words and then closed the book. He too had no telephone.

"Remember though, what I told you." He would not say Diana's name.

Caroline looked down at the notebook. "Yes, I remember. Max, I don't …"

"Ahh there you are!" Philip appeared at the table, smiling warmly. He had had a good meeting with a friend from seminary college and was looking forward to lunch.

"Philip, this is Max. He and I met in Cornwall, and we just happened to bump into each other again here."

Max got unsteadily to his feet and shook Philip's hand.

Caroline suddenly wanted to get Philip away from Max, before the questions started.

"Philip, I was going to suggest we have lunch somewhere else, there isn't much on the menu here and you must be hungry. I saw a hotel opposite the station entrance, perhaps we could go there?"

"Well, yes, I don't mind if you don't. Well, nice to meet you Max, we won't disturb your meal any further."

Caroline was standing now, putting her hat on and her notebook and pencil back into her bag, careful once more not to rest it on her wet bathing suit but keeping the rubber swim cap as a barrier. "Goodbye then Max. It was lovely to see you again. Do let me know if you are ever in Taunton won't you. No, don't get up, finish your sandwich," she touched his arm again gently and their eyes spoke every word ever needed between them.

Max might have said goodbye; Caroline swiftly turned and almost dragged Philip out of the tearoom and through the station entrance without listening. Max finished his sandwich and coffee deep in thought. How strange that he had only been thinking of her minutes before they had met again by chance. Was it chance? Max was not a religious man; he did not believe in divine intervention. It had been chance that had exploded the shell close enough to maim him but not close enough to finish him off. Chance had brought him and Caroline together in Cornwall, and yes, once again stepped in and brought them together briefly in a station tearoom on a damp October morning. He felt as if he had drunk several pints of beer. He did not trust his leg just yet to stand again and pay for his meal at the counter. Though he had little feeling in his left hand, his right hand had felt the warmth of Caroline's. She was alive. He wanted her as much as he had on the beach and in his bed that night. But: Diana.

Caroline tried very hard not to think of Max again that weekend. It was difficult in quiet interludes, and impossible when she retired to bed and was on her own, but largely Angelica and Grace kept her entertained. Mary noticed a subtle change in her friend when Caroline and Philip returned from Bath but said nothing. She was happy to have Caroline to talk to for those few days and although the weather kept them mostly indoors, the vicarage was large enough for Angelica to play happily while the two women chatted together. Grace was a contented baby. Like Angelica, her skin was a soft sugary brown and her hair dark and curled. Mary seemed relieved and relaxed that she was a girl, though Philip had hoped for a boy. Grace's christening would be in two weeks' time, and Caroline was honoured to be asked to be her godmother but decided to decline.

"It's not that I don't want to be," she explained to Philip and Mary over dinner on the Sunday, "but I shan't be able to get any more time away from work for a while. It's rather difficult to get here by train, I had three changes on the way up and tomorrow I shan't be home before three. But thank you so much for asking me."

"Not at all," said Philip, "you were our first choice."

"Have you considered Audrey?" Caroline asked.

Mary tilted her head and looked at Caroline, "No, we had not. But perhaps we should, Philip?"

"An excellent suggestion! It might help her feel more a part of our family."

When Caroline arrived back home the next day, there was a letter from her father and one from Midge waiting for her. The coal delivery had been while she had been away, which she had arranged through Ted Farthing. With the bunker at the back of the house now full, she hoped she would not need to purchase more until after Christmas. The rain had stopped, and Caroline opened the back door from the kitchen to the garden wide to let some air in while she stoked the range and got the fire alight again. She could hear voices over the garden wall which was seven feet high for privacy between the two houses and then dropped to four feet a little way out into the garden.

With the kettle on the hotplate, Caroline went outside and looked over the wall.

"I say, excuse me, Winnifred!"

Her neighbour was turning a mangle while Jonathan fed the laundry through the rollers. He was not doing it to Winnifred's satisfaction. She turned with a start when Caroline called to her.

"Yes? Just hold it for a moment Jonathan."

"Hello. I'm sorry to trouble you but I was wondering if your son might like to earn himself a bob or two."

"My Jonathan? Doing what exactly?" Winnifred asked suspiciously.

Caroline smiled her best smile and half turned back to her garden, sweeping her arm outwards. "I was rather hoping he might be able to run the lawn mower over this meadow I seem to have let happen! There is a mower in the shed, though I don't know the last time it was used."

Winnifred considered the proposition for a moment. She was still unsure what to make of Caroline, but as there had been no wild parties and the Austin was not noisy in the mornings when Caroline left for work, Winnifred had started to relax her guard. Jonathan had heard Caroline's request and had been looking for an excuse to talk to his neighbour.

"Can I please, Mother? I'm sure I could get the mower to work if it doesn't. Mr Mitchum said we should try and find things to repair if we could."

Winnifred yielded, "Well I suppose so, but change out of your uniform first!"

Jonathan bounded inside to get changed. Caroline was relieved; she had not been looking forward to manhandling the mower over such long grass by herself. She had considered asking Ted to help, but he and Irene had already been such good eggs, she was loath to impose on them any further.

"I should think it will only need one or two cuts this year, so it shouldn't interfere with Jonathan's school work," she said optimistically.

"Yes. He is not suited to manual work. Perhaps once you have it under control, you'll be able to tend it yourself."

"Or perhaps your husband might see to it for me occasionally?" Caroline replied, hopefully. She would really rather pay Jonathan an occasional shilling but failing that, Johnny might do it for free.

"He has enough to do looking after ours." Winnifred said with rather more force than she had intended. "What with his work hours," she added.

"Oh yes, I quite understand, being in the same boat myself."

Jonathan returned, dressed in long trousers and a collarless shirt, looking strangely much older than his twelve years.

"Shall I climb over?" he asked.

"No! You'll go round on the path. Is your gate unbolted Miss Munhead?"

"Yes, it is, and please do call me Caroline. Jonathan, the shed should be unlocked as well, I haven't got round to fitting a padlock yet."

Winnifred didn't stop to talk over the wall, and Caroline's kettle had started to sing so she went back into the kitchen but left the door open. She heard Jonathan open the side gate, then the shed, and after considerable clanging and grunting, the first sounds of a working lawnmower determinedly chewing up the over-long grass reassured Caroline that Jonathan would earn his shilling. She took it out of her purse and left it on the kitchen table, then went upstairs to unpack while the tea brewed.

She felt happy and light, as if a weight had been lifted from her. The only slight fly in her ointment was the inscription Max had left in her notebook. She had been so distracted by his physical presence, and then in company, that she hadn't looked at it until that evening when she had retired to her room at the vicarage. Sitting up in the bed that still smelled faintly of Celestine's cooking, Caroline had turned the pages of the little book until she found the one Max had written on.

I will write

No address of his own. No sweet words of love. It had taken her some moments to rationalise what she saw. His hand pressing on hers, his reminder of the fact he was not unencumbered; he was being cautious. And of course, Caroline should not have attempted to write to Max, for fear of his wife intercepting the letter however innocent the contents might be. He was right, she conceded. She would wait.

14 September 1928
Tanganyika

Dear Caroline,

Thank you so much for your recent letter, and the explanation of your new address. I won't pretend that I am not surprised, you and Noah seemed so well suited and happy together when we met him at Helen and Tommy's house. And yet, thinking back, perhaps there was something a little distant in you even then. I wondered if having James turn up had made you uncomfortable, but I suppose not.

In any case, you are once again mistress of your own abode! Do write and tell me all about the neighbours – they are one of the things I miss out here, and I never imagined I would. Oliver says he is very happy not to have people watching our every move, the Africans here are very respectful, but it would be nice once in a while to have someone to pass the time of day with, in a neighbourly fashion.

We shall be back in England for Christmas again. I think Oliver would be happy to come back to Africa, but really I have had enough of the experience now. He has secured a teaching position at a school in Winchester, and we shall be moving into a house in the town just before the new term begins. When I have the details confirmed I shall let you have our new address and you must come and stay. I'll be on my own for much of the time I expect.

Your job sounds terribly exciting. Have you met anyone famous yet? I have read that all the film stars fly everywhere these days. I should love to go up in an aeroplane one day, though our journey home will be mostly by boat. We stop at Cairo for one night and then continue across the Mediterranean Sea to Monaco where we pick up the train. I am travelling light with only two cases, but Oliver has been here for much longer and has amassed a collection of books to put the British Library to shame. I really think there will be little room for furniture in our new home, it will all be devoted to books!

Oh, before I forget, Luke is to be married. We are hoping to be back in time, but that all depends on the weather. His fiancée is a young nurse called Lizzy. Mark is staying on here for another year, and John is saving up for his own river boat. Of all of us, he was always the water baby.

Write to me at my parents' with your telephone number when you have it.

Best wishes

Midge

That didn't take Luke long, thought Caroline as she sipped her tea at the small kitchen table. There had been a brief time when Luke had hoped to entice Caroline into an engagement, and she had had to be very firm with him that she was not interested. She was happy for Midge to have found Oliver. He seemed a steady chap, and with a teaching post lined up they should be able to settle back into the British way of life without too much trouble.

Caroline pushed the thin blue sheet of paper back into the equally flimsy blue envelope. Jonathan was still battling in the back garden. The smell of the cut grass drifted into the kitchen. Caroline took another sip of tea and then opened the second envelope bearing her father's familiar handwriting.

29 September 1928
Cheltenham

My dearest Caroline,

I was satisfied to hear that you have now established a routine between your employment and home. Although I am still uncomfortable with your driving a motorcar by yourself, I understand that many young women now do so.

My recent visit to Dr Riley has led him to prescribe some tablets he thinks will aid the indigestion I have been experiencing recently. Though I keep to the diet he recommends, with Sara's help, some foods are becoming increasingly difficult to digest. He assures me it is nothing that you need worry about.

We were sadly informed two evenings ago of the passing of Captain McTimony. Mrs Monk knocked on our door at just after eight. It seems she was about to begin their evening routine of bathing and medication when she found the Captain to have died in his bed. It is, I feel, a merciful release. McTimony could not have been happy in his restricted state, however capable a nurse Mrs Monk has been to him. His stroke must have caused more damage than was evident to the untrained observer.

We shall all be attending the funeral. Sara will be accompanying Miss Kettle as she is not so steady on her feet. Ferris will arrange taxis I am told, and Mrs Monk will host the mourners afterwards in McTimony's apartment. With Vaughan Rickard's apartment still vacant, I feel it could be some time before we have any new neighbours.

Mrs Bassett tells me she is planning a trip abroad, to return to her homeland for some weeks in the new year. I have grown used to hearing her music in the evenings, and I know you also enjoyed her company and musical entertainment. Indeed, she asked me if there was any small gift that she could bring back for you from Russia. I must admit I was at a loss to suggest anything, my knowledge of the region being limited, and I have left it up to her judgement.

The agent has been most accommodating in allowing the installation of your telephone. It will be a comfort to me to know that we can be in more immediate contact should the need arise. Have you given any thought to where you might spend Christmas this year?

I look forward to next week's letter,
Take care my dear girl
Father

Christmas was still some weeks off, but Caroline knew that she would be able to spend a few days away from the airfield as the ground crew dispersed to their homes and families across the south of England. Tommy and Helen would spend some time in Plymouth, David was planning a trip to see his parents in Kent and Peter was going to his brother in the New Forest. Caroline had not asked Rupert his plans, she was trying to keep some professional distance to their relationship and give him no encouragement. The other member of the crew, Rodney, was hoping to fly across to France and make some business appointments. The company had still not made a profit, but they were much closer to being in the black and another investor had helped significantly by covering the cost of aviation fuel for three months.

Caroline smiled to herself over her father's continued use of 'we' and 'our' as if she still lived there with him. She had no preference at that moment between spending Christmas at Elmsworth or at Norwood Court with her father, or anywhere else. Jonathan came up to the kitchen door and broke her train of thought.

"Excuse me, Miss, but do you have any shears? I could do the edges of your lawn if you do, or I could use Father's if you don't."

"I really couldn't say. Do have a rummage in the shed and see what you can find in there. I don't think your mother would approve of you using your father's equipment on my garden."

"Oh, Mother is alright really, and I'm sure Father wouldn't mind, but I'll take a look." He lingered on the threshold for a moment.

Caroline turned in her chair to look at him, silhouetted in the sunlight, "Was there something else?"

"I … I was wondering, perhaps if you needed someone to help with your motor car … Oh I don't know, give it a polish some time …" he was blushing, but Caroline couldn't see his face clearly.

"Are you very interested in mechanical things?"

"Rather! I want to be an engineer when I leave school and I might have to go to the technical college Mr Mitchum says, but Mother wants me to be a lawyer or doctor or something like that. I'm far more interested in machines and engines."

Caroline smiled at the boy's enthusiasm.

"The chaps I work with look after my car for me if it needs anything doing, but why don't you ask Mr Farthing if he would show you his motor van? Perhaps on a Saturday morning when he's not on his delivery rounds."

"I hadn't thought of that! Yes, yes I will." Jonathan turned and ran across the lawn and began investigating the dark recesses of the shed for the shears.

The first visitor to Elmsworth that Caroline entertained was Daisy Clare. She arrived by train one Saturday, having left three dishes of chicken and fish for Gladstone her cat in the yard behind the bookshop to see him through the 36 hours she would be absent. Gladstone eyed them with suspicion, walked to the far end of the yard and sat facing the wall with his back to Daisy and the tip of his tail twitching as she closed the kitchen door to keep him outside.

Helen had mentioned the unfortunate Betty's demise to Daisy. Since then Daisy had been keen to visit the house and see if any residual spiritual energy could be detected. The only spirits that interested Helen came in bottles and she refused to discuss the matter further, wishing she had never mentioned it in the first place. And so, Daisy travelled alone: she was looking forward to seeing Caroline again.

As the two women left the railway station, Caroline stopped at the entrance to the Gaiety Theatre and looked closer at one of the posters on display for upcoming performances.

"Anything interesting?" Daisy asked.

Caroline pointed to a name on the poster, "I rather think I know that actress. Elsie Payne."

"From your acting days?"

Caroline laughed, "Oh Daisy, you make it sound as if I was a screen star like Clara Bow or Louise Brooks!"

"Well, you never know, there could be a huge crowd of Germans deep in Bavaria worshipping your image on a nightly basis. That was where James said it was being distributed, wasn't it?"

"Yes. I expect if they were worshipping any of us, it would have been Bella or Julia though. This play opens here next weekend, I think I might buy a ticket and see if it really is the Elsie I know."

They caught a bus from a little further along the street that took them to the end of Holway Road. Daisy remarked how useful it must be to have Farthing's on the corner and Caroline agreed.

"I have used my bicycle only a few times since I have been here, when I've needed something in town. Ted and Irene have almost everything one needs, it's truly an Aladdin's cave."

"I must remember to take some bread back with me, nothing will be open in Dunster by the time I get back tomorrow."

"We should pop in and buy some now then, Ted and Irene go to church on Sunday mornings and only open for an hour in the afternoon."

Their entrance to the shop was announced by a jangle of the bell over the door. Irene came from the back room wiping her hands on a tea towel. She saw Daisy first and was bemused by the woman standing before her wearing a dark felt hat with its wide brim, and her raincoat along with wellingtons on a day that promised no rain at all. Then Caroline emerged from behind a large display of yellow mustard tins that sported a familiar bullock, and Irene greeted her cheerily and asked how she could help.

"Do you have any bread left? And a penny's worth of sugar mice too please."

"You and your sugar mice!" Irene dropped six of the pink and white sweets into a small paper bag by their string tails and then turned to the breadbasket. "We've a cob and a square loaf, or three rolls."

Daisy chose the cob and Caroline paid for both items before Daisy could find her purse at the bottom of her bag.

"Thank you," Daisy said as the left the shop, "I will pay you back once I have unpacked."

"Nonsense. It's only a loaf of bread. Well, here we are, what do you think?"

"Is this your little motor car? How marvellous! I do like the blue colour, so much more cheerful than black." She took a step back to better view the front of the house. "I like how they all have names as well as numbers. Yours is Elmsworth, then Ivydene, Ashworth, Willowdene, Hazelworth and Hollydene. How clever. They all look very neat. Are your neighbours as welcoming as Irene?"

Caroline produced her front door key, "I have hardly been at home to get to know them. Shall we go inside?"

Once indoors, Caroline explained that she did not want to say more on the doorstep in case Winnifred could hear. "She is a little stand-offish with me, though her son Jonathan has done an admirable job in taming the back garden. At least it looks like a lawn again instead of a hay meadow."

"A widow?" It was a natural assumption for Daisy to make.

"Oh no, her husband Johnny is a much cheerier fellow. He is a carpenter and works long hours all over the town building houses. Let's get your things upstairs and then I'll put the kettle on. I'm so pleased you've come, Daisy."

"Do you use lavender polish?" Daisy asked as they climbed the stairs.

"No, why?"

"I can smell lavender. I didn't notice any bushes of it in your garden."

"No, I don't have any. Are you sure you can smell it?"

"Yes, can't you?"

"No, not at all. I can smell the carpet; it needs a jolly good beating over the line but I haven't had the will to bother with it yet. No lavender though."

They were now standing in the front bedroom which though in shade all day had a gay pink rose patterned wallpaper and dark pink curtains at the wide window.

"It's even stronger in here, are you sure you can't smell it Caroline?"

"Cross my heart. I wonder what it could be."

Daisy closed her eyes and spoke solemnly to the room, "I mean you no harm. I should like to stay just for one night and then I'll be on my way."

Caroline tried not to giggle. Daisy was clearly utterly serious. After a moment, Daisy opened her eyes and smiled.

"There, no more lavender smell. Sometimes you just need to reassure them. Now, did you mention tea?"

The following weekend as October drew to a close and the clocks were turned back an hour, Caroline sat in a plush red velvet seat six rows from the front in the Gaeity Theatre. It had been a wet Saturday, and Caroline had decided to drive across town rather than get wet walking to and waiting for buses. The play she was watching was not a good one, she decided. The theatre was almost full, but the audience appeared to share her assessment of the entertainment and after the interval several seats remained empty. The plot, such as it was, revolved around mistaken identity and a lot of short scenes with the actors coming and going through doors either side of the stage. With each slam of the door, the scenery wobbled precariously.

At the curtain call, a polite ripple of applause greeted the company as they took their bow, and not wanting to prolong the agony, they all skipped off into the wings as the house lights came up. Caroline put on her hat and gloves and joined the slow-moving procession out of the auditorium and through the foyer. Instead of returning to her car, she walked around the side of the theatre. A tall man wearing a raincoat but no hat on his bald head stood by the stage door smoking a cigarette.

"No autographs." He mumbled without removing the cigarette from his mouth.

"I am not here for an autograph. I was hoping to speak to my friend, Miss Elsie Payne, she is one of the company."

The doorman looked Caroline up and down and decided she would not cause any trouble. "Alright. In there, second door on the right, knock before you go in, Elsie is sharing with the other girls."

"Thank you."

Caroline stepped around the bulk of the man and entered the theatre. She did as she had been told and knocked on the second door to her right. It was opened by a short oriental woman who Caroline recognised as playing a maid in the show. Caroline asked for Elsie and had the door promptly closed in her face without a word from the other woman. Caroline was about to knock again when the door opened, and Elsie stood in front of her.

"Caroline! Is it really you! Oh my goodness, how wonderful to see you again!" Her familiar red curly hair had grown a little longer and now sat on her shoulders, her green eyes sparkled and her red painted mouth had the broadest smile showing white but crooked teeth. Elsie was wrapped in a kimono of pale blue silk and after a welcome hug, she asked if Caroline would mind waiting for five minutes while she dressed and then they could go and sit in the theatre bar. Caroline agreed and the dressing room door once again closed on her. She was not disappointed as the plume of cigarette smoke that emerged every time it opened was very strong smelling and would have made her eyes water if she had been invited inside.

Ten minutes later the two women were sat on chairs in the theatre bar, a pink gin and a side car on the table in front of them.

"I still can't believe it." Elsie said for the fifth time, "and you say you've only been here in Taunton for a few weeks?"

"Yes, and the time has flown by. I suppose it does when one is working, there never seems to be enough time to do the housework and cook meals, or even read a book for very long before I find I am falling asleep in my chair."

"But working at an airfield must be jolly exciting. All of those dashing pilots and famous travellers."

"Everyone seems to think so, but really no one truly famous has travelled with us since I have been there. It's just businessmen and an occasional wealthy woman who prefers to fly to Scotland than take the sleeper train. I spend more time answering the telephone and carrying boxes to and from the aeroplanes than anything else. Do you see anything of the others?"

"You mean the crowd from Dorset? Julia is in the West End at the moment, only a small part but she is getting on a bit poor thing," Elsie giggled, knowing Julia was only five years older than her. "Frank and I had a bit of a thing when we went to Andover, but it didn't last. It's simply too complicated when you're both in the business. I hear James has been in Wales."

"Yes, he and I write occasionally. He wants to return to Italy, he really seemed to like it there."

"He was sweet on you, but I see there was nothing doing." Elsie sipped her drink and smiled at Caroline.

"Well, I suppose I can tell you. He did propose to me. We were at a friend's wedding in Worcester."

"And you said no? Well, of course you did, he's not here and you've not got a ring on your finger, but whyever not?"

"Because he had convinced me he would not be a good husband for me. I am very fond of him, but he is so committed to his work. And then I was … well I suppose I was engaged for a while."

"You suppose? Oh Caroline, you can be so vague sometimes!" Elsie's raucous laugh turned heads in their direction and Caroline blushed in spite of herself.

"Well, you see, it was all rather awkward in the end. Noah, the man I was engaged to, had said at the start that we need not get married right away. He bought a house, and we were going to live together once the agreement ended on the cottage I had taken. But the closer we got to that date, the more everyone started talking about marriage for us and I'm afraid I got cold feet. I still feel awful about it."

"It was the same with Frank. He wanted to settle down after the Andover show, so he could write his plays in peace without moving around all the time. He wanted me to play house with him. I'm not ready for that. We had such a row one evening, the neighbours were banging on the walls. I might have said that his plays were boring. He didn't take it very well. I went back to Woolwich for a while and then hooked up with this company. The writing is still awful, but we travel around. We were in Ireland a few weeks ago, and we'll be in Grimsby after this," she drained her glass, "I do love it so, moving from place to place, pretending to be someone I'm not. Perhaps I was a gypsy in another life."

"I'd better be getting along Elsie. It's been lovely to see you again. Let me give you my telephone number in case you come to Taunton again." Caroline wrote her number on the back of a calling card for the airfield David had given her. They had had two hundred printed to promote the passenger routes.

"Thanks. Yes, if we come this way, I'll be sure to be in touch. Did you say you had a motor car? Could I have a lift to my digs please? This rain is no good for my hair!"

Caroline pulled the Austin in to the curb outside a four-storey building that looked for all the world as if it had been declared derelict a decade before.

"Are you sure this is a boarding house?" She asked as Elsie flipped open her compact and applied a layer of lipstick.

"Well, perhaps not a boarding house in the normal sense of the word. Us girls have a room here. I hope the others aren't back yet and I get first dibs on the bed."

"What do you mean? How many of you share the room?"

"Four of us. Lin, who you spoke to at the theatre, Joyce, Sally and me. Last one in has to sleep on the floor."

Whether Elsie had exaggerated the conditions or not, Caroline did not like the thought of her friend sharing a room in a building that could collapse at any moment.

"Elsie, I rather think you should stay with me while you're in Taunton. You can have your own room, and I'll give you the back door key so that you can let yourself in every night after the show."

"Oh, I couldn't possibly! You've only just moved in yourself, you said. I'll be alright here. It's only for another week."

"No, I insist. Go and collect your things. I'll wait here for you."

"Caroline, you're such a brick. Thank you. I won't be more than a couple of minutes."

There were several times over the course of the following week when Caroline regretted her impulsive offer to have Elsie stay with her. In truth they saw very little of each other, as Caroline left for work early in the morning and Elsie slept in until almost lunchtime. Then their paths crossed for a few minutes when Caroline returned home as Elsie was on her way out to the theatre. It was the evidence of Elsie that Caroline regretted. The stockings and underclothes hung over the bath, the depleted larder, the unwashed crockery in the kitchen sink.

On the final night of the Taunton leg of the show, Elsie arrived at Elmsworth at two in the morning, having been out celebrating with her cast members. She made such a noise coming through the rear gate, and then with her key in the kitchen door, Caroline was already wide awake when Elsie tripped over something in the kitchen with a crash. Caroline went down to help her friend, who declared loudly and repeatedly that she was the best Agnes Frost the company had ever had as they wobbled together up the stairs. A few minutes later, Elsie's snores rumbled along the landing. Back in her own bed, Caroline put a pillow over her left ear to try and muffle the noise. No more waifs and strays, she told herself as she waited for sleep to come.

8

ANOTHER TRAIN, ANOTHER NIGHT

The letter arrived the following Monday. The Bath postmark indicated the sender as there was no return address anywhere on the envelope or on the note inside.

26 October 1928
Dear Caroline

This is wrong of me, I know it, but I want to see you again. Will you meet me in Wells? I shall be on the bench at the Market Cross at 3pm on Saturday 3 November. I shall wait for an hour.

Yours
Max

Caroline carried the note and envelope into her sitting room and thumbed through her map book of the British Isles. She had heard of Wells and knew it must be quite close to Bath as the Bishop had oversight of both cities. Eventually she found it. A tiny place, perhaps an hour by train from Bath. Then she looked in the opposite direction on the map and guessed it would take her a little more than an hour and a half to get there and she might have to change at Glastonbury or Bridgwater. Or she could drive the Austin. He wanted to meet her. She found she was shaking and sat down on one of the upholstered chairs Helen had donated to Elmsworth. I must pull myself together, she thought. I am not a silly girl; I am a grown woman and able to make my own decisions and suffer the consequences. But what consequences would there be, she wondered.

She had been considering travelling up to Cheltenham the same weekend, it being the closest to the anniversary of her brother Freddie's death. She was going to ask her father if he would be at home when they spoke on the telephone that evening. Now she would be in Wells. There was no question in her mind that she would go to see Max. He had written as he had said he would.

Caroline had sausages with boiled potatoes, carrots and some thick gravy for her dinner at the kitchen table. She could hear the Collier's radio faintly from next door. Every day seemed to bring rain and her drive home had been a tiring one again. She washed up the dinner things and then took a cup of tea into the sitting room waiting for her father to telephone at seven thirty. They had agreed to take turns and halve the expense of the calls that way.

The conversation was not as light as they usually had. George explained the indigestion was not improved by Dr Riley's tablets and he had stopped taking them. Caroline could hear that it still troubled him and suggested that he see the doctor again and perhaps it was something more related to the diabetes he had been diagnosed with the year before. George snapped that he would in his own time, and then immediately apologised. He blamed the acid in his chest and the time of year, a reference to Freddie's death that Caroline had been hoping to avoid. After another five minutes of small chatter, they ended their call. Caroline was concerned; George had sounded in more discomfort than he had admitted, and it was most unlike him to be sharp with her. On the other hand, she had felt distracted and perhaps sounded disinterested in the conversation.

Caroline looked at the clock on the mantlepiece through the open sitting room door and made another call.

"Mrs Rich, could I speak to Helen please, it's Caroline Munhead ...," there was a moment where Caroline could hear conversation in the background and then Helen came to the telephone.

"Caroline, how lovely to hear from you. It is rather late in the evening, is everything alright?"

"Oh Helen, I don't know. I just wanted to talk to someone, and you know everything already so I'm afraid it had to be you. It can wait though, if you have company."

"Not at all, darling, it's only Daisy and Tommy can entertain her. Tell me everything..."

When Caroline went to bed that evening, she felt confused and bewildered. She had explained the accidental meeting with Max and how now he had asked to meet her. To her surprise Helen had been adamantly against the assignation. The fact that Max was married appeared to be the key to Helen's hostility, and she had ended their call by saying that Caroline must think long and hard about what she was proposing to do to Max's wife. The rebuke had stung Caroline as if Helen had physically struck her. She had stood with the telephone in her hand for almost two minutes after Helen had hung up.

The next day, after a poor night's sleep and another rainy journey to the airfield in the Austin, Caroline was not her usual chirpy, efficient self. Everyone noticed, particularly when Caroline told a passenger they could sit wherever they pleased as long as it wasn't in her office. Tommy told the others he would speak to her at lunchtime. The rain continued to pour down and the window of Caroline's office was obscured with condensation. Tommy opened the door gingerly and walked to Caroline's desk offering her a sandwich.

"Is something up old girl?" He asked as they ate.

Caroline finished her mouthful and looked at Tommy sitting on the edge of her desk. Could she bear another rebuke from someone she considered her friend? She bit her lip; she and Tommy had become good friends and surely he would be the very last person to judge her choice of relationship.

"Did Helen tell you that we spoke on the telephone last night?"

"That was you? Goodness what on earth did you say to her? She refused to discuss it with me, whatever it was but it put her in a thunderous mood!"

"I'm sorry about that. Do you remember the man I told you about when I went to Cornwall, to that artist retreat?"

"I remember he had made quite an impression on you, though please don't ask me to name him."

"I met him, quite by chance, when I was in Bath a few weeks ago. It was only for a few moments but … I gave him my address and he said he would write. Now he has and has asked me to meet him again. And I want to, but I wanted to talk to Helen about it last night and she completely overreacted. She hasn't even met Max!"

"Ahh yes, Max, that was the fellow's name. But wasn't he married?"

Caroline felt herself blush, partly with embarrassment and partly anger. "Everyone puts so much emphasis on marriage! And yet people lie and cheat and pretend all the time when they are married, it's not always something good and to be proud of. Florence married for money and that all went horribly wrong. Galina married for love and her husband was taken from her. And you and Helen…" She stopped, aware that she was about to criticise their marriage and she truly did not wish to. She understood their reasons. "I'm sorry, Tommy, but you see, I thought Helen would understand that sometimes marriages don't last or aren't what everyone thinks they are."

"I think she does, but have you considered that she is simply concerned that this Max will do to you what he is clearly willing to do to his wife?" He spoke quietly, without any hint of hostility in his voice. "They do say, once a liar always a liar. And he must have told lies somewhere, either to you or to his wife, or at the very least not been completely honest with one or even both of you."

Caroline had not considered that possibility. She took another bite of her sandwich and a drop of mustard fell onto her skirt.

"Oh blast it!"

"Here, use my handkerchief."

She wiped the yellow sauce and then handed the handkerchief back to Tommy.

"Thank you. It's one thing after another at the moment," she put the remains of her sandwich down on the desk. "Do you really think Max is lying?"

"I have no idea. I don't know the man. But we all care about you Caro, and no one would want to see your heart broken over a man who could not be honest and responsible. Helen perhaps cares more than most would, she is so very fond of you. But look here, I am not about to tell you never to see or speak to this Max again – how could I? I am many things, but I try not to be a hypocrite. I can speak from experience though, and I don't think you understand how difficult it can be having to keep a relationship a secret. When you want to shout from the rooftops how much you love someone, yet you can never even speak his name for fear that someone will find you out and cause trouble. Seeing others walk gaily arm in arm, or kissing on a street corner, yet being terrified that a touch or a look between you will give you away. It is hard on the nerves Caro, believe me."

"When I was with Max in Cornwall, he told me his wife no longer saw him as a man because of his injuries. He said she shrank at his touch. But Tommy all I want to do when I am with him is touch him." She could only ever have told Tommy that, she realised.

Tommy nodded, swallowing the last of his sandwich. He had heard many times other men say similar things about their wives, often before propositioning him. He also knew how blind love could be and it was obvious that Caroline would take no firm counsel to dissuade her from her path towards Max.

"Do one thing for me? No matter how much you love him, or he says he loves you, do not get yourself pregnant. If you need any … precautions, I will get some for you. I don't think I can give you any other advice. I don't think you really want any, do you?"

Now Caroline shook her head. "Not really. It has helped to talk about it with you, but no, I know what I want to do and if it all goes horribly wrong, I shall only have myself to blame."

"Not quite, dear heart, Max will share the blame if things go wrong whether he accepts it or not."

Max had decided he would stay the night in Wells, whether Caroline met him or not. He had been paid for three days work as a temporary counter assistant in a chemist and had not been sorry that his employment had been ended there as he felt exposed to the stares of the customers. Diana had looked at him with what he felt to be disappointment over dinner on the third evening; he had let her down again. He had given her one day's pay as housekeeping but kept the rest. Half of that he had handed over to the receptionist at the Overton Hotel an hour ago, for a small double room on the first floor with dinner at eight and breakfast at seven the next morning. It was an extravagance he could ill afford, but the thought of returning to Diana if Caroline did turn up was too much for him. He needed to keep some space between the two women, in his mind as well as physically.

Max was not happy with himself. He liked to think he had some standards of moral decency, some self-respect and dignity. Now here he sat, in the drizzle on a bench in the middle of Wells, a married man waiting for a young woman who was not his wife, because she had touched him and not been repulsed. He should leave, stand up now and walk back to the hotel. Get out of the rain and put an end to this foolish behaviour. He remained seated. The inhabitants of Wells moved around him, sounds muffled by the weather, all grey and dripping. He could see the clock outside the jeweller's said five minutes past three.

I should have driven the Austin, Caroline thought to herself for the tenth time that day. She had planned her journey to arrive in Wells at two-thirty that afternoon, but every train had been delayed so far and she was now twenty minutes behind schedule. She was hungry and there would be no time now to stop somewhere for a quick lunch. Annie would have packed her some sandwiches. Caroline wondered how Annie's pregnancy was progressing, she must be due any day. What would Annie think of Caroline going off to meet a married man? Caroline knew exactly the look that would be on Annie's face: one of surprise and disappointment. Annie was always one to do the right thing and stick to the rules. Tommy had been right about one thing; it would be difficult for her to talk to anyone about Max. Except perhaps Edna O'Neil. Edna had her own forbidden love affair, perhaps Caroline could confide in her. They had been to the cinema once more together and both enjoyed the other's company though their conversations had been brief and light-hearted after Edna's revelation about her relationship with Hugh.

The train came to a halt again and Caroline looked out of the carriage window in the hope of seeing a station platform, but once more it was just fields. She looked at her watch. He would wait the full hour; he had said so.

Max blew his nose. It was a quarter to four. The drizzle of before was now a steady rain, and despite his hat and upturned collar he could feel his clothes were becoming sodden. He had told her an hour, and he would see it to the last minute. His self-loathing had grown over the afternoon and was now a voice in his missing ear telling him how ridiculous he looked sitting there in the rain. He should be at home in the dry with his wife. He owed it to her to stop this nonsense. And yet, said another voice which Max was starting to believe was his own heart speaking, and yet Diana was not behaving as a wife should either. Did a good wife ignore her husband and his needs? Did a good wife ignore the 'in sickness and in health' element of their marriage vows?

He had been looking at his own shoes while the voices competed for his attention. A third voice caught him by surprise.

"You'll catch your death sitting in the rain, Max! I'm so sorry I'm late, the trains were all delayed and I shall have a devil of a time getting back again later, but here I am."

Caroline stood in front of him, a little out of breath, underneath her umbrella. Max roused himself and got to his feet unsteadily after so long sitting in one position.

"Shall we find somewhere out of the rain?" She asked.

"There is a café across the square. Thank you for coming Caroline. I wasn't sure if…"

"Weren't you?"

They looked at each other, both with expressions that were searching, concerned, afraid, determined. Now she was here, Max knew he would have waited until they pried his cold dead body from that bench. He offered her his arm, and she slipped her hand under his elbow. They walked carefully around the monument and on to the café with its double bay windows and lace half curtains.

Installed in a corner, Max having shed his wet coat, they ordered tea and toasted teacakes. The café was only half full, and Caroline kept her voice low when she spoke after the waitress had left their table.

"Why are we both here, Max?"

She had been thinking back on what Galina Bassett had told her some months before, that Caroline should find a man who shared her passions. Max and Caroline had certainly shared passion that one night in Cornwall but was that enough? Would they feel it again, and could it sustain them? She was coming to realise that Max was a man of measured words and she waited for his answer.

It was not until after the tea things had arrived that he felt able to speak the sentences he had been marshalling into some kind of order in his brain.

"I am not a successful man, Caroline. There is very little I can offer you by means of income or property. I don't even have a job at the moment, and I spend far too much time visiting doctors and hospitals. None of that mattered when we were in Cornwall. I couldn't hide my injuries, but it felt like nothing beyond that house mattered for those few days.

"Since I've been back in Bath, I have felt like a shadow of myself. As if I have no substance, and no drive. I have wondered if it is one reason why I've been unable to hold down a job. I have felt as though nothing matters anymore, but not in a good way. In a despondent way. Writers used to talk of melancholy, and I think I understand now what they meant. I don't think if I remain where I am I will be any different in a year's time. And I don't think I can bear it."

Their teacakes arrived. The waitress glanced at the unfilled teacups, then turned and went back to the counter.

"So you want to make some kind of change to your life, is that it?"

"I think I need something to make me change. To be a catalyst, to become the man I had been before … everything went wrong. Seeing you again, thinking about you in the weeks since seeing you, it has been like having a flashlight shone on a way sign at night, picking out the right road to take."

Caroline did not answer immediately. She stirred the tea leaves in the pot and poured out two cups. She added milk to her cup, but left Max to organise his own. Taking up her knife, she cut into the small pat of butter in its dish. It was soft and spread easily over her teacake halves. Max had not moved.

"I think I understand you," she said at last, "because I have also felt as if I have been drifting along since Cornwall. I have had no direction, despite rather a lot of people doing their best to guide me one way or another. I don't want you to think I have been moping around or unhappy, because that's not the case, but I have had no purpose. You're right, that week at the Bohenna's house was like nothing I have experienced before or since. In some ways it feels like a dream now, and yet here you are, here we are, again. What are we going to do about it all?"

Max took up his knife having seen how soft the butter was. He moved his numb left hand into position to steady the teacake and then spread a small amount of butter over the crisp, brown surface. Caroline watched him, noting how he moved deliberately as he had when glazing the tiles he had worked on in the afternoons near the Bohenna's beach. Instinctively she knew he would not want to be mothered or have his limited autonomy infringed.

"I don't want you to do anything you are not comfortable with. I think you are here because you want to be, but I am prepared for you to walk away at any moment, and I would have to let you go. I can hardly run after you." He smiled, despite the gravity of what he had just said.

"I'd like to finish my tea first, if it's all the same to you?" Caroline gave a small smile in return.

"There are things we need to talk about, and I don't think here is the right place to do that. I have no way of saying this without it sounding crass and presumptuous, but I have a hotel room booked for the night. I could explain that I wasn't sure if you would be able to join me or not, but we would have to pretend to be married I think."

Tommy's words of caution rang in Caroline's ears. She could stay, the train journey home would be hellish with the delays and the weather, but she had no overnight things. She would have to pretend, he said. No one knew her in Wells, and she assumed no one knew Max either.

Caroline was deep in thought as Max ate his teacake, when the café door opened and soldier in uniform entered noisily with a young woman. The girl made a fuss of her umbrella dripping everywhere and the soldier took off his cap and asked for two cups of coffee across the room before the waitress had time to arrive at their table. Caroline watched the soldier make sure his companion was comfortably seated before pulling out his own chair. As he sat, he looked across at Caroline and winked. He had a strong resemblance to Caroline's now long-dead brother, so much so that she shivered.

"Now, what's your fancy my dear?" The soldier asked, his voice filling the room.

"Oh Fred, I told you I'm on a diet! But if you insist…"

Caroline's teacake had turned to chalk in her mouth at the soldier's name. She took a gulp of tea to help her swallow and then looked at Max who was watching her intently.

"Yes," she said.

The receptionist at the hotel was suspicious of Max's story, particularly as the couple had no suitcases with them, but after looking Caroline up and down decided that she was not a woman of ill repute and added the suffix 'Mrs' to Max's account in the record book. The table for one was amended to a table for two at dinner and breakfast and the room key handed over. Caroline did not say a word and followed Max into the lift next to the staircase. On the first floor their room was at the far end of the corridor. Max unlocked the door and stepped back to let Caroline enter first.

They did not fall straight into bed. After removing their outer clothes and hanging them up to dry out, they sat side by side on one edge of the double bed and talked. Neither of them knew how to fully express the turmoil each was feeling. Eventually Max spoke of Diana by name; he described how cold she had become towards him, and how he hated to rely on her family as much as they had been.

"It is so strange," he said running his right hand through his hair, "I can talk to you easily, yet when I want to talk to

Diana, I have no words. They won't come out of my mouth though my brain is sometimes screaming them."

"I felt like that with Noah."

"Noah?"

"I had met a man, a Coastguard, in Watchet. We were going to live together, but the nearer the time came, the less I felt I could say to him."

"It is maddening. But I wonder even if I could say the words, whether she would understand. I don't think so."

"If you could find a job, and keep it, perhaps … Diana would be less distant with you?" Caroline felt awkward saying the other woman's name.

"We are beyond that now. She will never agree to a divorce though, even if I could afford one. It's something I don't fully understand; she must be as unhappy as I am and yet she won't let go. She resents me, or at least what the war did to me, and her silences often feel more spiteful than indifferent."

"I don't know what my father would think if he knew I was here with you. I think he might be rather disappointed. He's the only person whose opinion really matters to me."

"What about your friends?"

"They care about me of course, but they have their lives to live, and I have mine."

"I would hate myself if I upset your life in any way. It's one reason I suggested Wells to meet, I hoped you wouldn't know anyone here and could remain anonymous if you wanted."

"Well, I appear to be Mrs Bird now." Caroline smiled at the irony.

"Your father sounds a liberal sort."

"I suppose he is rather. He wants me to be happy, I know that much. He meets a lot of different people through his work, and I think he understands how the world has changed since he was young. He's not keen on me driving by myself, but I think he would forgive me almost anything if I were happy."

"And are you?"

Caroline could restrain herself no longer. She took Max's left hand in hers, knowing he could not feel her touch.

"In this moment, I am happy," she said. "And perhaps that is all we can have. Happiness moment by moment."

The next morning Caroline washed herself as best she could in the bathroom along the hallway while Max slept on. She had expected to feel ashamed, tarnished in some way. Yet, as with the morning after she and Max had spent the night together in Cornwall, all she felt was different. This time she would not lower her gaze at breakfast, because Mrs Bird would not have needed to. They had used the contraceptives that Tommy had slipped into her bag on Thursday before he returned to Minehead from the airfield. She had found them when she had looked for her house key on her doorstep in the pouring rain that evening. She had silently agreed with Tommy that a pregnancy would be the very worst outcome for her right at that moment.

Besides the immediate need for breakfast, they would have to decide what to do next. Pragmatically, Caroline felt she could spend one weekend a month in hotels similar to the Overton, moving from town to town around Somerset, for a short while at least. Perhaps a year. If she applied herself to producing some more paintings, particularly from her sketches of Tommy, she would be able to afford the expense. Max had been right, no one there knew her as anything other than Mrs Bird, and she could be better prepared to carry off the pretence next time by bringing a case. Next time. She looked at her reflection in the mirror above the basin. Just when she thought she had settled into a new life in Taunton, everything was changing again. Who was she becoming now? She had sounded more confident the night before describing how her father would forgive just about anything as long as Caroline was happy. In the cold light of day, she was less sure he would approve.

When she returned to the room Max was sitting up in bed smoking a cigarette. It was one thing Caroline disliked, not the act of smoking but how it made her clothes smell of smoke afterwards. The ground crew had been banned from smoking in her office, which they almost always respected.

"You didn't happen to notice if there was a razor in the bathroom at all?" he asked, "I didn't bring anything with me as my cover story was to be visiting an old pal and he would have had a spare."

"I didn't see one, no. What time is breakfast?"

"Seven. I'll go and look, sometimes people forget them, and they keep some in a cupboard somewhere. Could you pass me my clothes?"

"Are you sure you can afford the bill?" Caroline had gathered from Max's comments that money was at the very least tight for him.

"Just, yes."

"Max, let's be sensible about this, I can pay for half. It might make it easier for you to explain later..."

Max agreed it would be difficult to explain to Diana the expense of a hotel room, having told her he was visiting an old army pal. She had shrugged and continued reading the newspaper, hardly acknowledging his presence.

While Max went in search of shaving equipment, Caroline pushed a few coins into his trouser pocket.

They parted at the railway station.

"I am glad you are not driving home in this!" Max said as the rain hammered on the platform canopy.

"It's more convenient to drive, but I do find it tiring in the rain."

"Caroline, I don't know when I shall be able to see you again. Will you be alright?"

"I will be, yes. I am more concerned about you, but whenever you can get away again, just write and tell me where and when. Oh, I think this is my train."

They hesitated for a moment, then Max put his right arm around Caroline's waist and kissed her lips.

"Safe journey," he said.

Caroline said nothing but turned towards her train.

9

A DASH BACK TO CHELTENHAM

The telephone was ringing when Caroline arrived back at Elmsworth that Sunday, soaked through after walking across the town from the railway station to Holway Road. She nudged the front door closed behind her with her hip and pulled one glove off before taking up the receiver.

"Taunton 495, hello?"

"Miss Caroline? It's Sara, ma'am. I'm afraid to say your father's had a funny turn ... what? No, he's at home here. The doctor came and told him to go to bed ... He says you're not to, but that I should telephone you and let you know ... yes, I will ... yes, tomorrow, and he's changed your father's pills again ... well I offered to, but he said no ... Yes, alright. Goodbye."

Now Caroline felt the guilt that had been so elusive that morning. She had been cavorting with a married man while her father had been taken ill and needed her. She replaced the telephone on the hallway table and tried to take off her remaining glove. It stuck to her fingers and the effort was simply too much. Caroline burst into tears and slumped down on the stairs, feeling thoroughly wretched. She had worried about being so far from her father, especially after his illness the year before, and now her fears were justified. She had told Sara to sleep in Caroline's old room that night so that George would not be on his own and to ignore any protest he might make about it.

She blew her nose and stood up to unbutton her coat. Somewhere she knew she had Dr Riley's telephone number. It had been written down for her when she had first ventured to Midge's parents' house just before Christmas 1924, her first taste of the world outside of her restricted social activities. That was a lifetime ago she thought as she rummaged through receipts, letters and other papers on the small table in the sitting room that doubled as a writing desk. At last, she found the number and returned to the hallway.

Dr Riley was not at home, but she left a message for him to call her later that afternoon. When he did, Caroline learned that her father had suffered what the doctor called palpitations, and a shortness of breath, and had been instructed to go to bed and stay there for the rest of the weekend. Dr Riley would be visiting him again in the morning and would admit George to hospital if his condition had not improved. He agreed that it was a good idea for Sara to stay in the spare room that evening and tried to reassure Caroline that it was nothing too serious. He also agreed to telephone her again the following evening with an update. That would give Caroline the opportunity to explain the situation to the ground crew and prime them for her possible need to travel to Cheltenham at short notice.

Caroline's feelings had oscillated from one extreme to another over the course of twenty-four hours. She was exhausted and could not face cooking anything substantial for her dinner that evening. In truth she had little to choose from as she had not dared run across to Farthing's that afternoon in case she missed Dr Riley's telephone call. She stood in the pantry and surveyed her supplies. Half a loaf of bread, some cheese, butter, two tins of tomato soup, some potatoes, three carrots, seven eggs of assorted browns and creams, some powdered custard and in an old biscuit tin, three small fruit cakes in paper cases left from a batch she had made the weekend before. She picked up a tin of soup and took a cake from the tin.

As tired as she was, Caroline spent the evening washing out a few of her underclothes, polishing her shoes and sewing a button back on to a blouse. The radio kept her company as it always did now. She didn't think she would be able to sleep, but her body took over and only moments after laying down, she was snoring gently.

The ground crew were sympathetic to her plight. After offering condolences they left Caroline alone as much as possible that day. She kept busy making sure the week's passenger lists, deliveries and collections were all in order, with a growing feeling that she would go to Cheltenham the following day. The men could cope for a few days without her. She also decided that if she were to go, she would drive this time. As David pointed out, the Austin was reliable, and driving would mean she would have to concentrate on the road rather than dwell on the worst scenarios along the way.

The telephone call from Dr Riley confirmed Caroline's fears. He had decided to admit her father to the hospital as George's pulse was still racing despite his bed rest. George was complaining of cold hands and feet and was needing to urinate more frequently than usual. Caroline said she would be there the following day and would go straight to the hospital. Dr Riley cautioned her to drive sensibly and said he would be at the hospital to meet her. She had known the doctor all of her life, she trusted his judgement, but at the same time, was terrified that things were worse for her father than Dr Riley was letting on.

Caroline went over to Farthing's and caught Ted just as he was closing the shop for the evening. She explained she would be away for a few days and asked if he could keep an eye on the house for her.

"Of course, Miss. Nothing wrong I hope?"

"My father is ill. We only have each other, I need to be with him." As she spoke the words, she had to fight back tears. She felt very much alone already.

"Well now, let me see...," he went back into the shop and came out a moment later with two small paper bags. "Barley sugar twists, to keep your strength up, and one of Irene's steak and kidney pies in case you get hungry on the way."

"Oh Ted, that is so very kind of you. I didn't bring my purse with me..."

Ted held up his hand, "No need, no need. Just drive carefully and we'll make sure everything is alright here, don't you worry."

Caroline broke her journey into sections. The first was her usual route to the airfield, to make sure the crew had their final instructions for filing and payments due. David took the Austin to the nearest garage and filled it up for Caroline while she was talking to Peter and Tommy, and then she was on her way again, heading for Bristol. She stopped to use a public convenience at Cheddar, and then continued on to the centre of Bristol where she had a brief lunch. She topped up the Austin's fuel tank and then took the road out of Bristol to Yate, and onwards through Nailsworth and then to Stroud.

There she detoured from her route and pulled up outside the police houses. She needed to stretch her legs and use the toilet again, and hoped that her old workmate from

Sunningend Engineering would be at home. She heard the babies crying before she reached the door. Lottie's face was a picture of surprise and concern when she discovered Caroline on her doorstep.

"Lummy! You're the last person I expected to see. Come in, what's the matter? You look terrible!" Lottie stood back from the door to allow Caroline to enter.

"I'm sorry Lottie, I can't stay, I'm on my way to see Father at the hospital but I desperately need the lavatory. Would it be alright if I use yours?"

"Of course, you know where it is. And don't mind the twins. They were squabbling so I have put them in their cots to let them cry themselves to sleep. They will quieten down in a few minutes."

Lottie tried to convince Caroline to stay for a cup of tea, but Caroline explained that she was so close to Cheltenham now, she wanted to get going again and then have a proper rest later. She promised to call in again on her way home, and left Lottie in a considerably quieter house fifteen minutes later.

Now she took the winding road from Stroud uphill and through Painswick and then down again, past the Benedictine abbey and around the looping descent of Coopers Hill which, coming as it did towards the end of whole day's driving caused Caroline to slow to a crawl in some places. The rain was her constant companion and now it was growing dark she was concerned she would be unable to find her way for the very last portion of the journey. The lights of Leckhampton and then the edge of Cheltenham finally came into view, and Caroline pulled up outside the hospital at almost six o'clock.

Caroline found Dr Riley in his office near the entrance of the hospital. He explained that he now thought George had suffered a minor heart attack and that his heart was struggling to regain its natural rhythm.

"But he will be alright, won't he?" Caroline felt sick and her head was pounding.

"I think you should come and see him now, my dear," Doctor Riley led her along the corridor to the men's ward.

George lay in a bed on the right, just inside the door. He had a grey hue to his skin and his eyes were closed, though he was propped up on pillows with the head of the bed raised to support him in an almost sitting position. Caroline looked at Dr Riley, who smiled gentle at her and nodded his head in encouragement. She took a few steps towards the bed.

"Father?"

George's eyes opened slowly, and he turned his head towards her voice.

"Darling girl. I told Sara there was no need for you to come up."

"And I told her I would, regardless." Caroline sat on the chair next to the bed and took off her hat. "Now that I have the motor car, there would be no stopping me."

"You drove the whole way by yourself? Oh now Caroline, really…"

"Yes I did, with two or three stops along the way. I have spoken to Dr Riley, and he tells me it is your heart that is giving you trouble. He has you on warfarin and is confident you will be up and about in no time."

Dr Riley had said no such thing, but Caroline knew from her experience with her mother's illnesses that positivity was to be maintained with the patient even in the final moments. George was not persuaded but decided to go along with the deceit.

"I am sure after a few days here, I shall be able to go home again." His voice was paper thin, "You will stay at the apartment?"

"Yes. I might go and see Annie while I am here tomorrow before I come and see you again."

"I had meant to tell you in our next telephone conversation. Annie had a baby boy last week. I believe they are to call him either Dennis or Walter. Sara will know more."

"How wonderful, and perhaps you will be Godfather again to the baby as you are to Victor."

"Perhaps." George closed his eyes again for a moment. Caroline wondered if he had fallen asleep when he spoke again even more quietly, "If you need them, there are some papers in the left-hand drawer of my desk. The solicitor will handle everything."

Caroline could not speak for fear of crying. She took hold of George's cold hand and held it in both of her own. George squeezed her hands briefly.

"Freddie would have been proud of you, my girl, as I am." He whispered.

Half an hour later, Caroline was woken by Dr Riley's hand on her shoulder. She had fallen asleep in her chair, still holding on to her father's hand, her head resting against his shoulder.

"Caroline, I think you need to let go now."

She sat up, fuzzy with exhaustion. Slowly she realised that the coldness in her father's hand was more pronounced. She looked at his face and then his chest.

"Come along now..." Dr Riley gently took her hands away from George's and prompted her to stand. She looked at him dumbly. "Come into my office. I'll get you a glass of water." He led her away from the bed as a nurse drew the curtains around George.

Dr Riley had seen the situation a hundred times or more, yet Caroline's mute, stunned reaction reminded him so much of her mother's response to the death of Freddie. The difference now being, Caroline was the last of the Munheads and as such there was no immediate family who would take care of her. He was concerned that she would want to drive herself to Norwood Court, and while she sat silently in his office, he telephoned the railway station and arranged for a taxi to come and collect her instead. The Austin would be safe at the hospital until she was able to retrieve it.

He then telephoned Ferris the doorman at Norwood Court and asked if he had a number for Sara. Ferris knew the Johnson's did not have a telephone but on hearing the news about George he offered to personally make his way over to Rowanfield and bring the girl back to the apartments. Dr Riley agreed that this would be the best course of action and thanked Ferris before replacing the receiver. When he turned back to Caroline, to his relief she was crying into her handkerchief.

The rest of the week passed over and around Caroline. She was capable of the administration of the funeral arrangements and made two visits to her father's solicitor in the town to become acquainted with the contents of George's will. The staff at the Cheltenham and Gloucester Benefits Building Society sent a card of condolence and the acting manager, a Mr Foxton, offered to act on her behalf in all financial matters relating to George's estate. For much of the time, Caroline felt as if she were herself acting in a play. She felt outside of herself and detached from her inner anguish. She had become an orphan at the age of twenty-four.

Gradually, between bouts of crying over the smallest of things such as seeing George's shoes in the hallway waiting to be buffed, or finding the book he had been reading with the page marked by a strip of paper Caroline had painted a rose on years before as a bookmark, Caroline began to accept her situation. The rain had temporarily ceased, and the funeral director had been persuaded that Saturday morning would be the most suitable time to lay George to rest. Caroline had not wanted to receive the mourners at the apartment, and instead Dr Riley offered his house which Caroline gratefully accepted. This meant Caroline could escape back to the apartment if everything got too much for her. She did not feel she wanted to be polite to people she hardly knew.

The ceremony at Christ Church was brief. The mourners attended the plot at the cemetery in Prestbury where George was laid to rest with Elizabeth. They then moved singly, in pairs and in small groups to Dr Riley's house at Sydenham Villas. Jacob Jenks had been among them, paying his respects on behalf of Annie and the boys while she was still recovering from Dennis' birth. After an hour Caroline was about to tell Dr Riley that she wanted to leave, when a familiar figure appeared in the hallway, cap in hand and staring around at the mourners looking for her. Caroline made her way over to him.

"Bob. Thank you for coming."

"Caroline, I was so sorry to hear about your father. He was a good man."

Caroline produced the handkerchief that Bob and Lottie had given her the Christmas that her mother had died, "Once again, your gift has been useful. But tell me, how is the house coming along?"

They moved into the drawing room and Bob was handed a small glass of sherry by a young girl in a maid's uniform.

"It is watertight. The chickens don't like all this rain, but I shall get two or three more in the spring. But you don't want to hear about my chickens."

"Oh Bob, right now it is the only thing I want to hear about! This week has been so awful, and I am so glad you are here. I always told Father that I could depend upon you."

"You did? You can. You know I will always help you if ever I can. Is there anything I can do for you now?"

"Not materially, no, thank you. The solicitor and Mr Foxton have been most kind and Father had kept the most meticulous records of everything. But please, Bob, tell me about your chickens."

When Bob left the wake, he knew he would be unlikely to see Caroline again. She had told him of her plans to sell the apartment with Mr Foxton's assistance. She had no need to return to Cheltenham now that Philip and Mary Rose had moved away, unless she wanted to visit Annie and the children. He had listened to her description of her work at the airfield, and how she now drove herself around in her Austin and knew she had moved another step away from him. He was pleased for her and hoped she would be looked after by her friends. All the same, he wished he had been able to take her home and look after her himself.

It was only on her drive back to Taunton on Sunday 11 November, that Caroline realised the anniversary of Freddie's death had passed unmarked that year. She stopped again at Cheddar, and after spending a penny, she walked the short distance to the war memorial in the village. The poppy wreaths from that morning's service of remembrance fluttered in the strengthening wind. There were no Munheads on the memorial list of those lost in the war, but Caroline stood for a few moments as the rain began to fall once again.

"You are all together now, and I am still here," she said out loud. "I shan't forget."

How could I, she thought as she returned to the Austin, now there are two anniversaries in November so close to each other.

The ground crew understood loss. They understood Caroline's determination to return to work and made valiant attempts to treat her as if she had not just lost her last known living relative. There was a job to do, and after a week on their own, they all wanted Caroline to do it. Rupert asked David what he thought the chances were of Caroline investing some of her inheritance in the airfield, and David told him curtly that if he heard Rupert ask Caroline about it, he would give him a good thrashing. She knew the state of their finances, David said, and if she wanted to invest, she would volunteer the money herself without Rupert's encouragement.

The thought had crossed Caroline's mind. Until the apartment was sold, she had no idea the full extent of George's estate, but the solicitor Mr Embry had indicated it would be enough to purchase a house if she wished and provide an income of around one hundred and fifty pounds a year. Caroline had at first been astounded, but with her rudimentary maths she quickly understood that George had only continued to work after her mother's death because he wanted to leave Caroline with as much as possible. His reorganisation of their investment portfolio had proved a wise move, and those shares all now came to her. Provision for young Victor Jenks had been made with the sum equivalent to the amount that would have accrued over the years until his twenty-first birthday made over in George's will to his Godson. Mr Embry advised Caroline to make no impulsive purchases just yet unless absolutely necessary, but to wait until the affairs had been fully wound up. She was not rich, but she would be comfortable for as long as the investments held their worth.

Caroline asked Mr Foxton to advance the rent that would be due on Elmsworth until the end of January 1929 to the estate agent in Taunton. She gave him Edna's name and asked that he include an invitation for her to call on Caroline one evening. The arrangement for the rent would give her some time to decide whether to stay at Elmsworth and meant that she would not need to call in to the agent every Saturday and pay what was due. The account that George had opened for Caroline with Lloyds Bank in Cheltenham would enable her to draw funds virtually anywhere in the country. Naturally Mr Foxton hoped Caroline might leave her savings with the Cheltenham and Gloucester Building Society, and she agreed. Between Mr Foxton and Mr Embry, her finances would, she felt, be in safe hands.

She had not completely forgotten about Max, but he had receded in her mind while she dealt with her father's death. As things settled down again, Max began to move forwards in her thoughts. She wondered when she would hear from him, whether it would be before Christmas. Should she buy him a gift? No, he would have to keep whatever she bought him away from Diana and she didn't want to make things more difficult for him than they already were. One thing was clear to her now; no one else's opinion of her or her behaviour mattered. She no longer had to worry if her father would approve of Max.

Helen's reaction still troubled Caroline and she didn't know what to do to repair the damaged friendship. Tommy was little help; when he and Helen had argued, particularly after his arrest in Exeter, he had put physical distance between them for a while and only went back when he had a new plan to put to Helen. Caroline already had distance between herself and Helen, and there was no new plan. In the end, Caroline could see no other way than to visit Helen and try to explain again her position. She enlisted Tommy's help to make sure Helen would be at home and caught the train to Minehead on 24 November.

The weather was atrocious. The whole country was becoming bogged down in wet clothes, flooded roads and rail lines, and the endless grey skies. Caroline was admitted to the house overlooking Blenheim Gardens by Tommy who took her coat and told her Helen was in the sitting room. Mrs Rich the housekeeper was ill with flu. Tommy said if they wanted him to make tea, he would be in the kitchen reading his newspaper. Caroline opened the sitting room door.

"Hello Helen."

"Darling do come in and close the door. There is a frightful draft with it open." Helen was near the fireplace and had apparently been waiting only for Caroline's arrival as there was no open book or magazine nearby.

Caroline crossed the room and kissed Helen's cheek in greeting. Then she sat on the chair opposite.

"I was very sorry to hear about your father. It must have been such a shock for you."

"Yes, it all happened so fast."

"Better that way than to linger as Sophia did for years." Helen's sister had suffered from tuberculosis for several years before her death, only a few weeks after marrying her husband. "Shall we have tea? Or would you rather have something stronger?"

"It's a little early for that. Tea would be nice, thank you."

Helen stood up and went in search of Tommy, returning after a few moments with a plate of biscuits. She placed it on the coffee table and then lit a cigarette before she sat down again. Caroline decided to get straight to the point of her visit.

"Helen, when we spoke last, you made your feelings very clear to me about how you view Max. I don't want our friendship to be broken because of it."

Helen exhaled a stream of smoke, "Neither do I. I was perhaps a little forceful in my initial opinion. Tommy tells me you were rather upset and I apologise for that. Did you see this Max as you intended?"

"I did."

Helen sighed.

"Can I explain? Will you listen without getting angry with me?" Caroline sat forward in her seat, "Please?"

Tommy opened the sitting room door and brought in a tray of tea things. He sensed the mood of the room, said nothing, and left the two most important women in his life to their discussion.

"I will try,"

"I know how it will sound, I have thought how I would feel if a friend of mine were in a similar position, with … with a married man. I truly never thought I would see Max again after Cornwall. Helen, I cannot explain the attraction I feel towards him. I have never felt it with anyone else, not James and certainly not Noah."

Helen reached forward and poured the tea, "Go on," she said.

"Tommy pointed out to me that Max must be lying, or at least not telling the whole truth, to me or his wife. I asked Max, and I believe that he has not lied."

Helen looked up but said nothing. She wondered how much influence Caroline's recent reading material had had on her view of the situation. Helen was not a fan of Mrs Woolfe.

"I believe that he has not lied to his wife, but he has not told her everything. And I believe that his wife does not want to know. Of course, I only have Max's version of events, and I am not as experienced in relationships as you are, but what little experience I do have leads me to believe that Max's wife does not engage in conversation with him. As she will not speak to him, he does not elaborate to her." She sipped her tea, aware that Helen was listening intently.

"We talked for a long time when we met in Wells. Before anything else happened between us. Max said several times that he would understand if I wanted to leave, or if I was uncomfortable. He wasn't pleading or trying to make me feel sorry for him. We simply talked. He says his wife will not agree to a divorce, and he doesn't know how to persuade her. We have agreed to take it all one step at a time. I cannot contact him; I have to wait for him to contact me."

Helen stubbed out her cigarette in a heavy black Bakelite ashtray. Caroline appeared to have finished speaking and Helen had not changed her original opinion of Max or the position that Caroline had created for herself. However, she felt bad at how their telephone conversation had ended before, and really did not want to lose Caroline's friendship. Her skills at negotiation and compromise that she had been honing through her young career in politics would be needed now.

"You cannot contact him, or you will not?" she asked.

"Cannot. I don't have his address and they don't have a telephone."

"Do you not think it strange that he has not trusted you with his address?"

"I think … I think he is trying to protect his wife. I don't think Max wants to deliberately hurt her. He seems genuinely sad that his marriage has not been successful."

"And who is protecting you?"

"I don't think I need protecting. Honestly, I don't. The only person who I would truly not want to upset was my father.

I didn't have a chance to tell him about Max. Now that I am on my own, whatever I choose to do is my responsibility."

"Caro, forgive me for being vulgar, but you are now a woman of means, are you not? Who is protecting your interests?"

"My solicitor and the new manager who has replaced my father at the Building Society. Max doesn't know about my father's death though. He knows that I work, and that I live by myself, but he doesn't know about my other income. I did tell him about my art and how well it sells in London, but that's all."

Helen sat back and crossed her legs, "You are utterly serious about this fellow, aren't you. I simply want you to not be blinded by infatuation. I know what first love feels like. I know one can agree to all kinds of absurdities in the name of love. But if Max cannot get a divorce, what future do you see for yourself?"

"I am not looking into the future, Helen. I cannot. I think that is why I have been so unsettled this year; I have tried seeing a future and working towards it, but I simply am not able to. Plans can change. Promises can be broken. I want to take each day as it happens. And I now have the financial means to be able to do that."

"Yes, but what will you be working for? I assume you will continue at the airfield? They all seem to be happy with your work there according to Tommy. Do you want to purchase a house? Do you want to travel overseas? Do you want to… I don't know, fund an orphanage? You must have some idea of where you want to be in a year's time." Helen was struggling with the concept of living day by day. She had always had a goal, whether it was making a good impression at the next party, or obtaining an invitation to an event, and more recently gaining political power as a local councillor.

She had begun to think of her next steps and been having conversations with the Party about standing as the constituency MP in the future. Helen wanted to achieve and be recognised. Something she had so often failed to do with her parents.

Caroline by contrast had always had the attention of her parents, and for much of her life, too much attention. She had not needed to plan because her parents had planned for her. When the time had come to consider planning, Caroline had opted to grasp opportunity instead. It was her way.

"I will continue as I am now, until I decide to do something else. I might see another vacancy that interests me, or I might decide to fly to Paris or Amsterdam and explore Europe. I have no plan, but I know I want to spend time with Max when I can."

Helen drank her tea. A small part of her was envious of Caroline's sudden freedom. She still found the idea of an affair with a married man distasteful but accepted that Caroline had at least considered the other woman and accepted that the damage should be kept to a minimum. Helen would have to watch and wait, and hopefully not have to pick up any pieces of Caroline later.

"Won't you have a biscuit?" She smiled as genuinely as she could at Caroline, "and I will go and tell Tommy that he can come and warm himself by the fire. You'll stay for lunch?"

Caroline left Minehead with a sense of relief. Her friendship had been saved, and while she knew Helen would not welcome Max with open arms, she did at least understand a little more how Caroline felt. Tommy had also been relieved that the women had patched things up and hoped the affair with Max would not be a constant threat. He walked Caroline back through the town to the railway station and gave her a big hug in the ticket office.

"You know we both adore you," he said.

"I know, and I feel the same about you and Helen. See you on Tuesday."

10

A DECISION IS MADE

Max was in the dark little sitting room when Diana arrived home. He had no idea where she had been; she had gone out while he was on his daily search for employment. Diana pushed the sitting room door open further and walked in, saw Max in his chair and abruptly turned to leave again.

"Diana!"

She stopped, one hand on the doorknob, still facing the hallway outside.

"Diana, we need to talk. Please come and sit down."

She turned slowly but made no move towards the chair. Max's face was half in shadow, which made the space where his ear should have been more obvious. Diana resisted an urge to walk out of the room. How she hated seeing that side of his face; the scarred and patched surface, stretched smooth and then puckered and stitched like some macabre doll dismembered in a tug-of-war by two rival children. How she hated the weight of his numb arm on her skin. His useless leg attached to his useless body, which no one wanted to employ.

They had had dreams of children, dreams of a house on the edge of the city, which Max would have used his draughtsman skills to design and pay for. She would have entertained a small but select and influential group of friends, whose husbands would all have held similar positions. Bank managers, solicitors, doctors, respectable businessmen, their wives dressed in stylish but sensible outfits and involved in charitable enterprises. Max had thrown all of their dreams to the four winds and returned not once but twice from the war, unable to stand, unable to hear or see properly and unable to recapture those dreams and make them reality.

She could not forgive him for returning to the front a second time when he had been offered a discharge. She had pleaded with him; no one would thrust a white feather at him, no one would think him a coward. Yet now she felt his cowardice was at the core of his return to the front. He could not make their dreams come true, so he had run away, back to the men in the trenches, back to the mud and the guns and the blood, in the hope that the war might end what it had already damaged. She despised him for that. She despised him every time her father paid a bill on their behalf, every time her mother pressed a few coins into Diana's hand and whispered, "for the coal" or "for a bit of pork".

She despised Max for not being Franklin, her sister's husband, and she despised her sister Louise for achieving what Diana had not. Franklin had returned unscathed. Franklin had picked up where he had left off with his career as a veterinary surgeon. Franklin and Louise had married in the pretty parish church on a sunny summer's day and lived now just over the border with Wiltshire in Limpley Stoke. Of course, Franklin drank a little too much; that was to be expected of a man with his responsibilities.

Max had tricked her. He had promised he would return in a few months. He had been away for three years. He had promised her they would have children. She had endured his advances with that one goal in mind, yet it had become clear that he had tricked her there too. He had promised, as soon as he was healthy again, he would find work, they would move out of their little house and into a brighter cottage somewhere not dissimilar to Limply Stoke. They were still in Bath, ten years on.

"I prefer to stand," she said, her voice betraying none of the emotion she felt.

"Diana, we … I cannot continue with this hostility. I am sorry that our lives have not turned out the way we had hoped, but I have tried, so hard, to provide for us. I don't know what else I can do, but I know that you are not happy, and neither am I. Please Diana, will you consider a divorce?"

The indignity! The scorn she would be subjected to, the pity, the social stigma. This coward was trying to run away again! Her father had offered some months ago to pay for a divorce if Diana had wanted one, but she had said no then, and she would say no now. If Max thought he could just turn the page and begin a new chapter, then he was mistaken. He had made his bed, and he must lie in it.

"I will not." She almost spat the words. She turned to leave the room.

"Diana!" Max shouted. He had never raised his voice to her before. He struggled to get up out of the chair and followed her into the kitchen where she was filling the kettle with water.

"Diana, you can't keep walking away from this! Stop that for a moment. This is no way for two people to live. You cannot ignore me forever!"

"Ignore you?" Now it was her turn to shout, "Ignore you? How could that even be possible when everything in this marriage revolves around you?! Your needs, your wants, your hospital visits, your surgeries, your inability to find a job! All of this is always about you!"

Max was stung, and shocked by the anger of her accusations.

"Do you think I want to be like this? Do you think I enjoy being stared at, whispered about, poked and prodded like a joint of beef?" He saw the look she gave him, "My God, you do, don't you?"

"You chose to go back when you could have stayed. You gave no thought to me, to our marriage, to whether I could cope!"

"I had to go back – don't you understand, I had to face it all again to try and make sense of it all. So many of the boys were giving everything, I had to go back. What if we'd all said, 'well that's it then, I'll stay home now,' what kind of life would we have now?"

"We could have had a better one than this! You could have found another job; we could have had children…" the word caught in her throat.

"We would have been living under Fritz and God knows what nightmare society. I might not have found another job; we might not have ever been able to have children. For God's sake, I could have died over there!"

"I wish you had!" Diana screamed at him.

They stared at each other across the scrubbed kitchen table. Diana's wild eyes and the hatred she had for everything that she felt had happened to her in that moment burned into Max's own. He had had no idea how deeply her sense of injustice had taken root. He turned away awkwardly and left the kitchen.

"That's right! Run away again, just like you always do!" Diana shouted after him, swinging the kettle wildly and spilling water onto the floor.

Max climbed the stairs with difficulty, feeling that his legs had turned to lead. Diana hated him. It was not something he had been prepared for. He knew she had been unhappy but had thought it was because she still loved him, and he had let her down. Now he knew that love had long gone, trodden into the ground and buried under suffocating soil, with no marker to show it had ever existed. He pulled an old case out from underneath his bed and opened it. It contained some papers, including his final discharge papers, and his uniform. Three medals were pinned to the jacket. His silver British War medal, his Allied Victory medal with its bright rainbow ribbon, and his silver King's War Badge given to all soldiers who were discharged early from service.

He unpinned all three, then took the uniform out of the case and laid it on his bed. He returned the medals to the case, along with the discharge scroll and the other papers, then began adding the contents of his wardrobe. It took only a few minutes, and his clothes were not neatly folded. He looked around the room. The book on his bedside table went into the case, followed by his small bundle of pencils and sketch book. His grooming kit, pension book and post office account book, the photograph of his mother, his small telescope that he sometimes used to look into the night sky, the contents of the top drawer in his dresser, and finally the set of tiles he had glazed in Cornwall. He unwrapped them from the sacking, and rearranged them to lay flat against his clothes, using the sacking to protect them against the lid of the case as he closed it. He put on his coat and hat, picked up the case from the bed, and with a final glance around the room, he left.

On her way back through Taunton from the railway station, Caroline called into the estate agent's office to see Edna. They arranged to visit the cinema the following Friday, and Edna said how sorry she had been to hear of Caroline's father's passing. Caroline accepted the condolences and asked for the remaining balance on the telephone line installation to be billed to Mr Foxton.

On leaving the agent's office, Caroline picked up some groceries to see her through a couple of days before she would rely on Farthing's again. She bought some whitebait to fry for her dinner that evening, along with a skinned rabbit and some liver and kidney, a pound of brussels sprouts and a pound of chestnuts. Her basket full, she walked down South Street and into Holway Road.

Jonathan was in the street, riding his new bicycle up and down. It had been a birthday present, the week before but only now was the weather dry enough for him to try it out. He wobbled and had to keep putting his feet down. Caroline watched his progress as she neared Elmsworth, reminded of her own determined experience under Annie's supervision on her bicycle, now idle in the shed at the end of the garden.

"Hello Jonathan! That's a fine bicycle," she called as rode towards her.

He came to a juddering halt, applying the brakes a little too enthusiastically, "Good afternoon, Miss Munhead. Isn't it a wonderful machine!"

"Just be careful not to get too close to the motor cars."

"Oh, I shall. Miss Munhead, there was a man here earlier. He knocked on your door and asked me if I knew where you were."

"A man? I wonder who that could have been. Did he give you his name?"

"No. When I told him you went out rather a lot, he asked where the nearest pub was. I told him the Boatman and he gave me a sixpence and went off in that direction."

"Jonathan, what did the man look like?"

"Jolly strange. He had no ear!"

Caroline thanked the boy and hurried indoors. Her heart was thumping in her chest and she felt breathless. What was Max doing here? They had agreed that he would write, and they would meet elsewhere. She felt a little afraid, could she have misjudged him and now be in danger? She put her groceries away and stoked up the fire in the range. It would be dark soon; she decided to lay the fire in the sitting room. It was not something she did every evening, preferring to sit in the kitchen under the central room light if she had mending or washing to do. Weekends tended to be the exception, and when she was at home, Sunday afternoon by the fire with her knitting was how she usually spent her time.

She swept out the old ashes into her dustpan and tipped them into the steel dustbin beside the back door. Some of the old coal from the previous fire was saved onto a sheet of newspaper. More newspaper was scrunched up into lose balls and set on the grate. A layer of thin kindling wood went on top of the paper, then the old grey coals and finally some sticky black nuggets of fresh coal on the top. Caroline refilled the coal scuttle from the bunker in the back garden, and then brought in four split logs from her small store next to the bunker and set them down on the tiled hearth. She glanced at the mantle clock. It was almost four o'clock, and she decided to light the fire then to warm the sitting room for the evening. The matches were kept beside the clock, and Caroline struck one and held it to the newspaper through the edge of the grate in several places so that it would burn evenly. Satisfied that it would not go out, she replaced the matchbox and went to wash her hands.

In the Boatman, Max sat at a small round table with his second half pint of bitter in a handled glass. He had spent the train journey from Bath to Taunton rehearsing what he would say to Caroline on her doorstep. That she would not be at home hadn't occurred to him, yet the boy on the bicycle had said she was often not at home. The Austin was parked outside so he assumed she hadn't gone far. He wondered if he had misjudged Caroline, if she perhaps had another man or more in her sights and was at that moment walking arm in arm with someone. What would he do then? He could not go back to Bath, that was now out of the question. He would have to move on, perhaps spend the night on the station platform and then tomorrow head off somewhere, anywhere, and start again.

The barman came to collect some glasses and wipe down the tables as the other drinkers were moving off to their waiting homes.

"Can I get you another?" He asked Max.

"No thanks. I'd better get off."

"What are you selling?"

"Sorry?"

"Selling – in your case?"

"Oh, no, I'm not a salesman. I'm visiting a … someone. I was just waiting for them to return home."

"Ahh, I see. I thought perhaps you had some dusters or clothes pegs to sell. Always try and buy something from a fellow soldier."

"Sorry to disappoint you. I'll be getting along," Max drained his glass, put on his hat and made his way out into the glow of the streetlamps in their nightly combat against the darkness.

Caroline had busied herself with making up the spare bed which she hoped would not be needed, and with sweeping the stairs and ground floor of the house. She could stretch her groceries to feed two that evening and then top up her larder again at Farthing's the next day. If he stayed. He might not. He could be here to tell her that it was all too much, that he had made a mistake and they really would never see each other again.

She was in the kitchen, putting a little flour, salt and pepper into a saucer ready for the whitebait when she heard the knock at the front door. Wiping her hands on a tea towel, she went to answer it.

"Oh, Mr Collier, it's you!"

"Sorry to disturb you, Miss Munhead. Only Jonathan said there had been a strange fellow hanging around and asking after you earlier. I thought I'd just make sure everything was alright." He looked a little embarrassed now that he could see Caroline was in rude health.

"Yes, yes I am absolutely alright, thank you Mr Collier. I do appreciate your concern. One can't be too careful. But I know the fellow who was here earlier, and I rather hope he will be back again soon."

Johnny Collier was visibly relieved that he hadn't made a complete fool of himself. "Oh well, that's alright then. As long as he's not a ruffian trying his luck. You bang on the wall if he is though, and I'll come straight round."

"I'm sure there will be no need but thank you again. Good night."

"Good night."

Well, that would be the whole street aflame with gossip by the end of church tomorrow, Caroline thought as she returned to her fish. No doubt she would sink even lower in Winnifred's estimations once Johnny confirmed the 'strange fellow' was known to her. She sighed. It reminded her of the Thursday afternoon gossip exchange her mother had presided over with her acquaintances at their old house in Glencairn Road.

Caroline took an egg from the pantry, broke it into a cup and whisked it with a fork for a moment before setting the cup down on the kitchen table next to the saucer of flour. She would dip the small fish into the egg, then toss them in the flour, and stack them onto a third plate ready to shallow fry on the hotplate. She was about to begin her production line when another knock came from the front door.

Max had to put his case down to knock, then picked it up again and waited. He could see that Caroline was at home now with the lights on in the house. He hoped she did not have company. He was starting to feel that he should have warned her before arriving. It was too late now as the door opened.

"Come in, I was hoping you would come back…"

"Caroline, I hope I'm not …"

They had spoken at the same time, and Caroline smiled and moved back to let Max enter. He stepped from the dark to the light and set down his case on the hallway floor.

"I hope this isn't inconvenient."

"Not at all, but it is a surprise," Caroline registered that Max was not smiling. "Is something wrong?"

Max took off his hat slowly and looked at Caroline. She could not be more different to Diana, in looks, in behaviour, in substance. How could he drag her down with him?

"I … I think I have made a mistake. I'm sorry, Caroline." He replaced his hat and picked up his case as if to leave.

"What? Max, don't be absurd! Whatever the reason you are here, it's not a mistake. It simply can't be. Come along now, put your hat and coat on the peg and I will make some tea."

She slid past him and went into the kitchen, leaving Max in the hallway. Again, slowly, he took off his hat and shrugged off his coat. He tucked the case against the wall beneath the coat pegs and followed Caroline to the rear of the house.

"I was about to make some dinner. Are you hungry?"

He had not eaten since breakfast.

Caroline brought two potatoes from the pantry and sliced them thinly to go with the fried fish. They did not speak while she worked. Max felt overwhelmingly tired, mentally and physically from all that had happened that day. He watched Caroline's confident movements and was reassured by them. Caroline moved her large frying pan onto the hotplate and added dripping from an enamel mug. She put the kettle back onto the hotplate and added fresh tea leaves to the teapot. Only then did she turn to Max.

"Tell me what has happened, Max."

"Diana and I had a row this morning. I had to leave. I have left her."

"Oh, Max." Caroline sank into a chair and reached for his hand.

"She truly hates me. Hates what I have done to her, she said. She wished I had died at the front. I suppose that would have been a cleaner end to it all for her."

"She … she actually said that?"

"Yes. Well, screamed it at me to be accurate. I had no idea that she felt so strongly."

He looked utterly defeated.

"And so, your case …"

"I packed what was important to me. I can find a hotel or something. I just wanted to see you. To tell you."

"Do you have money for a hotel?"

"A little, enough for one or two nights."

"Then save it. You must stay here."

"But your neighbours, the gossip will …"

"Will run like wildfire, yes I know, and I honestly don't care. They already think I am a little odd for being here by myself and having my own motor car. At least this will just confirm their suspicions! Look, the bathroom is through there, go and wash your hands while I cook dinner and then when we've eaten, we can talk about what happens next."

It did not escape Caroline that her relationship with Noah had had similar beginnings. He had arrived on her doorstep exhausted and ill, in the middle of a summer storm, and she had nursed him for several days while he recovered. Yet she had never slept with Noah, despite what some women in Watchet had thought. She had never felt the desire to in the way she did with Max. Even now, she felt the need to touch him, but knew they must talk first.

They ate in companionable silence, and Max began to relax. He smiled as she poured more tea for them both and started to feel as if he had not turned Caroline's world upside down as well as his own, and Diana's. He had no idea what he would do about his wife. She would surely have realised by now that he had taken his belongings. It was strange, he thought, that he did not consider any of the furniture to be his. She could have it all and do with it as she pleased. He looked around the small kitchen at the odds and ends that Caroline had accumulated in her ten weeks of residence. There were dots of colour all around the room, from the teapot, the tea towel, the small vase on the mantle above the range, the red rag rug on the floor. He wondered how the rest of the house was furnished, and how different it would feel to the house he had left behind with its starched tablecloths and dark furniture.

"Will you give the fire a poke while I wash the dishes, please? You can turn the wireless on if you like." Caroline broke into his thoughts.

Max stood up, his chair scraping on the kitchen floor, and went into the sitting room, noting the dining room on the side of the house that Caroline rarely used. Before taking up the poker, he surveyed the sitting room with the same wonder as he had the kitchen. He did not know that Caroline had deliberately used light-coloured furnishings in there to counter the fact that the room was in constant shade. A large deep blue rug, slightly worn in places, almost covered the entire floor. Two armchairs stood on either side of the fireplace, which sported pale beige and cream glazed tiles. A blonde-wood mantle clock ticked solemnly onwards next to a box of Swan Vesta. A table near the window was covered with various letters, papers and envelopes and a folded copy of a newspaper. Two more small tables were beside the chairs, with small lamps. The wireless stood against the wall opposite the window. Max turned the knob, and the sound of an orchestra gently grew in volume. It was a comfortable room, he thought, and one that so obviously contained Caroline. The paintings of the sea on the walls, and the knitting in a basket by one of the chairs. Max returned to the fire and used the poker to stoke it before using tongs to add a few lumps of coal which immediately sent a plume of smoke up the chimney. Then he sat in the chair opposite the one he assumed Caroline favoured and waited for their discussion to begin.

Over glasses of brandy, either side of the fireplace, they talked until almost eleven o'clock. Neither of them knew how divorce proceedings were initiated, and Max felt sure that Diana would still not make any attempt to sever their marriage completely. Caroline talked for a while about the death of her father, and of her estimated inheritance. She explained that the rent had been paid for the next two months on Elmsworth to give her time to consider whether to stay on there. Max told her of his army pension, fifteen shillings a week in recompense for his injuries.

They considered possibilities such as Max finding his own lodgings for a while, but quickly dismissed that idea. Employment would be his first priority, though he was not optimistic given his poor luck in Bath. Caroline said he must stay with her until he found something, and then they could decide whether he would stay on or not. As she said it, she knew she would not want him to leave. As he agreed, he knew he would not want to go. Max was adamant that he did not want Caroline to be named in any divorce if Diana did decide to proceed with one. Caroline said she didn't care, but Max pointed out that if she needed to find another job one day, that piece of legal record could work against her, and she conceded.

Max understood that he would be alone in the house during the day while Caroline was at work, and that she already had engagements that he would not be able to attend with her. He decided that he would send Diana ten shillings a week from his pension until he found a job. Caroline agreed that would be appropriate. She did not think Max would add much expense to her overall outgoings, as the rent was already covered, and the Austin's running costs were within her means from her pay from the airfield.

When they had let the fire die down and talked themselves almost to sleep, they turned the lights out and went up to the back bedroom together.

By the end of the week, when Caroline had arranged to visit the cinema with Edna, Max had become familiar with Caroline's routine and was beginning to make himself useful while she was at work. Each morning he would get up early when she did and get the range going while she was in the bathroom. He would wave her off in the Austin, then carefully wash the breakfast things before shaving and dressing ready to go out. They had agreed that Max would have the back door key and use the side gate as Elsie had, not because Caroline was concerned with gossip but because it seemed the most practical solution until they could get another front door key cut.

Max had been introduced to Ted and Irene. Ted shook his hand warmly, and Irene discovered his love for liquorish. A shopkeeper could not afford to judge their customers, they had agreed privately later. Max bought a daily *Morning Echo* and studied the situations vacant column, circling possible opportunities in pencil while at the kitchen table. If there was a telephone number on the advert, he would make a call to arrange an interview. If there was none, he would ask Ted the whereabouts of the business in the town. He made a plan that on Thursday afternoon he would visit three business all within walking distance of each other and try to speak to the managers.

He was somewhat despondent by Friday. He had attended two interviews, but only one had seemed positive and he would have to wait to hear the outcome. Caroline remained positive and suggested that they take a drive into the country at the weekend and forget about jobs and other people for a few hours. He walked slowly into the town centre and cashed his pension slip for fifteen shillings at the post office, converting ten shillings into a postal order. This he pushed into an envelope that he had addressed to Diana, sealed it, added a stamp to the front, and dropped it into the letter box outside. He had eight shillings and three pence to his name but felt a strange sense of elation when he heard the envelope hit the other letters inside the post box. He was taking responsibility, doing the right thing.

When Caroline arrived home on Friday, Max had put two potatoes and two lamb chops in the oven to cook for their dinner. On the kitchen table was a small white paper bag.

"What's in there?" Caroline asked.

"I thought about flowers, but then Irene said you liked sugar mice."

"Oh, thank you!" She kissed him with a smile, and he laughed.

"If I had known the way to a woman's heart was through a pink mouse, life could have been so much easier," he said.

"Are you sure you don't mind not coming this evening?" Caroline asked over their meal.

"No, I don't mind. I have a bottle of beer and the wireless. I'm not sure about you walking home by yourself though."

"No, I shall drive, and then I can take Edna home as well. I know she lives in town, but I'd like to do that."

"Edna works at the agents who own this house, is that right?"

"Yes, it's her father's business. I'd better get a move on; I'm meeting her at seven!"

The women enjoyed the film programme, a comedy and a newsreel. As they got into the Austin afterwards, Edna told Caroline she had received a letter from Hugh that morning. The friend whose address they were using had dropped the letter into the office for her, wrapped inside a magazine.

"It's all very cloak and dagger, isn't it!" Observed Caroline.

"It has to be. But he sounded in good spirits and has been speaking to another chap there who wants to open a motor garage when he is released."

"Really? Does Hugh know anything about motor cars?"

"Oh yes, he loves messing about with them."

"Edna, I appreciate that you have taken me into your confidence over Hugh. My circumstances have changed recently as you know something of, and I want to tell you something that I need you to keep to yourself also, if you could."

"Of course. It's such a relief to be able to talk to someone about Hugh. You can tell me anything."

"A man I have known for a while has come to stay with me."

Edna was quiet for a moment, "When you say stay with you, do you mean …"

"Yes, I do."

"Well, that's not so shocking these days is it."

"No, perhaps not. There is a fly in the ointment though in that he is married."

"Oh."

Caroline started the engine and drove towards Edna's street.

"So, is he staying with you and then going back to his wife?" Edna asked, having digested the information.

"No. He is staying with me until we can work out what to do next. I shan't mind if he does stay for good, but he might want to have his own place for a while once he finds work."

"He doesn't have a job? What is he looking for?"

"That's another problem. You see he is disabled. He lost an ear and some of his sight, and the use of his left hand in the war. He finds it difficult to stand for very long too."

"I can see that would be a problem. What did he do before the war?"

"He was training to be a draughtsman."

"I suppose he can't drive."

"No, it would be impossible for him to steer and change gear with just one hand."

"I shall keep my eyes peeled for anything that might suit him."

"Thank you. Perhaps you would like to come to tea one Sunday and meet Max?"

"Yes, I should like that. Not this Sunday, it's Mother's birthday, but perhaps the week after?"

"That would be perfect. Goodness, we'll be into December by then too. Almost Christmas."

11

A MERRY CHRISTMAS

27 November 1928
Minehead, Somerset

Dear Midge,

So good to hear from you recently, and I hope this letter finds you at your parents in preparation for your next move to Winchester. You must bring Oliver to visit as soon as he has some holidays, I suppose that would be Easter which seems such a long way away. Perhaps you can convince him to play hooky and come for a long weekend?

I have another, more pressing reason to write to you, and I feel rather mean and underhand for doing so, but I hope as you read further you will understand my reasons. You will no doubt know of Caroline's father's passing. I am concerned that without his guiding hand, and without his stability, Caroline may descend into chaos and foolhardy decisions.

I fear she may already be on that path. Has she mentioned a man called Max to you at all? She met him when she went to that artists' colony in Cornwall, and now has been reunited with him – she says by accident but who can tell. You know I would not interfere under normal circumstances, and I would be the very last person to criticise a fellow female on her choice of partner. However, Max is a married man. I feel no good can come of this liaison while he remains married, and it rather sounds from the information Tommy has gleaned, that he is unlikely to be divorced any time soon.

Caroline has no concept of how this could impact her future. Goodness only knows how damaged she would be if she were to be named in divorce proceedings as the other woman! Max is also an invalid and unable to hold down any position that would support them both. I am so terribly sad that Caroline will end up carrying them both, working herself into an early grave while he drinks away her money and never makes an honest woman of her.

I never thought I would be so censorious but Caroline, along with you of course, is my oldest friend. If either of you needed me, I hope you know I would drop everything and fly to your aid. But in this instance, I simply do not know what to do to persuade Caroline to change her course. What can we do?

Do let me know your thoughts, and any further information if you have it.

Our love to Oliver
Your friend
Helen

Helen had been more disappointed than angry when Tommy told her Max had moved into Caroline's home. It wasn't so much the speed of things as the fact that Max was still legally joined to another woman. Helen only hoped that there were no children involved as that would have meant more expense from Caroline's home through Max to his now ex-wife. Tommy reassured her that no children had been mentioned, and he felt sure if any had existed, they would have been spoken of by now. He and Caroline often ate their lunch together and she confided in him how happy she was to have Max with her. Tommy shared some of Helen's concerns, but he was much less inclined to voice them as criticisms to Caroline.

Midge read Helen's letter while eating toast and marmalade at her parent's kitchen table at the vicarage in Pangbourne. She and Oliver had arrived two days before, after a fascinating but oh so tiring journey up from Africa through the Middle East and across half of Europe. Their belongings would follow them, but an exact date for their arrival had not been forthcoming from the shipping agent. His best estimate was sometime in January.

"News from your friends in the west?" Oliver asked, reaching for another slice of toast.

"Yes, from Helen. She is worried about Caroline." Midge took another bite of her toast and laid the letter flat on the table, "She has got herself mixed up with a married man."

"Oh dear. That sort of thing never ends well."

"No. It's funny, when we were all together last in Budleigh Salterton, before I went to Africa, Helen said she thought Caroline would have all kinds of escapades to make up for lost time as it were. I don't think any of us imagined it would come to this though."

"Lost time? Oh yes, I remember, she had nursed her mother or something like that hadn't she. Well, I suppose it is only natural to want to have adventures when one has been prevented before."

"And yet I can't help but think there must be some reasoning behind it all, some justification that Caroline knows of and perhaps Helen doesn't."

Oliver raised an eyebrow, "There can't be much justification in not honouring one's marriage vows, surely!"

"I know Helen is concerned, and I understand it, but I think I should like to wait and hear from Caroline the whole story before I leap to anyone's aid."

"Do you think perhaps Helen's concern is more for her association? This kind of scandal would damage someone's prospects in politics."

"Possibly, though the fact of Helen and Tommy's marriage being what it is would surely be more scandalous if that information every became public knowledge. No, I think she perhaps feels a small measure of responsibility for Caroline having encouraged her adventures. Caroline might be naïve, but she isn't stupid."

"It was your sensibleness that attracted me to you, you know," he smiled as he passed Midge the pot of marmalade. "Will you telephone her?"

"Not yet. Perhaps at the weekend."

Had Max not arrived at Elmsworth, Caroline would have had to ask for another day's holiday from the airfield to receive the delivery of the furniture and effects from her father's apartment. The letter from Mr Embry informed her that they would be arriving on Friday 7 December. The sale of the apartment had been advertised and several interested parties had enquired. Mr Embry felt sure it would realise the sum he had mentioned to Caroline, though she had been in the first tsunami of grief at the time and had not absorbed the information as quickly as she might otherwise have done. Looking at the figure neatly typed on the page, she felt overwhelmed as another wave of grief caught her unexpectedly on its crest.

Max looked up from the book he was reading, "Is it bad news?"

Caroline pulled her handkerchief from up her sleeve and wiped her eyes. "Not bad, no, it's from my solicitor. We shall have to make some room for the furniture from the apartment. I just … I just wish I still had my father instead of my inheritance." She was overtaken by sobs again.

Max put his book down and worked himself out of the chair. He couldn't crouch down, so he stood awkwardly by Caroline's side for a moment before seeming to come to a decision. He took her hands away from her eyes and pulled her gently to stand up with him. Then he put his arm around her, and she gave in to her grief. They stood there for some minutes until Caroline regained control. She looked up at Max with a blotchy face and red-rimmed eyes.

"I'm sorry."

"No need."

"I must look an absolute sight."

"You look like a girl who misses her father. I'm sorry you have had to deal with so much lately. I know I have added to it all; is there anything I can do to help more?"

Caroline sat back down, and Max returned to his chair opposite her. She blew her nose then picked up the letter again.

"It does seem to have all happened at once, and now with the King being ill as well …" she patted her eyes with her handkerchief, "If you could be here on Friday, that would be a great help. I assume the furniture will come by train and Mr Embry has arranged a carrier to collect it from the station and bring it here. I didn't want to keep everything, but Father's desk can go in the dining room along with the dining table for now, they should both fit. I think the chairs will be alright in here, and then my dressing table will need to be taken upstairs."

"Is it just furniture?"

"No, there will be kitchen things and lots of books which I suppose will also have to go into the dining room for now. And my paintings, and some smaller items, lamps, a side table, that kind of thing. We might find we are rather cramped here for a while, but I didn't want to sell everything off. Father's clothes will have gone to the Women's Section to distribute. I do hope Ferris was able to send word to Galina. The apartments will be quite empty when she returns. If she returns of course."

"Now, Galina was the woman who lived opposite you? The Russian lady?"

"That's right. She was rather fierce, always immaculately turned out and very sophisticated. But she gave me good advice and I did enjoy listening to her gramophone records."

"What music did she like?"

"Galina had a collection of music by the Russian composers. Borodin, Rimsky-Korsakov, and Mussorgsky mostly."

"And is that all you want me to do, let the carriers bring the furniture in on Friday?"

"Yes, thank you, that's all. For now, at least," she added with a small smile.

Max's search for employment was not bearing fruit. He had not expected it to immediately and had tried not to be too pessimistic when Caroline asked him each evening what he had found in the newspaper that day. Some days there was nothing new, and on those days, Max tried to find something meaningful to do in the house. He did not want Caroline to think he was content to live off her wages alone. His uncooperative hand made general tasks more difficult and, in some instances, impossible, but he found he rather enjoyed cleaning things. It gave him a sense of satisfaction to see the banister gleaming after he had polished it.

He also tried to have dinner either partially prepared or already cooking by the time Caroline got home, and that was something Caroline greatly appreciated particularly when she arrived home late. It meant they could eat before the evening concert started on the wireless.

The weekly envelopes continued to be filled with a postal order for ten shillings and dropped into the box outside the Post Office. Max had not included a letter with any of them and had no intention of telling Diana his new address. She would know he was in Taunton from the postmark on the envelopes. He doubted she would need or want to know anything more. He found that the only time he now thought of her was on his pension days. He wondered if she thought of him; he thought after the initial rage had been spent, Diana might be in a period of something akin to mourning. But how likely was that really, he countered himself, when they had hardly spoken to each other for several years.

It occurred to Max that Diana might have more difficulty in starting a new life than he was, given how consumed by her own feelings of hatred she had been. It had perhaps become her complete being – Max had no idea if Diana had friends that she confided in, but assumed she must have as she spent most of her days outside their home somewhere – and as such, would she find encouragement to start again, or would she assume the role of, for want of a better word, widow? Max still cared enough for Diana to not want her to become a melancholic caricature of a deserted woman. He wanted her to have an opportunity of a better life than they had found themselves sharing. He hoped she would see that too, in time.

As Christmas approached, the weather became colder and more extreme. Max was concerned that Caroline would become stuck in a flood or snowdrift in the Austin, and when the ground crew at the airfield began to express the same concerns, Caroline investigated the bus service between Taunton and Bridgwater to see if she could manage similar hours to her current routine. She would not be able to work as long hours as she had been, but everyone agreed they would rather she arrived and returned home safely. She found she missed driving the Austin, but at the same time she enjoyed riding along on the bus and gazing out of the window at whatever the weather happened to be doing that day.

The last flights home to the airfield were due back on the afternoon of Thursday 20 December. Tommy had decided not to drive from Minehead that week as he and Helen were hoping to go to her parents in Plymouth. With both planes safely in the hangar by half past two, Caroline wished the men a happy Christmas and set off for the bus stop as snow began to fall. She would not be needed there again until the new year and she was looking forward to sleeping in late and doing all the festive things she had promised herself.

Edna would be joining them for lunch on the Sunday before Christmas. She and Max had found they shared an interest in crosswords and had similar political sympathies, being largely liberal in their outlook. Caroline had not told Max about Edna's romance with Hugh, and reassured Edna that she would not unless Edna wanted her to. Edna said that perhaps after she had gone home Caroline might mention it and see how Max reacted to it. Max took it in his stride as Caroline assumed he would, though he did caution that they should be on their guard if they were ever to meet Hugh after his release.

To stock up with a few treats and a joint of beef for their Christmas lunch, Caroline walked slowly with Max to the Post Office on the first day of her holiday. Caroline had spent the evening before writing out her Christmas cards and was concerned that they would not reach their destinations in time, but the Postmaster assured her they would all be delivered on Christmas Eve. A steady stream of cards had been arriving at Elmsworth during December, and Max was intrigued by the number of people Caroline seemed to know. She had kept in touch with almost everyone she had met over the previous three years, although she had still not been able to find an address for Florence and Vaughan in Norfolk. Back in Bath, Max's Christmases had been spent at Diana's parent's house. They would receive a few cards which were displayed on the mantlepiece in the sitting room. This year, Max had tied some string between the pictures on the wall in the sitting room, and another length from the coat hooks to the mirror in the hallway, to accommodate the cards Caroline had been sent.

Caroline had not told Max exactly the state of her finances. He knew she had inherited some shares and savings from her father, and that she had a small yearly income from her own portfolio, plus the wages she earned at the airfield. He knew how much the rent was on Elmsworth, and how much the Austin cost to run. With every day that passed without him finding employment he was becoming more despondent that he would ever be able to contribute his share financially to their relationship.

On Christmas Eve, while Caroline was making pastry for some mince pies, Max went over to Farthing's to buy his *Morning Echo* and hand Ted and Irene the Christmas card Caroline had written for them. He returned with his newspaper and two bottles of beer, a gift from Ted to them both. As Caroline was busy at the kitchen table, Max took the newspaper into the dining room and spread it out on the table there, amongst the jumble of furniture and other items from the Cheltenham apartment. He smoked as he read through the local news and then went to get his pencil from the sitting room when he reached the situations vacant columns. A new advert caught his attention.

MEN OF GOOD CHARACTER AND WITH KEEN ATTENTION TO DETAIL REQUIRED FOR THE POSITION OF SAFETY INSPECTOR.

JOIN THE SAFETY MOVEMENT!

FULL TRAINING PROVIDED – FREE TRAVEL PASS INCLUDED.

APPLY AT YOUR LOCAL GWR STATION.

Max read the advertisement twice before circling it with his pencil. He knew he was running out of options and pride. He had been considering what manual positions he might be able to do, even for a short while, with his lack of mobility, hearing and his numb hand. He could push a broom but struggled to use a dustpan and brush without his own adaptations. He had tied a stick onto the handle of their dustpan so that he could keep it still with his foot while sitting on a chair and brush the debris into it with the large broom.

He looked out of the dining room window at the snowflakes swirling outside. He could hear Caroline humming to herself in the kitchen as she cut out circles of pastry and lay them into the baking tray hollows. How different it was living here with her. The house was light and bright, warm and welcoming. Caroline herself was outgoing, industrious, self-reliant. They could talk, or not, and he still felt that they were communicating. So different to the enforced silence and hostility that had enshrouded the house in Bath with Diana. Max thought back to the previous Christmas. Waking on Christmas morning after a silent evening in front of the fire in the sitting room; a silent breakfast alone, then waiting for Diana to appear in the hallway ready to walk the short distance to her parent's house. After brief welcomes and exchanges of insincere Christmas wishes, the walk to church. After church, they all had lunch – a mean affair with no alcohol – then he and Diana had walked home again in silence. No gifts were exchanged; his parents in law would have had to pay for their own to themselves.

Max smiled to himself thinking of the small bag of pink and white sugar mice he had hidden in the spare bedroom for Caroline. He had also managed to purchase a second-hand copy of Dorothy L Sayers' *Clouds of Witness*, now wrapped in some bright red crepe paper from Irene, who had also helped him tie the ribbon around it. Irene's brother had suffered similar physical injuries to Max in the war but had been unable to cope with his disfigurements and had lay down to die one evening on a railway track in Doncaster. Max looked down once again at the now circled advertisement.

In the kitchen Caroline began to spoon the sticky sweet mincemeat mixture into the pastry tarts with two teaspoons. She rarely made pastry, but it seemed to be the right consistency and she hoped the lids would stick down with a little milk brushed around the top of each tart. She was happy as she worked and could not remember having such a sense of contentment. Christmas this year would be a very different affair to the previous one where her father and Noah had sprung an engagement on her. She realised she had not missed Noah in weeks. She tried hard not to miss her father, but the grief was still very close to the surface. If Max hadn't arrived on her doorstep, she wondered what kind of Christmas she would have had by herself. Perhaps she would have invited Daisy to stay for a few days. She really must telephone Daisy while the mince pies were baking.

Caroline started humming a different carol, this time *The Holly and the Ivy.* Those would be pretty names for little girls, she thought absent-mindedly. She stopped mid-spoon. What if Max wanted a child? They had not talked about it and had both been very careful. She knew she did not want a child, who would naturally demand attention, prevent her from coming and going as she pleased and put an end to her exploration of the world near and far. The decision had been crystalising in her over recent months. She had felt no maternal stirrings when she visited Philip and Mary Rose and held baby Grace, or Lottie's twin girls or even Annie's sons Victor and Dennis when she had brought them to visit the apartment. Helen had said once how some women were born to be mothers. Caroline was certain she was not one of them. Could that be a problem between her and Max?

Later that evening, with the snow now laying three inches deep outside, Caroline and Max were in the sitting room listening to the wireless.

"Max, when would you usually give and receive Christmas presents?" Caroline asked.

Max put down the crossword he was slowly completing. "When there were presents, usually after lunch on Christmas day. What about your family?"

"Years ago, we would open them when we returned from church on Christmas Eve night. The last year we did that was the Christmas before Freddie went to war. More recently we have opened them after breakfast on Christmas morning and then gone to church. But since mother died, every year has been different."

"When would you like to open your gift this year?"

Caroline looked up at him in surprise, "I have something to open? Oh Max, I wasn't expecting anything!"

"Then I'm glad it will be a surprise. But when would you like to have it? Do you want to go to church tomorrow?"

Caroline considered for a moment. She was becoming less of a congregationalist as the years passed, and in Taunton she had not felt connected to any of the churches in the town.

"I don't think I do, if it's all the same to you?"

"I am in no hurry to go. If it keeps snowing, we may not be able to leave the house in any case."

"Then let's open our presents after breakfast tomorrow."

"I wasn't expecting anything either," Max said, a hint of concern in his voice. He hoped Caroline had not spent too much on him after covering all of the household expenses.

"Perhaps we should open them now? All this talk is making me very curious!"

"If we do, there will be nothing to open tomorrow."

"Yes, you're right of course. The excitement and anticipation of Christmas is what makes it, don't you think?"

"This year, yes."

Caroline had carefully wrapped Max's presents while he had been over at Farthing's on Sunday morning. She had bought him a new pair of black leather shoes having noticed that the soles on his current pair were rather thin. They were easy to wrap, snug as they were in their stiff cardboard box. The other item was much smaller, a silver cigarette case that she had had engraved with Max's initials. Though she disliked the way cigarette smoke clung to their clothes, it was a part of Max as much as the way he carefully combed his hair or liked his tea with no sugar and very little milk.

She encouraged Max to open one of her gifts to him first on Christmas morning in the sitting room after they had eaten breakfast and washed up the debris of the meal.

He chose the larger box and took the shoes out as if they were made of porcelain.

"These are very well made. Thank you." He managed to stop himself from saying how much they must have cost. "Now, you have this," he handed her the little white paper bag which Irene had tied closed with some narrow red ribbon.

Caroline guessed what was inside but pretended to be surprised, "Sugar mice! How delicious, thank you so much Max." She got up and crossed over to him, bending to kiss his cheek. "Now for this one," she turned and passed him the smaller parcel.

"Oh, two? When I get a job, you know I will make up for all of this don't you?" Max almost didn't want to accept a second gift, but he knew Caroline would be upset if he declined.

Caroline knelt beside his chair. "Max, I am not interested in you as someone to provide for me. I am perfectly capable of looking after myself. What I feel for you is not something that can be measured in material things. I want you to be as happy with me as I am with you, nothing more."

He nodded his head.

"So, open the present," Caroline said, smiling.

Max looked at her kneeling on the rug, her face beaming up at him as excited for him as if she had no idea what was inside the wrapping paper. Not beautiful, he thought, but everything. He pulled at the ribbon.

"Oh, my word! Caroline this is …"

"Please don't say it is too much, Max. I noticed that a lot of the men who fly with us have them and I wanted you to have one too. Turn it over, look!"

He did as she instructed and saw the engraving. He ran his finger over the letters as the case lay in his lap.

"Thank you. Thank you, Caroline. I shall be a spiv about town with these," he smiled.

Caroline got up and was about to go into the kitchen to begin preparing lunch when Max called her back. He had kept her second gift behind his back, and now felt relieved that he had prepared two gifts for her as she had for him.

"Another for me?" Caroline was genuinely surprised this time.

"The mice won't last long, so I thought I'd better get something that would." He smiled as she wrestled with the crepe paper.

"How wonderful, I don't have this one! How clever of you, thank you!"

Neither of them mentioned the wear on the cover or the creases on the spine.

Caroline had invited Daisy to visit the weekend between Christmas and the new year, to stay over on the Saturday night. Daisy was very curious to meet Max, having heard several sermons from Helen about the immorality of men who deserted their wives. Max was equally curious to meet Daisy, given Caroline's description of her as an 'erratically dressed bookseller'.

Max's suitcase was on a chair in the spare bedroom, where it had been since he had taken his few clothes out and hung them in the wardrobe in their own bedroom. Caroline went to move it to under the bed, but Max had not secured the clasps and as she lifted the handle, the contents began to spill out onto the floor. Caroline realised just in time, though not before spotting a wood and brass tube-shaped object now at the front of the case. With the case back safely on the chair, she lifted the lid carefully. It was Max's telescope.

When Caroline picked it up and understood the stacked brass rings at one end would extend to form the full length of the spyglass, she gave a small gasp. The spiritualist she had seen with Daisy and Noah at Dunster Castle had been right after all! It wasn't binoculars she had seen as Caroline had assumed at the time. Caroline carefully put the telescope back into the case, added the papers from the floor, and closed the clasps.

As Daisy would be arriving by train, and the snow continued to fall intermittently, Caroline said she would drive across town to the railway station. Max, saw an opportunity and said he would travel with Caroline, but then make his way home later. He offered to pick up some chops for their dinner on his way and Caroline said how thoughtful that would be of him.

After waving Caroline and the well-wrapped up Daisy off in the Austin, Max went back into the ticket office and asked if the Station Master was available. After waiting a few moments, he was shown into a small office behind the ticket counter. The Station Master was tall and thin with a dark moustache which was waxed and curled at the tips. Max couldn't help but notice the scar that ran across the man's right cheek, puckered and smooth like the space where Max's ear had been. The Station Master indicated for Max to sit down.

"So, you're here about the Safety Officer vacancy, is that it?"

"Yes, sir."

"What regiment were you in?" It was a common question between men of their age.

"Second Wiltshires, injured at Albers and then Arras. Yourself?"

"Somerset Yeomanry. Saw Palestine and then France." There was a moment's silence as they both tried not to remember. "You'll have had your basic mechanical safety training then?"

"Yes, and first aid. Though I would have to direct someone else these days and try not to get in their way."

"There are two kinds of positions the company is recruiting for. One is general line and rolling stock safety, and the other is workers' safety. For both, there is a written test, then those who pass will have to attend a three-day course in Bristol. Pass that, and they will find you a home station to work from. Any preference there?"

Max hadn't considered the job might be anywhere other than Taunton. Moment by moment, Caroline had said.

"No, no preference. Best not to count my chickens, eh?"

"Yes, well, we've had plenty of applications as I'm sure you'd expect," he took out his pocket watch and looked at the time. "If you're not in a hurry, you can take the written test now. There's a chap due to finish in five minutes."

Max agreed and was shown back out to the ticket office to wait. The test was one for basic literacy and numeracy, with a section at the end where the examinee could answer one of two scenarios with a few words about how they would approach and deal with the situation described. Max chose the second scenario where a worker had suffered a crush injury to his arm between two carriage couplings. He detailed applying pressure to any open bleeding wound, creating a splint if the elbow was undamaged and immobilising the arm. He was just finishing when the Station Master reappeared and told him his time was up.

"When will I hear how I've done?" Max asked putting his coat back on and picking up his hat.

"I have to send this off to Bristol. They will be in touch … good, you've put a telephone number on there as well as your address. They might telephone, but I expect they will let you know by letter, in a week to ten days. If you've heard nothing in a fortnight, assume you failed."

Max nodded, shook the other man's hand and went out into the grey, cold afternoon.

The Station Master glanced through Max's test answers. Better than many he'd seen so far, he thought. He put the paper on the table and took up a pencil. He made a short note at the top of the first page and folded the test in half before pushing it into an envelope which already contained several other papers.

12

THE SAFETY MAN

The weather did not improve as 1928 became 1929. Temperatures dropped each night, freezing the water in pipes, and animals and some unfortunate people who were unable to find shelter. The Thames and other rivers froze. Businesses struggled to move supplies around the country; while trains continued to run with a few frozen signal points delaying things, getting to and from stations was another matter entirely.

Caroline returned to work at the airfield, taking the bus service to and from Thurloxton as she had before Christmas. The road between Taunton and Bridgwater was a main route and mostly clear. Rodney was stuck in Lincolnshire after visiting friends, and Tommy would not be returning from Plymouth with Helen until the last week in January. The airfield was a carpet of white that David and Peter attempted to keep clear of snow using a large plough attachment they had designed, built and mounted onto the front of a small blue tractor. They took the decision to cancel the passenger flights until the weather improved, leaving Caroline to contact the would-be travellers and explain the situation, offering a full refund or bookings for later in the year. Most of the passengers were understanding as Caroline explained that their safety was of the utmost importance to the company.

Max had not told Caroline about the safety officer position. He knew she would get excited and say it was the perfect job for him, and he did not want to bear her disappointment as well as his own if he did not hear from the railway. He continued to circle the advertisements and inquired after two or three other positions while he waited.

When the letter arrived one Thursday morning towards the end of January, Max had almost given up hope of hearing anything. He picked the envelope up off the doormat and carried it into the sitting room to open it. The headed notepaper bore the crest of God's wonderful railway – the name Max and many others called the Great Western Railway company – in green ink on good quality cream paper. Max read the typed words. He put the sheet of paper down in his lap for a moment and rubbed his face with his right hand. Then he picked up the letter again and read it more slowly to make sure he understood the contents.

He had passed the test. He had passed the initial interview. Max assumed that was the questions that the Station Master had asked him about his training. He was now invited to attend three days of training at the Temple Meads station in Bristol beginning Monday 18 February. Caroline's twenty-fifth birthday. He would have to tell her when she got home that evening, and he hoped she would not be unhappy to spend her birthday alone. He simply could not turn this opportunity down.

Caroline was thrilled to hear his news that evening. The snow had cleared, and she was now driving herself to and from work again. Although she left and returned in the dark, she felt more confident behind the wheel than she had before. It occurred to her that she felt more confident all round and could not put her finger on why.

Once she had taken off her coat and shoes, it had become their routine for Max to refresh the teapot and Caroline would tell him about her day as they sat together at the kitchen table. She always encouraged him to tell her the most mundane things about his day in return. That Thursday evening she clapped her hands at the good news.

"That's wonderful! Truly darling, you made the right impression, and I am certain you will sail through the training as well!" She jumped up and put her arms around his neck, kissing the top of his head.

"Let's not get too carried away," Max said, making no move to dislodge Caroline's embrace.

"You don't sound quite as enthusiastic as you might," Caroline said, releasing him and sitting back down to pour their tea.

"I will have to go away for the training, to Bristol. I could go and come back each evening, but it starts on the eighteenth of February."

Caroline sipped her tea and Max waited.

"You will be very tired from studying all day and then walking to and from the railway station. I think you should take a hotel room in Bristol."

"But it's your birthday," he said with a frown.

"I shall have others. You might not get this opportunity again."

"Well, if you are sure, though I think I can manage the travelling."

"No, we can afford a hotel. Really, Max, it may still be frosty in the mornings and the very last thing we want is for you to slip over on your way to catch a train. That would be a very poor start for a safety officer, wouldn't it!" She chuckled, and he had to agree.

January slid into February and Caroline paid another two months' rent in advance on Elsmworth. If the inhabitants of Britain had thought December was cold, February had a nasty surprise for them. The Great Frost as it became known, was the coldest February for thirty years. The temperature dropped again to below zero degrees centigrade and for six consecutive days between 11–17 February it did not go above minus one; for several days it hovered around minus twelve. Hospitals were inundated with casualties from slips and falls, broken bones and concussions, taking people out of the workforce temporarily. Children and the elderly developed hypothermia and severe chilblains. Bodies began to accumulate in the undertakers' storerooms and people's parlours as the ground was too frozen to dig graves. Milk froze before it could be collected. Far from the idyllic Christmas card images of snowy scenes, the country was fast becoming sick and tired of the whiteness and cold.

Max and Caroline celebrated her birthday on the 16th with an afternoon trip to the cinema and a fish and chip supper afterwards. They talked about the death of the actress Lillie Langtry, the St Valentine's Day gangster shootings in Chicago, and more worrying news from America that the stock market there had fallen dramatically again. Max was concerned about Caroline's shares being affected and she promised she would telephone Mr Foxton and seek his reassurance while Max was in Bristol. Caroline had insisted that Max was not to buy her anything for her birthday and that she could wait until he was earning a wage again. She was acutely aware that the five shillings he had each week after he had sent Diana ten were mostly spent on his quest to find employment. She was not concerned for their situation, but she did not want unnecessary obligations to wear him down.

Caroline had convinced Max to travel up to Bristol on the afternoon of Sunday 17th so that he could find a hotel and settle in before his training started the next day. He had been reluctant, but she had insisted, pointing out that he might not have time during the day to find a room. Max arrived at Temple Meads at a little before four, and before leaving the station, made sure he knew where he had to report to the next morning. He made his way cautiously in the biting cold air past the tall buildings containing the great and good lawyers of the city, and found a small three-storey hotel called the Imperial in Redcliffe Street. Caroline had put three crisp pound notes into his hand as she kissed him goodbye that afternoon, and again he had protested but she insisted.

The training was, as Caroline had predicted, tiring. Max found himself in a group of nine other men of various ages and abilities from across Somerset and Gloucestershire. He was by far the most severely physically limited applicant in the group, but their instructor told them all on the first morning that they had passed their initial assessments and all of them had earned their place there. Some of their time was spent in their classroom, and some out on the tracks and around the station and goods yard. On the afternoon of the second day, they caught trams to the harbour to see the loading and unloading of ships to the waiting wagons. They wrote reports of what they had seen, and the instructor pointed out the hazards they had missed.

One young man did not return after the first day. The instructor received word that the man had decided he could not deal with potentially bloody scenes of bodies in contact with the fast-moving metal giants of the railway. Max had wondered how young the man had been when he first saw him. Not someone old enough to have served in the war, he concluded.

The afternoon of the third day was set aside for the final assessment. The group were taken to a siding shed and told to spend ten minutes making notes of any potential hazards they could see. They then returned to the classroom and had to write a full report including their recommendations on how to improve the safety of the location. Despite the cold, Max found he was sweating as he wrote his report. His right hand shook with the effort of using the pen and keeping the paper still with his left. He had had to memorise the scene as well as making scratchy notes with his sheet of paper resting on a stack of suitcases. At four, their reports were collected by the instructor, and they all shook each other's hands and wished each other good luck as they made their way out of the classroom. Max had checked out of the hotel that morning so that he could catch the train home as soon as the assessment was over.

He stood on the platform, his breath making a cloud in front of his face like all of the other passengers. Two women moved to stand a little way along the platform from him to his right, and he couldn't help but overhear their conversation.

"… and she still has no idea where he is living?"

"None at all! Yet he sends her money each week. It is most intriguing. She does not appear to be overly disappointed to be deserted."

"Better off without him by all accounts. What use is a man who cannot provide for his family?"

"Well, that appears to have been one of the sticking points. Not only could he not provide for his family, he could not give her the family she wanted!"

"These things happen of course, but such a shame when one or other of a couple wants children. Are you sure we are on the right platform, dear?"

"Yes, this is platform three, isn't it? Oh no, three is over there! Come along..."

Could there be another man locally who had left his wife yet still sent her money, and could not give her the child she had wanted? Max wondered how common his situation had been, with so many damaged men unable to find stable employment after the war. Surely the women must have been talking about someone else and not him. His mind wandered back to the conversation his second surgeon had had with him one afternoon in the hospital a few days after removing a large amount of shrapnel from his left leg and groin. He was 'unlikely to become a father' the doctor had told him, as if he were telling Max he might not have fish paste sandwiches for tea. Max had been more concerned at his ability to walk again. He was aware of course, how children usually followed a marriage, but had never specifically looked forward to having any. His parents were dead, he was their only surviving offspring, the name Bird would end with him. As Munhead would end with Caroline, he supposed. Did she want children? The question sent a shaft of ice into his stomach. What if she did? She was the best thing to have happened to Max in a very long time, but could she bear for it to be just the two of them and no more? Or would she decide she needed a man who could provide for her after all?

Max was walking slowly along South Street in Taunton when Caroline spotted him and pulled the Austin over. He got in, thankful to be out of the biting cold if only for a few moments.

"How did it go?" Caroline asked, pulling back out into the road.

"You were right about it being tiring. There were ten of us to start, one chap dropped out after the first day."

"Well, that will mean less competition."

"I suppose so. They didn't say how many positions there are, but I should hear one way or the other by the end of the month. I hope they don't keep me waiting too long."

"I'm sure you impressed them. Did they say which kind of safety officer they were considering you for?"

"No, but I expect it will be the rolling stock and yard role. I'd be more hindrance than help if someone fell off a platform and under a train. They gave me this booklet. Did you know there are more than thirty thousand accidents and deaths across all of the railways every year?"

"That's terrible! I had no idea it was such a dangerous job."

"But it doesn't have to be. If men are educated to spot the accidents waiting to happen, they can save another chap's life instead. A bit like in the army."

It wasn't until they had turned out the bedside lamps that evening that Max had arranged his thoughts sufficiently to talk to Caroline about the future. He knew she was tired and would have to be up at six the next morning, but he wanted to be sure they both felt the same way about having a family, or not.

They lay as they often did, with Max behind Caroline on their left sides so that Max could still hear whatever Caroline said. They often talked just before they fell asleep, even if they had spent all evening discussing something.

There was no better way than to come right out with it he decided, "You never mention it, but would you like to have a child one day?"

He felt her tense for a moment. Then she wriggled onto her back.

"Would you? Can you?"

"I don't think so. I was advised to still take precautions to be sure, but the doctors seem to think it is unlikely."

"Max, for a while now I have felt that a child would be such a huge responsibility, and such a change to everything. I'd sometimes thought I might like a dog, or perhaps a cat, but even those would mean I couldn't just go away somewhere if I suddenly felt like it. I don't think I would like one really. A child I mean, not a pet. If it happened, then we would just have to get on with it, but I'd rather it didn't. Do you think that makes me a bad person? Somehow not a real woman?"

He realised he had been holding his breath.

"Not at all a bad person, and you are very much a real woman Caroline. A sensible one."

"I wondered if perhaps I was being selfish." She said quietly, half to herself.

"Surely it would be selfish to have a child because you wanted one on a whim, but then left it with a nanny or relatives every time you went off somewhere."

"But if I had a child, I probably wouldn't have the money to be able to go off somewhere."

Max grinned in the darkness.

"And there is the matter of us not being married. It wouldn't really be fair on the child, would it?" Caroline turned her head to look at Max.

"If you really wanted to have one, and do everything the right way, then I would have to admit to adultery to obtain a divorce from Diana. I would have to name you. It wouldn't be fair on you or a child. These things tend to stick to a person."

"I have never known anyone who was divorced, have you?"

"No. But I have known rather a lot of couples who lived as we are now. I rather think it is becoming the norm."

"Another thing that wouldn't be fair is that you are so much older than I am."

"You make me sound ancient!"

"You are the same age as Freddie would have been.You'll be thirty-two in June."

"Men can have children much later in life though. I suppose it is nature's way, if the woman dies in childbirth, the man can continue his line with another."

"Marriages are meant to last forever."

"Sometimes they don't."

Max received an offer of employment from the Great Western Railway Company on the 27 February, as a full-time, permanent safety officer on a salary of four pounds and six shillings a week with free travel on the company's trains.There was only one problem with the offer, and he felt frustrated and impotent again in the face of fate's unruly nature. His position would be based at Plymouth station in Devon.

By the time Caroline arrived home, he had decided he would have to decline the offer. Perhaps he could ask to be considered if a vacancy appeared in Taunton instead, and in the meantime, he would keep looking. He had come so close; it was a bitter disappointment. He didn't even want to tell Caroline; he simply handed her the letter across the kitchen table. He watched her eyes widen, her smile grow, and then the frown he knew would follow appeared. She looked up at him.

"Plymouth?"

"I'll telephone them in the morning and turn it down. Perhaps they will keep my details in case something closer turns up."

"Don't be absurd, Max! You can't turn it down.You are perfect for the position, they can see that even if you can't."

"Caroline, we live in Taunton. That's too far to travel every day, and certainly too far for you to get to the airfield and back."

"Can we live on four pounds and six a week?"

"Not if you want to keep the Austin. It's not practical."

"There must be a way we can do this! You can't give up now," she poured more tea into her cup. Plymouth was by the sea, she remembered.

"What if you could take a room…"

"I suppose if I could find a room …"

They both laughed.

"When do you have to reply by?"

"Friday the eighth, to start on the following Tuesday."

"Then let me speak to Tommy tomorrow. He is sure to know of rooms to rent in Plymouth and if he doesn't, Helen will. You could stay there during the week, and then come home for weekends. I would miss you dreadfully, but perhaps I could try to find a job in the city as well."

"But I don't want you to uproot yourself on my behalf. You enjoy your job; I am the one causing all of the upset here."

"But I am not upset. I do enjoy my job at the airfield, I have learned so much there, but even with the drop in the shares, I … we could still live comfortably for a year or two on the savings I have now, and Elsa has been badgering me for some more paintings. When the apartment sells, perhaps we could buy a house in Plymouth if we both want to live there then. I found myself here in Taunton by accident really, and won't mind moving on to somewhere else."

Max took her hand. "You believe in me, don't you?"

"I do. And I will go wherever you need to go."

Helen and Daisy were drinking gin and tonic in Helen's conservatory in Minehead. A watery sun had been straining to make itself visible that afternoon and both women agreed to make the most of it while protected from the bitter wind that still coursed through the town.

"Have you heard from Caroline recently?" Helen asked, adopting an air of casual interest that Daisy saw cleanly through.

"We spoke on the telephone two evenings ago. I must say, she sounds so much happier now than when she was involved with Noah, don't you think?"

"I couldn't say dear, it has been some weeks since I heard from her."

"Did you remember to send her a birthday card?"

"Yes. Between you and Tommy, one had no hope of forgetting."

"Tommy will miss her when … I mean, if she ever leaves the airfield." Daisy tried to recover but knew she had given the game away.

"When? Why would Caroline leave? One imagines she will need to keep her position there with the state of the markets and the other expenses she must have these days."

"Helen don't be so acidic! Max is a very pleasant man, calm and quiet and rather intelligent. It is such a shame so many people cannot see past his disfigurement."

"I can ignore physical disfigurements, Daisy, it is the material imbalance I cannot ignore."

"Well I might as well tell you, seeing as you have no desire to keep in regular contact with Caroline yourself. Max has been offered a position with the Great Western Railway as a safety inspector. Unfortunately, he will be based in Plymouth, so it is likely they will be leaving Somerset later this year. And good luck to them I say. Caroline is a lovely girl."

Helen sighed. It was difficult to argue with Daisy on her final statement, Caroline was indeed a lovely girl and Helen missed her company more than she cared to admit to anyone, least of all herself. She felt an absurd sense of responsibility for her friend, and she had been annoyed at first when Daisy had gone to stay with the couple in Taunton. It didn't matter that she and Tommy were guests of her parents at that same moment.

"There is an airport in Plymouth." Helen said out loud though to herself.

Daisy said nothing.

Edna and Caroline had fallen into a habit of going to the cinema every other Friday evening. Caroline occasionally wondered why Max seemed to have no other friends but had not felt the need to ask him as yet. It was Edna who brought the question to her attention again as they left the Gaumont cinema and hurried to Caroline's Austin parked across the street. They had just seen a film where the leading man relied heavily on his slimmer, shorter, best friend to facilitate his attempts to woo the female lead.

"Has Max made any friends here yet?" Edna asked, getting out her handkerchief to blow her nose. She had picked up a cold that week and had almost cancelled their regular outing. Instead, she had sneezed frequently through the programme.

"No, I don't think so. Not besides Ted and Irene anyway."

"It's strange isn't it, how men don't seem to make friends in the same way women do."

"I wonder if it is something to do with their experiences in the war. To make friends and then see them all die, it must be worse in many ways than to lose one or two family members."

"Yes, it could be that. It's rather sad I think."

"Does Hugh have any friends?"

"He says there are men he talks to, but that no one in there are the sort of fellow he would want as a friend when he gets out. They are all criminals, after all."

Caroline refrained from pointing out the obvious.

"Will you go away, when he gets out? Away from Taunton?"

"I expect we'll have to. Between you and me, I don't think the chap Hugh spoke about who wanted to start a garage will come through on it. Perhaps we'll go further west like you and Max, maybe even into Cornwall. Or up to Bristol."

"But your father will be disappointed that you will be with Hugh."

"He'll probably have a heart attack!" Edna clapped her hand over her mouth and looked at Caroline with wide eyes, then said, "I'm sorry, that was insensitive of me."

Caroline pulled up outside of Edna's house.

"It's alright, dear. They are a very common thing to have, so I have learned. A man had one on one of the flights last week. The poor fellow died before they reached London."

"How ghastly!"

"Well, I shan't be moving away for a little while yet, so same time in two weeks?"

"Yes, good night Caroline!"

As she drove back to Holway Road, Caroline mulled over the question of Max's lack of friends. What if they had all died in the war? She knew Max's mother had died from the Spanish flu, and his father had died after a short non-descript illness two years later. He had no siblings, but what of the young men he had gone to school with? She asked Max as they undressed in the bedroom later that evening.

"Max, is there anyone who you would like to invite to stay when we find a new house?"

"We might not want to move to Plymouth, let's see how things go shall we?"

"Well, perhaps in the summer it might be nice to have some friends for drinks if we can tame the garden this year. Do you have anyone you would like to invite?"

Max sat on the edge of the bed with his back to Caroline. The scars on his left side like an embroidery of pain showed clearly in the light from the bedside lamp. Caroline climbed onto the bed and knelt behind him, putting her arms around his body and laying her head on his shoulder blade. He was still amazed every time she touched him. So many people had seen his body over the years with undisguised disgust or macabre fascination on their faces – when they could bear to look at him at all for more than a second – he still expected her to shrink away from him. That she reached out, often, had given him confidence over the recent months, and kept him going in his search for work when he might otherwise have given up completely.

"This might sound strange, but I haven't had much opportunity to make friends over the years, not since I was at school really. I had friends then of course, every young boy does. There were three of us that used to climb trees and play football together after school. Jimmy and Andrew. Then Jimmy's father died, and his mother took Jimmy and his little sisters away to live with her sister, I think in Leeds. Andrew and I would ride our bicycles for miles at weekends. He wanted to be scientist, he was obsessed with the planets and stars. He went to the higher elementary school when he was 12 and I went to a draughtsman's office as a post boy. We would see each other occasionally after that but his parents wanted him to get on and he was sent to the Trade School in Bristol. I suppose they didn't think I would amount to much." He gently unpeeled Caroline's arms from his torso and turned to get under the covers. She did the same.

"You didn't keep in touch with Andrew then?" Caroline asked when they had turned out the lamps.

"Not really. I would see him around Bath occasionally. He's still in Bristol I think, working for the Merchant's Technical College. And I was trying to learn how to be a draughtsman and spending most of my time with older men. As I say, I didn't have much chance to make friends my own age."

"And in the army? Freddie often wrote to me about the two chaps he spent a lot of time with. What were their names … Perkins was one … I can't remember the other."

Max was quite for a while and Caroline wondered if he had fallen asleep. She was about to turn over when he answered.

"There were lots of men around my age in the army. Some older, a few younger too. When I got to the training camp, the fellow next to me in the kit line became my friend. Will Butler. He died in our first battle at Ypres. By the time I was wounded at Aubers I had a couple of pals, Frank and Pots. Pots' first name I think was Terrence, but everyone called him Pots. I have no idea why, it wasn't his surname, that was Smith. I don't think they survived Aubers, I never saw them again and never heard anyone mention them.

"Men were coming and going all the time, the battalions were reformed and merged, you couldn't make long-lasting friendships in the way I think you mean. You got along with whoever happened to be next to you in the dugout or billet. We weren't there to make friends, Caroline.

"Then, when I was cut up bad at Arras, there was a chap in the next bed to me at the hospital in Sussex. Same sort of injuries, though where they left my arm on, they took his off at the shoulder, and he lost an eye completely. We would talk, share cigarettes. The nurses would wheel us out into the grounds in our wheelchairs together and leave us sitting under a tree. His name was John Palmer."

Another pause.

"What happened to him?" Caroline asked quietly, unsure whether she wanted to know the answer.

"He would have such nightmares. We all had them, but his seemed to take a real hold of him. He would talk about them during the next day as if they were still going on in is head sometimes. It got so bad that he didn't want to go to sleep. He begged the doctors to help him stay awake. Begged the nurses to give him something. I think one must have because he was awake for three days. The doctors found out, I never saw that nurse again, but they changed the drugs that John was on after that and for a while he seemed to be getting better. He still had the nightmares, but they didn't seem as bad for him. And then one day they found him in the bath house. He'd broken into the medicine store and overdosed on the stuff he'd used to stay awake.

"John was the last chap I would say was my friend."

"Perhaps you'll make a friend or two at the railway."

Tommy had provided details of a boarding house, two cheap hotels and the Salvation Army building in Plymouth for Max to find temporary accommodation. Max packed his case with more clothes than he had owned in a long time. Caroline had insisted on buying him a new suit and two shirts and had finished knitting the sweater she had started before Christmas for him. He left his new shoes at the bottom of the stairs, explaining that he did not want to get them covered with oil.

Max had spent twenty minutes on the telephone to his new manager while Caroline wrote down directions and other information Max relayed to her from his conversation.

Armed with the notes on a sheet of paper in his coat pocket, his pension book and post office book in his case and two pounds, seven shillings and three pence in his trouser pocket, Max locked the kitchen door behind him and left Elmsworth through the side gate. They had never got round to having a second front door key cut. He crossed the street to where Ted was waiting with the motor van's engine ticking over. Irene came out of the rear of the shop into the yard and gave Max a brown paper bag with small patches of grease on it containing a steak and kidney pie, still faintly warm, and then gave him a hug. Ted and Max got into the van and drove off to the railway station.

Max's first week in his new job was the most exhausting he had experienced since leaving the army. Everything was new and different, and he had to learn quickly. He was expected to know the handbook inside out by Friday and spent his evenings reading it laying on his narrow bed in the Hoe View Hotel, which in reality looked out only as far as the buildings on the opposite side of the street. Max could see nothing of Plymouth Hoe itself from his window. His hostess, Mrs Waring, was welcoming and remembered Tommy's name when Max said he was an acquaintance. She did not provide meals for her guests but allowed them to bring food in to consume in her dining room, which Max did each evening. He ate breakfast and lunch at the station canteen at a subsidised rate so that his main expense for the week other than his room was tram or bus fares to and from the station.

He quickly picked up on the tension between the Great Western Railway workers and those who worked for Southern Railway. There were often fights in the city pubs between the two groups of men, and as each company had its own football team, little was done to quell the rivalry. Max's boss, Chief Safety Officer Michael Teague, was a Cornishman.

A large man, Teague had a full beard and moustache that was bushy and red, yet his equally bushy eyebrows and thinning hair were pale straw yellow. He had given Max a tour of the goods yard on Max's first day and explained that his main task was to document any accidents, however small, that happened there. The day and night shifts had been informed of Max's arrival and it was only an hour later when the first accident occurred.

A young man, of uncertain age but who said he was fifteen, was brought to the Safety Office with his hand wrapped in a dirty rag. Blood was starting to seep through the covering. After taking a quick statement of the event, Max sent the man off to the Greenbank Infirmary. Max had already seen several instances of hazardous materials, untidy supplies and behaviour of the workers that he intended to tackle, but he decided he would use his first week to understand the most common injuries and accidents. If there was anything he could do to prevent those, that would provide the best start to his employment and Teague agreed when Max suggested it at the end of his first day.

After confirming with Mrs Waring that his room would be available for him the following week, Max made his way to the railway canteen on Friday morning feeling that his first week had gone well. The work was interesting yet not physically strenuous. He enjoyed using the typewriter to fill in the accident forms and make out his reports and no one seemed to mind that he could only type with one hand. Teague spent most of the day in his inner office on the telephone or out meeting with other managers, and Max was left by himself unless he ventured out into the yard. This he did two or three times each day, mainly so that the men became used to his presence. He tried to reassure them that he was not spying on them or there to make trouble.

As Max sat down to his mug of tea and bacon sandwich (which the girl who served the food had cut in half for him without him needing to ask), a small man wearing spectacles with thick lenses who Max felt he ought to recognise but couldn't remember a name for, took the seat opposite him at the table.

"So, you're the new safety man then."

Max put down his half of sandwich, wiped his fingers briefly on his trousers and offered his right hand to the other man.

"I am. Max Bird." His hand was given one shake, then let go as if it were contaminated.

"From up the line, I see."

Max could tell it was not meant as a compliment. "And you are?"

"George White. National Union of Railwaymen. I thought I should make you aware that any attempts to place undue restrictions on our brothers will lead to industrial action by our membership."

Max nodded. He had been warned by Teague about Mr White and had been expecting an interview. "What restrictions did you have in mind Mr White?"

The little man sniffed and attempted to increase his size by thrusting back his shoulders. "Anything that interferes with the established practices of our members. Unnecessary paperwork. Limiting the number of hours worked. Excessive extra duties."

"Tell me, Mr White, have you ever held a man's head together to stop his brain falling out of his scull? Have you ever seen a man's clothes and skin burnt off when he was engulfed in fuel that had seeped out of a container and caught alight as he flicked his cigarette end onto it? No?"

The other man's face had turned grey.

"Well I have, Mr White, and if there is anything I think can be done to stop me having to do either again, I will not hesitate to instruct your members for their own good. Tell your members, Mr White, they do not want to spend the rest of their lives dependent on others because of an accident that could have been prevented. Now, if you don't mind, I need to finish my breakfast and get to work."

Max picked up his sandwich half and took a bite, his eyes on George White daring him to stay and make further conversation. The little man's face had regained its colour and was now rising pink as he stood up.

"My members won't tolerate changes that see them lose wages, Mr Bird." He turned and marched out of the canteen.

It was almost nine o'clock on Friday evening when Max stepped through the kitchen doorway and was greeted with a kiss from Caroline and the smell of sausages. She took his coat and case while he sat at the kitchen table and ate his dinner. Caroline unpacked his case and put his shirts and underwear into a galvanised bucket with some soap flakes to soak overnight. She would get up early in the morning to wash them and get them hanging on the clothes horse to dry as quickly as possible. When she had finished, Max had pushed his empty plate away.

"Would you like to tell me about your week now, or save it until tomorrow?" Caroline asked.

Max rubbed his face with his right hand and stretched his legs out under the kitchen table.

"Do we have any beer? I should like a bottle and I will tell you some of it."

Caroline obliged him and poured a bottle of pale ale into a glass with a handle. He took a couple of gulps before he spoke.

"I think I can be of some use to the railway company. Perhaps not as much use to the union, but that doesn't concern me particularly. I answer to Teague, he's a big Cornishman. I've certainly seen some careless behaviour this week, and some men who should not be put in charge of anything sharp or mechanical. The most frequent accidents are simply men not paying full attention to the job at hand. The handbook will be most useful, it gives me a guide to work from, and something to point to if the fellows start to argue."

"Would they? If this is for their own good, why would they resist your efforts to help?"

Max smiled ruefully, "A man does not like to be told he is doing something the wrong way, even if he knows he is. Many of these men were too young to fight and have never had the benefit of army training. They haven't had to swallow their pride and let someone else show them a better way."

"Are they all much younger than you?"

"Many are your age; some are younger still. There are some older men too, though they have either already been injured and keep quiet for fear of ridicule, or else they take care of themselves but ignore their fellow workers. It's my job to encourage everyone to look out for everyone else." He took another large gulp of beer, "How has your week been?"

"Busy now that the weather has brightened a little. We are having to squeeze passengers in who had paid for their flights last month, and extra luggage means extra fuel. Peter was rather worried the other day that he might have to land in Cumbria to refuel just to make sure he could reach Scotland."

"Now that does sound dangerous! I'm glad you don't fly with them."

Caroline looked down for a moment. "Funny you should say that. They have asked me if I want to travel to Amsterdam next month. Tommy and Rodney are going to meet with some businessmen there, to talk about a Dutch office. They thought I might like to go with them, take notes of the meetings, that sort of thing."

"And do you?"

"I said I would think about it."

"Do they all know about my job, or just your friend Tommy?"

"They all know. I thought it only fair that I should tell them that I might need to look for something else. Oh, and that was the other thing that happened this week, Mr Embry has written to say the apartment has been sold."

"Do you think they are trying to tempt you to stay?"

Caroline shook her head, "I don't think so, I really think they want someone to tag along and remember everything they agree to."

13

A TASTE OF EUROPE

Max was still concerned for Caroline's safety on board the flight to Amsterdam but could raise no other objection. On the first Tuesday in April, Caroline handed her case to Tommy to stow in the cargo hold and climbed aboard the aeroplane with Rodney at the controls in the open pilot's seat. They were taking three other passengers on the flight, all men. Caroline took her seat towards the front of the passenger cabin and Tommy joined her after pulling up the steps and sealing the door.

This was to be a very important business trip and Caroline was incredibly nervous, not only because it was her first flight, but also because she would be expected to take detailed minutes of the meetings. She had been practicing with Tommy over their recent lunch breaks; he would read aloud a few paragraphs of an unfamiliar novel or a newspaper article and Caroline would transcribe as quickly and accurately as she could. She had begun to develop her own shorthand for common words.

The Sunray company was in discussion with both Imperial Airways and Hauge Airlines, and it seemed likely that it would be absorbed by one or other of them. Rodney had insisted on flying himself, and Tommy had a briefcase of documents that the two men would discuss with their Dutch counterparts. They would land at Schiphol and be driven to the town of Haarlem where they would stay the night before returning to Somerset the next day. Caroline had been in contact with Mr Visser's secretary at Hauge Airways, a Miss van Horst, and had the hotel address in the front of her notebook. They had been told their accommodation and meals would be charged to the Dutch airline, though Caroline had brought some petty cash with her for emergencies. She had no idea if the Dutch would honour British pounds sterling but felt sure that a national bank should if one were available nearby.

Caroline turned to look at her fellow passengers. All three were businessmen, dressed in well-tailored coats and suits with silk ties and gold watches on chains across their waistcoats. One smoked a cigarette as he read through some papers. Another had stretched out in his seat with his eyes closed and appeared to be determined to sleep through the journey. The last was hunched over a notebook on his lap, holding a pen in one hand and a sheaf of papers in the other. They had all been served coffee and sandwiches before the flight, as it would take around three hours to get to Schiphol and Sunray Air did not serve refreshments on-board.

The engine suddenly became louder, and the cabin began to rattle and shake. Caroline looked at Tommy in alarm.

"Don't worry old thing!" he shouted over the din, "Perfectly safe, just a lot of hot air!"

They began their taxi across the airfield, with every bump and divot in the grassy surface painfully covered. Despite her excitement, Caroline gripped the arms of her chair tightly while she stared out of the small window on her left. She felt Rodney turn the plane, and then begin to pick up speed as they careered across the grass. With a final jolt, they were in the air and climbing. Caroline felt a little sick, just as she had in Blackpool on the big wheel as it reached its full height and the gondola swung through and started its descent. Tommy patted her hand before taking out his cigarettes and lighter.

Caroline had had no expectations of what the flight might be like, but she could not have imagined air would be so full of bumps. They encountered turbulence after almost an hour in the sky which continued until they were a few minutes out of Schiphol. Tommy shouted that he had never known it so rough, having flown a grand total of three times previously. At first Caroline thought something on the aeroplane was broken but Tommy's calm reassurance helped her to relax as best she could. The landing was smoother, as the wheels touched down on a thin hard concrete surface rather than grass. When Rodney brought the plane to a halt near to the control tower, Caroline stood on legs that felt like jelly and made her way onto Dutch soil.

Tommy and Caroline walked with the other passengers to the terminal and after showing their brand-new passports, they looked around for someone who might be Miss van Horst. A tall, blonde woman approached them after a few moments, and introduced herself as Vivienne van Horst. Her English was conversational, and she ushered Tommy and Caroline into the lounge area to wait for Rodney to finish making the plane secure and find them. It was after one o'clock and Caroline could not stop her stomach from growling with hunger. She blushed and hoped Vivienne had not heard. She had.

"It is late for luncheon?" Vivienne asked.

Caroline blushed deeper red, "I am rather hungry I'm afraid."

"You stay."

Vivienne stood up and walked off towards a pair of glass doors. Rodney appeared while she was gone and declared he could eat a horse. Tommy reminded him not to joke too loudly, as he may well end up doing so. Caroline couldn't tell if they were teasing her or not but was relieved when Vivienne returned with a tray of coffee and pastries. The three ate and drank quickly, aware that they were due to meet Mr Visser at three o'clock and they still had to travel to Haarlem. When they had finished, Vivienne shepherded them out of the terminal and into a waiting car.

Caroline had been told that Holland was flat, but she was still amazed at just how level the countryside was. Canals criss-crossed the land and the sky was a pale grey. She saw windmills in the distance, their sails turning slowly in the sea breeze. Men and women rode bicycles, many with small trailers attached to the back to carry groceries, a piece of furniture, a child. Haarlem itself had as many waterways as it did roads. The buildings rose from the waterside three and four storeys high, with red painted roofs and yellow, white and cream frontages. The car drew up outside a hotel with a blue door. Caroline couldn't read the sign but Vivienne explained that it was the Hotel Europa and they would be staying there as well as meeting with Mr Visser in one of the rooms. The hotel also served dinner so they would have no need to venture anywhere else if they were tired from their journey. Caroline was beginning to like Vivienne with her halting English and asked her what 'thank you' was in Dutch.

"Bedankt," Vivienne said with a smile.

From what Caroline could understand from her notes, the meeting was a cordial one. Vivienne had also been present taking notes as the men talked, much faster and more proficiently than Caroline had. The meeting went on for just over two hours and ended with warm handshakes and back slapping. Mr Visser opened the door and led Tommy and Rodney out, as if Caroline and Vivienne were invisible. Caroline looked at Vivienne who was making some final notes.

"Vivienne, will we be eating with the men this evening?"

"I think no. Men talk more without women. You eat with me?"

"I would like to, yes. Do you live nearby? I would like to go to my room and change, so I could meet you in the lounge, perhaps?"

Vivienne looked at Caroline blankly. "No, you eat with me, no need to dress again. Now to my home we go."

"Oh, that's so very kind of you, if you're absolutely sure?"

Vivienne nodded vigorously and indicated for Caroline to walk with her. They left the hotel and walked along the canal-side road that was lit with many swaying lamps which were reflected as golden pennies in the water below. Caroline thought it was one of the prettiest things she had ever seen. A few minutes later, Vivienne unlocked a door of a three-storey building and Caroline followed her through. They went up two flights of stairs to the apartment on the top floor and Vivienne unlocked her own front door. She pointed to the shoes just inside the door as she took off her own, and Caroline understood and removed hers also. Music was playing quietly inside the apartment and a young man was sat at a table in the living room using a typewriter. A number of scrunched up sheets of paper were discarded across the wooden floor.

Vivienne introduced her fiancé Edvard, and then gently tugged at Caroline's sleeve to guide her through the double half-glazed doors into the kitchen.

"He writes. Will not stop until food. You sit. Coffee?"

"Yes please." Caroline would have preferred tea but had understood that coffee was by far the more common drink on the continent.

Vivienne placed a small pan on the stove to make coffee and then set about preparing a simple dinner of fried fish, boiled potatoes and cabbage. Caroline was very interested in the room, with its numerous cupboards and large window that looked out onto the canal. It was clear that Vivienne and Edvard used it as a dining room as well, and Caroline was happy to unfold the tablecloth Vivienne gave her and lay three places with cutlery and glasses. After a small number of embarrassed gestures, Caroline was shown to the small bathroom. When she returned to the kitchen, Edvard had taken his place and Vivienne was dishing up the meal onto their plates.

Edvard spoke less English than Vivienne, but through her he asked Caroline about her home and her work. She in turn asked what he was writing. Vivienne rolled her eyes and answered for him that it was a novel about a young man who went to war and came home to find his family had moved away without him. He then must find them again. Caroline said it must be very exciting to be writing a novel, but Vivienne shook her head.

"Painful," she said. "Always angry it not work."

Caroline wasn't sure if Vivienne meant Edvard was angry that the novel wouldn't work the way he wanted, or if Vivienne was angry because Edvard wasn't working. She wondered if it were both of those things as Vivienne cleared their plates away. Dessert was another new experience for

Caroline;Vla. She looked at the creamy mixture in her glass bowl and sniffed. It wasn't a smell she was familiar with at home, but the airport lounge had smelled vaguely similar, as had the hotel. Vivienne offered Caroline some small redcurrants and indicated that they were to be spooned into the cream. When she ate a spoonful of the mixture, the assault on her tastebuds was thrilling. The sweet custard-like pudding with the tart currants, and the warmth of the cinnamon that she had smelled blended wonderfully and she couldn't help but smile.

After the meal, Edvard returned to his typewriter while Vivienne and Caroline washed and dried the dishes. Vivienne offered more coffee, but Caroline said she should be getting back to the hotel as it had been a long day. After an exchange in Dutch that appeared to Caroline to be somewhat heated, Edvard and Vivienne both stood, and Vivienne said they would walk her back to the hotel together. The *cafés* and bars were busy with patrons of all ages eating, drinking and dancing. Vivienne and Edvard waved and greeted several people they knew as they walked along and Caroline thought what a friendly and relaxed community it was there on the edge of the North Sea.

When they reached the hotel entrance, Vivienne and Edvard kissed Caroline's cheeks three times each, which quite surprised her as they were only very new acquaintances. She waved them farewell and went into the hotel. It wasn't late by common standards, and Caroline wondered if Tommy and Rodney were still at dinner. She lingered in the lobby, trying to decide whether to put her head around the dining room door or to go straight up to her room and the novel that was waiting for her there. The desk clerk noticed and asked if she needed any help. His English was much more accomplished than Vivienne's had been.

"Do you know my companions, Mr Gersen-Fisch and Mr Cooper? I wondered if they were still at dinner. They were with a Mr Visser from Hague Air."

"Mr Visser has left just five minutes ago. I believe the gentlemen are in the bar, which is through those doors and turn left."

Caroline followed the directions and immediately spotted Tommy and Rodney sitting opposite each other on low leather armchairs. There was a bottle in a bucket of ice and two champagne glasses on the coffee table between them.

"Caro! We were just wondering where you had got to! Sorry to leave you to fend for yourself, old thing. Pull up a seat." Tommy sounded as if he had drunk a considerable amount already that evening.

"I saw you two go off to dinner with Mr Visser, and Vivienne invited me to dine with her. She has a lovely apartment overlooking the canal. Are you celebrating?"

Rodney waved at a waiter and asked for another champagne glass. "We are, although I do wonder if we are counting our chickens as they say. But Tommy insisted we should celebrate a good meeting if nothing else."

"Well why not? It's not every day one gets wined and dined by the chairman of an international aviation company."

"It seemed a jolly boring meeting if you ask me," Caroline turned a smaller chair around to face the two men and sat down. "A lot of talk of capital and investment and returns and what not. I'm certain I noted it all down accurately, but I haven't the foggiest idea what it all means."

Tommy took the bottle from the ice bucket and poured champagne into all three glasses.

"It means that Mr Visser is willing to part with a considerable amount of his fortune in order to help us extend our operation into Amsterdam and beyond into Germany.

His company has routes to Frankfurt and Berlin, and by joining with him, we get to use those routes as well. The best part is, we keep our own name. I did fear that he would want to swallow us up into Hague Air, didn't you Rodders?"

"I did. It's been happening all over the shop recently. Imperial Airways have grown enormously over the past two years buying up smaller companies with their airfields. I think it's what will swing it in Hague Air's favour with the other chaps when we tell them."

"So, let's celebrate being able to keep our own names!" Tommy lifted his glass and drank the contents in one go.

Caroline took a sip but knew she would sleep much better if she didn't drink any alcohol that evening.

"Will we have time for breakfast in the morning before we leave for Amsterdam?" She asked, placing her glass carefully on the coffee table next to the ice bucket.

Rodney lit a cigarette.

"I should think so. They serve here from six, and we need to be ready for the motor car at eight. Are you wanting to get off to bed?" He raised an eyebrow and Caroline, though not particularly good at noticing advances in her direction, saw and heard exactly what Rodney was thinking.

"You should probably make sure that Tommy gets to bed, Rodney. I am quite able to find my own. I think I shall go up now. Tommy, do make sure you drink some water as well as that champagne."

"Is Helen paying you to keep notes on me too?" He asked, good naturedly.

At breakfast, Tommy was yawning every other minute, but no worse for his celebration the night before. Rodney explained they had been drawn into a card game by some French businessmen and didn't get to bed until after two o'clock.

"Will you be alright to fly?" Caroline asked.

"Yes, yes, perfectly alright. It's a straight route." Rodney said with a chuckle that Caroline was not entirely convinced by. "Look here, I probably should apologise for last night, for suggesting … perhaps … well, you know."

"You know I am already spoken for." Caroline was amused by Rodney's apparent embarrassment. She would have expected Rupert to over-step the boundaries of politeness but not Rodney.

"Yes. Yes, and jolly lucky chap he is too. It was the drink. Nothing more. Won't happen again."

The car which had delivered them to Haarlem the day before arrived punctually to collect them at eight the next morning. Caroline had hoped to see Vivienne again, but only the driver was their company for the trip this time. When they arrived at Schiphol, Rodney left them to make sure the aeroplane was ready, and Caroline and Tommy had coffee in the waiting lounge. It was a brighter day. The sun streamed through the windows of the lounge and Caroline sat back comfortably in her chair and watched seagulls soar lazily in the blue sky outside. The lounge was busy with travellers; six would be returning with Sunray Air to Somerset including an elderly woman with a cat in a wicker hamper. The cat was a Siamese and yowled continuously, protesting at its confinement. Caroline hoped it would be carried in the cargo space rather than in the passenger cabin.

The sound of the aeroplane's engine was enough to drown out the cries of the Siamese cat. Tommy slept for most of the journey and feeling like a seasoned traveller on her second ever flight, Caroline was content to look out of her small window at the sea and then green countryside below. The return trip was via Croydon to collect some freight and drop off two of the businessmen. Rodney drank several cups of coffee before taking the controls again.

They arrived back at Thurloxton in a shower of rain, the clouds having increased as they neared Somerset. Caroline spent an hour typing up her notes from the meeting before leaving her office and dancing across the puddles to the Austin. In her luggage she had kept a linen napkin from the Hotel Europa which had a crest on one corner. She felt terribly guilty for what was clearly theft on an international scale, but she had wanted something to put in her keepsake box to remind her of her journey. She reasoned with herself that the Hotel must have hundreds of napkins and nobody would miss one. She still heard her late mother's disapproving voice in her ear that thieves should have their hands chopped off as she drove along the lanes towards Taunton that evening.

Max was relieved to find Caroline at home on Friday when he returned from Plymouth. He had not wanted to telephone during the week as Caroline had suggested; he did not want her to feel that he was questioning her judgement. He was, however, after a month of travelling to and from Plymouth each week, tired of the journey and on the Saturday morning over breakfast he proposed that Caroline arrange to go down with him and begin to look for somewhere for them both to live.

"We can find somewhere to rent if you're not sure about it all, but I don't think I want to be going to and fro like I have been for much longer." He said, breaking his boiled egg in half with his knife on a tea plate, before using his teaspoon to scoop out the contents of the shell against his left hand.

"I really didn't see very much of Plymouth besides Spooners when I visited Helen. I should like to have a look around. But perhaps I could travel down one Friday and come home again on the Sunday, and you could stay there instead which would save you travelling."

"I only have a small room. I don't think Mrs Waring would agree to me bringing a lady friend to stay." Max chuckled as he spoke, something he was doing more often these days he realised.

"Then let's stay somewhere else. There must be lots of hotels in Plymouth, it's a seaport after all. We can afford it for a weekend."

"You would have to be Mrs Bird of course."

"Of course. Will you choose somewhere, do you have time?"

"Yes, I can make a booking after work. There's a nice place along the road from Mrs Waring's that really does look out onto the Hoe."

"It will be lovely to see the sea again."

"But you saw the sea in Holland, didn't you?"

"Yes, but that wasn't our sea." Caroline said, wistfully.

They settled on the weekend before the May Day Bank Holiday Monday. It would mean Caroline could travel home on the Monday morning and Max could go to watch some of the Navy ships manoeuvring across the Sound and perhaps if his legs were strong enough, take a walk along the Barbican to look at the fishing boats on the quayside. It also meant that Helen would be in Plymouth as it was her mother's sixtieth birthday that weekend. Tommy had been cautiously dropping hints to Helen that she might invite Caroline and Max to the party that was being arranged, and Helen finally agreed. It was not that she didn't want to see Caroline, she argued, but that she could not condone her current relationship. Tommy had snapped back that Helen had no moral legs to stand on and walked out of the room before Helen could reply.

Caroline received the invitation with excitement, but Max was less enthusiastic. While at work or around town, he was able to somewhat disguise his disfigurement with a hat or a scarf. In polite company, he would necessarily be more exposed wearing a suit and no hat. He knew how many people shied away from him when they saw the hole where his ear should be. Children often pointed, particularly little boys he had noticed, whereas little girls would either cry or whisper to their mothers 'that man has no ear' while keeping their eyes firmly on him. It was worse when the children cried. It seemed to trigger some innate response in whoever was with the child, they would all steer their charge away muttering – or sometimes shouting – that he shouldn't be allowed out in public, frightening little children. At the railway yard there were no small children, and no women to be offended by his battle scars. He was thankful for that.

Max met Caroline off the train as a fine misty rain fell across Plymouth. He carried her case, and she did not protest as she once might have but slipped her hand under his left elbow. She had packed her long blue evening dress for the party and had bought Max a new dress shirt and jacket. It would be a while before he could pay for one himself out of his wages, Caroline had said, and his work jacket smelled of engine oil. They walked slowly across the city, through Plymouth's main shopping streets towards the Hoe. It was as busy as Bristol had been, with buses, trams and horse carts vying with motor cars for space on the roads, many of which still had cobbled surfaces. Groups of men stood around on street corners and outside pubs, some in naval uniforms from a range of countries. They smoked and talked, whistling at pretty girls who hurried by with one eye on their reflection in the shop windows.

Max might not have been able to afford a new suit jacket, or to pay for their hotel for the weekend, but he had been able to book them a table for dinner that night at the Swiss Café. It was the most talked-about restaurant in the city where celebrities visiting Plymouth could be seen to dine. The owners were Italian but had felt Swiss sounded more trans-European. They served pies, pastries, chops and steaks, with a range of beers and wines. The décor was green and gold, and the waiters wore crisp white jackets, similar to those on board the cruise liners now regularly docking at nearby Devonport. Teague had suggested that Max might like to take 'Mrs Bird' there and had given him the name of the second chef who happened to be a neighbour of Teague's. So it had been arranged, and after Caroline had changed at their hotel, they walked back towards George Street for their dinner.

The menu, much to both their reliefs, was written in English. Noting that several other diners that night were either missing an arm or hand, Max selected a steak with boiled potatoes and three vegetables, and Caroline chose a fillet of cod in a parsley sauce. They both had beer, Caroline did not want a whole bottle of wine to herself. As the house band struck up a jaunty jazz number, the couple finished their meal with slices of cherry pie and custard. Caroline would have liked to dance, but she knew Max would feel self-conscious shuffling around while others kicked high and waved their arms with gay abandon. Instead, they agreed to return to their hotel and have a cocktail in the bar before bed.

It was still raining the fine drizzle that coated everything with a felt blanket of dampness. Caroline's hat preserved her hair but began to drip as they arrived at their hotel.

"What a lively place that was. Thank you for arranging it all, Max. The only sad thing was to see those people waiting around outside. I suppose they beg for the scraps when the café closes each night. I have seen them do the same in Taunton when Edna and I come out of the picture house, but never so many as there were here."

"Times are hard. We are lucky, Caroline. We both have work, you have your inheritance. We don't live beyond our means."

"I know I have been very fortunate that my father made such arrangements for me, before and after his death. And Victor, Annie's eldest son, should also have the benefit of Father's prudence. I can't remember if I told you that there was a one hundred pounds bequest to Victor in Father's will? It is in trust, naturally, until he is twenty-one, and should gain a significant amount of interest over the years."

"No, you didn't say."

"Father was godfather to Victor. And in my will I have a made a quarter share of my estate to Angelica." Caroline stopped in the hallway as they were approaching their room, "I shall have to see about changing my will won't I, now that we … are whatever we are."

"For this weekend we are Mr and Mrs Bird." Max opened their room door, and they went inside.

Caroline took off her coat and hat, "Yes, but in the eyes of the law, if anything should happen to me, you would not receive anything from my estate unless I specifically include you in my will. I shall have to speak to Mr Embry when I go back to Taunton."

"I know some people might think so, but I am not after your money."

Max sat on the edge of the bed and undid his shoes. Caroline waited until he had slipped them off, and then went to him, putting her arms around his neck.

"I know you're not. I didn't really have any money when we first met. Do we care very much what other people think of us?"

Max sighed, "It's never going to be easy for us, you know that. People will always gossip. People are afraid of how I look. You might not have noticed the stares and whispers this evening, but I did. And they don't only look at me. They will pity you – yes, I know it's ridiculous, but they will all the same. Men will wonder if they can tempt you away and once they get to know our situation women will call you a loose woman, perhaps even to your face. I'm lucky to have my job, but you might find it more difficult to secure one here. So many more people are looking for work now. Caroline, it doesn't matter so much if we care or not; it's what others think of us that will dictate our fortunes."

"No one will tempt me away, Max." Caroline said firmly. "And I have never been interested in gossiping women. I want us to be happy together wherever we are, that's all that matters. One moment at a time."

Max said nothing. He knew what he had said was true, and he knew Caroline's naïveté was a precious thing.

When one is looking for a new home, it is often better not to view property on a gloriously sunny day. This is particularly the case in the west country where, although they do experience sunny days, the more common condition is the grey blanket of misty drizzle that had shrouded Plymouth since Caroline's arrival the day before. Max had taken advice from Teague as to the areas of Plymouth he and Caroline might consider making their home. They would be taking buses and trams across the city, starting from the Theatre terminus at Derry's clock, a short walk from their hotel.

After a light breakfast, they set off first for St Budeaux, which sat on the hill above the river Tamar, overlooking Brunel's feat of engineering that was the rail bridge across the river. Caroline was not impressed by the houses strung up and across the hillside, and the smell that came from the riverbanks as the tide was low. Had it been a sunny day, her perception might have been swayed by the extensive views to Dartmoor in the north and Cornwall to the west, but as it was that day there were no views to be had.

They journeyed southwest, past the growing new housing development of North Prospect to Milehouse junction, then changed trams and rode around Central Park to the area of Peverell. Caroline liked this area better, the houses seemed well proportioned and had rear access by cobbled alleys as well as formal front entrances with wide doors. Many of the houses here had two windows in the bay for the sitting room and main bedroom above, and the roads, while still on a hill, sloped less steeply. The couple saw two notices of properties that were available to rent along Holland Road, and one for sale in Hyde Park Road. Caroline made a note of each in her pocket notebook.

From Peverell, Max and Caroline continued towards Mannamead. This would be the closest of the areas to the station yard where Max worked, and equidistant to the growing goods depot at Laira. They walked slowly along Compton Avenue from Mannamead Road towards Seymour Road. Here, past the church of Emmanuel on the corner, they found a range of houses, some built recently and a few that were thirty or forty years older. One or two were set way back from the street with winding paths or terraced front gardens that reminded Caroline of the house in Watchet that Noah had bought. She was fighting down a wave of guilt when they came to a detached bungalow that had a for sale sign tied to the driveway gate.

Caroline stopped to take a closer look, which caught Max off guard, and he swayed unsteadily as she let go of his arm.

"I wish you would give me some warning when you want to stop like that!"

"I'm sorry, but just look at it Max! Do you think we could have a look through the windows? There doesn't seem to be anyone living there."

Max pushed open the gate that opened onto the driveway along the side of the house which led to a garage at the far end of the property. The grass on either side was tall and studded with yarrow and dandelions, and the privet and laurel hedge that separated it from its neighbour to the right needed a trim. The porch over the front door was supported by four slender columns topped with an arch of ornate ironwork; one either side of the door and one at each corner of the bungalow. On the far side of the front door, a bay protruded with its roof pointing up and out, reminding Caroline of a castle tower.

They crept along the driveway to the rear of the bungalow and discovered a small, concreted area outside what they assumed was the kitchen door, a coal bunker, and more overgrown lawn with a pink camelia desperately trying to flower amid the abandonment. Max wandered away to look at the garage, while Caroline stood on tip toe and tried to see into the the windows. She was startled to hear a voice from above.

"I say! Excuse me, can I help you?"

Caroline looked up to see a woman in a house coat holding a duster at her open window.

"Hello there! We noticed the for-sale sign and thought we'd be ever so cheeky and take a look round."

"Wait there, I'll come down." The woman closed the window and disappeared before Caroline could answer.

Max joined Caroline and they made their way back to the front of the plot, where the woman from next door arrived, minus her house coat. She stopped in surprise when she saw Max, and then visibly pulled herself together and held out her hand.

"Mildred Roscommon, most people call me Milly. I have the key here if you'd like to look inside."

Max shook Milly's hand, "Max Bird, and this is Caroline."

"We'd love to look inside if you're sure it's no trouble," Caroline said quickly. She was almost laughing at their apparent good fortune.

Milly unlocked the front door and let them in as she explained that the previous owner who had had the bungalow built, was now in India and had decided to sell. The hallway ran the length of the building, with a small room immediately to the right that had a floor to ceiling narrow window. The room with the circular bay was a sitting room to the left and had a tiled fireplace. Further along the hall was a dining room, two large bedrooms and one smaller room. The hall then branched off and a separate toilet and bathroom plus the kitchen that Caroline had seen from the outside were at the rear right corner of the property. The floors throughout were wooden, and most of the walls painted in a pale-yellow paint.

"I have the solicitor's details if you are interested in taking it," Milly said when Max and Caroline found her again by the front door.

"Do you know how much the sale price is?" Caroline asked.

"I'm afraid I don't. Bill, my husband, might know, he was always friendly with Mr Harmer."

"I think we should take the details if you have them Mrs Roscommon."

"Of course. I'll lock up here, we don't want any undesirables finding their way in!"

Milly led them out of the garden and into her own. She opened the front door to her detached house and asked them to wait in what she called the parlour while she went to find the solicitor's address. Max would have liked to sit down, but as a seat hadn't explicitly been offered, he felt it might seem rude to do so. If Milly were to be their new neighbour, he didn't want to start by making a bad impression.

The room was full of china ornaments and photographs in frames. Dark Edwardian furniture crowded around the fireplace and Caroline felt it was out of place in the newly built house with its large windows and generous proportions. She understood that as she and her father had done, old furniture would have been brought into a new home until replacements could be found.

"Here we are, I knew it was Mutley Plain but I can never remember the number. Prescott is his name." She handed the sheet of paper to Max who folded it and put it in his pocket.

"Thank you. Well, we should be getting along now, we won't keep you Mrs Roscommon."

"Thank you for letting us see inside, it was very nice to meet you," Caroline shook the other woman's hand once more as they returned to the hallway.

Once outside, and with Milly's door firmly closed, Caroline slipped her hand under Max's left elbow as they walked back towards Mannamead Road.

"What did you think of it?"

Max had turned to look at Caroline, knowing she would want to talk, so that he could watch her lips as well as try to hear what she said. It was always awkward when they walked together; he needed his right arm to be free to help propel himself along and keep his balance, but it meant not always hearing what Caroline said on his left.

"I don't know. It felt rather large, perhaps too large for us." Max was acutely aware that most of the housing stock being built in the city and across the country was designed for families, with children.

"There would be room for us to paint, that odd front room was bright enough with the tall window. And we'll always need spare rooms for when friends come to stay."

"I think we should go and see that estate agent that we saw in Peverell. There might be other properties that we could look at tomorrow, from the outside at least."

Caroline was a little disappointed at Max's lack of enthusiasm but agreed.

Lady Rosalind's birthday party was due to begin at seven that evening. Helen was in the dining room where a buffet had been laid out for the guests to help themselves. Her parents had argued earlier that afternoon over William's inability to return home from Aden for the auspicious occasion. Lady Rosalind naturally wanted her elder son there, Colonel Postgate had pointed out that should William return there were several men in the city who would make it their business to seek him out and either reclaim a debt owed, challenge him to a duel over some offence taken, or force him to the nearest church to make an honest woman out of a slip of a girl. The Colonel was happier the more distance he could put between his errant son and the rest of the family.

Jolyon came into the dining room as Helen was turning a plate of small savoury pastries. Her younger brother by three years (there were only eleven months between Helen and William), Jolyon was the brains of the family. He worked for the navy, based at Devonport dockyard as a legal clerk and was studying to become a solicitor. He was slim, as his father had once been, but had Lady Rosalind's olive skin and dark hair as did his sisters. Roberta, their eldest sister, was in the kitchen with the cook and maids giving them their final instructions for the evening. Helen and Jolyon had both wondered if there might be a male companion for Roberta, but her status as spinster now seemed to be a permanent one.

"Alicia will be here any time now," Jolyon said, pushing his spectacles higher on his nose and casting a glance over the food. It was the first time he had invited the daughter of Chief Petty Officer Mortimer currently on-board HMS Furious somewhere in the north Atlantic, to meet his parents and sisters. Alicia lived with her mother and younger sister in a three-story house in Devonport, and the two young people had met at the cinema six months earlier.

"Don't be so nervous, darling, everyone will adore her, I'm sure." Helen had never met Alicia but felt sure Jolyon's choice of sweetheart would not be as troublesome as William's usually were, despite being only sixteen years old. She offered Jolyon a cigarette and they both lit up from Helen's lighter.

"Has Tommy gone to collect your friends?" Jolyon asked, peering out of the window at the last pinkish glow of the sunset. The rain had stopped around six and the clouds lifted enough to give the sun a brief moment of extravagance.

Helen chose not to correct the plural. "Yes, they are staying at a hotel near the Hoe. He has been quite the engineer recently between Caroline and I. One wonders what plot or surprise he will force next."

"I haven't met her, have I? Oh, don't look so exasperated Helen, I can't be expected to remember every one of your friends!"

"I admit, I do know rather a lot of people, but Caroline is one of my oldest friends darling, you have heard me talk about her even though you have never met her."

"Describe her to me so that I shall pretend to recognise her."

"She is almost as tall as I am, not quite so slender; her hair is a common brown, cut to her shoulders and has an unruly nature." Helen looked off into the distance, picturing Caroline when they had last been happy in each other's company. "She has eyes that are rather too large and open, not the sort of eyes that could ever keep a secret, though Caro rarely tries. She has a love of swimming, though goodness knows why, and is an artist, or a secretary, or a seamstress as the notion takes her."

"She sounds rather interesting. And her husband?"

Helen drew on her cigarette. Jolyon would have to be told, to avoid any embarrassment later. "They are not married, darling. I believe Max is employed by the Great Western Railway Company, but Tommy could probably give you more information if you want it."

A motor car pulled into the gravel driveway outside the window. "She's here!" Jolyon turned and hurried from the room to open the front door to his love. Helen watched the young girl step out of the vehicle, the door held for her by a man in a grey suit and cap. Alicia wore a knee-length cream dress with a light overcoat of brown, cream stockings and black shoes. Her blond hair was cut very short and around her head was a cream band with a small feather sticking up on one side. Helen saw the girl's face light up with a smile as Jolyon went to meet her with a kiss on her cheek.

Helen stubbed out her cigarette in an ashtray and went to meet her potential sister-in-law.

Max was, in the end, grateful for Caroline's gift of a new jacket for the evening. Though Caroline had described the Postgate's villa in Lipson to him, neither of them knew what kind of party it would be. Caroline had suspected there would be older women that Lady Rosalind knew from her political and charity work, and perhaps some family friends. She felt a little nervous about seeing Helen again, despite their reconciliation. She was also aware of how people reacted to Max, and as she did not know the company they were entering, she was worried that someone might make a scene. Tommy, as ever, was on her side. He shook Max's hand warmly when he arrived at the hotel to collect them, having been fully briefed on Max's appearance and disabilities. He chattered on during the trip back to Lipson, and Max asked him several questions about the safety of the aeroplanes that Sunray Air operated.

There were several motor cars in the driveway of the villa when Tommy turned in off the road. Caroline and Max waited for Tommy while he took off his driving gloves and left them in his car, then they all entered the party together. There was music playing from a phonogram in one room where chairs and tables had been pushed back to create a dance floor. People were standing in small groups, drinking and chatting in their finery. In the dining room, some guests were helping themselves to the buffet, piling their small china plates with slices of pie, assorted fruit and hot sausages before finding a seat at one of the tables to eat their food.

Lady Rosalind sat in her favourite chair by the open French doors in the morning room, a glass of whiskey in her hand and a smile on her powdered face. She was joined by a rotating precession of guests wishing her many happy returns and kissing her rouged cheeks. Roberta was on hand to whisper the names of those her mother could not immediately remember, and to accept any small gifts that had been brought.

After making sure Caroline and Max had a drink, Tommy had left them to seek out Helen. Caroline was hungry, so they first went into the dining room and Max took a seat while Caroline filled two plates for them. After they had eaten and made conversation with various other guests who joined them at their table, they left their empty glasses and went in search of Lady Rosalind. Caroline as usual had her hand through Max's left arm. It felt natural to her, and it meant Max was free to use his good right arm to shake hands, take a drink or anything else he might need to do in company. They approached Lady Rosalind in her chair, and the older woman's eyes sparkled as she recognised Caroline.

"Many happy returns, Lady Rosalind."

"Thank you my dear! So good to see you again."

Roberta bent to whisper in Lady Rosalind's ear, "I don't know who these people are, Mother."

Lady Rosalind waved her daughter away, "This is Helen's young friend, Caroline, and her companion, so I understand." She looked at Max keenly, taking in his features as if she were appraising a racehorse. "One of our brave soldiers." She said in a kind tone.

"Lady Rosalind, this is Max Bird."

Max held out his hand and was surprised at the firmness of the older woman's grasp, "Happy birthday, Lady Rosalind. Such a lively party."

"Thank you, Max. I do love to see people enjoying themselves. Are you enjoying yourself?"

Max understood that she was not referring to the party alone. "I am, thank you."

An older couple had moved to stand behind Max and Caroline and Roberta smiled at them over Max's shoulder.

"Well, you young things will be wanting to find Helen no doubt. She is in the garden. And Caroline," Lady Rosalind reached out for Caroline's hand, "understand that she cares about you, that is all."

"Yes, yes I do, Lady Rosalind, thank you."

They found Helen and Tommy, smoking and sitting on white-painted iron chairs around a matching table on the lawn behind a rose bed. Tommy offered Max a cigarette as he and Caroline sat on the two vacant chairs. They all sat in silence for a few moments. It was Max who spoke first.

"Thank you for inviting us to the party, Helen."

"Mother was quite insistent that Caroline should come." Helen crossed her legs beneath her apricot chiffon dress. She wore a matching apricot cape that tied at the neck, the colour contrasting with her dark hair and olive skin.

"I was surprised that she remembered me, it's been four years since I last saw her."

"Helen's been talking about you to her rather a lot recently," blurted Tommy, earning a sharp look from Helen that he chose to ignore. "Lady Ros thought you might want to stay at the house in Tavistock while you were down here, but I explained you'd only be here for the weekend as we need you back at the airfield."

"How kind of her. We are quite comfortable at the hotel though. We've spent much of today wandering around Plymouth looking at houses, haven't we?" She smiled at Max.

Tommy sensed something was afoot. "Max, have you met my brother-in-law Jolyon? He is just by the door with his young lady. Shall we?"

The men got up and walked back to the house. Helen blew out cigarette smoke and turned to Caroline.

"Mother thinks I am being too hard on you."

"You've told her about Max and I? About our situation?"

"She is the wisest woman I know. She pointed out that Max was not creeping about between two houses, that he had made as clean a break of things as is possible when one cannot afford a divorce. I felt such a cad holding out while Tommy gushed at how happy you have been since Max moved in with you. But you do understand how worried I have been for you darling, don't you?"

"I do. I think I would have felt the same if the shoe were on the other foot."

"I remember your reaction when we told you we were to be married. Thinking back, I can understand how shocked you were, and yet now everything is as if we were a normal couple. Tommy adores you. Can you forgive my harshness?"

Caroline looked at her friend, then looked across the garden to where Max, Tommy and Jolyon stood in the light from the morning room. Three men so very different from each other, each with their own impediments.

"He sends Diana money every week from his pension. Ten shillings. He doesn't think he can have children and I don't want any. I had felt that before I moved to Taunton, but I am sure of it now. There is something about him that makes me feel I can take on the world, Helen. I don't want to rescue him or mother him, and he wouldn't stand for it. He wants nothing from me except me. There are no presumptions, no expectations, no demands."

"I understand he has a job now here in Plymouth. At the railway. Is that why you've been looking at houses?"

"Yes. It's so very tiring for him to come home and go back again each weekend. I so enjoy working at the airfield, and the trip to Holland was such an experience, but I miss the sea and I have money now to buy a house somewhere.

It would help Max feel … useful again. He needs to keep his job, and I don't need to work for a while at least. I've paid the rest that I owed on the Austin, there's nothing keeping me in Taunton now."

Helen lit another cigarette, the end glowing golden in the darkness as she inhaled.

"There is an airport here in Plymouth, I'm sure you know that. I have been thinking about asking Papa for a motor car, rather like yours. It's not entirely necessary around town, but with Tommy away during the week it would be useful to visit Daisy for example." She turned to face Caroline suddenly. "Do you love him?"

"I think I do, yes." There was no hesitation in Caroline's response.

"Let's go and dance, shall we?" Helen took hold of Caroline's hand across the table.

"And see if Alicia wants to join us."

They linked arms as they crossed the lawn to rejoin the party.

14

BALANCE IN ALL THINGS

Caroline's last day with Sunray Air was Friday 2 August 1929. The rent on Elmsworth was paid up until the end of August, and Caroline was planning to visit her friends in Bradford-on-Avon, Cheltenham and north Somerset that month while the final details of her house purchase were completed. Max was still travelling up and down the railway tracks each Friday and Sunday, and while finding it ever more tiring, was focused on the day they could move into the bungalow on Compton Avenue together. Though they had looked at two other properties in Peverell, it had been clear that Caroline's heart belonged to the bungalow and Max had not put up any more resistance to the idea.

Caroline's solicitor, Mr Embry, and then Mr Foxton at the Building Society, had taken a considerable amount of convincing that purchasing a house was what Caroline should be using the bulk of her ready cash to do. Concerns were raised about her ability to run a home, which she pointed out she had been doing for some time now, and whether Plymouth was a suitable area for her to reside. Caroline suspected that both older men would have preferred her to return closer to Cheltenham and it reminded her of the conversation she had had with Lady Victoria in the Clarion Club in London. Vic had said how despite her fortune, she was unable to chart her own course in the world. Caroline had nowhere near as much wealth as Vic had had, but now understood the constraints placed on a woman despite her outward independence. The fact she could not have obtained a mortgage on the property in her own right should she have needed or wanted one was further evidence of her restricted sex.

Mr Harmer's solicitor had been able to contact him in India without much difficulty and had taken instruction to sell at four hundred and fifty pounds. This was a little more than the sale of the apartment had generated, but still left Caroline with savings of close to seven hundred pounds plus the income from her now substantial shares portfolio. She had been depositing her wages from the airfield into her post office savings account each Saturday morning, while Max withdrew his pension and made out the postal order to Diana. Mr Embry and Mr Foxton knew of her post office account's existence, but Caroline flatly refused to discuss with them how much it contained. Even Max did not know. It was one of only a handful of truly independent things that belonged to her, and she was determined to keep it that way.

Mr Embry had also been reluctant to agree to the changes that Caroline wanted to make to her will in favour of Max. It was only when Caroline, exasperated with his objections over the telephone, said that she would take her business elsewhere if he refused, did he agree to take her instruction. Now, in the event of her death, Max would receive a half share of her estate after any duties were paid, with Annie and Angelica receiving the other two quarter shares. She added a small gift of fifty pounds for baby Grace, and twenty-five pounds each for Lottie's twin girls Alice and Edith.

Max had taken charge of arranging the transportation of the contents of Elmsworth to Plymouth, aided by Edna and her contacts through the estate agency. A Taunton removals company would use their steam lorry to collect the furniture and take it to Plymouth, while their smaller vehicles would transport the crates of books, kitchen ware and other small items to the railway station where they would be packed onto a train and retrieved in Plymouth by a second removals company. Max had arranged with Teague and one of the day shift managers that three able men could be used to offload and load the removal lorry from the train at Plymouth for an extra three shillings each that day out of Max's own pocket. The steam lorry would take two to three days to make the eighty-mile journey, dependent on obtaining sufficient coal and water along the route. Max felt he would rather pay for that job to be done by professionals and not have everything transported by train.

On Caroline's last day at Sunray Air, the ground crew presented her with a bouquet of flowers and the promise of a free return trip to anywhere the company serviced, whenever Caroline wanted to claim it. She had mentioned to a few of their regular customers and delivery drivers that she would be leaving, and several had sent cards to the airfield wishing her bon voyage to pastures new. Caroline was sad to be leaving them all and found herself crying two or three times as she said goodbye to everyone that day, but as she drove out of the airfield gates in the sunny summer heat, she felt a delicious sense of freedom.

The first full week of August Caroline devoted to producing two canvases to send to Elsa and Bobby in London. She had started one over her Christmas holiday and wanted to finish that and use up her remaining blank canvas so that they would not be damaged in transit to Plymouth. Working from her old sketches, she became so absorbed in her work that she missed lunch altogether and had an early dinner two days running. When she was happy with both paintings, she decided to show Max before she packaged them up. She wrote a short note to Elsa to warn her to expect the canvases the following week, and then took a bottle of beer out into the back garden to enjoy the early evening sun while a potato baked in the oven for her dinner.

Jonathan Collier was also in his back garden next door, with his bicycle upside down. He was greasing the chain, and heard Caroline bring her kitchen chair outside. He stood up, wiping his hands on a rag, and leaned on the lower portion of the brick wall that separated the two gardens.

"Good evening, Miss Munhead!"

"Good evening, Jonathan. Are you working on your bicycle?"

"Yes, the chain keeps slipping off, so I've been trying to sort it out."

"Would you mind giving our grass one final trim sometime next week please? I shan't be at home, but you know where the shed key is, and I can leave your shilling on the windowsill here."

"Yes, I can. I'm saving up for a crystal wireless kit. Oh, did you say a final trim?" The boy suddenly looked worried.

"Yes, I'm afraid I shall be moving out some time this month and relocating to Devonshire. But there will be a steam removals lorry to collect our furniture, you might be interested in looking at it as long as you don't get in the men's way."

"A steam lorry! Gosh, yes I would like that. And I promise not to get too close. Mother would be cross if I got coal or oil on my clothes."

"Well look out for it won't you. I think that was your mother calling you just then."

Jonathan went into his own kitchen as Caroline sipped her glass of beer. Winnifred had never been particularly keen on Jonathan talking to Caroline over the garden wall, and usually found an excuse to call him inside if she noticed that they were. Caroline wondered what kind of neighbours Mildred and Bill Roscommon would be, and what neighbours they might have on the other side of the bungalow. She had mentioned to Max that she would like to attend Emmanuel church in order to meet some of the locals, and Max had turned his nose up and said he was not interested in going with her. Max usually discussed religion in abstract terms with her, never personal ones and she had come to understand that what little faith had been instilled in him as a child had been blasted out of him on the battlefields.

When she showed him the two canvases in the spare bedroom that weekend, he nodded appreciatively.

"I like the way you make the charcoal flow across the surface. I remember your sketches of Ed Bohenna, how tentative they were compared to the boldness you show now. You've come a long way."

"What happened to the sketch you made of me that day?" Caroline asked as they went back downstairs.

"I left it in Cornwall at the Bohenna's. I couldn't take it home."

At the bottom of the stairs Caroline turned and put her arms around Max's waist.

"I should like to go back to Cornwall, perhaps next year. St Ives bay was so beautiful in the sunlight."

Max kissed the top of her head. "Perhaps we can take a cottage for a week there. Somewhere secluded. But look,

Caroline, there is something we need to discuss, something that I have been thinking about since we went to your friend's party."

Caroline looked up, saw the slight furrow in Max's brow, and said, "Let me make a pot of tea and then tell me."

Max had spent some time talking to Jolyon and Tommy at Lady Rosalind's birthday party while Caroline, Helen and Alicia danced together. Max had mentioned that he was still married; he knew Tommy was already aware and when he learned that Jolyon was hoping to become a solicitor he wondered if he might know about divorce law. Jolyon had explained that it wasn't his area of expertise, but that adultery was usually the only route to a decree absolute if the husband could prove it. Max had shaken his head and said the adultery was not on his wife's side. After a pause, Jolyon said that a woman would normally need to prove adultery on the part of her husband but also other reasons such as desertion or cruelty. It would not be enough that Max was no longer living with Diana, Jolyon explained, if he were still maintaining the home. It had to be a complete break.

Max had been ruminating on this information ever since, particularly each time he sent off the postal order to Diana for ten shillings.

"So you see, according to Jolyon, if I keep sending her the money, she wouldn't be able to prove sufficient grounds for divorce even if she wanted to. Yet if I don't send it, I don't know that I can live with my own conscience. She would be left with nothing and none of this is her fault really." Max rubbed his hand over his face and then took out his cigarettes.

As he lit up, Caroline said, "Do you think you ought to ask her again for a divorce? It's been almost a year since you left."

"I won't have you pay for it. It's bad enough that you would be named in it."

"Perhaps if you stop sending her the money, she will change her mind and start proceedings. But then how would she find you – we'll be in Plymouth in a couple of weeks."

"I don't know. I don't know what I'm going to do yet, I just wanted you to know how things stand."

Caroline's first trip that August was to Bradford-on-Avon. She spent three nights with Philip and Mary Rose and the children and was interested to find that Audrey no longer wore the uniform that she had brought with her from the orphanage. Mary explained that she and Philip had decided to formally adopt Audrey and that the church had agreed. The girl still did not speak, and rarely smiled, but had developed a good relationship with Angelica and was particularly attentive to Grace. Mary felt comfortable leaving her daughters in Audrey's care when she went to the shops or to visit the friends she was starting to make in her own right, and Caroline agreed that it seemed to be a good solution for everyone.

Caroline had already told Philip and Mary about Max by letter and was expecting Philip to offer some spiritual guidance at some point during her stay. It came as they were all sitting in the vicarage garden, watching Audrey play with Angelica and her dolls.

"The house in Plymouth, will you be renting?" Philip asked as a means of turning their conversation to Max.

"No, I have purchased it. There was enough money from Father's estate." Caroline looked at Philip, "I have made provision for Max in my will, should anything happen."

"Caroline, you know that I cannot condone your current domestic situation. I am sure Max is a perfect gentleman, but one cannot ignore the fact that in God's eyes you are both committing a dreadful sin. Him more so, for not only living with you but deserting his wife to do so."

"I don't want to fall out with you Philip, I understand that you care and that of course your beliefs are sacred to you. But God felt it necessary to let my brother die. God felt it necessary to make me an orphan – and Audrey too – and God felt it necessary to allow Max to be horrifically wounded in battle. Why would God do those things and yet be upset that Max and I are sharing a bed without being married?"

Philip was silent. His God had also seen it necessary to take his and Mary's son Mark with whooping cough. It was difficult to see Him as a merciful and loving God at times, Philip conceded.

Mary, who had been sitting with her head tilted back and her eyes closed offered, "Perhaps God would be happier if Max were to divorce his wife, since the law allows for it, though he would not approve of you marrying him even then, Miss Caroline."

"Divorce is not acceptable to many in the church, despite the government permitting it," Philip frowned, "but divorcees can marry in a civil ceremony if they wish to. It is a most difficult subject."

"It is not something that was planned. It has just happened. Max is trying to make the best of it all and I am not handing over all my worldly possessions to him just like that. The house is mine. Max is not bringing any debts with him and is making no demands of me. I had hoped you would be happy for us Philip, though I understand that it conflicts with your vocation."

"I am happy for you both Miss Caroline. I would not want anyone to have to stay somewhere that they are not wanted." Said Mary, still with her eyes closed.

Philip sighed, "I still cannot condone it, but I would never want to see you unhappy Caroline. You have a special part in our little family, and I would be very sorry if anything were to affect our relationship."

"Thank you," Caroline knew this was as close to wishing her and Max well that Philip was likely to get.

When Caroline returned home from the Rose's, there were a pile of letters on the doormat.

7 August 1929
York

Dear Caroline,

Thought I would drop you a quick line before I move on again, and see how things are working out between you and your new chap. I can't pretend to understand your reasons, but I wish you happiness nonetheless. As long as a man is working, he retains a certain self-esteem, so it was good to hear that Max had secured a position with the Great Western Railway. Is he still employed there? Do you get free rail travel as a perk of his job?

As I say, I am about to move on once again, so if you want to reply, send your letter to me care of

Pavel Svoboda
Pellicova 669/67,
602 00 Brno-střed-Staré
Brno, Czechoslovakia

I am going to stay with the friend I met while in Italy, and his wife Marta. They have just had a baby boy and Pavel wishes to be rescued! He also has some people for me to meet and has been working at a theatre in the city for the past year so it should be a good way for me to increase my contacts across Europe.

Unfortunately, I won't be flying! Far too expensive for me I'm afraid, I shall be taking the good old iron horse once more. Tommy says you have been a real asset to his airline. I can see it is definitely the way to travel in future, so much faster at least, but one would have to sell a lot of film reels to make that a reality.

Fancy you seeing Elsie again like that! I miss the old crowd sometimes. We all live such nomadic existences, it's impossible to keep in touch for long. And good for Julia landing a role in London. I always felt she would get better parts as an older actress. Frank is in Liverpool at the moment I believe, but I have no idea about the others.

Please do write and tell me your news Caroline. We might not have been right for each other, but I do still look forward to hearing from you.

Yours ever

James

First Italy, now Czechoslovakia! Caroline smiled as she pushed the letter back into its envelope. She was happy for James, happy that he was following his career as a film and theatre director wherever it led him, and happy that she had made the right decision to turn down his marriage proposal. Their times apart would have been much greater than the ones she and Max currently endured, and she did not think she would have been in the same position that she now was with her own motor car and independence had she become James' wife.

There were other letters from Midge and from Lina, Tommy's cousin several times removed, who Caroline exchanged

Christmas cards and a summer letter with each year. She had met both Lina and James at a house party given by Helen's cousin Gordon during her first year of exploring the independence she now cherished so dearly. Lina had married a young man called Albert whom she had also met at the house party, and after producing twin girls had now also given Albert a son and heir to the fortune the young man was cultivating through securing a seat in Parliament. It had been after Lina and Albert's wedding in Worcester that James had proposed to Caroline. She pondered the curious nature of the movements of the people she now considered to be her friends, and how they resembled a chess game with some moving ever forwards and others criss-crossing the board in all directions.

Midge had travelled the furthest, geographically speaking. Her trip to Africa to work with some church missionaries had led to her marriage to Oliver. Now they were 'camped' as Midge had referred to their large house, in Winchester and Oliver was apparently enjoying his new role as House Master at a small boy's school in the city. Caroline had wanted to visit them but had decided that Winchester would need to be a train journey rather than taking the Austin, and it would have to wait until she and Max were settled in Plymouth.

The following week, Caroline did take the Austin back to Stroud and Cheltenham to visit her friends there. She felt a sadness to be retracing the route she had taken to be with her father, and a strong sense of not returning to the same place that she had known for so long as a young girl. Things had changed in Cheltenham, buildings were different, new houses were being built, factories were rising all around the town with new industries to cater for the growing demand in motor vehicles and domestic appliances.

Caroline stayed at the Queens Hotel for two nights and spent the day with her old housemaid Annie and Annie's two sons in their home. The trees along Tennyson Road and Milton Road were in full leaf and the quiet streets shimmered in the summer heat. As Caroline turned off the Austin's engine outside the Jenks' house she sat for a moment and listened to the birds chirping and the distant clip clip of someone trimming a hedge with some shears. She understood why Annie had so wanted one of these new houses to raise her family in. Her reverie was broken by Annie's front door opening and Victor running out to the garden gate, followed by his little brother Dennis shouting 'car!' with glee.

Before going onwards to Stroud, Caroline called in to Norwood Court and spent a few moments talking to Ferris the doorman. She learned that Miss Kettle was again away from home and would be very sad to have missed Caroline's visit. Galina Bassett was still travelling in eastern Europe, but Caroline left her new Plymouth address with Ferris and asked him to give it to both ladies on their return. Though she was determined to stay in touch with them and Annie, Caroline left Cheltenham with the feeling it would be some time before she returned again. She headed over Cooper's Hill to Painswick and had lunch in the inn near to the church. She wandered around the churchyard with its numerous yew trees clipped into what reminded Caroline of chubby thumbs sticking up as Victor had been taught to do by his father. She continued to Stroud, where she took a room at the Imperial Hotel near the railway station and then drove up to the Police houses where Lottie and Eric lived with their twin girls, Alice and Edith.

Lottie suggested taking the girls to a small park a short walk away, and Caroline readily agreed to the exercise having been sat in the Austin for much of the previous two days. The girls were dressed and strapped into their large pram, and Lottie expertly manoeuvred it out of the house and down the garden path into the street. They spent an hour in the park, with the girls running across the grass and playing on the swings and slide before returning home for refreshments.

Lottie looked to have aged by ten years, Caroline thought. Having twin girls without the aid of a nanny or close relatives nearby was difficult and it showed on Lottie's face and her red raw hands. And yet Lottie was proud of her home and her family and assured Caroline that as the girls got older, they were becoming easier to care for. They slept through the night now and were weaned, so it was only really the never-ending washing of laundry that was still time consuming.

Caroline asked if Eric might watch the children that evening so that Lottie could go to the cinema with her. Lottie said she would ask and said she would be outside the Picture House in Kings Street at seven if Eric had got home in time and agreed. He obliged on both counts, and the women enjoyed a programme of two comedies with tubs of ice cream during the interval. That, at least to Caroline, felt like old times again.

Back in Taunton, Caroline once again set about packing up her life into crates and boxes ready to move to another new home. She was genuinely excited this time and had been browsing magazines and brochures looking for items to fill the rooms with. She had asked Max to open an account at Spooner's for them so that she could make some of the larger purchases as she saw them. It had prompted them to once again discuss what she should call herself.

"If I open the account, it will be in my name. For you to use it, they will expect you to be Mrs Bird." Max had pointed out.

"But they won't allow me to open one myself," Caroline had said with exasperation. "The only reason I have my bank account and my savings account are because my father opened them for me, and now Mr Foxton oversees the savings and is co-signatory on the bank account if I want to withdraw funds from there. Sometimes I do think it would be better to be poor, then at least one has all of one's cash in one place and can get to it and spend it however one pleases!"

"Your Post Office account is in your name though, isn't it?"

"Yes. They do at least allow that."

"Why not close your bank account and have the cheque paid into your Post Office account? Then you'll be able to at least get to your cash as you put it. You can always settle the account in cash if you go to the top floor in Spooner's. And you'll still have your savings account with the Building Society and Mr Foxton."

"Of course, you clever thing! That would solve having to answer any difficult questions when paying for things there. And I can leave Mr Foxton to manage the income from my shares as he has been, and to send me a cheque twice a year or pay it into my savings account there."

"Well, only if you need it. Your Post Office account doesn't pay you any interest, remember. I think you should keep some of your money in an account that does."

"True. But this still doesn't resolve what I will be known as to our neighbours and new friends in Plymouth. I suppose they will assume that I am Mrs Bird."

"It's what people naturally do."

"It's not true though." Caroline said quietly.

"Listen, I've decided, when we move, I shall stop sending Diana any money. Jolyon was right, it needs to be a clean break if we are to have any hope of encouraging her to petition for a divorce. I'm not happy about it, but I will do it. You are already Mrs Bird to me, Caroline, but from this moment let everyone else think so too. I can't propose marriage, but I don't want things to be difficult for you because of me."

Max had taken the last Monday and Tuesday in August off work so that he could travel down to Plymouth with Caroline in the Austin once the last of their possessions were out of Elmsworth. They dropped the keys into the estate agent's office and said a tearful goodbye to Edna with promises that she must visit them as soon as she could. Then they were on their way, driving along the lanes and some newer stretches of road to Exeter where they stopped for lunch and then on to Plymouth. Max had obtained a second-hand bed and two kitchen chairs that one of the men from the yard had been keen to dispose of. The rest of their furniture would arrive in the next day or two.

It was late afternoon when Caroline pulled into the driveway and turned off the Austin's engine. They had agreed to have a fish supper that evening from a fried fish and pies shop on Mannamead Road as they had no plates or cutlery to use, and only their clothes, toiletries and a few final small items in the Austin with them.

"Here we are then Mrs Bird," Max said, looking out at the brown pebble-dashed side of the bungalow.

"Here we are indeed, Mr Bird. Shall we go in?"

They had been inside no more than twenty minutes and were just about to walk down the Avenue to get their supper when there was a knock at the door. Caroline, being in the rounded sitting room, was closest to the door and went to answer it.

"Mildred! Won't you come in?"

"Please, do call me Milly. I saw your car and thought this might be the big day, so I've made you a few sandwiches and a flask of tea. I know I was simply gasping for a brew when we moved in and not a kettle or teapot on hand for hours!" She thrust a wicker basket at Caroline with a beaming smile.

"That's very thoughtful of you, thank you. I'm afraid as you can see, we can't offer you a seat or anything else just yet. Everything will hopefully be arriving tomorrow."

Max joined them in the hallway.

"Milly has brought us some tea, Max."

"Well, that's very kind. Perhaps you and your husband would like to have dinner one evening when we're settled in?"

Caroline was surprised at Max's invitation but said nothing.

"That would be lovely, I'm sure Bill would like that. Now I won't disturb you any further, just pop the basket back when you've finished with it. Good evening!"

When Caroline closed the door, she turned and with a raised eyebrow asked Max, "Inviting people to dinner already?"

"We're going to need all the friends we can get, particularly our neighbours. Anyway, I get the feeling Mildred will be someone who knows everyone's business around here so we might as well get her to make our introductions. Might save a bit of awkwardness in the long run." Max was thinking of his own appearance and how if people had some warning, they often were better able to treat him on equal terms.

"Shall we take the chairs outside and have a drink?" Caroline lifted the lid of the basket a little way and looked at the sandwiches wrapped in baking parchment while her stomach growled.

It took the rest of the week for all of their furniture and other belongings to make their way to Compton Avenue. Max returned to work with a new sense of pride that he was providing for them both by paying for the utilities and household expenses now despite the house itself being Caroline's. He felt useful, which in turn prompted him to think about how he could be useful around their home as well in a practical way. He had a rudimentary knowledge of motor engines, and on his way home one day he called in at the city library and took out a book on car maintenance. He knew he would never be able to change a wheel should it be needed but hoped there would be some small activities he could perform now that the Austin was not being regularly checked by the ground crew.

Max also wanted to buy a lawn mower. The lawn around the bungalow was level and he felt he would be able to manage a manual machine, though he would prefer one with a small petrol engine. After talking to some of the men at the yard, he placed an order for an Atco petrol model at ten pounds and four shillings, and eagerly awaited its delivery.

Caroline had offered to drive Max to and from work in the Austin now that she was no longer travelling to her own employment. Max admitted that it was tiring for him to walk that far even once a day, but they compromised with Caroline taking him to the station in the morning, and then Max would ride the bus along Mutley Plain and up Mannamead Road to go home for two pence a day. It would leave Caroline able to come and go as she pleased, he reasoned.

Once Caroline had unpacked as much of their belongings as would be immediately needed, she set about obtaining the soft furnishings that she felt would make the bungalow a more comfortable home. The floorboards throughout the bungalow were relatively new and in good condition so they agreed to have only a few rugs where their feet might be cold in the winter. Having been to the house auction in

Williton with Daisy, Caroline read the *Plymouth Echo* avidly each evening looking for sales and clearances, jumble sales, auctions and individual bargains. She also kept to her word and went to meet the vicar at Emmanuel church. Reverend Edward Frogmore greeted Caroline warmly and explained the workmen that she could see on her visit were rehanging one of the bells in the tower.

It was the first time that Caroline had introduced herself out loud as Mrs Bird and she had to battle nerves at being struck down by some invisible hand for not being entirely truthful to a man of God. She reasoned that if she could say it to the vicar, she could say it to anyone. It was through Reverend Frogmore that Caroline learned of the parish magazine, the mother's morning on Wednesdays (at which she simply smiled and nodded), Sunday School after the morning service for an hour, and the up-coming harvest festival service. An inscription caught Caroline's eye, and the Reverend explained that the small chapel to one side of the church had been dedicated to the fallen of the Great War and in particular two Jago brothers who had been killed two years apart in France. Caroline found herself telling him about Freddie, and then a little about Max. The visit that she had thought might take fifteen minutes turned into an hour.

Milly was also a valuable source of local knowledge as Max had predicted. It seemed as if she had been waiting for someone like Caroline to appear in order to have a good friend at hand rather than a string of acquaintances. Milly had been a shop assistant in the music department of one of the smaller stores in Devonport before she married Bill Roscommon. Bill worked as an insurance clerk and was a keen follower of Plymouth Argyle football club. Caroline was just wondering how the couple could afford to live on Compton Avenue in their detached three-bedroom, two storey home when Milly volunteered that she had been left a small sum by an elderly relative which meant they had been able to get a mortgage on good terms over twenty-five years.

Caroline kept her answers vague to start with, quickly understanding that Milly would talk to anyone about anything given half a chance. She did mention Helen's parents as being acquaintances, and Milly was suitably impressed. She had read Lady Rosalind's name several times in the *Western Morning News* she said in connection with good works around the city. One difference between them quickly emerged; while Milly was content to stay at home and not work, Caroline was beginning to miss the company and constant flow of new people she had experienced at Sunray Air. Over coffee in Milly's kitchen one morning, Caroline mentioned that she used to work as an office manager at an airline.

"Would you want that sort of position again?" Milly asked, pushing a plate of Rich Tea biscuits towards Caroline across the kitchen table.

"Something like it I think, yes. Though perhaps to just do a few hours a week, not a full-time position. Now that Max is working, I should like to be at home more."

"You know that we have an airport out at Roborough? There are sometimes positions advertised in the *News*. Shall I let you know if I see anything?"

"Would you? Thanks awfully, that would be a great help. But anything interesting, even if it's not at the airport, do tell me."

The neighbours on the other side of the bungalow were an older couple who were renting the house. Richard and Catherine Ward kept themselves to themselves, with Richard happily tending his garden when not working for the Plymouth Coal and Steamship Company based at Sutton harbour. Caroline wished them a 'Good day!' whenever she saw them, but that was an infrequent event.

Caroline made a point to call on Lady Rosalind after she and Max had been at the bungalow for a couple of weeks. She arrived without an appointment and had only just been able to find the Postgate's villa again after getting lost on her way to Lipson. She was prepared to find Lady Rosalind either out or indisposed but was shown into the drawing room by an elderly maid after giving up her coat and hat. After a few minutes, Lady Rosalind entered the room.

"My dear! How delightful to see you again so soon. We shall have tea shortly, Jones is a little slow these days."

"Thank you. Did you enjoy your birthday party? It seems such a long time ago now."

"It was a splendid evening. So many old friends, and new friends too." Her eyes sparkled and she smiled kindly at Caroline, "And how is your young man?"

Caroline couldn't help but giggle, to hear Max described as a young man.

"He is very well, thank you. I came to tell you that we have bought a house at Mannamead and intend to stay in Plymouth for a while at least."

"That is very interesting news. Do you intend to work as well?"

"Not straight away, which is the other reason I wanted to speak with you, Lady Rosalind. I was wondering if there were any good causes you could recommend that I could become involved in. I'm not one for politics like Helen I'm afraid, but I have helped with the Women's Section in Cheltenham."

"My dear, there is always work to be done."

And so, after a number of introductions, Caroline found herself devoting Thursday mornings to the Ways and Means committee of the Virginia House Settlement in Looe Street near the Barbican, and Thursday afternoons to helping with reading and writing classes for young men and women who were disabled or of low ability despite some school attendance. The Settlement had been the idea of Lord and Lady Astor, and in the four years since its opening had become a valuable and well-used resource by the Plymouth inhabitants. Max was happy that Caroline had found something worthwhile to do and said that several of the men at the yard had attended one or more of the many clubs that operated out of the Settlement, such as sports and sailing.

As Caroline preferred to read the local evening newspaper, it was the national news broadcasts that kept her informed about the world outside of Plymouth. She and Max would listen after dinner in the sitting room, and towards the end of September they began to hear troubling news from the stock market in America. Milly had mentioned it when she and Caroline were having tea the day before and had said how concerned Bill was as he had a small portfolio of shares that were what they hoped to live off when he eventually retired. Caroline hadn't considered that she might be affected until that point. Max suggested that she telephone Mr Foxton to determine whether any of Caroline's shares were in companies that were traded on Wall Street.

That evening as they listened to the increasingly troubling news together, Max asked what Mr Foxton had said.

"He said he would have to look at the portfolio, but that indications are we shall not be as badly affected as the Americans might. He said it really all depends on how low the prices go. I don't really understand, but apparently it doesn't matter if my shares are traded in London or New York; if their price is reduced then the dividends will be less. He couldn't say by how much."

"Perhaps it was the best thing you could have done, to buy this place when you did."

"Well yes, Mr Foxton did say that too, though only if we don't intend to sell it. We might never get back what we paid for it."

"You. It's your house Caroline. You might not get back what you paid."

"Don't you think of it as ours? Not even now that we've been here a few months?"

Max tapped the end of his cigarette into the ashtray, "It's our home, yes. I suppose it's all semantics, home, house, where we live. But it is your money Caroline, and I don't like the sound of the reports of how much the stock prices are dropping."

"Do you think we should start cutting back on things? Or perhaps I should buy more food in tins each week and build up a store cupboard. Milly has a whole shelf of tinned vegetables in her pantry."

"Perhaps a bit of both would be a sensible idea," replied Max.

Caroline grew more conscious of what she was spending each time she went to the little row of shops on Mannamead Road. She had tried not to let Max see how concerned Mr Foxton had sounded to her on the telephone, but he had warned her that some of her shares were in companies that might not survive a prolonged drop in the market or even a recession. Everyone would suffer, he had said, it simply depended by how much. Caroline had never been extravagant, and she and Max were content to stay at home during the week in their sitting room and read or Max would attempt the crossword in the newspaper. At weekends if the weather was fine, they might take the bus into town, or drive out onto Dartmoor and have tea in a village before driving back home again. Max had been to watch Plymouth Argyle play with Bill two or three times on a Saturday afternoon but preferred to stay at home when he wasn't at work. The stares and comments wore down his confidence easily, despite the men at the yard now accepting him as he was and Caroline's staunch support.

On Sunday mornings, Max would stay home while Caroline went to Emmanuel church. He would mow the lawns around the bungalow if the grass was dry or practice his sketching by drawing the Austin or the view from the French windows of the dining room out to the garden. He wished he could wield a spade or fork and put some of the space to use by growing vegetables, but his left leg was not strong enough and his left hand was still numb.

When Max returned home on Tuesday 29 October 1929, the news of the previous day's losses on Wall Street had been on all of the newspaper boards. The mood at the yard was stoic; rich people would probably still be alright but the poor and working classes would suffer as they always did. A cold wind blew at his back as he walked up Compton Avenue and for the first time that year, he thought he might need some knitted gloves. Perhaps Caroline could make him a set with a hat and scarf to match. He smiled in spite of the nagging worry about Caroline's finances and the security of his own job. It was so nice to be with someone who cared and wanted to make things better. He wondered if he would ever really get used to it.

Caroline was in the kitchen when he opened the front door. The aroma of pork chops mingled with the sweet smell of baked cakes, and the windows had a film of condensation on them.

"You've been busy!" Max said as he kissed Caroline on the cheek. She was washing up the debris of her baking in the sink.

"I wanted to try the recipe for rock cakes that Mrs Dawson gave me on Sunday. It's chops for dinner and probably mashed potatoes and carrots; the potatoes are going to mush anyway. That last bag really hasn't been very good, I must mention it to Mr Cawthorne. Oh, there's a letter on the dining room table for you. It has a Bath postmark but there is not return address on the envelope. It's rather a thick envelope."

Max frowned and went to retrieve it. He opened it slowly, using the paper knife as he sat at the table, and eventually extracted the contents.

21 October 1929, Bath

Dear Sir,

We are acting under instruction for Mrs Diana Alice Bird, in the matter of her petition for divorce on the grounds of desertion and adultery. You will find enclosed the details of her grounds against you and also her terms for a settlement.

An assizes court hearing is scheduled for Monday November 4 at the Council Chambers in Wells, Somerset, and you are required to attend with or without legal representation as is your right. Should you wish to contest the terms set out in the enclosed documents, we anticipate the hearing will run over the course of a week.

There is no need for you to acknowledge this letter personally. Official summons will be issued to you in due course. We are willing to communicate through your own legal representative to proceed with the matter at hand.

Your obedient servants

Messers Godwin, Clarence and Banks, Solicitors.

Max lay the letter on the table and ran his hand over his face. So, Jolyon had been right; Diana had needed the extra cause of desertion to move her to take action. Her father would no doubt be paying for her solicitor as he would not be permitted to act for her himself, but perhaps she had also found someone else that she wanted to spend the rest of her life with. Max listened to Caroline humming to herself in the kitchen. He wanted to be free of Diana, but this was the worst possible time to have to find money for court costs. They were managing on his wages, but only because they were being careful, and the house and car were paid for. Max suspected that Caroline's finances were in as perilous a state as everyone else's at that time and she either didn't realise it or didn't want to acknowledge it.

Caroline appeared in the doorway drying her hands on a tea towel.

"Who was it from?"

"Diana's solicitor." He handed her the letter.

"But how did they know you were here? You haven't sent Diana any money since we moved, how could they know that we weren't in Taunton anymore?"

"It's not difficult for the police or private investigators to track a man down if he isn't hiding, and I certainly haven't been hiding. I pay my insurance stamp at work, I cash in my pension, even the account we opened at Spooner's. Bird isn't a particularly common surname."

"I suppose not. But does this mean you will have to go to Wells?"

"That's what it says. I haven't read the petition yet, but I can imagine what's in it."

"Will Diana be there too?"

"I think she has to be, yes."

"Well then I will go with you."

It was what Max had feared. "No, really Caroline, I would prefer you not to. It's bad enough to be accused of adultery, bad enough to be admitting it, without having you there too for the news hacks to write nasty comments about."

"You can't go on your own!"

"I can. I have faced worse."

That evening, the news programme on the wireless brought more bad tidings. The stock market crash on Wall Street had exceeded everyone's expectations, the newsreader told Max and Caroline as they listened in silence. Hundreds of thousands of dollars had been wiped off the value of shares, and other markets were following suit around the globe. When they went to bed that night, neither of them spoke very much. They were both mulling over the events of the day and what they could mean for them, in the immediate and longer-term future.

15

A FINAL FLOURISH

Max felt he had no choice but to confide in Teague about his situation. He would have preferred to discuss it with his neighbour Bill, or even with young Jolyon, but as he would need some time off work to attend the hearing, he decided he may as well make a clean breast of it with his manager. Caroline had agreed not to discuss it with anyone in their immediate vicinity. She liked Milly a lot but had already realised that she would tell anyone anything and was not someone with whom to trust a secret.

Much as Max had done with selecting Teague to share his burden, Caroline spent the next morning mentally working through her friends to find one who would not only be sympathetic but also not broadcast her personal details to all and sundry. She so desperately wanted to talk to Helen, but she feared disturbing their delicate reconciliation. She felt that Midge would be in a difficult position, given her religious upbringing and connection to the church. Annie and Lottie had both given Caroline the distinct impression that their views on divorce were not favourable, and

Mary Rose while almost certainly understanding Caroline's situation, would feel such loyalty to Philip and the church that Caroline placed her firmly in the mental bucket of 'not to be troubled with it all'.

If James had been nearer, she would have considered him, but the thought of writing it all down and then possibly having to wait for weeks for a reply was anathema to her. That left only two options: Daisy Clare, and Edna O'Neil. Edna would be at work, and while Daisy would have opened her bookshop, it was never so busy that she would not answer the telephone and chat for a few minutes.

"Hello Daisy, it's Caroline."

"Caroline! Lovely to hear from you, is everything alright, dear?"

"Not exactly, no. I suppose you've heard the news?"

"Gosh, yes! And from what you've told me before it must affect you quite badly. How are you bearing up?"

"I think I shall have to find a job. The dividends are due to be paid in January, but it sounds as if I shall be lucky to receive just a few pounds. Thankfully Max's job has a good wage, but … oh Daisy, Max's wife has started divorce proceedings against him. He has to go to trial and won't let me go with him. He says there will be reporters and he wants to keep me away from it all. But he is terribly worried about it, I can tell."

"Oh Lord, that's all you need on top of the crash. Max is right though; you really shouldn't go. Is he … are you … named in the petition?"

"No. We read through it carefully last night. She is using both adultery and desertion as her complaint, both of which are fair. They had very little property, she is insisting that Max have no claim on any of their furniture but he really doesn't want any of it in any case. Max won't contest it at all, but he still has to go, and we shall have to pay for a solicitor, and probably his wife's costs as well. It could be hundreds of pounds just when we can least afford it."

"Do you have a good lawyer?"

"Max is going to ask his manager today. We only know the fellow who sold the house to us down here, and I couldn't possibly ask Mr Embry."

"I do know a chap, but you probably want someone more local to you. When is the trial?"

"The fourth of November, which of course is the anniversary of Freddie's death as well and so close to Father's passing. I might have to sell the Austin." Caroline felt the tears forming along her lashes and pulled her handkerchief out from up her cardigan sleeve.

"Now that would be a shame, just when you've got used to having it. But the fourth is next week, that's really not long to prepare."

"Max thinks his father-in-law might have had some influence over the trail date."

"I suppose a mortgage on the bungalow is out of the question?"

"It would have to be in Max's name. We might have to consider it. I have no idea how much trials cost, Daisy. One never expects to need to know these things.

"Quite. Look here, would you like to come and stay while the trial is on? Or perhaps I should come down to you? If Max isn't contesting it, I should think it will be all over in a couple of days, and I can make myself scarce when Max returns."

"Would you? I think I should prefer to stay here, but it would be good to have you here if you can spare a couple of days away from the shop."

"Of course I can. Now, this call will be costing you a pretty penny, so let's say I shall come down on … yes, Sunday is the third, so I shall make my way to Plymouth then and I will write when I have checked the timetables and have the exact time. Keep your chin up, dear."

"Thank you, Daisy, you are a good friend."

Teague put down the report he had been reading and took off his spectacles. He looked at the man sitting in the chair on the other side of the desk and not for the first time wondered how much more life would throw at him. Teague thought Max was a good fellow, dependable, conscientious, calm in a crisis as he had proven only a few days before when a young lad in the yard had been badly scalded. Naturally Teague had had some reservations when Max was first sent to him, you never could tell how the war had affected someone and the physical injuries were often not the worst of it. But Max was good at his job and Teague felt a duty of care towards him.

Being a family man, with six children under the age of twelve at home, Teague also knew how marriage was meant to be for life. It had to be worked at, and divorce was an admission of failure. Though not quite the scandal it once was, it was still rare enough among those of their class that it would cause idle chatter and speculation. Having that stamp of finality on a marriage was somehow far more of a stain than simply taking up with another partner.

"Monday you say?"

"Yes, and I was hoping to see if I could find a solicitor in my lunch break later."

"Do you need one, if you're just going to agree to it all? You could represent yourself and save the expense."

"I could. No doubt I will have to pay Diana's costs, so perhaps that would be a better approach."

"I can't say I'm happy about it all. Marriage is a commitment."

"I'd rather not go into details," Max rubbed his face with his right hand, "but Caroline is not the reason."

"Is she named?"

"No."

"There is that, then. Well, if I say no, and you've been summoned, you'll be arrested for not turning up and that won't help anyone. Take the week, unpaid mind, and clear your head before you come back. This is not a job that you can be distracted on."

"Thank you, sir."

Max got up to return to his own desk. Teague called him back.

"I'm sure you don't want it to be yard gossip, so I'd be careful who you tell. Let's say you've a funeral to attend, an elderly aunt. In Doncaster."

"Doncaster?"

"I've an aunt there. I'll remember it."

"Thank you."

Max ate his lunch in the old carriage that served the purpose of a break room for those who worked in the railway yard. He had decided to follow Teague's suggestion and forgo legal representation. He would simply attend the court, agree to everything and hope that it would all be over swiftly. He felt sure that Diana's solicitor must know of Caroline, given the bungalow deeds were in her name. He could only think that they had not named her because they did not need to. The phrase used in the petition had been 'person or persons unknown'. Naming her would have meant she would also be expected to defend herself and could prolong the trial. Max believed that Diana would want everything over with as quickly as possible; she might wish him dead, but she would not want to spend day upon day in a court room to be gawped at by reporters.

He watched the rivulets of rain trickle slowly down the carriage window. If they blamed it on his injuries, he would agree. If they said he had become mentally unbalanced he would go along with them. If they called him a cad, a scoundrel, a selfish wastrel, he would nod and not argue otherwise. He had been called much worse over the years, by his drill sergeant amongst others, and he knew his character was flawed. It would be just one more situation where he was placed on show, to be stared at, talked about, and ridiculed in public. If he had never met Caroline, would he still be in Bath now, he wondered. Possibly there would have been some other woman eventually that he might have turned to. The doctor who had recommended the painting retreat could not have foreseen where that therapy would eventually lead.

A young boy, short for his fourteen years and with a baby's face burst into the carriage, and shouted to Max.

"Mr Bird! You'm come quick, Tom's got his arm stuck under a load!" He was jigging from one foot to the other.

Max screwed up his paper bag and dropping it into the barrel that served as a rubbish bin, said, "Show me where he is then."

Daisy arrived at lunchtime. She met Caroline and Max in the open ticket hall of Plymouth station and wished Max good luck as he went off to catch his train towards Wells. As she and Caroline walked out to the Austin, stepping around and over the puddles that had appeared again overnight, Daisy could see the concern on Caroline's face.

"You can let it all out now that he's gone, dear." She said once they were safely in Caroline's kitchen and the teapot filled.

"I will not cry, Daisy. And if I do, it will be tears of frustration at the ridiculousness of it all."

"It is, as they say, a solemn vow. One has to be, is meant to be absolutely sure when one agrees to be married."

"But how can one ever be sure? Max married when he was eighteen. When I was eighteen, I had no interest in men at all, I would have been horrified if someone had told me I must spend the rest of my life with a man."

"Well, from what you have told me, you were rather a late starter in that department. Young girls did marry, as young as fourteen or fifteen if there was a need to. You know what I mean. Now of course, with the Age of Marriage Act that Helen was so keen on being passed earlier this year, everyone must be at least sixteen. I have often wondered at the rush to marry, especially when not precipitated by an imminent birth."

"Max was going to war. He thought it would be the right thing to do, so that Diana would at least receive a pension should anything happen to him."

Daisy poured the tea. "When it is all over, do you plan to marry him?"

"I don't think so. I don't feel that I need to. I know Max simply wants to break off that part of his life and I can't imagine he would want to go through it all again."

"You talk as if you think you might not be with him in the future," Daisy frowned.

"Who can tell, Daisy? That's rather my point. I am very happy with Max, I can't imagine not being with him and I've never felt such strong feelings for anyone," she began to blush, but ignored it and continued, "but people change, I might change or Max might, and I would never want to keep him with me if that's not what he wanted too. Especially as I have seen what it did to Max with Diana. Honestly Daisy, when we met in Cornwall, he was so quiet, so … intense. As if he was carrying a great weight. And now, at least until the petition arrived, he seemed to be less downtrodden."

Daisy smiled kindly at her friend and patted her hand. "Let us hope that it will all be over quickly then, and that you don't have to sell the Austin to cover the expenses. With the crash, I'm not sure you would find a buyer easily in any case. Now, what are your plans for us for tomorrow?"

Although it was too cold to swim, Caroline suggested that she and Daisy might drive to the coast. They drove out of the city and east, across the river Plym and then southeast towards Newton Ferrers and Noss Mayo. Caroline thought the beach that she and Tommy had discovered the year before might be too much of a walk in the wet and windy weather, and so decided to make do with the sandy edges of the river Yealm instead. Daisy was enchanted by the twin villages on either side of the river, and when they found a small book shop, she insisted on going inside and making herself known to the owner. They had lunch in a small café and then returned to the car.

Despite the dark clouds, Caroline wanted to show Daisy some of south Dartmoor. They drove north after lunch to Ivybridge and then skirted the edge of the moor to Yelverton. Caroline pulled over and turned off the engine for a moment so that they could get out and look at the view.

"It is quite breath-taking in the better weather," Caroline said into the wind.

"One always imagines one is climbing a hill when one travels north from anywhere, and it appears we really did all the way from the sea earlier. Yet it didn't feel like it, driving along the lanes. Suddenly you find you are much higher. I wonder if you could see the sea on a very clear day?"

"Perhaps not from this spot, but I think it is possible from parts of the golf course, and of course from one of the tors."

"They have a golf course here?"

"Oh yes, and another in Tavistock. It's all the rage."

A sudden squall forced them back into the Austin and Caroline headed for home.

Max telephoned that evening to say he would be returning the following day. The trial had been concluded and he would be sent the bill for the court costs separately to the bill from Diana's solicitor. He did not want to say any more on the telephone and Caroline did not press him to. Daisy said she would go with Caroline to the station and make her way home so as not to intrude on what she perceived would be an emotional reunion. Caroline did not try too hard to persuade her to stay.

So, as they had the Sunday before, Tuesday saw Daisy and Max exchange a brief greeting before one departed by train and the other returned to the bungalow with Caroline. Max was silent for the short journey to Compton Avenue. He carried his case indoors and unpacked while Caroline made tea. She was just sniffing the jug of milk when he joined her in the kitchen.

"I think this is still alright. I must ask Milly if she can leave a note for the milk delivery man and ask him to call here. I know we don't drink very much, but a fresh pint each morning would be so convenient."

"Sit down for a minute, would you." Max looked as he had when she had met him in Cornwall and her heart felt like lead in her chest as she put the jug on the table and sat on the chair next to his. She took his right hand in hers and waited for him to speak.

"It will cost us just over two hundred pounds in all." He said quietly, looking down at their hands.

"Was it so terrible?"

"I am glad that you weren't there, though I would have given much to have been with you afterwards. The assizes are held in the council chambers, not as you would imagine a formal court. Perhaps you've never seen a formal court?"

Caroline shook her head.

"No, of course, why should you have. Still the judge was a real judge, and as I was not contesting the petition there was no need for a jury. That did not stop Diana's solicitor doing his best to draw out the proceedings, presumably to make his bill as large as possible. He suggested that there had been numerous instances of infidelity and I did not correct him. He became rather angry at one point; I think he was hoping for some kind of big revelation or a battle of words. The only thing I corrected him on was his assertion that I had left Diana penniless. I explained I had sent her the greater portion of my pension weekly until only recently. I saw the judge nodding after I had spoken, I think he understood my reasons."

"Were the reporters there?"

"One or two. I doubt anyone here will know about it, but anyone who knew us, Diana and I, in Bath will almost certainly be reading about it today."

"And is that it, truly over? We pay the bills, and you won't hear any more?"

"It seems that way, yes."

"Well, it's not as much as we'd feared. I don't think I shall need to sell the Austin. I can telephone Mr Foxton tomorrow and ask him to expect the bills to be forwarded and paid immediately."

Max shook his head. "This is not your bill to pay, Caroline. I have asked to pay the court costs by two instalments, and I shall make a similar arrangement with Diana's solicitors."

"Don't be silly darling, I have the money. Surely you don't want this all to linger over us?"

"I don't want you to have to pay for my … mistakes."

Caroline frowned. "I rather think I may be the cause of some of them. The least I can do is help you."

"It will take much of the rest of your savings. You might not receive any dividend payment next year."

"I shall get a job. I had been thinking about it in any case. I shall enquire about everything in the *Western Morning News* tomorrow." She smiled, trying desperately to encourage Max to stay afloat and not disappear under a wave of depression.

"Caroline ... I'm sorry. It seems I keep taking and taking from you and your kindness and generosity must surely have reached their limits."

"Max, we always knew it could be this way. You have promised me nothing. Daisy doesn't think we'll be able to sell the Austin anyway, she says no one will have the money to buy it since the crash. Darling, we have a home, you have your job, and I will find some work somewhere. We will find our way through this, and I'm sure by next summer we shall look back and laugh at how serious this all seems now."

They stood up. Max put his good arm around her and kissed her forehead.

"I need a bath. I want to wash it all off of me and start again clean. Keep the pot warm."

Max returned to work the following day, not wanting to stretch Teague's patience if he should discover the trial had only lasted a day. Caroline pored over the situations vacant columns in the morning newspaper, though for her determination to apply for all of the jobs listed she found that very few would really be suitable for her. She could feed herself and Max, but her cookery skills were not worthy of payment, she felt certain. She had hoped to see some kind of seamstress position, or an administration vacancy but there were none. The majority of the advertisements were for male positions, or for skilled and qualified individuals.

Undeterred, Caroline composed a letter enquiring after any possible vacancies and listing her experience as an office manager at the airfield. She addressed the envelope to the Managing Director at the Roborough Airport, Plymouth, and fixed a stamp to the front. She held it in her hands for a moment, closed her eyes and sent a prayer to God, to her father, to anyone who might be listening, that there might be an opening for her there. Then she opened her eyes, looked at her watch, and decided to take the letter to the post box outside the Emmanuel church straight away.

On Thursday she returned to Virginia House and the hustle and bustle of the classrooms and refectory were a welcome distraction for her. She mentioned to one or two women there that she might be interested in a part time paid position, should one become available that they might hear about, but she felt awkward doing so. The poverty of the families that the Settlement assisted and the wealth of the women who volunteered both felt alien to her.

When the bill for the court costs arrived, Max explained that he could pay half from his small savings immediately, and then would need to pay the other half by the time the assizes sat again the following spring. This was by far the smaller portion of the overall expense of the divorce. Caroline had spent the day working on another canvas and had a smudge of charcoal on her cheek.

"If I can get this one finished, I'll have two to send up to Elsa and Bobby. They might not sell for quite as much as the others, but it will help."

"You are determined to pay aren't you." Max said, taking out his handkerchief and wiping the smudge away from her face.

"Well, why don't you send one or two of your sketches as well?"

"I don't think they are the kind of subjects that your friends would be interested in selling. But perhaps... no, forget it."

"What?"

Max hesitated. The idea had come to him so suddenly, he had no time to consider the implications.

"Max?" Caroline stood smiling at him, her hair tucked behind her ears and her old painting overall tied around her like a dressing gown.

"I could draw you."

Caroline's mouth opened as if she were about to speak but no words emerged. They held each other's gaze for some moments while they both considered the proposal. Caroline was the first to break the silence.

"You mean, the same way that I draw Tommy?"

"That's the kind of painting Elsa and Bobby sell, isn't it?"

"Yes."

"We could try, perhaps just one. If we change our minds, then, well, perhaps we can keep it in the bedroom."

"You wouldn't mind other people, other men, seeing me that way?"

"Everyone knows what bodies look like. Most people have enough imagination even when we are fully clothed. Unless you're not happy with the idea."

"I don't know. I hadn't considered it before. But, well, I don't think I could model the way Phyllis Bohenna did, but as I'd only be sitting for you..."

"The truth is, I don't think I can get more hours at the yard, and I don't expect to find a second job when so many men now are looking. I know you have been looking too, darling, but there have been no bites have there?"

Caroline shook her head with a sigh, "No, nothing at all."

"This might be the only way I can cover the divorce. And you would still be helping, just not with your own money."

"Then let's do it. Dinner will be ready shortly, but let's start tonight. We can set up the easel in the sitting room, it will be warmer in there than in here." Her eyes sparkled with excitement. Caroline knew Max could draw well; his style was less bold than her own and displayed more of his draughtsman background. She was curious to see how he would draw more than her face.

They moved one armchair so that it was just in front of the side window in the sitting room and drew back the long curtain so that it exposed some of the window and the black night beyond. The fire was built up so that Caroline would not get cold, and she undressed in the bedroom before wrapping herself in her dressing gown and returning to where Max was securing the canvas onto the easel.

"How would you like me to sit?"

"I thought you might like to read a book. I can capture you in semi profile, looking down. It should be an easy enough pose to hold, and you can of course turn the pages when you need to. And use the foot stool, I think that will help the work feel relaxed. It's how I ..." He stopped, aware Caroline was watching him intently.

She untied the dressing gown and let it fall to the floor. Caroline stepped forwards, put her hand on his shoulder and kissed his mouth.

"We'll make this work." Caroline said, her voice little more than a whisper. Then she turned, picked up the novel she had been reading earlier that afternoon, and took up her position in the chair.

If you enjoyed this story, please leave a rating
or review on Amazon or Goodreads.com

Thank you!